Get the eBooks FREE!

(PDF, ePub, Kindle, and liveBook all included)

We believe that once you buy a book from us, you should be able to read it in any format we have available. To get electronic versions of this book at no additional cost to you, purchase and then register this book at the Manning website.

Go to https://www.manning.com/freebook and follow the instructions to complete your pBook registration.

That's it!
Thanks from Manning!

Praise for the First Edition

A deluge of practical advice about applying Docker to problems you have right now.
—From the Foreword to the first edition by Ben Firshman, Docker, Inc.

Filled with 4-star recipes!

—Chad Davis, SolidFire

You'll love Docker after reading this book.

—José San Leandro, OSOCO

Packed with Docker tricks of the developer trade.

—Kirk Brattkus, Net Effect Technologies

Extremely good sets of tips for using docker. Really useful and pragmatic and addresses real world docker issues.

—Amazon customer

Easy to read and follow. I have a much better understanding of the internal working of Docker after reading this book.

—Amazon customer

Docker in Practice

SECOND EDITION

IAN MIELL
AIDAN HOBSON SAYERS

MANNING
Shelter Island

For online information and ordering of this and other Manning books, please visit
www.manning.com. The publisher offers discounts on this book when ordered in quantity.
For more information, please contact

> Special Sales Department
> Manning Publications Co.
> 20 Baldwin Road
> PO Box 761
> Shelter Island, NY 11964
> Email: orders@manning.com

⊗ Recognizing the importance of preserving what has been written, it is Manning's policy to have
the books we publish printed on acid-free paper, and we exert our best efforts to that end.
Recognizing also our responsibility to conserve the resources of our planet, Manning books are
printed on paper that is at least 15 percent recycled and processed without the use of elemental
chlorine.

Manning Publications Co.
20 Baldwin Road
PO Box 761
Shelter Island, NY 11964

Development editor:	Jenny Stout
Review editor:	Ivan Martinović
Project manager:	Vincent Nordhaus
Copyeditor:	Andy Carroll
Proofreader:	Keri Hales
Technical proofreader:	Jose San Leandro
Typesetter:	Gordan Salinovic
Cover designer:	Marija Tudor

ISBN 9781617294808
Printed and bound by CPI Group (UK) Ltd, Croydon, CR0 4YY
2 3 4 5 6 7 8 9 10 – CPI – 24 23 22 21 20 19

contents

preface

In September 2013, while browsing *Hacker News*, I stumbled across an article in *Wired* about a new technology called "Docker."[1] As I read it, I became increasingly excited as I realized Docker's revolutionary potential.

The company I'd worked at for over a decade was struggling to deliver software quickly enough. Provisioning environments was a costly, time-consuming, manual, and inelegant affair. Continuous integration was barely existent, and setting up development environments was an exercise in patience. As my job title included the words "DevOps Manager," I was peculiarly motivated to solve these problems!

I recruited a couple of motivated coworkers (one of them now my coauthor) via a company mailing list, and together our skunkworks team labored to turn a beta tool into a business advantage, reducing the high costs of VMs and enabling new ways of thinking about building and deploying software. We even built and open sourced an automation tool (ShutIt) to suit our organization's delivery needs.

Docker gave us a packaged and maintained tool that solved many problems that would have been effectively insuperable had we taken it upon ourselves to solve them. This was open source at its best, empowering us to take on a challenge using our spare time, overcoming technical debt, and learning lessons daily. Lessons not only about Docker, but about continuous integration, continuous delivery, packaging, automation, and how people respond to speedy and disruptive technological change.

---

[1] http://www.wired.com/2013/09/docker/

For us, Docker is a remarkably broad tool. Wherever you run software using Linux, Docker can impact it. This makes writing a book on the subject challenging, as the landscape is as broad as software itself. The task is made more onerous by the extraordinary rate at which the Docker ecosystem is producing solutions to meet the needs that emerge from such a fundamental change in software production. Over time, the shape of problems and solutions became familiar to us, and in this book, we've endeavored to pass on this experience. This will enable you to figure out solutions to your specific technical and business constraints.

Giving talks at meetups we're struck by how quickly Docker has become effective within organizations willing to embrace it. This book mirrors how we used Docker, going from our desktops, through the DevOps pipeline, all the way to production. Consequently, this book is sometimes unorthodox, but as engineers we believe that purity must sometimes give way to practicality, especially when it comes to saving money! Everything in this book is based on real lessons from the field, and we hope you benefit from our hard-won experience.

—IAN MIELL

acknowledgments

This book couldn't have been written without the support, sacrifice, and patience of those closest to us. Special mention is due to Stephen Hazleton, whose tireless efforts with us to make Docker useful for our customers informed much of the book's contents.

Several Docker contributors and staff were kind enough to review the book at different stages and provided much useful feedback, including the following people who read the book in manuscript form: Benoît Benedetti, Burkhard Nestmann, Chad Davis, David Moravec, Ernesto Cárdenas Cangahuala, Fernando Rodrigues, Kirk Brattkus, Pethuru Raj, Scott Bates, Steven Lembark, Stuart Woodward, Ticean Bennett, Valmiky Arquissandas, and Wil Moore III. José San Leandro acted as our technical proofreader and we are grateful for his sharp eye.

Finally, this book also owes a great deal to the Manning editorial team, who went out of their way to push us into making the book not just good enough, but the best it could be. We hope the pride they took in their work rubbed off on us.

IAN MIELL   To Sarah, Isaac, and Rachel for putting up with the late-night coding, a father glued to a laptop screen, and the eternal "Docker this, Docker that, Docker blah, blah," and to my parents for encouraging me from an early age to question the status quo. And for buying me that Spectrum.

AIDAN HOBSON SAYERS   To Mona for the support and encouragement, my parents for their wisdom and motivating words, and my coauthor for that fateful "Has anyone tried this Docker thing?" e-mail.

about this book

Docker is arguably the fastest-growing software project ever. Open-sourced in March 2013, by 2018 it had gained nearly 50,000 GitHub stars and over 14,000 forks. It has accepted significant numbers of pull requests from the likes of Red Hat, IBM, Microsoft, Google, Cisco, and VMWare.

Docker has hit this critical mass by responding to a vital need for many software organizations: the ability to build software in an open and flexible way and then deploy it reliably and consistently in different contexts. You don't need to learn a new programming language, buy expensive hardware, or do much in the way of installation or configuration to build, ship, and run applications portably with Docker.

Docker in Practice, second edition, takes you through real-world examples of Docker usage using techniques we've employed in various contexts. Where possible, we've tried to elucidate these techniques without requiring knowledge of other technologies before reading. We've assumed readers have an understanding of basic development techniques and concepts, such as the ability to develop some structured code, and some awareness of software development and deployment processes. In addition, we've assumed a knowledge of core source-control ideas, and a basic understanding of network fundamentals such as TCP/IP, HTTP, and ports. Anything less mainstream will be explained as we go.

Starting with a rundown of Docker fundamentals in part 1, in part 2 we focus on using Docker in development on a single machine. In part 3 we move on to Docker use within a DevOps pipeline, covering continuous integration, continuous delivery, and testing. Part 4 looks at how to run Docker containers in a scalable way with orchestration. The last part covers running Docker in production, focusing on the options for standard production operations, as well as what can go wrong and how to deal with it.

Docker is such a broad, flexible, and dynamic tool that keeping up with its fast-evolving landscape is not for the faint-hearted. We've endeavored to give you an understanding of critical concepts through real-world applications and examples, with the aim of giving you the power to critically evaluate future tools and technologies within the Docker ecosystem with confidence. We've tried to make the book an enjoyable tour of the many ways we've seen Docker make our lives easier and even fun. Immersing ourselves in Docker has introduced us to many interesting software techniques spanning the entire software lifecycle in a stimulating way, and we hope that this is an experience you'll share.

Roadmap

This book consists of 16 chapters divided into 5 parts.

Part 1 lays down the groundwork for the rest of the book, introducing Docker and getting you to run some basic Docker commands. Chapter 2 spends some time on getting you familiar with Docker's client-server architecture and how to debug it, which can be useful for identifying issues with unconventional Docker setups.

Part 2 focuses on familiarizing you with Docker and getting the most out of Docker on your own machine. An analogy with a concept you may be familiar with, virtual machines, is used as the basis for chapter 3, to give you an easier route into getting started using Docker for real. Chapters 4, 5, and 6 then detail several Docker techniques we've found ourselves using on a daily basis to build images, run images, and manage Docker itself. The final chapter in this part explores the topic of building images in more depth by looking at configuration management techniques.

Part 3 begins looking at uses of Docker in a DevOps context, from using it for automation of software builds and tests to moving your built software to different places. This part concludes with a chapter on the Docker virtual network, which introduces Docker Compose and covers some more advanced networking topics, like network simulation and Docker network plugins.

Part 4 examines the topic of orchestrating containers. We'll take you on a journey from a single container on a single host to a Docker-based platform running on a "data center as an operating system." Chapter 13 is an extended discussion of the areas that must be considered when choosing a Docker-based platform, and it doubles as a guide to what enterprise architects think about when implementing technologies like this.

Part 5 covers a number of topics for using Docker effectively in a production environment. Chapter 14 addresses the important topic of security, explaining how to lock down processes running inside a container and how to restrict access to an externally exposed Docker daemon. The final two chapters go into detail on some key practical information for running Docker in production. Chapter 15 demonstrates how to apply classic sysadmin knowledge in the context of containers, from logging to

resource limits, and chapter 16 looks at some problems you may encounter and provides some steps for debugging and resolution.

The appendixes contain details for installing, using, and configuring Docker in
different ways, including inside a virtual machine and on Windows.

About the code

The source code for all tools, applications, and Docker images we've created for use in
this book is available on GitHub under the "docker-in-practice" organization: https://
github.com/docker-in-practice/. Images on the Docker Hub under the "dockerin-
practice" user https://hub.docker.com/u/dockerinpractice/ are typically automated
builds from one of the GitHub repositories. Where we've felt the reader may be interested in further study of some source code behind a technique, a link to the relevant
repository has been included in the technique discussion. The source code is also
available from the publisher's website at www.manning.com/books/docker-in-prac-
tice-second-edition.

A significant number of the code listings in the book illustrate a terminal session
for the reader to follow, along with corresponding output from commands. There are
a couple of things to note about these sessions:

- Long terminal commands may use the shell line-continuation character, (\), to
  split a command over multiple lines. Although this will work in your shell if you
  type it out, you may also omit it and type the command on one line.
- Where a section of output doesn't provide extra useful information for the discussion, it may be omitted and an ellipsis inserted ([…]) in its place.

Book Forum

Purchase of *Docker in Practice, Second Edition* includes free access to a private web forum
run by Manning Publications where you can make comments about the book, ask
technical questions, and receive help from the author and other users. To access the
forum, go to www.manning.com/books/docker-in-practice-second-edition. You can
also learn more about Manning's forums and the rules of conduct at https://
forums.manning.com/forums/about.

Manning's commitment to its readers is to provide a venue where a meaningful
dialog between individual readers and between readers and the author can take place.
It is not a commitment to any specific amount of participation on the part of the
author, whose contributions to the forum remain voluntary (and unpaid). We suggest
you ask the author challenging questions, lest his interest stray.

about the cover illustration

The figure on the cover of *Docker in Practice, Second Edition,* is captioned "Man from Selce, Croatia." The illustration is taken from a reproduction of an album of Croatian trad itional costumes from the mid-nineteenth century by Nikola Arsenovic, published by the Ethnographic Museum in Split, Croatia, in 2003. The illustrations were obtained from a helpful librarian at the Ethnographic Museum in Split, itself situated in the Roman core of the medieval center of the town: the ruins of Emperor Diocletian's retirement palace from around AD 304. The book includes finely colored illustrations of figures from different regions of Croatia, accompanied by descriptions of the costumes and of everyday life.

Dress codes and lifestyles have changed over the last 200 years, and the diversity by region, so rich at the time, has faded away. It's now hard to tell apart the inhabitants of different continents, let alone of different hamlets or towns separated by only a few miles. Perhaps we have traded cultural diversity for a more varied personal life—certainly for a more varied and fast-paced technological life.

Manning celebrates the inventiveness and initiative of the computer business with book covers based on the rich diversity of regional life of two centuries ago, brought back to life by illustrations from old books and collections like this one.

Part 1

Docker fundamentals

Part 1 of this book consists of chapters 1 and 2, which get you started using Docker and cover its fundamentals.

Chapter 1 explains the origin of Docker along with its core concepts, such as images, containers, and layering. Finally, you'll get your hands dirty by creating your first image with a Dockerfile.

Chapter 2 introduces some useful techniques to give you a deeper understanding of Docker's architecture. Taking each major component in turn, we'll cover the relationship between the Docker daemon and its client, the Docker registry, and the Docker Hub.

By the end of part 1 you'll be comfortable with core Docker concepts and will be able to demonstrate some useful techniques, laying a firm foundation for the remainder of the book.

Discovering Docker

1

This chapter covers

- What Docker is
- The uses of Docker and how it can save you time and money
- The differences between containers and images
- Docker's layering feature
- Building and running a to-do application using Docker

Docker is a platform that allows you to "build, ship, and run any app, anywhere." It has come a long way in an incredibly short time and is now considered a standard way of solving one of the costliest aspects of software: deployment.

Before Docker came along, the development pipeline typically involved combinations of various technologies for managing the movement of software, such as virtual machines, configuration management tools, package management systems, and complex webs of library dependencies. All these tools needed to be managed and maintained by specialist engineers, and most had their own unique ways of being configured.

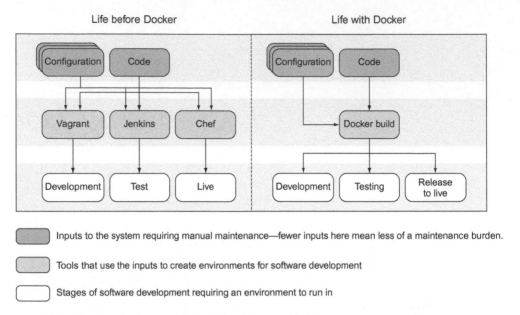

Figure 1.1   How Docker has eased the tool maintenance burden

Docker has changed all of this, allowing different engineers involved in this process to effectively speak one language, making working together a breeze. Everything goes through a common pipeline to a single output that can be used on any target—there's no need to continue maintaining a bewildering array of tool configurations, as shown in figure 1.1.

At the same time, there's no need to throw away your existing software stack if it works for you—you can package it up in a Docker container as-is, for others to consume. As a bonus, you can see how these containers were built, so if you need to dig into the details, you can.

This book is aimed at intermediate developers with some knowledge of Docker. If you're OK with the basics, feel free to skip to the later chapters. The goal of this book is to expose the real-world challenges that Docker brings and to show how they can be overcome. But first we're going to provide a quick refresher on Docker itself. If you want a more thorough treatment of Docker's basics, take a look at *Docker in Action* by Jeff Nickoloff (Manning, 2016).

In chapter 2 you'll be introduced to Docker's architecture more deeply, with the aid of some techniques that demonstrate its power. In this chapter you're going to learn what Docker is, see why it's important, and start using it.

1.1   *The what and why of Docker*

Before we get our hands dirty, we'll discuss Docker a little so that you understand its context, where the name "Docker" came from, and why we're using it at all!

1.1.1 What is Docker?

To get an understanding of what Docker is, it's easier to start with a metaphor than a technical explanation, and the Docker metaphor is a powerful one. A *docker* was a laborer who moved commercial goods into and out of ships when they docked at ports. There were boxes and items of differing sizes and shapes, and experienced dockers were prized for their ability to fit goods into ships by hand in cost-effective ways (see figure 1.2). Hiring people to move stuff around wasn't cheap, but there was no alternative.

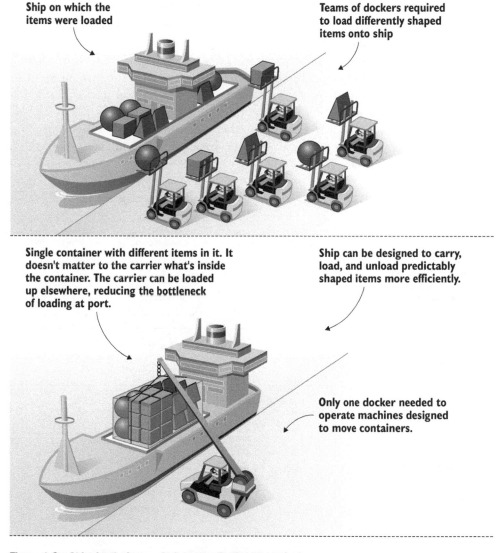

Figure 1.2   Shipping before and after standardized containers

This should sound familiar to anyone working in software. Much time and intellectual energy is spent getting metaphorically odd-shaped software into differently-sized metaphorical ships full of other odd-shaped software, so they can be sold to users or businesses elsewhere.

Figure 1.3 shows how time and money can be saved with the Docker concept. Before Docker, deploying software to different environments required significant effort. Even if you weren't hand-running scripts to provision software on different machines (and plenty of people do exactly that), you'd still have to wrestle with configuration management tools that manage state on what are increasingly fast-moving environments starved of resources. Even when these efforts were encapsulated in VMs, a lot of time was spent managing the deployment of these VMs, waiting for them to boot, and managing the overhead of resource use they created.

With Docker, the configuration effort is separated from the resource management, and the deployment effort is trivial: run `docker run`, and the environment's image is pulled down and ready to run, consuming fewer resources and contained so that it doesn't interfere with other environments.

You don't need to worry about whether your container is going to be shipped to a Red Hat machine, an Ubuntu machine, or a CentOS VM image; as long as it has Docker on it, it'll be good to go.

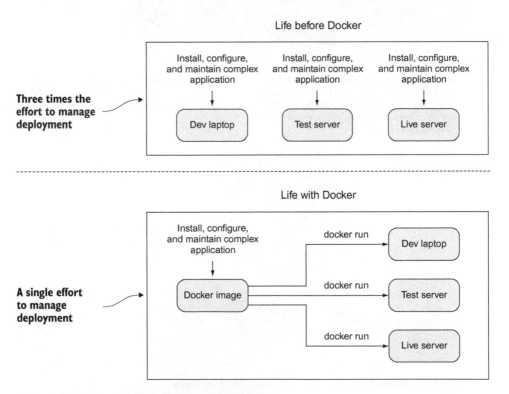

Figure 1.3 Software delivery before and after Docker

1.1.2 What is Docker good for?

Some crucial practical questions arise: why would you use Docker, and for what? The short answer to the "why" is that for a modicum of effort, Docker can save your business a lot of money quickly. Some of these ways (and by no means all) are discussed in the following subsections. We've seen all of these benefits firsthand in real working contexts.

REPLACING VIRTUAL MACHINES (VMs)

Docker can be used to replace VMs in many situations. If you only care about the application, not the operating system, Docker can replace the VM, and you can leave worrying about the OS to someone else. Not only is Docker quicker than a VM to spin up, it's more lightweight to move around, and due to its layered filesystem, you can more easily and quickly share changes with others. It's also firmly rooted in the command line and is eminently scriptable.

PROTOTYPING SOFTWARE

If you want to quickly experiment with software without either disrupting your existing setup or going through the hassle of provisioning a VM, Docker can give you a sandbox environment in milliseconds. The liberating effect of this is difficult to grasp until you experience it for yourself.

PACKAGING SOFTWARE

Because a Docker image has effectively no dependencies for a Linux user, it's a great way to package software. You can build your image and be sure that it can run on any modern Linux machine—think Java, without the need for a JVM.

ENABLING A MICROSERVICES ARCHITECTURE

Docker facilitates the decomposition of a complex system to a series of composable parts, which allows you to reason about your services in a more discrete way. This can allow you to restructure your software to make its parts more manageable and pluggable without affecting the whole.

MODELING NETWORKS

Because you can spin up hundreds (even thousands) of isolated containers on one machine, modeling a network is a breeze. This can be great for testing real-world scenarios without breaking the bank.

ENABLING FULL-STACK PRODUCTIVITY WHEN OFFLINE

Because you can bundle all the parts of your system into Docker containers, you can orchestrate these to run on your laptop and work on the move, even when offline.

REDUCING DEBUGGING OVERHEAD

Complex negotiations between different teams about software delivered is a commonplace within the industry. We've personally experienced countless discussions about broken libraries; problematic dependencies; updates applied wrongly, or in the wrong order, or even not performed at all; unreproducible bugs; and so on. It's likely you have too. Docker allows you to state clearly (even in script form) the steps for debugging a problem on a system with known properties, making bug and environment reproduction a much simpler affair, and one normally separated from the host environment provided.

DOCUMENTING SOFTWARE DEPENDENCIES AND TOUCHPOINTS

By building your images in a structured way, ready to be moved to different environments, Docker forces you to document your software dependencies explicitly from a base starting point. Even if you decide not to use Docker everywhere, this documentation can help you install your software in other places.

ENABLING CONTINUOUS DELIVERY

Continuous delivery (CD) is a paradigm for software delivery based on a pipeline that rebuilds the system on every change and then delivers to production (or "live") through an automated (or partly automated) process.

Because you can control the build environment's state more exactly, Docker builds are more reproducible and replicable than traditional software building methods. This makes implementing CD much easier. Standard CD techniques, such as Blue/Green deployment (where "live" and "last" deployments are maintained on live) and Phoenix deployment (where whole systems are rebuilt on each release), are made trivial by implementing a reproducible Docker-centric build process.

You now know a bit about how Docker can help you. Before we dive into a real example, let's go over a couple of core concepts.

1.1.3 Key concepts

In this section we're going to cover some key Docker concepts, which are illustrated in figure 1.4.

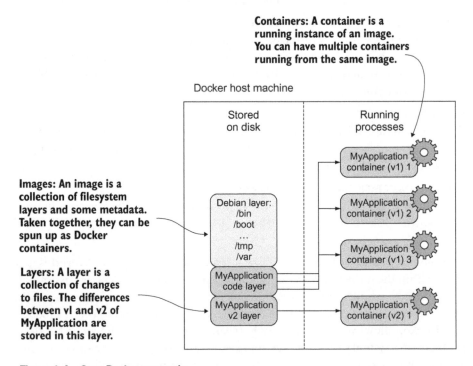

Figure 1.4   Core Docker concepts

It's most useful to get the concepts of images, containers, and layers clear in your mind before you start running Docker commands. In short, *containers* are running systems defined by *images*. These images are made up of one or more *layers* (or sets of diffs) plus some metadata for Docker.

Let's look at some of the core Docker commands. We'll turn images into containers, change them, and add layers to new images that we'll commit. Don't worry if all of this sounds confusing. By the end of the chapter it will all be much clearer.

KEY DOCKER COMMANDS

Docker's central function is to build, ship, and run software in any location that has Docker. To the end user, Docker is a command-line program that they run. Like git (or any source control tool), this program has subcommands that perform different operations. The principal Docker subcommands you'll use on your host are listed in table 1.1.

Table 1.1 Docker subcommands

Command	Purpose
docker build	Build a Docker image
docker run	Run a Docker image as a container
docker commit	Commit a Docker container as an image
docker tag	Tag a Docker image

IMAGES AND CONTAINERS

If you're unfamiliar with Docker, this may be the first time you've come across the words "container" and "image" in this context. They're probably the most important concepts in Docker, so it's worth spending a bit of time to make sure the difference is clear. In figure 1.5 you'll see an illustration of these concepts, with three containers started up from one base image.

One way to look at images and containers is to see them as analogous to programs and processes. In the same way a process can be seen as an "application being executed," a Docker container can be viewed as a Docker image in execution.

If you're familiar with object-oriented principles, another way to look at images and containers is to view images as classes and containers as objects. In the same way that objects are concrete instances of classes, containers are instances of images. You can create multiple containers from a single image, and they are all isolated from one another in the same way objects are. Whatever you change in the object, it won't affect the class definition—they're fundamentally different things.

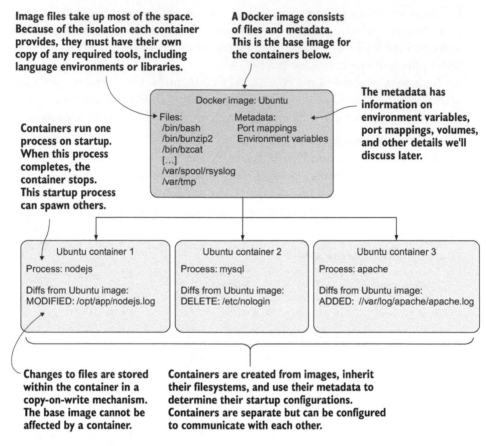

Image files take up most of the space. Because of the isolation each container provides, they must have their own copy of any required tools, including language environments or libraries.

A Docker image consists of files and metadata. This is the base image for the containers below.

Docker image: Ubuntu

Files:
/bin/bash
/bin/bunzip2
/bin/bzcat
[...]
/var/spool/rsyslog
/var/tmp

Metadata:
Port mappings
Environment variables

The metadata has information on environment variables, port mappings, volumes, and other details we'll discuss later.

Containers run one process on startup. When this process completes, the container stops. This startup process can spawn others.

Ubuntu container 1

Process: nodejs

Diffs from Ubuntu image:
MODIFIED: /opt/app/nodejs.log

Ubuntu container 2

Process: mysql

Diffs from Ubuntu image:
DELETE: /etc/nologin

Ubuntu container 3

Process: apache

Diffs from Ubuntu image:
ADDED: //var/log/apache/apache.log

Changes to files are stored within the container in a copy-on-write mechanism. The base image cannot be affected by a container.

Containers are created from images, inherit their filesystems, and use their metadata to determine their startup configurations. Containers are separate but can be configured to communicate with each other.

Figure 1.5   Docker images and containers

1.2   *Building a Docker application*

We're going to get our hands dirty now by building a simple to-do application (todoapp) image with Docker. In the process, you'll see some key Docker features like Docker-files, image re-use, port exposure, and build automation. Here's what you'll learn in the next 10 minutes:

- How to create a Docker image using a Dockerfile
- How to tag a Docker image for easy reference
- How to run your new Docker image

A to-do app is one that helps you keep track of things you want to get done. The app we build will store and display short strings of information that can be marked as done, presented in a simple web interface. Figure 1.6 shows what we'll achieve by doing this.

The details of the application are unimportant. We're going to demonstrate that from the single short Dockerfile we're about to give you, you can reliably build, run,

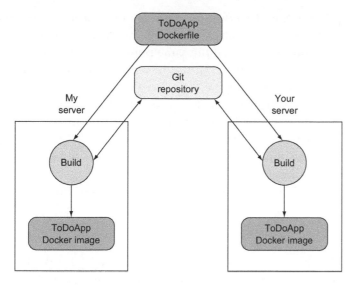

Figure 1.6   Building a Docker application

stop, and start an application in the same way on both your host and ours without needing to worry about application installations or dependencies. This is a key part of what Docker offers—reliably reproduced and easily managed and shared development environments. This means no more complex or ambiguous installation instructions to follow and potentially get lost in.

> **NOTE**   This to-do application will be used a few times throughout the book, and it's quite a useful one to play with and demonstrate, so it's worth familiarizing yourself with it.

1.2.1   Ways to create a new Docker image

There are four standard ways to create Docker images. Table 1.2 itemizes these methods.

Table 1.2   Options for creating Docker images

Method	Description	See technique
Docker commands / "By hand"	Fire up a container with `docker run` and input the commands to create your image on the command line. Create a new image with `docker commit`.	See technique 15
Dockerfile	Build from a known base image, and specify the build with a limited set of simple commands.	Discussed shortly
Dockerfile and configuration management (CM) tool	Same as Dockerfile, but you hand over control of the build to a more sophisticated CM tool.	See technique 55
Scratch image and import a set of files	From an empty image, import a TAR file with the required files.	See technique 11

The first "by hand" option is fine if you're doing proofs of concept to see whether your installation process works. At the same time, you should keep notes about the steps you're taking so that you can return to the same point if you need to.

At some point you're going to want to define the steps for creating your image. This is the Dockerfile option (and the one we'll use here).

For more complex builds, you may want to go for the third option, particularly when the Dockerfile features aren't sophisticated enough for your image's needs.

The final option builds from a null image by overlaying the set of files required to run the image. This is useful if you want to import a set of self-contained files created elsewhere, but this method is rarely seen in mainstream use.

We'll look at the Dockerfile method now; the other methods will be covered later in the book.

1.2.2 *Writing a Dockerfile*

A Dockerfile is a text file with a series of commands in it. Listing 1.1 is the Dockerfile we'll use for this example. Create a new folder, move into it, and create a file called "Dockerfile" with these contents.

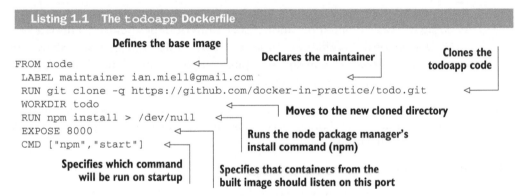

Listing 1.1 The `todoapp` Dockerfile

You begin the Dockerfile by defining the base image with the FROM command. This example uses a Node.js image so you have access to the Node.js binaries. The official Node.js image is called `node`.

Next, you declare the maintainer with the LABEL command. In this case, we're using one of our email addresses, but you can replace this with your own reference because it's your Dockerfile now. This line isn't required to make a working Docker image, but it's good practice to include it. At this point, the build has inherited the state of the node container, and you're ready to work on top of it.

Next, you clone the todoapp code with a RUN command. This uses the specified command to retrieve the code for the application, running `git` within the container. Git is installed inside the base node image in this case, but you can't take this kind of thing for granted.

Now you move to the new cloned directory with a `WORKDIR` command. Not only does this change directories within the build context, but the last `WORKDIR` command determines which directory you're in by default when you start up your container from your built image.

Next, you run the node package manager's install command (npm). This will set up the dependencies for your application. You aren't interested in the output in this example, so you redirect it to /dev/null.

Because port 8000 is used by the application, you use the `EXPOSE` command to tell Docker that containers from the built image should listen on this port.

Finally, you use the `CMD` command to tell Docker which command will be run when the container is started up.

This simple example illustrates several key features of Docker and Dockerfiles. A Dockerfile is a simple sequence of a limited set of commands run in strict order. It affects the files and metadata of the resulting image. Here the `RUN` command affects the filesystem by checking out and installing applications, and the `EXPOSE`, `CMD`, and `WORKDIR` commands affect the metadata of the image.

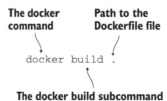

Figure 1.7   Docker `build` command

1.2.3   *Building a Docker image*

You've defined your Dockerfile's build steps. Now you're going to build the Docker image from it by typing the command in figure 1.7. The output will look similar to this:

Each command results in a new image being created, and the image ID is output.

Docker uploads the files and directories under the path supplied to the docker build command.

Each build step is numbered sequentially from I and is output with the command.

```
Sending build context to Docker daemon  2.048kB
 Step 1/7 : FROM node
  ---> 2ca756a6578b
 Step 2/7 : LABEL maintainer ian.miell@gmail.com
 ---> Running in bf73f87c88d6
 ---> 5383857304fc
Removing intermediate container bf73f87c88d6
 Step 3/7 : RUN git clone -q https://github.com/docker-in-practice/todo.git
 ---> Running in 761baf524cc1
 ---> 4350cb1c977c
Removing intermediate container 761baf524cc1
Step 4/7 : WORKDIR todo
 ---> a1b24710f458
Removing intermediate container 0f8cd22fbe83
Step 5/7 : RUN npm install > /dev/null
 ---> Running in 92a8f9ba530a
npm info it worked if it ends with ok
 [...]
npm info ok
```

To save space, each intermediate container is removed before continuing.

Debug of the build is output here (and edited out of this listing).

```
 ---> 6ee4d7bba544
Removing intermediate container 92a8f9ba530a
Step 6/7 : EXPOSE 8000
 ---> Running in 8e33c1ded161
 ---> 3ea44544f13c
Removing intermediate container 8e33c1ded161
Step 7/7 : CMD npm start
 ---> Running in ccc076ee38fe
 ---> 66c76cea05bb
Removing intermediate container ccc076ee38fe
Successfully built 66c76cea05bb
```

The final image ID for this build, ready to tag

You now have a Docker image with an image ID ("66c76cea05bb" in the preceding example, but your ID will be different). It can be cumbersome to keep referring to this ID, so you can tag it for easier reference, as shown in figure 1.8.

Type the preceding command, replacing the 66c76cea05bb with whatever image ID was generated for you.

You can now build your own copy of a Docker image from a Dockerfile, reproducing an environment defined by someone else!

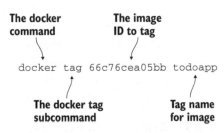

The docker command

The image ID to tag

```
docker tag 66c76cea05bb todoapp
```

The docker tag subcommand

Tag name for image

Figure 1.8   Docker `tag` subcommand

1.2.4   *Running a Docker container*

You've built and tagged your Docker image. Now you can run it as a container:

Listing 1.2   `docker run` output for todoapp

```
$ docker run -i -t -p 8000:8000 --name example1 todoapp
 npm install
npm info it worked if it ends with ok
npm info using npm@2.14.4
npm info using node@v4.1.1
npm info prestart todomvc-swarm@0.0.1

> todomvc-swarm@0.0.1 prestart /todo
 > make all

npm install
npm info it worked if it ends with ok
npm info using npm@2.14.4
npm info using node@v4.1.1
npm WARN package.json todomvc-swarm@0.0.1 No repository field.
npm WARN package.json todomvc-swarm@0.0.1 license should be a valid SPDX
➥ license expression
npm info preinstall todomvc-swarm@0.0.1
npm info package.json statics@0.1.0 license should be a valid SPDX license
➥ expression
```

The docker run subcommand starts the container, -p maps the container's port 8000 to the port 8000 on the host machine, --name gives the container a unique name, and the last argument is the image.

The output of the container's starting process is sent to the terminal.

```
npm info package.json react-tools@0.11.2 No license field.
npm info package.json react@0.11.2 No license field.
npm info package.json node-
    jsx@0.11.0 license should be a valid SPDX license expression
npm info package.json ws@0.4.32 No license field.
npm info build /todo
npm info linkStuff todomvc-swarm@0.0.1
npm info install todomvc-swarm@0.0.1
npm info postinstall todomvc-swarm@0.0.1
npm info prepublish todomvc-swarm@0.0.1
npm info ok
if [ ! -e dist/ ]; then mkdir dist; fi
cp node_modules/react/dist/react.min.js dist/react.min.js

LocalTodoApp.js:9:     // TODO: default english version
LocalTodoApp.js:84:            fwdList = this.host.get('/TodoList#'+listId);
 // TODO fn+id sig
TodoApp.js:117:        // TODO scroll into view
TodoApp.js:176:        if (i>=list.length()) { i=list.length()-1; } // TODO
➥ .length
local.html:30:    <!-- TODO 2-split, 3-split -->
model/TodoList.js:29:        // TODO one op - repeated spec? long spec?
view/Footer.jsx:61:        // TODO: show the entry's metadata
view/Footer.jsx:80:            todoList.addObject(new TodoItem()); // TODO
➥ create default
view/Header.jsx:25:        // TODO list some meaningful header (apart from the
➥ id)
```

```
npm info start todomvc-swarm@0.0.1
```

Press Ctrl-C here to terminate the process and the container.

```
> todomvc-swarm@0.0.1 start /todo
> node TodoAppServer.js

Swarm server started port 8000
^Cshutting down http-server...  ◄──────
 closing swarm host...
swarm host closed
npm info lifecycle todomvc-swarm@0.0.1~poststart: todomvc-swarm@0.0.1
npm info ok
$ docker ps -a                                              ◄──
 CONTAINER ID  IMAGE     COMMAND      CREATED        STATUS PORTS  NAMES
b9db5ada0461  todoapp  "npm start"  2 minutes ago  Exited (0) 2 minutes ago
➥        example1
$ docker start example1        ◄─
 example1
$ docker ps
CONTAINER ID  IMAGE    COMMAND     CREATED        STATUS
➥ PORTS               NAMES
b9db5ada0461  todoapp  "npm start"  8 minutes ago  Up 10 seconds
➥ 0.0.0.0:8000->8000/tcp  example1
 $ docker diff example1        ◄──
 C /root
C /root/.npm
C /root/.npm/_locks
C /root/.npm/anonymous-cli-metrics.json
```

Run this command to see containers that have been started and removed, along with an ID and status (like a process).

Restart the container, this time in the background.

Run the ps command again to see the changed status.

The docker diff subcommand shows you what files have been affected since the image was instantiated as a container.

```
C /todo
 A /todo/.swarm
 A /todo/.swarm/_log
 A /todo/dist
 A /todo/dist/LocalTodoApp.app.js
 A /todo/dist/TodoApp.app.js
 A /todo/dist/react.min.js
C /todo/node_modules
```

The /todo directory has been changed (C).

The /todo/.swarm directory has been added (A).

The `docker run` subcommand starts up the container. The `-p` flag maps the container's port 8000 to the port 8000 on the host machine, so you should now be able to navigate with your browser to http://localhost:8000 to view the application. The `--name` flag gives the container a unique name you can refer to later for convenience. The last argument is the image name.

Once the container has been started, you can press Ctrl-C to terminate the process and the container. You can run the `ps` command to see the containers that have been started but not removed. Note that each container has its own container ID and status, analogous to a process. Its status is `Exited`, but you can restart it. After you do, notice how the status has changed to `Up` and the port mapping from container to host machine is now displayed.

The `docker diff` subcommand shows you which files have been affected since the image was instantiated as a container. In this case, the todo directory has been changed (C), and the other listed files have been added (A). No files have been deleted (D), which is the other possibility.

As you can see, the fact that Docker "contains" your environment means that you can treat it as an entity on which actions can be predictably performed. This gives Docker its breadth of power—you can affect the software lifecycle from development to production and maintenance. These changes are what this book will cover, showing you in practical terms what can be done with Docker.

Next you're going to learn about layering, another key concept in Docker.

1.2.5 *Docker layering*

Docker layering helps you manage a big problem that arises when you use containers at scale. Imagine what would happen if you started up hundreds—or even thousands—of the to-do app, and each of those required a copy of the files to be stored somewhere.

As you can imagine, disk space would run out pretty quickly! By default, Docker internally uses a copy-on-write mechanism to reduce the amount of disk space required (see figure 1.9). Whenever a running container needs to write to a file, it records the change by copying the item to a new area of disk. When a Docker commit is performed, this new area of disk is frozen and recorded as a layer with its own identifier.

This partly explains how Docker containers can start up so quickly—they have nothing to copy because all the data has already been stored as the image.

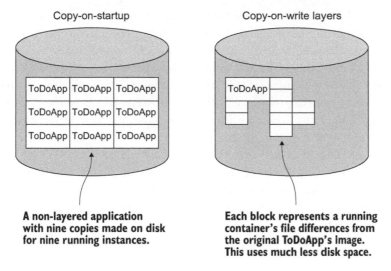

Figure 1.9   Docker filesystem layers

> **TIP** Copy-on-write is a standard optimization strategy used in computing. When you create a new object (of any type) from a template, rather than copying the entire set of data required, you only copy data over when it's changed. Depending on the use case, this can save considerable resources.

Figure 1.10 illustrates that the to-do app you've built has three layers you're interested in. The layers are static, so if you need to change anything in a higher layer, you can just build on top of the image you wish to take as a reference. In the to-do app, you built from the publicly available node image and layered changes on top.

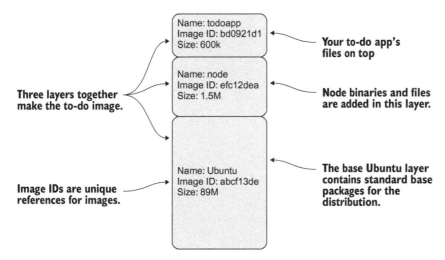

Figure 1.10   The todoapp's filesystem layering in Docker

All three layers can be shared across multiple running containers, much as a shared library can be shared in memory across multiple running processes. This is a vital feature for operations, allowing you to run numerous containers based on different images on host machines without running out of disk space.

Imagine that you're running the to-do app as a live service for paying customers. You can scale up your offering to a large number of users. If you're developing, you can spin up many different environments on your local machine at once. If you're moving through test, you can run many more tests simultaneously, and far more quickly than before. All these things are made possible by layering.

By building and running an application with Docker, you've begun to see the power that Docker can bring to your workflow. Reproducing and sharing specific environments and being able to land these in various places gives you both flexibility and control over development.

Summary

- Docker is an attempt to do for software what containerization did for the shipping industry: reducing the cost of local differences through standardization.
- Some of the uses for Docker include prototyping software, packaging software, reducing the cost of testing and debugging environments, and enabling DevOps practices such as continuous delivery (CD).
- You can build and run a Docker application from a Dockerfile using the commands `docker build` and `docker run`.
- A Docker image is the template for a running container. This is similar to the difference between a program executable and a running process.
- Changes to running containers can be committed and tagged as new images.
- Images are created from a layered filesystem, which reduces the space used by Docker images on your host.

Understanding Docker: Inside the engine room

This chapter covers

- Docker's architecture
- Tracing the internals of Docker on your host
- Using the Docker Hub to find and download images
- Setting up your own Docker registry
- Getting containers to communicate with each other

Grasping Docker's architecture is key to understanding Docker more fully. In this chapter you'll get an overview of Docker's major components on your machine and on the network, and you'll learn some techniques that will develop this understanding.

In the process, you'll learn some nifty tricks that will help you use Docker (and Linux) more effectively. Many of the later and more advanced techniques in this book will be based on what you see here, so pay special attention to what follows.

2.1   *Docker's architecture*

Figure 2.1 lays out Docker's architecture, and that will be the centerpiece of this chapter. We're going to start with a high-level look and then focus on each part, with techniques designed to cement your understanding.

Docker on your host machine is (at the time of writing) split into two parts—a daemon with a RESTful API and a client that talks to the daemon. Figure 2.1 shows your host machine running the Docker client and daemon.

> **TIP** A RESTful API uses standard HTTP request types such as GET, POST, DELETE, and others to represent resources and operations on them. In this case images, containers, volumes, and the like are the represented resources.

You invoke the Docker client to get information from or give instructions to the daemon; the daemon is a server that receives requests and returns responses from the client using the HTTP protocol. In turn, it will make requests to other services to send and receive images, also using the HTTP protocol. The server will accept requests from the command-line client or anyone else authorized to connect. The daemon is also

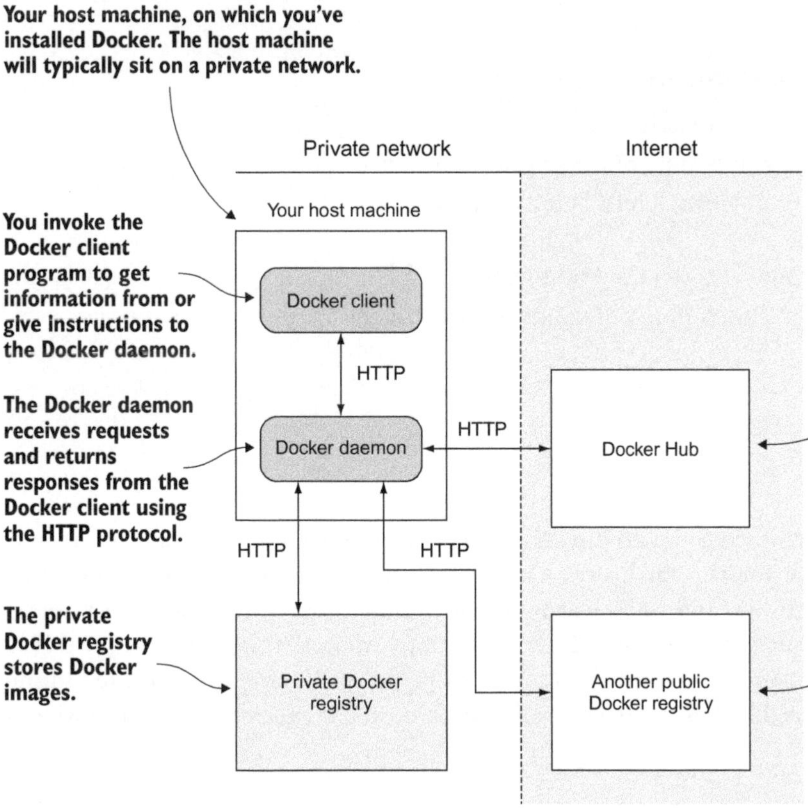

Your host machine, on which you've installed Docker. The host machine will typically sit on a private network.

You invoke the Docker client program to get information from or give instructions to the Docker daemon.

The Docker daemon receives requests and returns responses from the Docker client using the HTTP protocol.

The private Docker registry stores Docker images.

The Docker Hub is a public registry run by Docker, Inc.

Other public registries can also exist on the internet.

Figure 2.1   Overview of Docker's architecture

responsible for taking care of your images and containers behind the scenes, whereas the client acts as the intermediary between you and the RESTful API.

The private Docker registry is a service that stores Docker images. These can be requested from any Docker daemon that has the relevant access. This registry is on an internal network and isn't publicly accessible, so it's considered private.

Your host machine will typically sit on a private network. The Docker daemon will call out to the internet to retrieve images if requested.

The Docker Hub is a public registry run by Docker Inc. Other public registries can also exist on the internet, and your Docker daemon can interact with them.

In the first chapter we said that Docker containers can be shipped to anywhere you can run Docker—this isn't strictly true. In fact, containers will run on the machine only if the *daemon* can be installed.

The key point to take from figure 2.1 is that when you run Docker on your machine, you may be interacting with other processes on your machine, or even services running on your network or the internet.

Now that you have a picture of how Docker is laid out, we'll introduce various techniques relating to the different parts of the figure.

2.2 The Docker daemon

The Docker daemon (see figure 2.2) is the hub of your interactions with Docker, and as such it's the best place to start gaining an understanding of all the relevant pieces. It controls access to Docker on your machine, manages the state of your containers and images, and brokers interactions with the outside world.

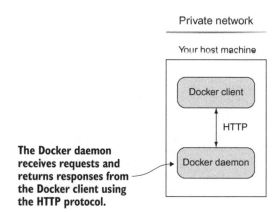

The Docker daemon receives requests and returns responses from the Docker client using the HTTP protocol.

Figure 2.2   The Docker daemon

TIP   A *daemon* is a process that runs in the background rather than under the direct control of the user. A *server* is a process that takes requests from a client and performs the actions required to fulfill the requests. Daemons are frequently also servers that accept requests from clients to perform actions for them. The `docker` command is a client, and the Docker daemon acts as the server doing the processing on your Docker containers and images.

Let's look at a couple of techniques that illustrate how Docker effectively runs as a daemon, and how your interactions with it using the docker command are limited to simple requests to perform actions, much like interactions with a web server. The first technique allows others to connect to your Docker daemon and perform the same actions you might on your host machine, and the second illustrates that Docker containers are managed by the daemon, not your shell session.

TECHNIQUE 1 **Open your Docker daemon to the world**

Although by default your Docker daemon is accessible only on your host, there can be good reason to allow others to access it. You might have a problem that you want someone to debug remotely, or you may want to allow another part of your DevOps workflow to kick off a process on a host machine.

> **WARNING** Although this can be a powerful and useful technique, it's considered insecure. A Docker socket can be exploited by anyone with access (including containers with a mounted Docker socket) to get root privileges.

PROBLEM

You want to open your Docker server up for others to access.

SOLUTION

Start the Docker daemon with an open TCP address.

Figure 2.3 gives an overview of how this technique works.

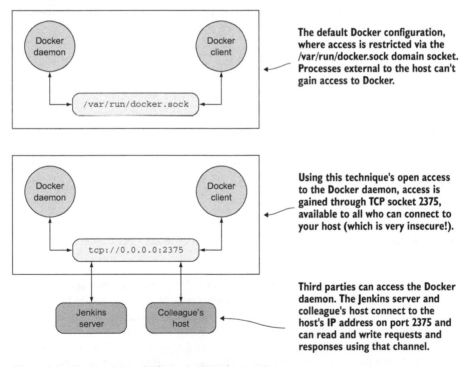

Figure 2.3 Docker accessibility: normal and opened up

Before you open up the Docker daemon, you must first shut the running one down. How you do this will vary depending on your operating system (non-Linux users should see appendix A). If you're not sure how to do this, start with this command:

```
$ sudo service docker stop
```

If you get a message that looks like this,

```
The service command supports only basic LSB actions (start, stop, restart,
try-restart, reload, force-reload, status). For other actions, please try
to use systemctl.
```

then you have a systemctl-based startup system. Try this command:

```
$ systemctl stop docker
```

If that works, you shouldn't see any output from this command:

```
$ ps -ef | grep -E 'docker(d| -d| daemon)\b' | grep -v grep
```

Once the Docker daemon has been stopped, you can restart it manually and open it up to outside users with the following command:

```
$ sudo docker daemon -H tcp://0.0.0.0:2375
```

This command starts as a daemon (docker daemon), defines the host server with the -H flag, uses the TCP protocol, opens up all IP interfaces (with 0.0.0.0), and opens up the standard Docker server port (2375).

You can connect from outside with the following command:

```
$ docker -H tcp://<your host's ip>:2375 <subcommand>
```

Or you can export the DOCKER_HOST environment variable (this won't work if you have to use sudo to run Docker—see technique 41 to find out how to remove this requirement):

```
$ export DOCKER_HOST=tcp://<your host's ip>:2375
$ docker <subcommand>
```

Note that you'll also need to do one of these from inside your local machine as well, because Docker is no longer listening in the default location.

If you want to make this change permanent on your host, you'll need to configure your startup system. See appendix B for information on how to do this.

> **WARNING** If you use this technique to make your Docker daemon listen on a port, be aware that specifying the IP as 0.0.0.0 gives access to users on all network interfaces (both public and private), which is generally considered insecure.

DISCUSSION

This is a great technique if you have a powerful machine dedicated to Docker inside a secure private local network, because everyone on the network can easily point Docker tools to the right place—DOCKER_HOST is a well-known environment variable that will inform most programs that access Docker where to look.

As an alternative to the somewhat cumbersome process of stopping the Docker service and running it manually, you could combine mounting the Docker socket as a volume (from technique 45) with using the socat tool to forward traffic from an external port—simply run `docker run -p 2375:2375 -v /var/run/docker.sock:/var/run/docker.sock sequenceid/socat`.

You'll see a specific example of something this technique allows later in the chapter, in technique 5.

TECHNIQUE 2 **Running containers as daemons**

As you get familiar with Docker (and if you're anything like us), you'll start to think of other use cases for Docker, and one of the first of these is to run Docker containers as background services.

Running Docker containers as services with predictable behavior through software isolation is one of the principal use cases for Docker. This technique will allow you to manage services in a way that works for your operation.

PROBLEM

You want to run a Docker container in the background as a service.

SOLUTION

Use the -d flag to the `docker run` command, and use related container-management flags to define the service characteristics.

Docker containers—like most processes—will run by default in the foreground. The most obvious way to run a Docker container in the background is to use the standard & control operator. Although this works, you can run into problems if you log out of your terminal session, necessitating that you use the nohup flag, which creates a file in your local directory with output that you have to manage... You get the idea: it's far neater to use the Docker daemon's functionality for this.

To do this, you use the -d flag.

```
$ docker run -d -i -p 1234:1234 --name daemon ubuntu:14.04 nc -l 1234
```

The -d flag, when used with `docker run`, runs the container as a daemon. The -i flag gives this container the ability to interact with your Telnet session. With -p you publish the 1234 port from the container to the host. The --name flag lets you give the container a name so you can refer to it later. Finally, you run a simple listening echo server on port 1234 with netcat (nc).

You can now connect to it and send messages with Telnet. You'll see that the container has received the message by using the `docker logs` command, as shown in the following listing.

Listing 2.1 Connecting to the container netcat server with Telnet

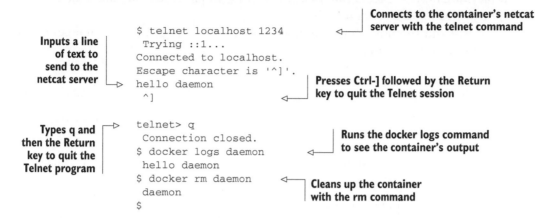

You can see that running a container as a daemon is simple enough, but operationally some questions remain to be answered:

- What happens to the service if it fails?
- What happens to the service when it terminates?
- What happens if the service keeps failing over and over?

Fortunately Docker provides flags for each of these questions!

NOTE Although restart flags are used most often with the daemon flag (-d), it's not a requirement to run these flags with -d.

The docker run--restart flag allows you to apply a set of rules to be followed (a so-called "restart policy") when the container terminates (see table 2.1).

Table 2.1 Docker restart flag options

Policy	Description
no	Don't restart when the container exits
always	Always restart when the container exits
unless-stopped	Always restart, but remember explicitly stopping
on-failure[:max-retry]	Restart only on failure

The no policy is simple: when the container exits, it isn't restarted. This is the default.
The always policy is also simple, but it's worth discussing briefly:

```
$ docker run -d --restart=always ubuntu echo done
```

This command runs the container as a daemon (-d) and always restarts the container on termination (--restart=always). It issues a simple echo command that completes quickly, exiting the container.

If you run the preceding command and then run a docker ps command, you'll see output similar to this:

```
$ docker ps
CONTAINER ID        IMAGE                       COMMAND                     CREATED
    STATUS                      PORTS                       NAMES
69828b118ec3        ubuntu:14.04        "echo done"                 4 seconds ago
    Restarting  (0) Less than a second ago                         sick_brattain
```

The docker ps command lists all the running containers and information about them, including the following:

- When the container was created (CREATED).
- The current status of the container—usually this will be Restarting, because it will only run for a short time (STATUS).
- The exit code of the container's previous run (also under STATUS). 0 means the run was successful.
- The container name. By default, Docker names containers by concatenating two random words. Sometimes this produces odd results (which is why we typically recommend giving them a meaningful name).

Note that the STATUS column also informed us that the container exited less than a second ago and is restarting. This is because the echo done command exits immediately, and Docker must continually restart the container.

It's important to note that Docker reuses the container ID. It doesn't change on restart, and there will only ever be one entry in the ps table for this Docker invocation.

Specifying unless-stopped is almost the same as always—both will cease restarting if you run docker stop on a container, but unless-stopped will make sure that this stopped status is remembered if the daemon restarts (perhaps if you restart your computer), whereas always will bring the container back up again.

Finally, the on-failure policy restarts only when the container returns a non-zero exit code (which normally means failing) from its main process:

```
$ docker run -d --restart=on-failure:10 ubuntu /bin/false
```

This command runs the container as a daemon (-d) and sets a limit on the number of restart attempts (--restart=on-failure:10), exiting if this is exceeded. It runs a simple command (/bin/false) that completes quickly and will definitely fail.

If you run the preceding command and wait a minute, and then run docker ps -a, you'll see output similar to this:

```
$ docker ps -a
CONTAINER ID        IMAGE                     COMMAND              CREATED
➧     STATUS                          PORTS                NAMES
b0f40c410fe3        ubuntu:14.04          "/bin/false"         2 minutes ago
➧     Exited (1) 25 seconds ago                            loving_rosalind
```

DISCUSSION

Creating services to run in the background often comes with the difficulty of making sure the background service won't crash in unusual environments. Because it's not immediately visible, users may not notice that something isn't working correctly.

This technique lets you stop thinking about the incidental complexity of your service, caused by the environment and handling restarts. You can focus your thinking on the core functionality.

As a concrete example, you and your team might use this technique to run multiple databases on the same machine and avoid having to write instructions for setting them up or to have terminals open to keep them running.

TECHNIQUE 3   **Moving Docker to a different partition**

Docker stores all the data relating to your containers and images under a folder. Because it can store a potentially large number of different images, this folder can get big fast!

If your host machine has different partitions (as is common in enterprise Linux workstations), you may encounter space limitations more quickly. In these cases, you may want to move the directory from which Docker operates.

PROBLEM

You want to move where Docker stores its data.

SOLUTION

Stop and start the Docker daemon, specifying the new location with the -g flag.

Imagine you want to run Docker from /home/dockeruser/mydocker. First, stop your Docker daemon (see appendix B for a discussion on how to do this). Then run this command:

```
$ dockerd -g /home/dockeruser/mydocker
```

A new set of folders and files will be created in this directory. These folders are internal to Docker, so play with them at your peril (as we've discovered!).

You should be aware that this command will appear to wipe the containers and images from your previous Docker daemon. Don't despair. If you kill the Docker process you just ran, and restart your Docker service, your Docker client will be pointed back at its original location, and your containers and images will be returned to you. If you want to make this move permanent, you'll need to configure your host system's startup process accordingly.

DISCUSSION

Aside from the obvious use case for this (reclaiming space on disks with limited disk space), you could also use this technique if you wanted to strictly partition sets of images and containers. For example, if you have access to multiple private Docker registries with different owners, it might be worth the extra effort to make sure you don't accidentally give private data to the wrong person.

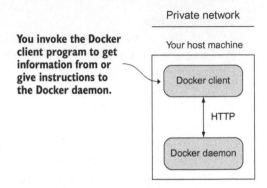

You invoke the Docker client program to get information from or give instructions to the Docker daemon.

Figure 2.4   The Docker client

2.3   *The Docker client*

The Docker client (see figure 2.4) is the simplest component in the Docker architecture. It's what you run when you type commands like `docker run` or `docker pull` on your machine. Its job is to communicate with the Docker daemon via HTTP requests.

In this section you're going to see how you can snoop on messages between the Docker client and server. You'll also see a way of using your browser as a Docker client and a few basic techniques related to port mapping that represent baby steps toward orchestration, discussed in part 4 of this book.

TECHNIQUE 4   Using socat to monitor Docker API traffic

Occasionally the `docker` command may not work as you expect. Most often, some aspect of the command-line arguments hasn't been understood, but occasionally there are more serious setup problems, such as the Docker binary being out of date. In order to diagnose the problem, it can be useful to view the flow of data to and from the Docker daemon you're communicating with.

> **NOTE** Don't panic! The presence of this technique doesn't indicate that Docker needs to be debugged often, or that it's in any way unstable! This technique is here primarily as a tool for understanding Docker's architecture, and also to introduce you to socat, a powerful tool. If, like us, you use Docker in a lot of different locations, there will be differences in the Docker versions you use. As with any software, different versions will have different features and flags, which can catch you out.

PROBLEM

You want to debug a problem with a Docker command.

SOLUTION

Use a traffic snooper to inspect the API calls and craft your own.

In this technique you'll insert a proxy Unix domain socket between your request and the server's socket to see what passes through it (as shown in figure 2.5). Note that you'll need root or sudo privileges to make this work.

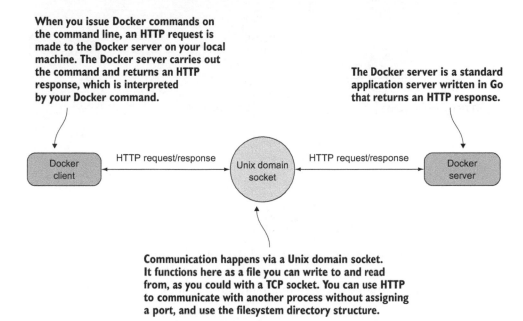

When you issue Docker commands on the command line, an HTTP request is made to the Docker server on your local machine. The Docker server carries out the command and returns an HTTP response, which is interpreted by your Docker command.

The Docker server is a standard application server written in Go that returns an HTTP response.

Communication happens via a Unix domain socket. It functions here as a file you can write to and read from, as you could with a TCP socket. You can use HTTP to communicate with another process without assigning a port, and use the filesystem directory structure.

Figure 2.5   Docker's client/server architecture on your host

To create this proxy, you'll use socat.

> **TIP** socat is a powerful command that allows you to relay data between two data channels of almost any type. If you're familiar with netcat, you can think of it as netcat on steroids. To install it, use the standard package manager for your system.

```
$ socat -v UNIX-LISTEN:/tmp/dockerapi.sock,fork \
  UNIX-CONNECT:/var/run/docker.sock &
```

In this command, -v makes the output readable, with indications of the flow of data. The UNIX-LISTEN part tells socat to listen on a Unix socket, fork ensures that socat doesn't exit after the first request, and UNIX-CONNECT tells socat to connect to Docker's Unix socket. The & specifies that the command runs in the background. If you usually run the Docker client with sudo, you'll need to do the same thing here as well.

The new route that your requests to the daemon will travel can be seen in figure 2.6. All traffic traveling in each direction will be seen by socat and logged to your terminal, in addition to any output that the Docker client provides.

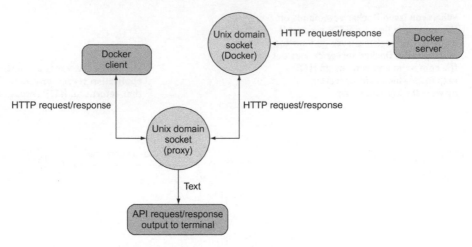

Figure 2.6   Docker client and server with socat inserted as a proxy

The output of a simple docker command will now look similar to this:

```
$ docker -H unix:///tmp/dockerapi.sock ps -a          ◁── The command you issue
 > 2017/05/15 16:01:51.163427  length=83 from=0 to=82      to see the request and
GET /_ping HTTP/1.1\r                                       response
Host: docker\r
User-Agent: Docker-Client/17.04.0-ce (linux)\r
\r
< 2017/05/15 16:01:51.164132  length=215 from=0 to=214
HTTP/1.1 200 OK\r
Api-Version: 1.28\r
Docker-Experimental: false\r
Ostype: linux\r
Server: Docker/17.04.0-ce (linux)\r
Date: Mon, 15 May 2017 15:01:51 GMT\r
Content-Length: 2\r                               The HTTP request
Content-Type: text/plain; charset=utf-8\r         begins here, with
\r                                                the right angle
OK> 2017/05/15 16:01:51.165175  length=105 from=83 to=187  ◁── bracket on the left.
 GET /v1.28/containers/json?all=1 HTTP/1.1\r
Host: docker\r
User-Agent: Docker-Client/17.04.0-ce (linux)\r
\r
< 2017/05/15 16:01:51.165819  length=886 from=215 to=1100  ◁── The HTTP response
 HTTP/1.1 200 OK\r                                begins here, with
Api-Version: 1.28\r                               the left angle
Content-Type: application/json\r                  bracket on the left.
Docker-Experimental: false\r
Ostype: linux\r
Server: Docker/17.04.0-ce (linux)\r
Date: Mon, 15 May 2017 15:01:51 GMT\r
Content-Length: 680\r
\r
[{"Id":"1d0d5b5a7b506417949653a59deac030ccbcbb816842a63ba68401708d55383e",
➥ "Names":["/example1"],"Image":"todoapp","ImageID":
```

```
⇨   "sha256:ccdda5b6b021f7d12bd2c16dbcd2f195ff20d10a660921db0ac5bff5ecd92bc2",
⇨   "Command":"npm start","Created":1494857777,"Ports":[],"Labels":{},
⇨   "State":"exited","Status":"Exited (0) 45 minutes ago","HostConfig":
⇨   {"NetworkMode":"default"},"NetworkSettings":{"Networks":{"bridge":
⇨   {"IPAMConfig":null,"Links":null,"Aliases":null,"NetworkID":
⇨   "6f327d67a38b57379afa7525ea63829797fd31a948b316fdf2ae0365faeed632",
⇨   "EndpointID":"","Gateway":"","IPAddress":"","IPPrefixLen":0,
⇨   "IPv6Gateway":"","GlobalIPv6Address":"","GlobalIPv6PrefixLen":0,
⇨   "MacAddress":""}},"Mounts":[]}]
    CONTAINER ID        IMAGE                   COMMAND             CREATED
⇨       STATUS                          PORTS               NAMES
    1d0d5b5a7b50        todoapp                 "npm start"         45 minutes ago
⇨       Exited (0) 45 minutes ago                           example1
```

The JSON content of the response from the Docker server

The output as normally seen by the user, interpreted by the Docker client from the preceding JSON

The specifics of the preceding output will change with the Docker API's growth and development. When you run the preceding command, you'll see later version numbers and different JSON output. You can check your client and server versions of the API by running the `docker version` command.

> **WARNING** If you ran socat as root in the previous example, you'll need to use sudo to run the `docker -H` command. This is because the dockerapi.sock file is owned by root.

Using socat is a powerful way to debug not only Docker, but any other network services you might come across in the course of your work.

DISCUSSION

It's possible to come up with a number of other use cases for this technique:

- Socat is quite a Swiss Army knife and can handle quite a number of different protocols. The preceding example shows it listening on a Unix socket, but you could also make it listen on an external port with `TCP-LISTEN:2375,fork` instead of the `UNIX-LISTEN:…` argument. This acts as a simpler version of technique 1. With this approach there's no need to restart the Docker daemon (which would kill any running containers). You can just bring the socat listener up and down as you desire.
- Because the preceding point is so simple to set up and is temporary, you can use it in combination with technique 47 to join a colleague's running container remotely and help them debug an issue. You can also employ the little-used `docker attach` command to join the same terminal they started with `docker run`, allowing you to collaborate directly.
- If you have a shared Docker server (perhaps set up with technique 1) you could use the ability to expose externals and set up socat as the broker between the outside world and the Docker socket to make it act as a primitive audit log, recording where all requests are coming from and what they're doing.

It can be difficult to sell new technologies, so simple and effective demonstrations are invaluable. Making the demo hands-on is even better, which is why we've found that creating a web page that allows users to interact with a container in a browser is a great technique. It gives newcomers their first taste of Docker in an easily accessible way, allowing them to create a container, use a container terminal in a browser, attach to someone else's terminal, and share control. The significant "wow" factor doesn't hurt either!

PROBLEM

You want to demonstrate the power of Docker without requiring users to install it themselves or run commands they don't understand.

SOLUTION

Start the Docker daemon with an open port and Cross-Origin-Resource Sharing (CORS) enabled, and then serve the docker-terminal repository in your web server of choice.

The most common use of a REST API is to expose it on a server and use JavaScript on a web page to make calls to it. Because Docker happens to perform all interaction via a REST API, you should be able to control Docker in the same way. Although it may initially seem surprising, this control extends all the way to being able to interact with a container via a terminal in your browser.

We've already discussed how to start the daemon on port 2375 in technique 1, so we won't go into any detail on that. Additionally, CORS is too much to go into here. If you're unfamiliar with it, refer to *CORS in Action* by Monsur Hossain (Manning, 2014). In short, CORS is a mechanism that carefully bypasses the usual restriction of JavaScript that limits you to only accessing the current domain. In this case, CORS allows the daemon to listen on a different port from where you serve your Docker terminal page. To enable CORS, you need to start the Docker daemon with the option `--api-enable-cors` alongside the option to make it listen on a port.

Now that the prerequisites are sorted, let's get this running. First, you need to get the code:

```
git clone https://github.com/aidanhs/Docker-Terminal.git
cd Docker-Terminal
```

Then you need to serve the files:

```
python2 -m SimpleHTTPServer 8000
```

The preceding command uses a module built into Python to serve static files from a directory. Feel free to use any equivalent you prefer. Now visit http://localhost:8000 in your browser and start a container.

Figure 2.7 shows how the Docker terminal connects up. The page is hosted on your local computer and connects to the Docker daemon on your local computer to perform any operations.

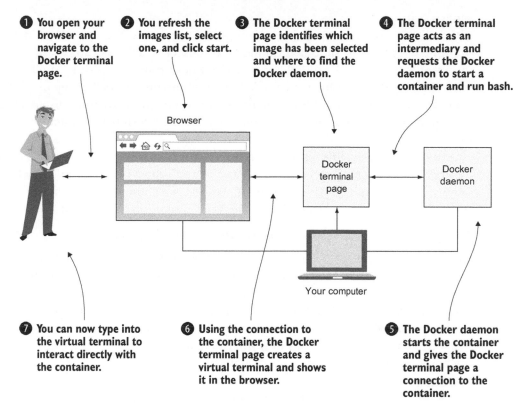

1 You open your browser and navigate to the Docker terminal page.

2 You refresh the images list, select one, and click start.

3 The Docker terminal page identifies which image has been selected and where to find the Docker daemon.

4 The Docker terminal page acts as an intermediary and requests the Docker daemon to start a container and run bash.

Browser

Docker terminal page

Docker daemon

Your computer

7 You can now type into the virtual terminal to interact directly with the container.

6 Using the connection to the container, the Docker terminal page creates a virtual terminal and shows it in the browser.

5 The Docker daemon starts the container and gives the Docker terminal page a connection to the container.

Figure 2.7   How the Docker terminal works

It's worth being aware of the following points if you want to give this link to other people:

- The other person must not be using a proxy of any kind. This is the most common source of errors we've seen—Docker terminal uses WebSockets, which don't currently work through proxies.
- Giving a link to `localhost` obviously won't work—you'll need to give out the external IP address.
- Docker terminal needs to know where to find the Docker API—it should do this automatically based on the address you're visiting in the browser, but it's something to be aware of.

TIP If you're more experienced with Docker, you might wonder why we didn't use a Docker image in this technique. The reason is that we're still introducing Docker and didn't want to add to the complexity for readers new to Docker. Dockerizing this technique is left as an exercise for the reader.

DISCUSSION

Although we originally used this technique as an exciting demo for Docker (having multiple people easily share a terminal on disposable machines can be difficult to set up, even with terminal multiplexers), we've found some interesting applications in some unrelated areas. One example is using it to monitor a small group of trainees in some task at the command line. There's no need for you or them to install anything; just open your browser and you can connect to their terminal to jump in and give them a hand at any time!

On a similar note, this has some strengths in collaboration. In the past, when we've wanted to share a bug with a coworker, we've reproduced the bug in a Docker container so we can track it down together. With this technique, there's no need to go through a possible "but why do I want Docker?" discussion beforehand.

TECHNIQUE 6 **Using ports to connect to containers**

Docker containers have been designed from the outset to run services. In the majority of cases, these will be HTTP services of one kind or another. A significant proportion of these will be web services accessible through the browser.

This leads to a problem. If you have multiple Docker containers running on port 80 in their internal environment, they can't all be accessible on port 80 on your host machine. This technique shows how you can manage this common scenario by exposing and mapping a port from your container.

PROBLEM

You want to make multiple Docker container services available on a port from your host machine.

SOLUTION

Use Docker's -p flag to map a container's port to your host machine.

In this example we're going to use the tutum-wordpress image. Let's say you want to run two of these on your host machine to serve different blogs.

Because a number of people have wanted to do this before, someone has prepared an image that anyone can acquire and start up. To obtain images from external locations, you can use the `docker pull` command. By default, images will be downloaded from the Docker Hub:

```
$ docker pull tutum/wordpress
```

Images will also be retrieved automatically when you try to run them if they're not already present on your machine.

To run the first blog, use the following command:

```
$ docker run -d -p 10001:80 --name blog1 tutum/wordpress
```

This `docker run` command runs the container as a daemon (`-d`) with the publish flag (`-p`). It identifies the host port (`10001`) to map to the container port (`80`) and gives the container a name to identify it (`--name blog1 tutum/wordpress`).

You can do the same for the second blog:

```
$ docker run -d -p 10002:80 --name blog2 tutum/wordpress
```

If you now run this command,

```
$ docker ps | grep blog
```

you'll see the two blog containers listed, with their port mappings, looking something like this:

```
$ docker ps | grep blog
9afb95ad3617  tutum/wordpress:latest  "/run.sh" 9 seconds ago
➥ Up 9 seconds   3306/tcp, 0.0.0.0:10001->80/tcp  blog1
31ddc8a7a2fd  tutum/wordpress:latest  "/run.sh" 17 seconds ago
➥ Up 16 seconds  3306/tcp, 0.0.0.0:10002->80/tcp  blog2
```

You'll now be able to access your containers by navigating to http://localhost:10001 and http://localhost:10002.

To remove the containers when you're finished (assuming you don't want to keep them—we'll make use of them in the next technique), run this command:

```
$ docker rm -f blog1 blog2
```

You should now be able to run multiple identical images and services on your host by managing the port allocations yourself, if necessary.

> **TIP** It can be easy to forget which port is the host's and which port is the container's when using the -p flag. We think of it as being like reading a sentence from left to right. The user connects to the host (-p) and that host port is passed to the container port (host_port:container_port). It's also the same format as SSH's port-forwarding commands, if you're familiar with them.

DISCUSSION

Exposing ports is an incredibly important part of many use cases of Docker, and you'll come across it a number of times throughout this book, especially in part 4, where containers talking to each other is part of everyday life.

In technique 80 we'll introduce you to virtual networks and explain what they do behind the scenes and how they direct the host ports to the right container.

TECHNIQUE 7 **Allowing container communication**

The last technique showed how you can open up your containers to the host network by exposing ports. You won't always want to expose your services to the host machine or the outside world, but you will want to connect containers to one another.

This technique shows how you can achieve this with Docker's user-defined networks feature, ensuring outsiders can't access your internal services.

PROBLEM

You want to allow communication between containers for internal purposes.

SOLUTION

Employ user-defined networks to enable containers to communicate with each other.

User-defined networks are simple and flexible. We have a couple of WordPress blogs running in containers from the previous technique, so let's take a look at how we can reach them from another container (rather than from the outside world, which you've seen already).

First you'll need to create a user-defined network:

```
$ docker network create my_network
0c3386c9db5bb1d457c8af79a62808f78b42b3a8178e75cc8a252fac6fdc09e4
```

This command creates a new virtual network living on your machine that you can use to manage container communication. By default, all containers that you connect to this network will be able to see each other by their names.

Next, assuming that you still have the blog1 and blog2 containers running from the previous technique, you can connect one of them to your new network on the fly.

```
$ docker network connect my_network blog1
```

Finally, you can start up a new container, explicitly specifying the network, and see if you can retrieve the first five lines of HTML from the landing page of the blog.

```
$ docker run -it --network my_network ubuntu:16.04 bash
root@06d6282d32a5:/# apt update && apt install -y curl
[...]
root@06d6282d32a5:/# curl -sSL blog1 | head -n5
<!DOCTYPE html>
<html xmlns="http://www.w3.org/1999/xhtml" lang="en-US" xml:lang="en-US">
<head>
        <meta name="viewport" content="width=device-width" />
        <meta http-equiv="Content-Type" content="text/html; charset=utf-8" />
root@06d6282d32a5:/# curl -sSL blog2
curl: (6) Could not resolve host: blog2
```

> **TIP** Giving containers names is very useful for assigning memorable host-names you can later refer to, but it's not strictly necessary—if connections are only outgoing, then you probably won't need to look up the container. If you find you *do* want to look up the host and haven't assigned a name, you can resort to using the short image ID as listed in the terminal prompt (unless it has been overridden with a hostname) or in the docker ps output.

Our new container was successfully able to access the blog we connected to my_network, displaying some of the HTML of the page we'd see if we visited it in the browser. On the other hand, our new container couldn't see the second blog. Because we never connected it to my_network, this makes sense.

DISCUSSION

You can use this technique to set up any number of containers in a cluster on their own private network, only requiring that the containers have some way of discovering each other's names. In technique 80 you'll see a method of doing this that integrates well with Docker networks. Meanwhile, the next technique will start much smaller, demonstrating some benefits of being able to make an explicit connection between a single container and the service it provides.

One additional point of note is the interesting final state of the blog1 container. All containers are connected to the Docker bridge network by default, so when we asked for it to join my_network, it did so *in addition to* the network it was already on. In technique 80 we'll look at this in more detail to see how *network straddling* can be used as a model for some real-world situations.

TECHNIQUE 8   **Linking containers for port isolation**

In the previous technique you saw how to get containers to communicate with user-defined networks. But there's an older method of declaring container communication—Docker's link flag. This isn't the recommended way of working anymore, but it has been part of Docker for a long time, and it's worth being aware of in case you encounter it in the wild.

PROBLEM

You want to allow communication between containers without using user-defined networks.

SOLUTION

Use Docker's linking functionality to allow the containers to communicate with each other.

Taking up the torch of the WordPress example, we're going to separate the MySQL database tier from the WordPress container, and link these to each other without port configuration or creating a network. Figure 2.8 gives an overview of the final state.

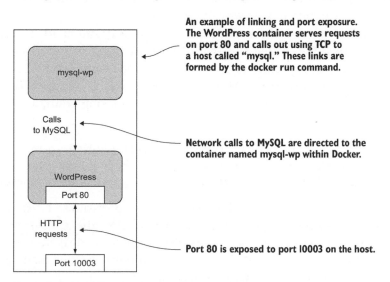

Figure 2.8   WordPress setup with linked containers

NOTE Why bother with linking if you can already expose ports to the host and use that? Linking allows you to encapsulate and define the relationships between containers without exposing services to the host's network (and potentially, to the outside world). You might want to do this for security reasons, for example.

Run your containers in the following order, pausing for about a minute between the first and second commands:

```
$ docker run --name wp-mysql \
  -e MYSQL_ROOT_PASSWORD=yoursecretpassword -d mysql
$ docker run --name wordpress \
  --link wp-mysql:mysql -p 10003:80 -d  wordpress
```

First you give the MySQL container the name `wp-mysql` so you can refer to it later. You also must supply an environment variable so the MySQL container can initialize the database (`-e MYSQL_ROOT_PASSWORD=yoursecretpassword`). You run both containers as daemons (`-d`) and use the Docker Hub reference for the official MySQL image.

In the second command you give the WordPress image the name `wordpress` in case you want to refer to it later. You also link the wp-mysql container to the WordPress container (`--link wp-mysql:mysql`). References to a `mysql` server within the Word-Press container will be sent to the container named `wp-mysql`. You also use a local port mapping (`-p 10003:80`), as discussed in technique 6, and add the Docker Hub reference for the official WordPress image (`wordpress`). Be aware that links won't wait for services in linked containers to start; hence the instruction to pause between commands. A more precise way of doing this is to look for "mysqid: ready for connections" in the output of `docker logs wp-mysql` before running the WordPress container.

If you now navigate to http://localhost:10003, you'll see the introductory Word-Press screen and you can set up your WordPress instance.

The meat of this example is the `--link` flag in the second command. This flag sets up the container's host file so that the WordPress container can refer to a MySQL server, and this will be routed to whatever container has the name `wp-mysql`. This has the significant benefit that different MySQL containers can be swapped in without requiring any change at all to the WordPress container, making configuration management of these different services much easier.

NOTE The containers must be started up in the correct order so that the mapping can take place on container names that are already in existence. Dynamic resolution of links is not (at the time of writing) a feature of Docker.

In order for containers to be linked in this way, their ports must be specified as exposed when building the images. This is achieved using the `EXPOSE` command within the image build's Dockerfile. The ports listed in `EXPOSE` directives in Docker-files are also used when using the `-P` flag ("publish all ports." rather than `-p`, which publishes as a specific port) to the `docker run` command.

By starting up different containers in a specific order, you've seen a simple example of Docker orchestration. Docker orchestration is any process that coordinates the running of Docker containers. It's a large and important subject that we'll cover in depth in part 4 of this book.

By splitting your workload into separate containers, you've taken a step toward creating a microservices architecture for your application. In this case you could perform work on the MySQL container while leaving the WordPress container untouched, or vice versa. This fine-grained control over running services is one of the key operational benefits of a microservices architecture.

DISCUSSION

This kind of precise control over a set of containers is not often needed, but it can be useful as a very straightforward and easy-to-reason-about way to swap out containers. Using the example from this technique, you might want to test a different MySQL version—the WordPress image doesn't need to know anything about this, because it just looks for the mysql link.

2.4 *Docker registries*

Once you've created your images, you may want to share them with other users. This is where the concept of the *Docker registry* comes in.

The three registries in figure 2.9 differ in their accessibility. One is on a private network, one is open on a public network, and another is public but accessible only to those registered with Docker. They all perform the same function with the same API, and this is how the Docker daemon knows how to communicate with them interchangeably.

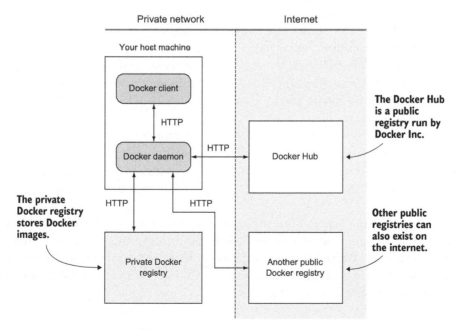

Figure 2.9   A Docker registry

A Docker registry allows multiple users to push and pull images from a central store using a RESTful API.

The registry code is, like Docker itself, open source. Many companies (such as ours) set up private registries to store and share their proprietary images internally. This is what we'll discuss before we look more closely at Docker Inc.'s registry.

TECHNIQUE 9   Setting up a local Docker registry

You've seen that Docker Inc. has a service where people can share their images publicly (and you can pay if you want to do it privately). But there are a number of reasons you may want to share images without going via the Hub—some businesses like to keep as much in-house as possible, maybe your images are large and transferring them over the internet will be too slow, or perhaps you want to keep your images private while you experiment and don't want to commit to paying. Whatever the reason, there's a simple solution.

PROBLEM

You want a way to host your images locally.

SOLUTION

Set up a registry server on your local network. Simply issue the following command on a machine with plenty of disk space:

```
$ docker run -d -p 5000:5000 -v $HOME/registry:/var/lib/registry registry:2
```

This command makes the registry available on port 5000 of the Docker host (-p 5000:5000). With the -v flag, it makes the registry folder on your host (/var/lib/registry) available in the container as $HOME/registry. The registry's files will therefore be stored on the host in the /var/lib/registry folder.

On all of the machines that you want to access this registry, add the following to your daemon options (where HOSTNAME is the hostname or IP address of your new registry server): --insecure-registry HOSTNAME (see appendix B for details on how to do this). You can now issue the following command: docker push HOSTNAME:5000/image:tag.

As you can see, the most basic level of configuration for a local registry, with all data stored in the $HOME/registry directory, is simple. If you wanted to scale up or make it more robust, the repository on GitHub (https://github.com/docker/distribution/blob/v2.2.1/docs/storagedrivers.md) outlines some options, like storing data in Amazon S3.

You may be wondering about the --insecure-registry option. In order to help users remain secure, Docker will only allow you to pull from registries with a signed HTTPS certificate. We've overridden this because we're fairly comfortable that we can trust our local network. It goes without saying, though, that you should be much more cautious about doing this over the internet.

DISCUSSION

With registries being so easy to set up, a number of possibilities arise. If your company has a number of teams, you might suggest that everyone start up and maintain a registry on a spare machine to permit some fluidity in storing images and moving them around.

This works particularly well if you have an internal IP address range—the `--insecure-registry` command will accept CIDR notation, like `10.1.0.0/16`, for specifying a range of IP addresses that are permitted to be insecure. If you're not familiar with this, we highly recommend you get in touch with your network administrator.

2.5 *The Docker Hub*

The Docker Hub (see figure 2.10) is a registry maintained by Docker Inc. It has tens of thousands of images on it ready to download and run. Any Docker user can set up a free account and store public Docker images there. In addition to user-supplied images, official images are maintained for reference purposes.

Your images are protected by user authentication, and there's a starring system for popularity, similar to GitHub's. The official images can be representations of Linux distributions like Ubuntu or CentOS, preinstalled software packages like Node.js, or whole software stacks like WordPress.

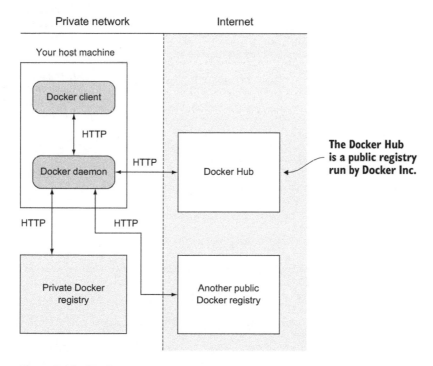

Figure 2.10   The Docker Hub

TECHNIQUE 10   Finding and running a Docker image

Docker registries enable a social coding culture similar to GitHub's. If you're interested in trying out a new software application, or looking for a new one that serves a particular purpose, Docker images can be an easy way to experiment without interfering with your host machine, provisioning a VM, or having to worry about installation steps.

PROBLEM

You want to find an application or tool as a Docker image and try it out.

SOLUTION

Use the docker search command to find the image to pull, and then run it.

Let's say you're interested in playing with Node.js. In the following example we searched for images matching "node" with the docker search command:

The description is the uploader's explanation of the purpose of the image.

The output of docker search is ordered by the number of stars.

```
$ docker search node
NAME                       DESCRIPTION
⇒ STARS       OFFICIAL   AUTOMATED
node                                  Node.js is a JavaScript-based platform for...
⇒  3935       [OK]
 nodered/node-red-docker   Node-RED Docker images.
⇒  57                      [OK]
  strongloop/node           StrongLoop, Node.js, and tools.
⇒  38                      [OK]
   kkarczmarczyk/node-yarn   Node docker image with yarn package manage...
⇒  25                      [OK]
 bitnami/node              Bitnami Node.js Docker Image
⇒  19                      [OK]
siomiz/node-opencv        _/node + node-opencv
⇒  10                      [OK]
dahlb/alpine-node         small node for gitlab ci runner
⇒  8                       [OK]
cusspvz/node              Super small Node.js container (~15MB) ba...
⇒  7                       [OK]
anigeo/node-forever       Daily build node.js with forever
⇒  4                       [OK]
seegno/node               A node docker base image.
⇒  3                       [OK]
starefossen/ruby-node     Docker Image with Ruby and Node.js installed
⇒  3                       [OK]
urbanmassage/node         Some handy (read, better) docker node images
⇒  1                       [OK]
xataz/node                very light node image
⇒  1                       [OK]
centralping/node          Bare bones CentOS 7 NodeJS container.
⇒  1                       [OK]
joxit/node                Slim node docker with some utils for dev
⇒  1                       [OK]
bigtruedata/node          Docker image providing Node.js & NPM
⇒  1                       [OK]
```

Official images are those trusted by Docker Hub.

Automated images are those built using Docker Hub's automated build feature.

```
1science/node            Node.js Docker images based on Alpine Linux
    1                    [OK]
domandtom/node           Docker image for Node.js including Yarn an...
    0                    [OK]
makeomatic/node          various alpine + node based containers
    0                    [OK]
c4tech/node              NodeJS images, aimed at generated single-p...
    0                    [OK]
instructure/node         Instructure node images
    0                    [OK]
octoblu/node             Docker images for node
    0                    [OK]
edvisor/node             Automated build of Node.js with commonly u...
    0                    [OK]
watsco/node              node:7
    0                    [OK]
codexsystems/node        Node.js for Development and Production
    0                    [OK]
```

Once you've chosen an image, you can download it by performing a `docker pull` command on the name:

```
$ docker pull node              ◁──────────    Pulls the image
 Using default tag: latest                     named node from
latest: Pulling from library/node              the Docker Hub
5040bd298390: Already exists
fce5728aad85: Pull complete
76610ec20bf5: Pull complete
9c1bc3c30371: Pull complete
33d67d70af20: Pull complete            This message is seen if Docker has pulled a new image (as
da053401c2b1: Pull complete            opposed to identifying that there's no newer image than
05b24114aa8d: Pull complete            the one you already have). Your output may be different.
Digest:
 ➥ sha256:ea65cf88ed7d97f0b43bcc5deed67cfd13c70e20a66f8b2b4fd4b7955de92297
Status: Downloaded newer image for node:latest       ◁────────
```

Then you can run it interactively using the `-t` and `-i` flags. The `-t` flag creates a TTY device (a terminal) for you, and the `-i` flag specifies that this Docker session is interactive:

```
$ docker run -t -i node /bin/bash
root@c267ae999646:/# node
> process.version
'v7.6.0'
>
```

> **TIP**   You can save keystrokes by replacing `-t -i` with `-ti` or `-it` in the preceding call to `docker run`. You'll see this throughout the book from here on.

Often there will be specific advice from the image maintainers about how the image should be run. Searching for the image on the http://hub.docker.com website will take you to the page for the image. The Description tab may give you more information.

> **WARNING** If you download an image and run it, you're running code that you
> may not be able to fully verify. Although there is relative safety in using
> trusted images, nothing can guarantee 100% security when downloading and
> running software over the internet.

Armed with this knowledge and experience, you can now tap the enormous resources
available on Docker Hub. With literally tens of thousands of images to try out, there's
much to learn. Enjoy!

DISCUSSION

Docker Hub is an excellent resource, but sometimes it can be slow—it's worth pausing
to decide how to best construct your Docker search command to get the best results.
The ability to do searches without opening your browser offers you quick insight into
possible items of interest in the ecosystem, so you can better target the documentation
for images that are likely to fulfill your needs.

When you're rebuilding images, it can also be good to run a search every now and
again to see if a stars count suggests that the Docker community has begun to gather
around a different image than the one you're currently using.

Summary

- You can open up the Docker daemon API to outsiders, and all they need is
  some way to make a HTTP request—a web browser is enough.
- Containers don't have to take over your terminal. You can start them up in the
  background and come back to them later.
- You can make containers communicate, either with user-defined networks (the
  recommended approach), or with links to very explicitly control inter-container
  communication.
- Because the Docker dacmon API is over HTTP, it's fairly easy to debug it with
  network monitoring tools if you're having issues.
- One particularly useful tool for debugging and tracing network calls is `socat`.
- Setting up registries isn't just the domain of Docker Inc.; you can set up your
  own on a local network for free private image storage.
- Docker Hub is a great place to go to find and download ready-made images,
  particularly ones provided officially by Docker Inc.

Part 2

Docker and development

In part 1, you learned Docker's core concepts and architecture by example. Part 2 will take you from this base and demonstrate ways Docker can be used in development.

Chapter 3 covers using Docker as a lightweight virtual machine. This is a controversial area. Although there are critical differences between virtual machines and Docker containers, development can be sped up considerably in many cases by using Docker. It's also an effective means of getting familiar with Docker before we move into more advanced Docker usage.

Chapters 4, 5, and 6 cover over 20 techniques to make building, running, and managing Docker containers more effective and efficient. In addition to building and running containers, you'll learn about persisting data with volumes and keeping your Docker host in order.

Chapter 7 covers the important area of configuration management. You'll use Dockerfiles and traditional configuration management tools to get control of your Docker builds. We'll also cover the creation and curation of minimal Docker images to reduce image bloat. By the end of this part you'll have a wealth of useful techniques for single-use Docker and be ready to take Docker into a DevOps context.

Using Docker as a
lightweight virtual machine

3

Virtual machines (VMs) have become ubiquitous in software development and deployment since the turn of the century. The abstraction of machines to software has made the movement and control of software and services in the internet age easier and cheaper.

> **TIP** A virtual machine is an application that emulates a computer, usually to run an operating system and applications. It can be placed on any (compatible) physical resources that are available. The end user experiences the software as though it were on a physical machine, but those managing the hardware can focus on larger-scale resource allocation.

Docker isn't a VM technology. It doesn't simulate a machine's hardware and it doesn't include an operating system. A Docker container is not, by default, constrained to specific hardware limits. If Docker virtualizes anything, it virtualizes the environment in which services run, not the machine. Moreover, Docker can't easily run Windows software (or even that written for other Unix-derived operating systems).

From some standpoints, though, Docker can be used much as a VM. For developers and testers in the internet age, the fact that there's no init process or direct hardware interaction is not usually of great significance. And there are significant commonalities, such as its isolation from the surrounding hardware and its amenability to more fine-grained approaches to software delivery.

This chapter will take you through the scenarios in which you could use Docker as you previously might have used a VM. Using Docker won't give you any obvious functional advantages over a VM, but the speed and convenience Docker brings to the movement and tracking of environments can be a game-changer for your development pipeline.

3.1   *From VM to container*

In an ideal world, moving from VMs to containers would be a simple matter of running configuration management scripts against a Docker image from a distribution similar to the VM's. For those of us who aren't in that happy state of affairs, this section will show how you can convert a VM to a container—or containers.

TECHNIQUE 11   Converting your VM to a container

The Docker Hub doesn't have all possible base images, so for some niche Linux distributions and use cases, people need to create their own. For example, if you have an existing application state in a VM, you may want to put that state inside a Docker image so that you can iterate further on that, or to benefit from the Docker ecosystem by using tooling and related technology that exists there.

Ideally you'd want to build an equivalent of your VM from scratch using standard Docker techniques, such as Dockerfiles combined with standard configuration management tools (see chapter 7). The reality, though, is that many VMs aren't carefully configuration-managed. This might happen because a VM has grown organically as people have used it, and the investment needed to recreate it in a more structured way isn't worth it.

PROBLEM
You have a VM you want to convert to a Docker image.

SOLUTION
Archive and copy the filesystem of the VM and package it into a Docker image.

First we're going to divide VMs into two broad groups:

- *Local VM*—VM disk image lives on and VM execution happens on your computer.
- *Remote VM*—VM disk image storage and VM execution happen somewhere else.

The principle for both groups of VMs (and anything else you want to create a Docker image from) is the same—you get a TAR of the filesystem and ADD the TAR file to / of the scratch image.

TIP The ADD Dockerfile command (unlike its sibling command COPY) unpacks TAR files (as well as gzipped files and other similar file types) when they're placed in an image like this.

TIP The *scratch* image is a zero-byte pseudo-image you can build on top of. Typically it's used in cases like this where you want to copy (or add) a complete filesystem using a Dockerfile.

We'll now look at a case where you have a local VirtualBox VM.

Before you get started, you need to do the following:

1 Install the qemu-nbd tool (available as part of the qemu-utils package on Ubuntu).
2 Identify the path to your VM disk image.
3 Shut down your VM.

If your VM disk image is in the .vdi or .vmdk format, this technique should work well. Other formats may experience mixed success. The following code demonstrates how you can turn your VM file into a virtual disk, which allows you to copy all the files from it.

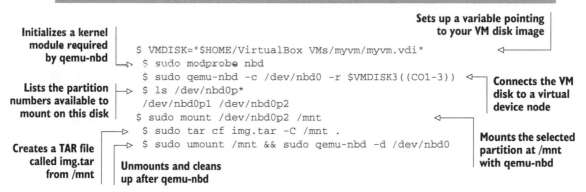

Listing 3.1   Extracting the filesystem of a VM image

```
$ VMDISK="$HOME/VirtualBox VMs/myvm/myvm.vdi"
$ sudo modprobe nbd
$ sudo qemu-nbd -c /dev/nbd0 -r $VMDISK
$ ls /dev/nbd0p*
/dev/nbd0p1 /dev/nbd0p2
$ sudo mount /dev/nbd0p2 /mnt
$ sudo tar cf img.tar -C /mnt .
$ sudo umount /mnt && sudo qemu-nbd -d /dev/nbd0
```

Sets up a variable pointing to your VM disk image

Initializes a kernel module required by qemu-nbd

Connects the VM disk to a virtual device node

Lists the partition numbers available to mount on this disk

Mounts the selected partition at /mnt with qemu-nbd

Creates a TAR file called img.tar from /mnt

Unmounts and cleans up after qemu-nbd

NOTE To choose which partition to mount, run sudo cfdisk /dev/nbd0 to see what's available. Note that if you see LVM anywhere, your disk has a non-trivial partitioning scheme—you'll need to do some additional research into how to mount LVM partitions.

If your VM is kept remotely, you have a choice: either shut down the VM and ask your operations team to perform a dump of the partition you want, or create a TAR of your VM while it's still running.

If you get a partition dump, you can mount this fairly easily and then turn it into a TAR file as follows:

Listing 3.2 Extracting a partition

```
$ sudo mount -o loop partition.dump /mnt
$ sudo tar cf $(pwd)/img.tar -C /mnt .
$ sudo umount /mnt
```

Alternatively, you can create a TAR file from a running system. This is quite simple after logging into the system:

Listing 3.3 Extracting the filesystem of a running VM

```
$ cd /
$ sudo tar cf /img.tar --exclude=/img.tar --one-file-system /
```

You now have a TAR of the filesystem image that you can transfer to a different machine with scp.

> **WARNING** Creating a TAR from a running system may seem like the easiest option (no shutdowns, installing software, or making requests to other teams), but it has a severe downside—you could copy a file in an inconsistent state and hit strange problems when trying to use your new Docker image. If you must go this route, first stop as many applications and services as possible.

Once you've got the TAR of your filesystem, you can add it to your image. This is the easiest step of the process and consists of a two-line Dockerfile.

Listing 3.4 Adding an archive to a Docker image

```
FROM scratch
ADD img.tar /
```

You can now run docker build . and you have your image!

> **NOTE** Docker provides an alternative to ADD in the form of the docker import command, which you can use with cat img.tar | docker import - new_image _name. But building on top of the image with additional instructions will require you to create a Dockerfile anyway, so it may be simpler to go the ADD route, so you can easily see the history of your image.

You now have an image in Docker, and you can start experimenting with it. In this case, you might start by creating a new Dockerfile based on your new image, to experiment with stripping out files and packages.

Once you've done this and are happy with your results, you can use `docker export` on a running container to export a new, slimmer TAR that you can use as the basis for a newer image, and repeat the process until you get an image you're happy with.

The flow chart in figure 3.1 demonstrates this process.

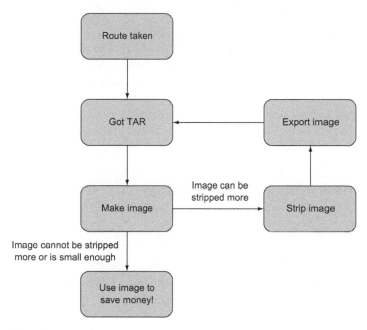

Figure 3.1   Image-stripping flowchart

DISCUSSION

This technique demonstrates a few fundamental principles and techniques that are useful in contexts other than converting a VM to a Docker image.

Most broadly, it shows that a Docker image is essentially a set of files and some metadata: the `scratch` image is an empty filesystem over which a TAR file can be laid. We'll return to this theme when we look at *slim* Docker images.

More specifically, you've seen how you can ADD a TAR file to a Docker image, and how you can use the `qemu-nbd` tool.

Once you have your image, you might need to know how to run it like a more traditional host. Because Docker containers typically run one application process only, this is somewhat against the grain, and it's covered in the next technique.

TECHNIQUE 12   **A host-like container**

We'll now move on to one of the more contentious areas of discussion within the Docker community—running a host-like image, with multiple processes running from the start.

This is considered bad form in parts of the Docker community. Containers are not virtual machines—there are significant differences—and pretending there aren't can cause confusion and issues down the line.

For good or ill, this technique will show you how to run a host-like image and discuss some of the issues around doing this.

NOTE Running a host-like image can be a good way to persuade Docker refuseniks that Docker is useful. As they use it more, they'll understand the paradigm better and the microservices approach will make more sense to them. At the company we introduced Docker into, we found that this monolithic approach was a great way to move people from developing on dev servers and laptops to a more contained and manageable environment. From there, moving Docker into testing, continuous integration, escrow, and DevOps workflows was trivial.

Differences between VMs and Docker containers

These are a few of the differences between VMs and Docker containers:

- Docker is application-oriented, whereas VMs are operating-system oriented.
- Docker containers share an operating system with other Docker containers. In contrast, VMs each have their own operating system managed by a hypervisor.
- Docker containers are designed to run one principal process, not manage multiple sets of processes.

PROBLEM

You want a normal host-like environment for your container with multiple processes and services set up.

SOLUTION

Use a base container designed to run multiple processes.

For this technique you're going to use an image designed to simulate a host, and provision it with the applications you need. The base image will be the phusion/baseimage Docker image, an image designed to run multiple processes.

The first steps are to start the image and jump into it with docker exec.

Listing 3.5   Running the phusion base image

Starts the image in the background

Returns the ID of the new container

```
user@docker-host$ docker run -d phusion/baseimage
3c3f8e3fb05d795edf9d791969b21f7f73e99eb1926a6e3d5ed9e1e52d0b446e
user@docker-host$ docker exec -i -t 3c3f8e3fb05d795 /bin/bash
root@3c3f8e3fb05d:/#
```

The prompt to the started container terminal

Passes the container ID to docker exec and allocates an interactive terminal

In this code, docker run will start the image in the background, starting the default command for the image and returning the ID of the newly created container.

You then pass this container ID to docker exec, which is a command that starts a new process inside an already running container. The -i flag allows you to interact with the new process, and -t indicates that you want to set up a TTY to allow you to start a terminal (/bin/bash) inside the container.

If you wait a minute and then look at the processes table, your output will look something like the following.

Listing 3.6 Processes running in a host-like container

The bash process started by docker exec and acting as your shell

Runs a ps command to list all the running processes

A simple init process designed to run all the other services

```
root@3c3f8e3fb05d:/# ps -ef
  UID   PID  PPID  C STIME TTY      TIME CMD
  root    1     0  0 13:33 ?    00:00:00 /usr/bin/python3 -u /sbin/my_init
  root    7     0  0 13:33 ?    00:00:00 /bin/bash
  root  111     1  0 13:33 ?    00:00:00 /usr/bin/runsvdir -P /etc/service
  root  112   111  0 13:33 ?    00:00:00 runsv cron
  root  113   111  0 13:33 ?    00:00:00 runsv sshd
  root  114   111  0 13:33 ?    00:00:00 runsv syslog-ng
  root  115   112  0 13:33 ?    00:00:00 /usr/sbin/cron -f
  root  116   114  0 13:33 ?    00:00:00 syslog-ng -F -p /var/run/syslog-ng.pid
    --no-caps
  root  117   113  0 13:33 ?    00:00:00 /usr/sbin/sshd -D
  root  125     7  0 13:38 ?    00:00:00 ps -ef
```

runsvdir runs the services defined in the passed-in /etc/service directory.

The ps command currently being run

The three standard services (cron, sshd, and syslog) are started here with the runsv command.

You can see that the container starts up much like a host, initializing services such as cron and sshd that make it appear similar to a standard Linux host.

DISCUSSION

Although this can be useful in initial demos for engineers new to Docker or genuinely useful for your particular circumstances, it's worth being aware that it's a somewhat controversial idea.

The history of container use has tended toward using them to isolate workloads to "one service per container." Proponents of the host-like image approach argue that this doesn't violate that principle, because the container can still fulfill a single discrete function for the system within which it runs.

More recently, the growing popularity of both the Kubernetes' pod and docker-compose concepts has made the host-like container relatively redundant—separate containers can be conjoined into a single entity at a higher level, rather than managing multiple processes using a traditional init service.

The next technique looks at how you can break up such a monolithic application into microservice-style containers.

<hr>

TECHNIQUE 13   **Splitting a system into microservice containers**

We've explored how to use a container as a monolithic entity (like a classical server) and explained that it can be a great way to quickly move a system architecture onto Docker. In the Docker world, however, it's generally considered a best practice to split up your system as much as possible until you have one service running per container and have all containers connected by networks.

The primary reason for using one service per container is the easier separation of concerns through the single-responsibility principle. If you have one container doing one job, it's easier to put that container through the software development lifecycle of development, test, and production while worrying less about its interactions with other components. This makes for more agile deliveries and more scalable software projects. It does create management overhead, though, so it's good to consider whether it's worth it for your use case.

Putting aside the discussion of which approach is better for you right now, the best-practice approach has one clear advantage—experimentation and rebuilds are much faster when using Dockerfiles, as you'll see.

PROBLEM

You want to break your application up into distinct and more manageable services.

SOLUTION

Create a container for each discrete service process.

As we've touched upon already, there's some debate within the Docker community about how strictly the "one service per container" rule should be followed, with part of this stemming from a disagreement over the definitions—is it a single process, or a collection of processes that combine to fulfill a need? It often boils down to a statement that, given the ability to redesign a system from scratch, microservices is the route most would chose. But sometimes practicality beats idealism—when evaluating Docker for our organization, we found ourselves in the position of having to go the monolithic route in order get Docker working as quickly and easily as possible.

Let's take a look at one of the concrete disadvantages of using monoliths inside Docker. First, the following listing shows you how you'd build a monolith with a database, application, and web server.

NOTE   These examples are for explanation purposes and have been simplified accordingly. Trying to run them directly won't necessarily work.

Listing 3.7   Setting up a simple PostgreSQL, NodeJS, and Nginx application

```
FROM ubuntu:14.04
RUN apt-get update && apt-get install postgresql nodejs npm nginx
WORKDIR /opt
COPY . /opt/                                    # {*}
```

```
RUN service postgresql start && \
    cat db/schema.sql | psql && \
    service postgresql stop
RUN cd app && npm install
RUN cp conf/mysite /etc/nginx/sites-available/ && \
    cd /etc/nginx/sites-enabled && \
    ln -s ../sites-available/mysite
```

> **TIP** Each Dockerfile command creates a single new layer on top of the previous one, but using `&&` in your `RUN` statements effectively ensures that several commands get run as one command. This is useful because it can keep your images small. If you run a package update command like `apt-get update` with an install command in this way, you ensure that whenever the packages are installed, they'll be from an updated package cache.

The preceding example is a conceptually simple Dockerfile that installs everything you need inside the container and then sets up the database, application, and web server. Unfortunately, there's a problem if you want to quickly rebuild your container—any change to any file under your repository will rebuild everything starting from the {*} onwards, because the cache can't be reused. If you have some slow steps (database creation or `npm install`), you could be waiting for a while for the container to rebuild.

The solution to this is to split up the COPY . /opt/ instruction into the individual aspects of the application (database, app, and web setup).

Listing 3.8 Dockerfile for a monolithic application

```
FROM ubuntu:14.04
RUN apt-get update && apt-get install postgresql nodejs npm nginx
WORKDIR /opt
COPY db /opt/db                                     -+
RUN service postgresql start && \                   |- db setup
    cat db/schema.sql | psql && \                   |
    service postgresql stop                         -+
COPY app /opt/app                                   -+
RUN cd app && npm install                           |- app setup
RUN cd app && ./minify_static.sh                    -+
COPY conf /opt/conf                                 -+
RUN cp conf/mysite /etc/nginx/sites-available/ && \  +
    cd /etc/nginx/sites-enabled && \                |- web setup
    ln -s ../sites-available/mysite                 -+
```

In the preceding code, the COPY command is split into two separate instructions. This means the database won't be rebuilt every time code changes, as the cache can be reused for the unchanged files delivered before the code. Unfortunately, because the caching functionality is fairly simple, the container still has to be completely rebuilt every time a change is made to the schema scripts. The only way to resolve this is to move away from sequential setup steps and create multiple Dockerfiles, as shown in listings 3.9 through 3.11.

Listing 3.9   Dockerfile for the postgres service

```
FROM ubuntu:14.04
RUN apt-get update && apt-get install postgresql
WORKDIR /opt
COPY db /opt/db
RUN service postgresql start && \
    cat db/schema.sql | psql && \
    service postgresql stop
```

Listing 3.10   Dockerfile for the nodejs service

```
FROM ubuntu:14.04
RUN apt-get update && apt-get install nodejs npm
WORKDIR /opt
COPY app /opt/app
RUN cd app && npm install
RUN cd app && ./minify_static.sh
```

Listing 3.11   Dockerfile for the nginx service

```
FROM ubuntu:14.04
RUN apt-get update && apt-get install nginx
WORKDIR /opt
COPY conf /opt/conf
RUN cp conf/mysite /etc/nginx/sites-available/ && \
    cd /etc/nginx/sites-enabled && \
    ln -s ../sites-available/mysite
```

Whenever one of the db, app, or conf folders changes, only one container will need to be rebuilt. This is particularly useful when you have many more than three containers or there are time-intensive setup steps. With some care, you can add the bare minimum of files necessary for each step and get more useful Dockerfile caching as a result.

In the app Dockerfile (listing 3.10), the operation of npm install is defined by a single file, package.json, so you can alter your Dockerfile to take advantage of Dockerfile layer caching and only rebuild the slow npm install step when necessary, as follows.

Listing 3.12   Faster Dockerfile for the nginx service

```
FROM ubuntu:14.04
RUN apt-get update && apt-get install nodejs npm
WORKDIR /opt
COPY app/package.json /opt/app/package.json
RUN cd app && npm install
COPY app /opt/app
RUN cd app && ./minify_static.sh
```

Now you have three discrete, separate Dockerfiles where formerly you had one.

DISCUSSION

Unfortunately, there's no such thing as a free lunch—you've traded a single simple Dockerfile for multiple Dockerfiles with duplication. You can address this partially by adding another Dockerfile to act as your base image, but some duplication is not uncommon. Additionally, there's now some complexity in starting your image—in addition to EXPOSE steps making appropriate ports available for linking and altering of Postgres configuration, you need to be sure to link the containers every time they start up. Fortunately there's tooling for this called *Docker Compose*, which we'll cover in technique 76.

So far in this section you've taken a VM, turned it into a Docker image, run a host-like container, and broken a monolith into separate Docker images.

If, after reading this book, you still want to run multiple processes from within a container, there are specific tools that can help you do that. One of these—Supervisord—is treated in the next technique.

TECHNIQUE 14 **Managing the startup of your container's services**

As is made clear throughout the Docker literature, a Docker container is *not* a VM. One of the key differences between a Docker container and a VM is that a container is designed to run one process. When that process finishes, the container exits. This is different from a Linux VM (or any Linux OS) in that it doesn't have an init process.

The init process runs on a Linux OS with a process ID of 1 and a parent process ID of 0. This init process might be called "init" or "systemd." Whatever it's called, its job is to manage the housekeeping for all other processes running on that operating system.

If you start to experiment with Docker, you may find that you want to start multiple processes. You might want to run cron jobs to tidy up your local application log files, for example, or set up an internal memcached server within the container. If you take this path, you may end up writing shell scripts to manage the startup of these sub-processes. In effect, you'll be emulating the work of the init process. Don't do that! The many problems arising from process management have been encountered by others before and have been solved in prepackaged systems.

Whatever your reason for running multiple processes inside a container, it's important to avoid reinventing the wheel.

PROBLEM

You want to manage multiple processes within a container.

SOLUTION

Use Supervisor to manage the processes in your container.

We'll show you how to provision a container running both Tomcat and an Apache web server, and have it start up and run in a managed way, with the Supervisor application (http://supervisord.org/) managing process startup for you.

First, create your Dockerfile in a new and empty directory, as the following listing shows.

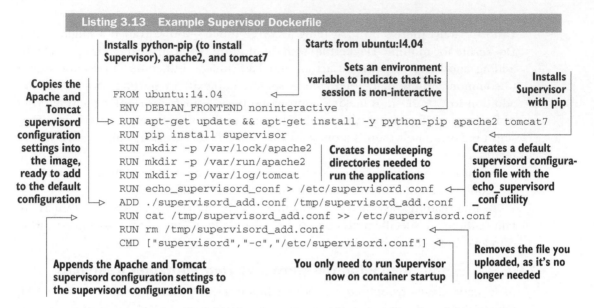

Listing 3.13 Example Supervisor Dockerfile

Starts from ubuntu:14.04

Installs python-pip (to install Supervisor), apache2, and tomcat7

Sets an environment variable to indicate that this session is non-interactive

Installs Supervisor with pip

Copies the Apache and Tomcat supervisord configuration settings into the image, ready to add to the default configuration

```
FROM ubuntu:14.04
ENV DEBIAN_FRONTEND noninteractive
RUN apt-get update && apt-get install -y python-pip apache2 tomcat7
RUN pip install supervisor
RUN mkdir -p /var/lock/apache2
RUN mkdir -p /var/run/apache2
RUN mkdir -p /var/log/tomcat
RUN echo_supervisord_conf > /etc/supervisord.conf
ADD ./supervisord_add.conf /tmp/supervisord_add.conf
RUN cat /tmp/supervisord_add.conf >> /etc/supervisord.conf
RUN rm /tmp/supervisord_add.conf
CMD ["supervisord","-c","/etc/supervisord.conf"]
```

Creates housekeeping directories needed to run the applications

Creates a default supervisord configuration file with the echo_supervisord _conf utility

Appends the Apache and Tomcat supervisord configuration settings to the supervisord configuration file

You only need to run Supervisor now on container startup

Removes the file you uploaded, as it's no longer needed

You'll also need configuration for Supervisor, to specify what applications it needs to start up, as shown in the next listing.

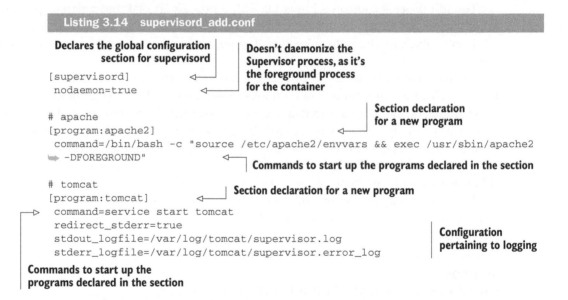

Listing 3.14 supervisord_add.conf

Declares the global configuration section for supervisord

Doesn't daemonize the Supervisor process, as it's the foreground process for the container

```
[supervisord]
nodaemon=true


# apache
[program:apache2]
command=/bin/bash -c "source /etc/apache2/envvars && exec /usr/sbin/apache2
➥ -DFOREGROUND"

# tomcat
[program:tomcat]
command=service start tomcat
redirect_stderr=true
stdout_logfile=/var/log/tomcat/supervisor.log
stderr_logfile=/var/log/tomcat/supervisor.error_log
```

Section declaration for a new program

Commands to start up the programs declared in the section

Section declaration for a new program

Configuration pertaining to logging

Commands to start up the programs declared in the section

You build the image using the standard single-command Docker process because you're using a Dockerfile. Run this command to perform the build:

```
docker build -t supervised .
```

You can now run your image!

Listing 3.15   Run the supervised container

**Starts up the
Supervisor
process**

**Maps the container's port 80 to the host's port
9000, gives the container a name, and specifies
the image name you're running, as tagged with
the build command previously**

**Starts up the
Supervisor
process**

```
$ docker run -p 9000:80 --name supervised supervised      ◁─┐
 2015-02-06 10:42:20,336 CRIT Supervisor running as root (no user in config
┌─▷ ➥ file)
│   2015-02-06 10:42:20,344 INFO RPC interface 'supervisor' initialized
│   2015-02-06 10:42:20,344 CRIT Server 'unix_http_server' running without any
│  ➥ HTTP authentication checking
│   2015-02-06 10:42:20,344 INFO supervisord started with pid 1          ◁───┘
│    2015-02-06 10:42:21,346 INFO spawned: 'tomcat' with pid 12    │ Starts up the
│    2015-02-06 10:42:21,348 INFO spawned: 'apache2' with pid 13   │ managed processes
│    2015-02-06 10:42:21,368 INFO reaped unknown pid 29
│   2015-02-06 10:42:21,403 INFO reaped unknown pid 30
│   2015-02-06 10:42:22,404 INFO success: tomcat entered RUNNING state, process
│  ➥ has stayed up for > than 1 seconds (startsecs)
│    2015-02-06 10:42:22,404 INFO success: apache2 entered RUNNING state, process
│  ➥ has stayed up for > than 1 seconds (startsecs)
```

**Managed processes have been deemed by
Supervisor to have successfully started.**

If you navigate to http://localhost:9000, you should see the default page of the
Apache server you started up.

To clean up the container, run the following command:

```
docker rm -f supervised
```

DISCUSSION

This technique used Supervisor to manage multiple processes in your Docker
container.

If you're interested in alternatives to Supervisor, there's also `runit`, which was used
by the phusion base image covered in technique 12.

3.2   *Saving and restoring your work*

Some people say that code isn't written until it's committed to source control—it
doesn't always hurt to have the same attitude about containers. It's possible to save
state with VMs by using snapshots, but Docker takes a much more active approach in
encouraging the saving and reusing of your existing work.

We'll cover the "save game" approach to development, the niceties of tagging,
using the Docker Hub, and referring to specific images in your builds. Because these
operations are considered so fundamental, Docker makes them relatively simple and
quick. Nonetheless, this can still be a confusing topic for Docker newbies, so in the
next section we'll take you through the steps to a fuller understanding of this subject.

The "save game" approach: Cheap source control

If you've ever developed any kind of software, you've likely exclaimed, "I'm sure it was working before!" at least once. Perhaps your language was not as sober as this. The inability to restore a system to a known good (or maybe only "better") state when you're hurriedly hacking away at code to hit a deadline or fix a bug is the cause of many broken keyboards.

Source control has helped significantly with this, but there are two problems in this particular case:

- The source may not reflect the state of your "working" environment's filesystem.
- You may not be willing to commit the code yet.

The first problem is more significant than the second. Although modern source control tools like Git can easily create local throwaway branches, capturing the state of your entire development filesystem isn't the purpose of source control.

Docker provides a cheap and quick way to store the state of your container's development filesystem through its commit functionality, and that's what we're going to explore here.

PROBLEM
You want to save the state of your development environment.

SOLUTION
Regularly commit your container so you can recover state at that point.

Let's imagine you want to make a change to your to-do application from chapter 1. The CEO of ToDoCorp isn't happy and wants the title of the browser to show "ToDoCorp's ToDo App" instead of "Swarm+React - TodoMVC."

You're not sure how to achieve this, so you probably want to fire up your application and experiment by changing files to see what happens.

Listing 3.16   Debugging the application in a terminal

```
$ docker run -d -p 8000:8000 --name todobug1 dockerinpractice/todoapp
 3c3d5d3ffd70d17e7e47e90801af7d12d6fc0b8b14a8b33131fc708423ee4372
$ docker exec -i -t todobug1 /bin/bash 2((C07-2))
```

The docker run command starts the to-do application in a container in the background (-d), mapping the container's port 8000 to port 8000 on the host (-p 8000:8000), naming it todobug1 (--name todobug1) for easy reference, and returning the container ID. The command started in the container will be the default command specified when the dockerinpractice/todoapp image was built. We've built it for you and made it available on the Docker Hub.

The second command will start /bin/bash in the running container. The name todobug1 is used, but you can also use the container ID. The -i makes this exec run interactively, and -t makes sure that the exec will work as a terminal would.

Now you're in the container, so the first step in experimenting is to install an editor. We prefer vim, so we used these commands:

```
apt-get update
apt-get install vim
```

After a little effort, you realize that the file you need to change is local.html. You therefore change line 5 in that file as follows:

```
<title>ToDoCorp's ToDo App</title>
```

Then word comes through that the CEO might want the title to be in lowercase, as she's heard that it looks more modern. You want to be ready either way, so you commit what you have at the moment. In another terminal you run the following command.

Listing 3.17   Committing container state

**Turns the container you
created earlier into an image**

```
$ docker commit todobug1
  ca76b45144f2cb31fda6a31e55f784c93df8c9d4c96bbeacd73cad9cd55d2970
```

**The new image ID of the
container you've committed**

You've now committed your container to an image that you can run from later.

> **NOTE**   Committing a container only stores the state of the filesystem at the time of the commit, not the processes. Docker containers aren't VMs, remember! If your environment's state depends on the state of running processes that aren't recoverable through standard files, this technique won't store the state as you need it. In this case, you'll probably want to look at making your development processes recoverable.

Next, you change local.html to the other possible required value:

```
<title>todocorp's todo app</title>
```

Commit again:

```
$ docker commit todobug1
071f6a36c23a19801285b82eafc99333c76f63ea0aa0b44902c6bae482a6e036
```

You now have two image IDs that represent the two options (ca76b45144f2 cb31f da6a31e55f784c93df8c9d4c96bbeacd73cad9cd55d2970 and 071f6a36c23a19801285 b82eafc99333c76f63ea0aa0b44902c6bae482a6e036 in our example, but yours will be different). When the CEO comes in to evaluate which one she wants, you can run up either image and let her decide which one to commit.

You do this by opening up new terminals and running the following commands.

Listing 3.18   Running up both committed images as containers

Maps the container's port 8000 to the host's
port 8001 and specifies the lowercase image ID

```
$ docker run -p 8001:8000 \
ca76b45144f2cb31fda6a31e55f784c93df8c9d4c96bbeacd73cad9cd55d2970
$ docker run -p 8002:8000 \
071f6a36c23a19801285b82eafc99333c76f63ea0aa0b44902c6bae482a6e036
```

Maps the container's port 8000 to the host's port
8002 and specifies the uppercase image ID

In this way you can present the uppercase option as available on http://localhost
:8001 and the lowercase option on http://localhost:8002.

> **NOTE** Any dependencies external to the container (such as databases,
> Docker volumes, or other services called) aren't stored on commit. This tech-
> nique doesn't have any external dependencies so you don't need to worry
> about that.

DISCUSSION

This technique demonstrated `docker commit`'s functionality, and how it might be used
in a development workflow. Docker users tend to be directed toward using `docker
commit` only as part of a formal `commit-tag-push` workflow, so it's good to remember
that it has other uses too.

We find this to be a useful technique when we've negotiated a tricky sequence of
commands to set up an application. Committing the container, once successful, also
records your bash session history, meaning that a set of steps for regaining the state
of your system is available. This can save a *lot* of time! It's also useful when you're
experimenting with a new feature and are unsure whether you're finished, or when
you've recreated a bug and want to be as sure as possible that you can return to the
broken state.

You may well be wondering whether there's a better way to reference images than
with long random strings of characters. The next technique will look at giving these
containers names you can more easily reference.

TECHNIQUE 16   Docker tagging

You've now saved the state of your container by committing, and you have a random
string as the ID of your image. It's obviously difficult to remember and manage the
large numbers of these image IDs. It would be helpful to use Docker's tagging functionality to give readable names (and tags) to your images and remind you what they
were created for.

Mastering this technique will allow you to see what your images are for at a glance,
making image management on your machine far simpler.

PROBLEM

You want to conveniently reference and store a Docker commit.

SOLUTION

Use the `docker tag` command to name your commits.

In its basic form, tagging a Docker image is simple.

> **Listing 3.19 A simple `docker tag` command**

This gives your image a name that you can refer to, like so:

```
docker run imagename
```

This is much easier than remembering random strings of letters and numbers!

If you want to share your images with others, there's more to tagging than this, though. Unfortunately, the terminology around tags can be rather confusing. Terms such as *image name* and *repository* are used interchangeably. Table 3.1 provides some definitions.

Table 3.1 Docker tagging terms

Term	Meaning
Image	A read-only layer.
Name	The name of your image, such as "todoapp."
Tag	As a verb, it refers to giving an image a name. As a noun, it's a modifier for your image name.
Repository	A hosted collection of tagged images that together create the filesystem for a container.

Perhaps the most confusing terms in this table are "image" and "repository." We've been using the term *image* loosely to mean a collection of layers that we spawn a container from, but technically an image is a single layer that refers to its parent layer recursively. A *repository* is hosted, meaning that it's stored somewhere (either on your Docker daemon or on a registry). In addition, a repository is a collection of tagged images that make up the filesystem for a container.

An analogy with Git can be helpful here. When cloning a Git repository, you check out the state of the files at the point you requested. This is analogous to an image. The repository is the entire history of the files at each commit, going back to the initial commit. You therefore check out the repository at the head's "layer." The other "layers" (or commits) are all there in the repository you've cloned.

In practice, the terms "image" and "repository" are used more or less interchangeably, so don't worry too much about this. But be aware that these terms exist and are used similarly.

What you've seen so far is how to give an image ID a name. Confusingly, this name isn't the image's "tag," although people often refer to it as that. We distinguish between the action "to tag" (verb) and the "tag" (noun) you can give to the image name. This tag (noun) allows you to name a specific version of the image. You might add a tag to manage references to different versions of the same image. For example, you could tag an image with a version name or the date of commit.

A good example of a repository with multiple tags is the Ubuntu image. If you pull the Ubuntu image and then run docker images, you'll get output similar to the following listing.

> **Listing 3.20   An image with multiple tags**

```
$ docker images
REPOSITORY        TAG          IMAGE ID        CREATED          VIRTUAL SIZE
ubuntu            trusty       8eaa4ff06b53    4 weeks ago      192.7 MB
ubuntu            14.04        8eaa4ff06b53    4 weeks ago      192.7 MB
ubuntu            14.04.1      8eaa4ff06b53    4 weeks ago      192.7 MB
ubuntu            latest       8eaa4ff06b53    4 weeks ago      192.7 MB
```

The Repository column lists the hosted collection of layers called "ubuntu". Often this is referred to as the "image." The Tag column here lists four different names (trusty, 14.04, 14.04.1, and latest). The Image ID column lists identical image IDs. This is because these differently tagged images are identical.

This shows that you can have a repository with multiple tags from the same image ID. In theory, though, these tags could later point to different image IDs. If "trusty" gets a security update, for example, the image ID may be changed with a new commit by the maintainers and tagged with "trusty", "14.04.2", and "latest".

The default is to give your image a tag of "latest" if no tag is specified.

> **NOTE** The "latest" tag has no special significance in Docker—it's a default for tagging and pulling. It *doesn't* necessarily mean that this was the last tag set for this image. The "latest" tag of your image may be an old version of the image, as versions built later may have been tagged with a specific tag like "v1.2.3".

DISCUSSION

In this section we covered Docker image tagging. In itself, this technique is relatively simple. The real challenge we've found—and focused on here—is navigating the loose use of terminology among Docker users. It's worth re-emphasizing that when people talk about an image, they might be referring to a tagged image, or even a repository. Another particularly common mistake is referring to an image as a container: "Just download the container and run it." Colleagues at work who have been using Docker for a while still frequently ask us, "What's the difference between a container and an image?"

In the next technique you'll learn how to share your now-tagged image with others using a Docker image hub.

<hr>

TECHNIQUE 17   ## Sharing images on the Docker Hub

Tagging images with descriptive names would be even more helpful if you could share these names (and images) with other people. To satisfy this need, Docker comes with the ability to easily move images to other places, and Docker Inc. created the Docker Hub as a free service to encourage this sharing.

> **NOTE**   To follow this technique, you'll need a Docker Hub account that you have logged into previously by running `docker login` on your host machine. If you haven't set one up, you can do so at http://hub.docker.com. Just follow the instructions to register.

PROBLEM

You want to share a Docker image publicly.

SOLUTION

Use the Docker Hub registry to share your image.

As with tagging, the terminology around registries can be confusing. Table 3.2 should help you understand how the terms are used.

Table 3.2   Docker registry terms

Term	Meaning
Username	Your Docker registry username.
Registry	Registries hold images. A registry is a store you can upload images to or download them from. Registries can be public or private.
Registry host	The host on which the Docker registry runs.
Docker Hub	The default public registry hosted at https://hub.docker.com.
Index	The same as a registry host. It appears to be a deprecated term.

As you've seen previously, it's possible to tag an image as many times as you like. This is useful for "copying over" an image so that you have control of it.

Let's say your username on the Docker Hub is "adev". The following three commands show how to copy the "debian:wheezy" image from the Docker Hub to be under your own account.

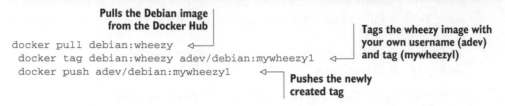

You now have a reference to the Debian wheezy image you downloaded that you can maintain, refer to, and build on.

If you have a private repository to push to, the process is identical, except that you must specify the address of the registry before the tag. Let's say you have a repository that's served from http://mycorp.private.dockerregistry. The following listing will tag and push the image.

The preceding commands won't push the image to the public Docker Hub but will push it to the private repository, so that anyone with access to resources on that service can pull it.

DISCUSSION

You now have the ability to share your images with others. This is a great way to share work, ideas, or even issues you're facing with other engineers.

Just as GitHub isn't the only publicly available Git server, Docker Hub isn't the only publicly available Docker registry. But like GitHub, it's the most popular. For example, RedHat has a hub at https://access.redhat.com/containers.

Again, like Git servers, public and private Docker registries might have different features and characteristics that make one or the other appeal to you. If you're evaluating them, you might want to think about things like cost (to buy, subscribe to, or maintain), adherence to APIs, security features, and performance.

In the next technique, we'll look at how specific images can be referenced to help avoid issues that arise when the image reference you're using is unspecific.

TECHNIQUE 18 **Referring to a specific image in builds**

Most of the time you'll be referring to generic image names in your builds, such as "node" or "ubuntu" and will proceed without problem.

If you refer to an image name, it's possible that the image can change while the tag remains the same, as paradoxical as it sounds. The repository name is only a reference, and it may be altered to point to a different underlying image. Specifying a tag with the colon notation (such as `ubuntu:trusty`) doesn't remove this risk either, as security updates can use the same tag to automatically rebuild vulnerable images.

Most of the time you'll want this—the maintainers of the image may have found an improvement, and patching security holes is generally a good thing. Occasionally, though, this can cause you pain. And this is not merely a theoretical risk: this has happened to us on a number of occasions, breaking continuous delivery builds in a way that's difficult to debug. In the early days of Docker, packages would be added to and removed from the most popular images regularly (including, on one memorable occasion, the disappearance of the `passwd` command!), making builds that previously worked suddenly break.

PROBLEM

You want to be sure that your build is from a specific and unchanging image.

SOLUTION

To be absolutely certain that you're building against a given set of files, specify a specific image ID in your Dockerfile.

Here's an example (which will likely not work for you):

> **Listing 3.23 Dockerfile with a specific image ID**

Builds from a specific image (or layer) ID

Runs commands within this image to record the image you built from within a file in the new image

```
FROM 8eaa4ff06b53    ◁─┐
 RUN echo "Built from image id:" > /etc/buildinfo
 RUN echo "8eaa4ff06b53" >> /etc/buildinfo
 RUN echo "an ubuntu 14.4.01 image" >> /etc/buildinfo
 CMD ["echo","/etc/buildinfo"]    ◁──
```

The built image will by default output the information you recorded in the /etc/buildinfo file.

To build from a specific image (or layer) ID like this, the image ID and its data must be stored locally on your Docker daemon. The Docker registry won't perform any kind of lookup to find the image ID in layers of images available to you on the Docker Hub, or in any other registry you may be configured to use.

Note that the image you refer to need not be tagged—it could be any layer you have locally. You can begin your build from any layer you wish. This might be useful for certain surgical or experimental procedures you want to perform for Dockerfile build analysis.

If you want to persist the image remotely, it's best to tag and push the image to a repository that's under your control in a remote registry.

> **WARNING**   It's worth pointing out that almost the opposite problem can occur when a Docker image that was previously working suddenly does not. Usually this is because something on the network has changed. One memorable example of this was when our builds failed to `apt-get update` one morning. We assumed it was a problem with our local deb cache and tried debugging without success until a friendly sysadmin pointed out that the particular version of Ubuntu we were building from was no longer supported. This meant that the network calls to `apt-get update` were returning an HTTP error.

DISCUSSION

Although it might sound a little theoretical, it's important to understand the advantages and disadvantages of being more specific about the image you want to build or run.

Being more specific makes the result of your action more predictable and debuggable, as there's less ambiguity about which Docker image is or was downloaded. The disadvantage is that your image may not be the latest available, and you may therefore miss out on critical updates. Which state of affairs you prefer will depend on your particular use case and what you need to prioritize in your Docker environment.

In the next section, you'll apply what you've learned to a somewhat playful real-world scenario: winning at 2048.

3.3   *Environments as processes*

One way of viewing Docker is to see it as turning environments into processes. VMs can be treated in the same way, but Docker makes this much more convenient and efficient.

To illustrate this, we'll show you how the speedy spin-up, storage, and recreation of container state can allow you to do something otherwise (almost) impossible—winning at 2048!

TECHNIQUE 19   **The "save game" approach: Winning at 2048**

This technique is designed to provide you with a little light relief while showing you how Docker can be used to revert state easily. If you're not familiar with 2048, it's an addictive game where you push numbers around a board. The original version is available online at http://gabrielecirulli.github.io/2048 if you want to get acquainted with it first.

PROBLEM

You want to save container state regularly in order to revert to a known state if necessary.

SOLUTION

Use `docker commit` to "save game" whenever you are unsure whether you will survive in 2048.

We've created a monolithic image on which you can play 2048 within a Docker container that contains a VNC server and Firefox.

To use this image you'll need to install a VNC client. Popular implementations include TigerVNC and VNC Viewer. If you don't have one, a quick search for "vnc client" on the package manager on your host should yield useful results.

To start up the container, run the following commands.

Listing 3.24   Start the 2048 container

> **Run the imiell/win2048
> image as a daemon**

```
$ docker run -d -p 5901:5901 -p 6080:6080 --name win2048 imiell/win2048  ⊲──┘
 $ vncviewer localhost:1                    ⊲──┐ Use VNC to get GUI access
                                                 to the container
```

First you run a container from the imiell/win2048 image that we've prepared for you. You start this in the background and specify that it should open two ports (5901 and 6080) to the host. These ports will be used by the VNC server started automatically inside the container. You also give the container a name for easy use later: win2048.

You can now run your VNC viewer (the executable may differ depending on what you have installed) and instruct it to connect to your local computer. Because the appropriate ports have been exposed from the container, connecting to localhost will actually connect to the container. The :1 after localhost is appropriate if you have no X displays on your host, other than a standard desktop—if you do, you may need to choose a different number and look at the documentation for your VNC viewer to manually specify the VNC port as 5901.

Once you're connected to the VNC server, you'll be prompted for a password. The password for VNC on this image is "vncpass". You'll then see a window with a Firefox tab and a 2048 table preloaded. Click on it to give it focus, and play until you're ready to save the game.

To save the game, you tag the named container after committing it:

Listing 3.25   Commit and tag the game state

An image ID was generated by committing the win2048 container, and now you want to give it a unique name (because you may be creating a number of these images). To do this, you can use the output of date +%s as part of the image name. This outputs the number of seconds since the first day of 1970, providing a unique (for our purposes), constantly increasing value. The $(command) syntax just substitutes the output of command at that position. If you prefer, you can run date +%s manually and paste the output as part of the image name instead.

You can then continue playing until you lose. Now comes the magic! You can return to your save point with the following commands.

Listing 3.26   Return to the saved game

```
$ docker rm -f win2048
$ docker run -d -p 5901:5901 -p 6080:6080 --name win2048 my2048tag:$mytag
```

$mytag is a tag selected from the docker images command. Repeat the tag, rm, and run steps until you complete 2048.

DISCUSSION

We hope that was fun. This example is more fun than practical, but we have used—and seen other developers use—this technique to great effect, especially when their environments are complex and the work they're doing is somewhat forensic and tricky.

Summary

- You can create a Docker container that looks like a "normal" host. Some consider this to be bad practice, but it may benefit your business or fit your use case.
- It's relatively easy to convert a VM to a Docker image to make the initial move to Docker.
- You can supervise services on your containers to mimic their previous VM-like operation.
- Committing is the correct way to save your work as you go.
- You can specify a particular Docker image to build from by using its build ID.
- You can name your images and share them with the world on the Docker Hub for free.
- You can even use Docker's commit capability to win at games like 2048!

Building images

This chapter covers

- Some basics of image creation
- Manipulating the Docker build cache for fast and reliable builds
- Configuring timezones as part of an image build
- Running commands directly on your containers from the host
- Drilling down into the layers created by an image build
- Using the more advanced ONBUILD feature when building and using images

To get beyond the basics of using Docker, you'll want to start creating your own building blocks (images) to pull together in interesting ways. This chapter will cover some of the important parts of image creation, looking at practicalities that you might otherwise stumble over.

4.1 Building images

Although the simplicity of Dockerfiles makes them a powerful time-saving tool, there are some subtleties that can cause confusion. We'll take you over a few time-saving features and their details, starting with the ADD instruction. Then we'll cover the Docker build cache, how it can let you down, and how you can manipulate it to your advantage.

Remember to refer to the official Docker documentation for complete Dockerfile instructions at https://docs.docker.com.

TECHNIQUE 20   Injecting files into your image using ADD

Although it's possible to add files within a Dockerfile using the RUN command and basic shell primitives, this can quickly become unmanageable. The ADD command was added to the list of Dockerfile commands to address the need to put large numbers of files into an image without fuss.

PROBLEM

You want to download and unpack a tarball into your image in a concise way.

SOLUTION

Tar and compress your files, and use the ADD directive in your Dockerfile.

Create a fresh environment for this Docker build with mkdir add_example && cd add_example. Then retrieve a tarball and give it a name you can reference later.

Listing 4.1   Downloading a TAR file

```
$ curl \
https://www.flamingspork.com/projects/libeatmydata/
➥ libeatmydata-105.tar.gz > my.tar.gz
```

In this case we've used a TAR file from another technique, but it could be any tarball you like.

Listing 4.2   Adding a TAR file to an image

```
FROM debian
RUN mkdir -p /opt/libeatmydata
ADD my.tar.gz /opt/libeatmydata/
RUN ls -lRt /opt/libeatmydata
```

Build this Dockerfile with docker build --no-cache . and the output should look like this:

Listing 4.3   Building an image with a TAR file

```
$ docker build --no-cache .
Sending build context to Docker daemon 422.9 kB
Sending build context to Docker daemon
Step 0 : FROM debian
 ---> c90d655b99b2
Step 1 : RUN mkdir -p /opt/libeatmydata
 ---> Running in fe04bac7df74
 ---> c0ab8c88bb46
Removing intermediate container fe04bac7df74
```

```
Step 2 : ADD my.tar.gz /opt/libeatmydata/
 ---> 06dcd7a88eb7
Removing intermediate container 3f093a1f9e33
Step 3 : RUN ls -lRt /opt/libeatmydata
 ---> Running in e3283848ad65
/opt/libeatmydata:
total 4
drwxr-xr-x 7 1000 1000 4096 Oct 29 23:02 libeatmydata-105

/opt/libeatmydata/libeatmydata-105:
total 880
drwxr-xr-x 2 1000 1000    4096 Oct 29 23:02 config
drwxr-xr-x 3 1000 1000    4096 Oct 29 23:02 debian
drwxr-xr-x 2 1000 1000    4096 Oct 29 23:02 docs
drwxr-xr-x 3 1000 1000    4096 Oct 29 23:02 libeatmydata
drwxr-xr-x 2 1000 1000    4096 Oct 29 23:02 m4
-rw-r--r-- 1 1000 1000    9803 Oct 29 23:01 config.h.in
[...edited...]
-rw-r--r-- 1 1000 1000    1824 Jun 18  2012 pandora_have_better_malloc.m4
-rw-r--r-- 1 1000 1000     742 Jun 18  2012 pandora_header_assert.m4
-rw-r--r-- 1 1000 1000     431 Jun 18  2012 pandora_version.m4
 ---> 2ee9b4c8059f
Removing intermediate container e3283848ad65
Successfully built 2ee9b4c8059f
```

You can see from this output that the tarball has been unpacked into the target directory by the Docker daemon (the extended output of all the files has been edited). Docker will unpack tarfiles of most standard types (.gz, .bz2, .xz, .tar).

It's worth observing that although you can download tarballs from URLs, they'll only be unpacked automatically if they're stored in the local filesystem. This can lead to confusion.

If you repeat the preceding process with the following Dockerfile, you'll notice that the file is downloaded but not unpacked.

Listing 4.4   Directly adding of the TAR file from the URL

```
FROM debian
RUN mkdir -p /opt/libeatmydata                    The file is retrieved from
ADD \                                             the internet using a URL.
 https://www.flamingspork.com/projects/libeatmydata/libeatmydata-105.tar.gz \
/opt/libeatmydata/
 RUN ls -lRt /opt/libeatmydata
```

The destination directory is indicated by the directory name and a trailing slash. Without the trailing slash, the argument is treated as a filename for the downloaded file.

Here's the resulting build output:

```
Sending build context to Docker daemon 422.9 kB
Sending build context to Docker daemon
Step 0 : FROM debian
 ---> c90d655b99b2
```

```
Step 1 : RUN mkdir -p /opt/libeatmydata
 ---> Running in 6ac454c52962
 ---> bdd948e413c1
Removing intermediate container 6ac454c52962
Step 2 : ADD \
https://www.flamingspork.com/projects/libeatmydata/libeatmydata-105.tar.gz
➥ /opt/libeatmydata/
Downloading [==================================================>] \
419.4 kB/419.4 kB
 ---> 9d8758e90b64
Removing intermediate container 02545663f13f
Step 3 : RUN ls -lRt /opt/libeatmydata
 ---> Running in a947eaa04b8e
/opt/libeatmydata:
total 412
-rw------- 1 root root 419427 Jan  1  1970 \
libeatmydata-105.tar.gz
  ---> f18886c2418a
Removing intermediate container a947eaa04b8e
Successfully built f18886c2418a
```

> **The libeatmydata-l05.tar.gz file has been downloaded and placed in the /opt/libeatmydata directory without being unpacked.**

Note that without the trailing slash in the ADD line in the previous Dockerfile, the file would be downloaded and saved with that filename. The trailing slash indicates that the file should be downloaded and placed in the directory specified.

All new files and directories are owned by root (or whoever has group or user IDs of 0 within the container).

Whitespace in filenames

If your filenames have whitespace in them, you'll need to use the quoted form of ADD (or COPY):

```
ADD "space file.txt" "/tmp/space file.txt"
```

DISCUSSION

The ADD Dockerfile instruction is quite a workhorse, with a number of different pieces of functionality you can take advantage of. If you're going to write more than a couple of Dockerfiles (which you likely will as you go through this book), it's worth reading the official Dockerfile instructions documentation—there aren't many (18 instructions are listed in the documentation at the time of writing at https://docs.docker .com/engine/reference/builder) and you'll only use a few of them regularly.

People often ask about adding compressed files without extracting them. For this you should use the COPY command, which looks exactly like the ADD command but doesn't unpack any files and won't download over the internet.

TECHNIQUE 21   **Rebuilding without the cache**

Building with Dockerfiles takes advantage of a useful caching feature: steps that have already been built are only rebuilt if the commands have changed. The next listing shows the output of a rebuild of the to-do app from chapter 1.

Listing 4.5   Rebuilding with the cache

```
$ docker build .
Sending build context to Docker daemon  2.56 kB
Sending build context to Docker daemon
Step 0 : FROM node
 ---> 91cbcf796c2c
Step 1 : MAINTAINER ian.miell@gmail.com
 ---> Using cache
  ---> 8f5a8a3d9240
 Step 2 : RUN git clone -q https://github.com/docker-in-practice/todo.git
 ---> Using cache
 ---> 48db97331aa2
Step 3 : WORKDIR todo
 ---> Using cache
 ---> c5c85db751d6
Step 4 : RUN npm install > /dev/null
 ---> Using cache
 ---> be943c45c55b
Step 5 : EXPOSE 8000
 ---> Using cache
 ---> 805b18d28a65
Step 6 : CMD npm start
 ---> Using cache
 ---> 19525d4ec794
Successfully built 19525d4ec794
```

> **Indicates you're using the cache**
>
> **Specifies the cached image/layer ID**
>
> **The final image is "rebuilt," but in reality nothing has changed.**

As useful and time-saving as this is, it's not always the behavior you want.

Taking the preceding Dockerfile as an example, imagine you'd changed your source code and pushed it to the Git repository. The new code wouldn't be checked out, because the git clone command hasn't changed. As far as the Docker build is concerned, it's the same, so the cached image can be reused.

In these cases, you'll want to rebuild your image without using the cache.

PROBLEM

You want to rebuild your Dockerfile without using the cache.

SOLUTION

To force a rebuild without using the image cache, run your docker build with the --no-cache flag. The following listing runs the previous build with --no-cache.

Listing 4.6   Forcing a rebuild without using the cache

```
$ docker build --no-cache .
 Sending build context to Docker daemon  2.56 kB
Sending build context to Docker daemon
```

> **Rebuilds the Docker image, ignoring cached layers with the --no-cache flag**

```
Step 0 : FROM node                  No mention of caching this time
 ---> 91cbcf796c2c
Step 1 : MAINTAINER ian.miell@gmail.com              Intervening images have
 ---> Running in ca243b77f6a1          <───         a different ID than in the
  ---> 602f1294d7f1                    <───         previous listing.
 Removing intermediate container ca243b77f6a1
Step 2 : RUN git clone -q https://github.com/docker-in-practice/todo.git
 ---> Running in f2c0ac021247
 ---> 04ee24faaf18
Removing intermediate container f2c0ac021247
Step 3 : WORKDIR todo
 ---> Running in c2d9cd32c182
 ---> 4e0029de9074
Removing intermediate container c2d9cd32c182
Step 4 : RUN npm install > /dev/null
 ---> Running in 79122dbf9e52
npm WARN package.json todomvc-swarm@0.0.1 No repository field.
 ---> 9b6531f2036a
Removing intermediate container 79122dbf9e52
Step 5 : EXPOSE 8000
 ---> Running in d1d58e1c4b15
 ---> f7c1b9151108
Removing intermediate container d1d58e1c4b15
Step 6 : CMD npm start
 ---> Running in 697713ebb185
 ---> 74f9ad384859
Removing intermediate container 697713ebb185
Successfully built 74f9ad384859           <───  A new image is built.
```

The output shows no mention of caching, and each intervening layer ID is different from the output in listing 4.5.

Similar problems can occur in other situations. We were flummoxed early on using Dockerfiles when a network blip meant that a command didn't retrieve something properly from the network, but the command didn't error. We kept calling docker build, but the resulting bug wouldn't go away! This was because a "bad" image had found its way into the cache, and we didn't understand the way Docker caching worked. Eventually we figured it out.

DISCUSSION

Removing caching can be a useful sanity check once you've got your final Dockerfile, to make sure it works from top to bottom, particularly when you're using internal web resources in your company that you may have changed while iterating on the Docker-file. This situation doesn't occur if you're using ADD, because Docker will download the file every time to check if it has changed, but that behavior can be tiresome if you're pretty sure it's going to stay the same and you just want to get going with writing the rest of the Dockerfile.

TECHNIQUE 22   **Busting the cache**

Using the --no-cache flag is often enough to get around any problems with the cache, but sometimes you'll want a more fine-grained solution. If you have a build that takes a long time, for example, you may want to use the cache up to a certain point, and then invalidate it to rerun a command and create a new image.

PROBLEM

You want to invalidate the Docker build cache from a specific point in the Dockerfile build.

SOLUTION

Add a benign comment after the command to invalidate the cache.

Starting with the Dockerfile in https://github.com/docker-in-practice/todo (which corresponds to the Step lines in the following output), we've done a build and then added a comment in the Dockerfile on the line with CMD. You can see the output of doing docker build again here:

```
$ docker build .                                          ◄─┐ A "normal"
 Sending build context to Docker daemon   2.56 kB           docker build
Sending build context to Docker daemon
Step 0 : FROM node
 ---> 91cbcf796c2c
Step 1 : MAINTAINER ian.miell@gmail.com
 ---> Using cache
 ---> 8f5a8a3d9240
Step 2 : RUN git clone -q https://github.com/docker-in-practice/todo.git
 ---> Using cache
 ---> 48db97331aa2
Step 3 : WORKDIR todo
 ---> Using cache
 ---> c5c85db751d6
Step 4 : RUN npm install
 ---> Using cache
 ---> be943c45c55b
Step 5 : EXPOSE 8000                             ◄─┐ Cache is used
 ---> Using cache                                    up to here.
 ---> 805b18d28a65                                                Cache has been invalidated,
Step 6 : CMD ["npm","start"] #bust the cache    ◄─┐ but the command is effectively
 ---> Running in fc6c4cd487ce                        unchanged.
 ---> d66d9572115e                              ◄─┐ A new image has
 Removing intermediate container fc6c4cd487ce       been created.
Successfully built d66d9572115e
```

The reason this trick works is because Docker treats the non-whitespace change to the line as though it were a new command, so the cached layer is not re-used.

You may be wondering (as we did when we first looked at Docker) whether you can move Docker layers from image to image, merging them at will as though they were change sets in Git. This isn't possible at present within Docker. A layer is defined as a change set from a given image only. Because of this, once the cache has been broken, it can't be re-applied for commands re-used later in the build. For this reason, you're advised to put commands that are less likely to change nearer the top of the Docker-file if possible.

DISCUSSION

For the initial iteration on a Dockerfile, splitting up every single command into a separate layer is excellent for speed of iteration, because you can selectively rerun parts of the process, as shown in the previous listing, but it's not so great for producing a small final image. It's not unheard-of for builds with a reasonable amount of complexity to approach the hard limit of 42 layers. To mitigate this, once you have a working build you're happy with, you should look at the steps in technique 56 for creating a production-ready image.

TECHNIQUE 23 **Intelligent cache-busting using build-args**

In the previous technique you saw how the cache can be busted mid-build by changing the relevant line.

In this technique we're going to take things a step further by controlling whether or not the cache is busted from the build command.

PROBLEM

You want to bust the cache on demand when performing a build, without editing the Dockerfile.

SOLUTION

Use the ARG directive in your Dockerfile to enable surgical cache-busting.

To demonstrate this, you're again going to use the Dockerfile at https://github .com/docker-in-practice/todo, but make a minor change to it.

What you want to do is control the busting of the cache before the `npm install`. Why would you want to do this? As you've learned, by default Docker will only break the cache if the command in the Dockerfile changes. But let's imagine that updated npm packages are available, and you want to make sure you get them. One option is to manually change the line (as you saw in the previous technique), but a more elegant way to achieve the same thing involves using the Docker ARGS directive and a bash trick.

Add the ARG line to the Dockerfile as follows.

Listing 4.7   Simple Dockerfile with bustable cache

```
WORKDIR todo
ARG CACHEBUST=no        ⊲──┤ The ARG directive sets an
 RUN npm install            environment variable for the build.
```

In this example, you use the ARG directive to set the CACHEBUST environment variable and default it to no if it's not set by the `docker build` command.

Now build that Dockerfile "normally":

```
$ docker build .
Sending build context to Docker daemon   2.56kB
Step 1/7 : FROM node
latest: Pulling from library/node
aa18ad1a0d33: Pull complete
```

```
15a33158a136: Pull complete
f67323742a64: Pull complete
c4b45e832c38: Pull complete
f83e14495c19: Pull complete
41fea39113bf: Pull complete
f617216d7379: Pull complete
cbb91377826f: Pull complete
Digest: sha256:
➥ a8918e06476bef51ab83991aea7c199bb50bfb131668c9739e6aa7984da1c1f6
Status: Downloaded newer image for node:latest
 ---> 9ea1c3e33a0b
Step 2/7 : MAINTAINER ian.miell@gmail.com
 ---> Running in 03dba6770157
 ---> a5b55873d2d8
Removing intermediate container 03dba6770157
Step 3/7 : RUN git clone https://github.com/docker-in-practice/todo.git
 ---> Running in 23336fd5991f
Cloning into 'todo'...
 ---> 8ba06824d184
Removing intermediate container 23336fd5991f
Step 4/7 : WORKDIR todo
 ---> f322e2dbeb85
Removing intermediate container 2aa5ae19fa63
Step 5/7 : ARG CACHEBUST=no
 ---> Running in 9b4917f2e38b
 ---> f7e86497dd72
Removing intermediate container 9b4917f2e38b
Step 6/7 : RUN npm install
 ---> Running in a48e38987b04
npm info it worked if it ends with ok
[...]
added 249 packages in 49.418s
npm info ok
 ---> 324ba92563fd
Removing intermediate container a48e38987b04
Step 7/7 : CMD npm start
 ---> Running in ae76fa693697
 ---> b84dbc4bf5f1
Removing intermediate container ae76fa693697
Successfully built b84dbc4bf5f1
```

If you build it again with exactly the same docker build command, you'll observe that
the Docker build cache is used, and no changes are made to the resulting image.

```
$ docker build .
Sending build context to Docker daemon    2.56kB
Step 1/7 : FROM node
 ---> 9ea1c3e33a0b
Step 2/7 : MAINTAINER ian.miell@gmail.com
 ---> Using cache
 ---> a5b55873d2d8
Step 3/7 : RUN git clone https://github.com/docker-in-practice/todo.git
 ---> Using cache
 ---> 8ba06824d184
```

```
Step 4/7 : WORKDIR todo
 ---> Using cache
 ---> f322e2dbeb85
Step 5/7 : ARG CACHEBUST=no
 ---> Using cache
 ---> f7e86497dd72
Step 6/7 : RUN npm install
 ---> Using cache
 ---> 324ba92563fd
Step 7/7 : CMD npm start
 ---> Using cache
 ---> b84dbc4bf5f1
Successfully built b84dbc4bf5f1
```

At this point you decide that you want to force the npm packages to be rebuilt. Perhaps a bug has been fixed, or you want to be sure you're up to date. This is where the ARG variable you added to the Dockerfile in listing 4.7 comes in. If this ARG variable is set to a value never used before on your host, the cache will be busted from that point.

This is where you use the build-arg flag to docker build, along with a bash trick to force a fresh value:

```
$ docker build --build-arg CACHEBUST=${RANDOM} .      ◄─┐  Run docker build with the build-
 Sending build context to Docker daemon 4.096 kB         arg flag, setting the CACHEBUST
Step 1/9 : FROM node                                     argument to a pseudo-random
 ---> 53d4d5f3b46e                                       value generated by bash
Step 2/9 : MAINTAINER ian.miell@gmail.com
 ---> Using cache
 ---> 3a252318543d
Step 3/9 : RUN git clone https://github.com/docker-in-practice/todo.git
 ---> Using cache
 ---> c0f682653a4a
Step 4/9 : WORKDIR todo                     Because the ARG CACHEBUST=no
 ---> Using cache                           line itself has not changed, the
 ---> bd54f5d70700                          cache is used here.
Step 5/9 : ARG CACHEBUST=no      ◄─┘
   ---> Using cache
 ---> 3229d52b7c33
Step 6/9 : RUN npm install       ◄─┐    Because the CACHEBUST arg was
   ---> Running in 42f9b1f37a50        set to a previously unset value,
npm info it worked if it ends with ok  the cache is busted, and the npm
npm info using npm@4.1.2                install command is run again.
npm info using node@v7.7.2
npm info attempt registry request try #1 at 11:25:55 AM
npm http request GET https://registry.npmjs.org/compression
npm info attempt registry request try #1 at 11:25:55 AM
[...]
Step 9/9 : CMD npm start
 ---> Running in 19219fe5307b
 ---> 129bab5e908a
Removing intermediate container 19219fe5307b
Successfully built 129bab5e908a
```

Note that the cache is busted on the line *following* the ARG line, not the ARG line itself. This can be a little confusing. The key thing to look out for is the "Running in" phrase—this means that a new container has been created to run the build line in.

The use of the ${RANDOM} argument is worth explaining. Bash provides you with this reserved variable name to give you an easy way of getting a value between one and five digits long:

```
$ echo ${RANDOM}
19856
$ echo ${RANDOM}
26429
$ echo ${RANDOM}
2856
```

This can come in handy, such as when you want a probably unique value to create files just for a specific run of a script.

You can even produce a much longer random number if you're concerned about clashes:

```
$ echo ${RANDOM}${RANDOM}
434320509
$ echo ${RANDOM}${RANDOM}
1327340
```

Note that if you're not using bash (or a shell that has this RANDOM variable available), this technique won't work. In that case, you could use the date command instead to produce a fresh value:

```
$ docker build --build-arg CACHEBUST=$(date +%s)  .
```

DISCUSSION

This technique has demonstrated a few things that will come in handy when using Docker. You've learned about using the --build-args flag to pass in a value to the Dockerfile and bust the cache on demand, creating a fresh build without changing the Dockerfile.

If you use bash, you've also learned about the RANDOM variable, and how it can be useful in other contexts than just Docker builds.

TECHNIQUE 24   **Intelligent cache-busting using the ADD directive**

In the previous technique you saw how the cache could be busted mid-build at a time of your choosing, which was itself a level up from using the --no-cache flag to ignore the cache completely.

Now you're going to take it to the next level, so that you can automatically bust the cache only when it's necessary to. This can save you a lot of time and compute—and therefore money!

PROBLEM

You want to bust the cache when a remote resource has changed.

SOLUTION

Use the Dockerfile ADD directive to only bust the cache when the response from a URL changes.

One of the early criticisms of Dockerfiles was that their claim of producing reliable build results was misleading. Indeed, we took this very subject up with the creator of Docker back in 2013 (http://mng.bz/B8E4).

Specifically, if you make a call to the network with a directive in your Dockerfile like this,

```
RUN git clone https://github.com/nodejs/node
```

then by default the Docker build will perform this once per Docker daemon. The code on GitHub could change substantially, but as far as your Docker daemon is concerned, the build is up to date. Years could pass, and the same Docker daemon will still be using the cache.

This may sound like a theoretical concern, but it's a very real one for many users. We've seen this happen many times at work, causing confusion. You've already seen some solutions to this, but for many complex or large builds, those solutions are not granular enough.

THE SMART CACHE-BUSTING PATTERN

Imagine you have a Dockerfile that looks like the following listing (note that it won't work! It's just a Dockerfile pattern to show the principle).

> Listing 4.8   An example Dockerfile

Installs a series of packages as a prerequisite

```
FROM ubuntu:16.04
RUN apt-get install -y git and many other packages
 RUN git clone https://github.com/nodejs/node
 WORKDIR node
RUN make && make install
```

Clones a regularly changing repository (nodejs is just an example)

Runs a make and install command, which builds the project

This Dockerfile presents some challenges to creating an efficient build process. If you want to build everything from scratch each time, the solution is simple: use the --no-cache argument to docker build. The problem with this is that each time you run a build you're repeating the package installation in the second line, which is (mostly) unnecessary.

This challenge can be solved by busting the cache just before the git clone (demonstrated in the last technique). This raises another challenge, however: what if the Git repository hasn't changed? Then you're doing a potentially costly network transfer, followed by a potentially costly make command. Network, compute, and disk resources are all being used unnecessarily.

One way to get around this is to use technique 23, where you pass in a build argument with a new value every time you know that the remote repository has changed. But this still requires manual investigation to determine whether there has been a change, and intervention.

What you need is a command that can determine whether the resource has changed since the last build, and only then bust the cache.

THE ADD DIRECTIVE—UNEXPECTED BENEFITS

Enter the ADD directive!

You're already familiar with ADD, as it's a basic Dockerfile directive. Normally it's used to add a file to the resulting image, but there are two useful features of ADD that you can use to your advantage in this context: it caches the contents of the file it refers to, and it can take a network resource as an argument. This means that you can bust the cache whenever the output of a web request changes.

How can you take advantage of this when cloning a repository? Well, that depends on the nature of the resource you're referencing over the network. Many resources will have a page that changes when the repository itself changes, but these will vary from resource type to resource type. Here we'll focus on GitHub repos, because that's a common use case.

The GitHub API provides a useful resource that can help here. It has URLs for each repository that return JSON for the most recent commits. When a new commit is made, the content of the response changes.

Listing 4.9 Using ADD to trigger a cache bust

It doesn't matter where the output of the file goes, so we send it to /dev/null.

The URL that changes when a new commit is made

```
FROM ubuntu:16.04
ADD https://api.github.com/repos/nodejs/node/commits
➥ /dev/null
 RUN git clone https://github.com/nodejs/node
 [...]
```

The git clone will take place only when a change is made.

The result of the preceding listing is that the cache is busted only when a commit has been made to the repo since the last build. No human intervention is required, and no manual checking.

If you want to test this mechanism with a frequently changing repo, try using the Linux kernel.

Listing 4.10 Adding the Linux kernel code to an image

The ADD command, this time using the Linux repository

```
FROM ubuntu:16.04
ADD https://api.github.com/repos/torvalds/linux/commits /dev/null
 RUN echo "Built at: $(date)" >> /build_time
```

Outputs the system date into the built image, which will show when the last cache-busting build took place

If you create a folder and put the preceding code into a Dockerfile, and then run the following command regularly (every hour, for example), the output date will change only when the Linux Git repo changes.

> **Listing 4.11   Building a Linux code image**

Builds the image and gives it
the name linux_last_updated

Outputs the contents of
the /build_time file from
the resulting image

```
$ docker build -t linux_last_updated .
 $ docker run linux_last_updated cat /build_time
```

DISCUSSION

This technique demonstrated a valuable automated technique for ensuring builds only take place when necessary.

It also demonstrated some of the details of how the ADD command works. You saw that the "file" could be a network resource, and that if the contents of the file (or network resource) change from a previous build, a cache bust takes place.

In addition, you also saw that network resources have related resources that can indicate whether the resource you're referencing has changed. Although you could, for example, reference the main GitHub page to see if there are any changes there, it's likely that the page changes more frequently than the last commit (such as if the time of the web response is buried in the page source, or if there's a unique reference string in each response).

In the case of GitHub, you can reference the API, as you saw. Other services, such as BitBucket, offer similar resources. The Kubernetes project, for example, offers this URL to indicate which release is stable: https://storage.googleapis.com/kubernetes-release/release/stable.txt. If you were building a Kubernetes-based project, you might put an ADD line in your Dockerfile to bust the cache whenever this response changes.

TECHNIQUE 25   Setting the right time zone in your containers

If you've ever installed a full operating system, you'll know that setting the time zone is part of the process of setting it up. Even though a container isn't an operating system (or a virtual machine), it contains the files that tell programs how to interpret the time for the configured timezone.

PROBLEM

You want to set the time zone correctly for your containers.

SOLUTION

Replace the container's localtime file with a link to the time zone you want.

The following listing demonstrates the problem. It doesn't matter where in the world you run this, the container will show the same time zone.

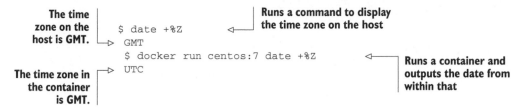

Listing 4.12   Container starting with wrong time zone

The time zone on the host is GMT.

The time zone in the container is GMT.

Runs a command to display the time zone on the host

Runs a container and outputs the date from within that

```
$ date +%Z
GMT
$ docker run centos:7 date +%Z
UTC
```

The container contains the files that determine which time zone is used by the container to interpret the time value it gets. The actual time used is, of course, tracked by the host operating system.

The next listing shows how you can set the time zone to the one you want.

Listing 4.13   Dockerfile for replacing the centos:7 default time zone

Removes the existing localtime symlink file

Starts from the centos image we just looked at

```
FROM centos:7
RUN rm -rf /etc/localtime
RUN ln -s /usr/share/zoneinfo/GMT /etc/localtime
CMD date +%Z
```

Replaces the /etc/localtime link with a link to the time zone you want

Shows the time zone of your container as the default command to run

In listing 4.13 the key file is /etc/localtime. This points to the file that tells the container which time zone to use when it's asked for the time. The default time given is in the UTC time standard, which is used if the file doesn't exist (the minimal BusyBox image, for example, doesn't have it).

The following listing shows the output of building the preceding Dockerfile.

Listing 4.14   Building a time-zone-replacing Dockerfile

```
$ docker build -t timezone_change .                    Builds the container
 Sending build context to Docker daemon 62.98 kB
Step 1 : FROM centos:7
7: Pulling from library/centos
45a2e645736c: Pull complete
Digest: sha256:
➥ c577af3197aacedf79c5a204cd7f493c8e07ffbce7f88f7600bf19c688c38799
Status: Downloaded newer image for centos:7
 ---> 67591570dd29
Step 2 : RUN rm -rf /etc/localtime
 ---> Running in fb52293849db
 ---> 0deda41be8e3
Removing intermediate container fb52293849db
Step 3 : RUN ln -s /usr/share/zoneinfo/GMT /etc/localtime
 ---> Running in 47bf21053b53
```

```
 ---> 5b5cb1197183
Removing intermediate container 47bf21053b53
Step 4 : CMD date +%Z
 ---> Running in 1e481eda8579
 ---> 9477cdaa73ac
Removing intermediate container 1e481eda8579
Successfully built 9477cdaa73ac
$ docker run timezone_change          ◁——— Runs the container
  GMT              ◁——┐
                      └ Outputs the specified time zone
```

In this way you can specify the time zone to use within—and only within—your container. Many applications depend on this setting, so it comes up not infrequently if you're running a Docker service.

There's another problem that this container-level time granularity can solve. If you're working for a multinational organization and run many different applications on servers based in data centers around the world, the ability to change the time zone in your image and trust that it will report the right time wherever it lands is a useful trick to have to hand.

DISCUSSION

Because the point of Docker images is explicitly to provide a consistent experience no matter where you run your container, there are a number of things you may stumble across if you do want varied results depending on where an image is deployed.

As an example, if you're automatically producing CSV spreadsheets of data for users in different locations, they may have certain expectations of the data format. American users might expect dates in the mm/dd format, whereas Europeans might expect dates in dd/mm format, and Chinese users might expect dates in their own character set.

In the next technique we'll consider locale settings, which affect how dates and times are printed in the local format, among other things.

TECHNIQUE 26   Locale management

In addition to time zones, locales are another aspect of Docker images that can be relevant when building images or running containers.

> **NOTE** A locale defines which language and country settings your programs should use. Typically a locale will be set in the environment through the LANG, LANGUAGE, and locale-gen variables, and through variables beginning with LC_, such as LC_TIME, whose setting determines how the time is displayed to the user.

> **NOTE** An encoding (in this context) is the means by which text is stored as bytes on a computer. A good introduction to this subject is available from W3C here: https://www.w3.org/International/questions/qa-what-is-encoding. It's worth taking the time to understand this subject, as it comes up in all sorts of contexts.

PROBLEM

You're seeing encoding errors in your application builds or deployments.

SOLUTION

Ensure the langugage-specific environment variables are correctly set in your Dockerfile.

Encoding issues aren't always obvious to all users, but they can be fatal when building applications.

Here are a couple of examples of typical encoding errors when building applications in Docker.

Listing 4.15 Typical encoding errors

```
MyFileDialog:66: error: unmappable character for encoding ASCII

UnicodeEncodeError: 'ascii' codec can't encode character u'\xa0' in
position 20: ordinal not in range(128)
```

These errors can kill a build or an application stone dead.

> **TIP** A non-exhaustive list of key words to look out for in the error are "encoding," "ascii," "unicode," "UTF-8," "character," and "codec." If you see these words, chances are you're dealing with an encoding issue.

WHAT DOES THIS HAVE TO DO WITH DOCKER?

When you set up a full-blown operating system, you're typically guided through a setup process that asks you to confirm your preferred time zone, language, keyboard layout, and so on.

Docker containers, as you know by now, aren't full-blown operating systems set up for general use. Rather they're (increasingly) minimal environments for running applications. By default, therefore, they may not come with all the setup you're used to with an operating system.

In particular, Debian removed their dependency on the locales package in 2011, which means that, by default, there's no locale setup in a container based on a Debian image. For example, the following listing shows a Debian-derived Ubuntu image's default environment.

Listing 4.16 Default environment on an Ubuntu container

```
$  docker run -ti ubuntu bash
root@d17673300830:/# env
HOSTNAME=d17673300830
TERM=xterm
LS_COLORS=rs=0 [...]
HIST_FILE=/root/.bash_history
PATH=/usr/local/sbin:/usr/local/bin:/usr/sbin:/usr/bin:/sbin:/bin
PWD=/
SHLVL=1
HOME=/root
_=/usr/bin/envj
```

There are no LANG or similar LC_ settings available in the image by default.

Our Docker host is shown in the next listing.

Listing 4.17   LANG setting on Docker host OS

```
$ env | grep LANG
LANG=en_GB.UTF-8
```

There's a LANG setting in our shell that informs applications that the preferred encoding in our terminal is British English, with text encoded in UTF-8.

To demonstrate an encoding issue, we'll create a file locally that contains a UTF-8-encoded UK currency symbol (the UK's pound sign), and then show how the interpretation of that file changes depending on the terminal's encoding.

Listing 4.18   Creating and showing a UTF-8-encoded UK currency symbol

```
$ env | grep LANG
LANG=en_GB.UTF-8
$ echo -e "\xc2\xa3" > /tmp/encoding_demo   ◁─┐   Uses echo with the -e flag to output
 $ cat /tmp/encoding_demo                         two bytes into a file, which represent
 £                                                a UK pound sign

                                            Cats the file; we'll
                                            see a pound sign.
```

In UTF-8, a pound sign is represented by two bytes. We output these two bytes using echo -e and the \x notation and redirect output into a file. When we cat the file, the terminal reads the two bytes and knows to interpret the output as a pound sign.

Now if we change our terminal's encoding to use the Western (ISO Latin 1) encoding (which sets up our local LANG also) and output the file, it looks quite different:

Listing 4.19   Demonstrating the encoding problem with the UK currency symbol

```
$ env | grep LANG
 LANG=en_GB.ISO8859-1        The LANG environment variable is now set to
 $ cat /tmp/encoding_demo    Western (ISO Latin l), which is set by the terminal.
 Â£
                             The two bytes are interpreted differently, as two
                             separate characters that are displayed to us.
```

The \xc2 byte is interpreted as a capital *A* with a circumflex on top, and the \xa3 byte is interpreted as a UK pound sign!

> **NOTE** We say "we" rather than "you" above deliberately! Debugging and controlling encodings is a tricky affair, which can depend on a combination of the running application's state, the environment variables you have set up, the running application, and all of the preceding factors that create the data you're examining!

As you've seen, encodings can be affected by the encoding set in the terminal. Getting back to Docker, we noted that no encoding environment variables were set by default in our Ubuntu container. Because of this, you can get different results when running the same commands on your host or in a container. If you see errors that seem to relate to encodings, you may need to set them in your Dockerfile.

SETTING UP ENCODINGS IN A DOCKERFILE

We'll now look at how you can control the encoding of a Debian-based image. We've chosen this image because it's likely to be one of the more common contexts. This example will set up a simple image that just outputs its default environment variables.

Listing 4.20 Setting up a Dockerfile example

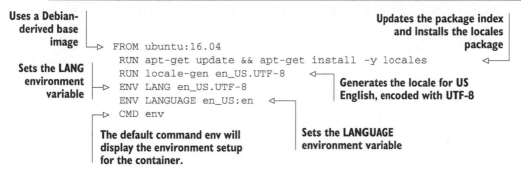

Uses a Debian-derived base image

Updates the package index and installs the locales package

Sets the **LANG** environment variable

Generates the locale for US English, encoded with UTF-8

```
FROM ubuntu:16.04
RUN apt-get update && apt-get install -y locales
RUN locale-gen en_US.UTF-8
ENV LANG en_US.UTF-8
ENV LANGUAGE en_US:en
CMD env
```

The default command env will display the environment setup for the container.

Sets the **LANGUAGE** environment variable

You may be wondering what the differences between the LANG and LANGUAGE variables are. Briefly, LANG is the default setting for the preferred language and encoding settings. It also provides a default when applications look for the more specific LC_* settings. LANGUAGE is used to provide an ordered list of languages preferred by applications if the principal one isn't available. More information can be found by running man locale.

Now you can build the image, and run it to see what's changed.

Listing 4.21 Building and running the encoding image

```
$ docker build -t encoding .          ◁—— Builds the encoding Docker image
 [...]
$ docker run encoding                 ◁—— Runs the built Docker image
 no_proxy=*.local, 169.254/16
LANGUAGE=en_US:en                     ◁┐  The LANGUAGE variable is
 HOSTNAME=aa9d6c8a3ff5                   │  set in the environment
HOME=/root
HIST_FILE=/root/.bash_history
PATH=/usr/local/sbin:/usr/local/bin:/usr/sbin:/usr/bin:/sbin:/bin
LANG=en_US.UTF-8                      ◁┐  The LANG variable is
 PWD=/                                   │  set in the environment
```

DISCUSSION

Like the previous time zone technique, this technique illustrates an issue that catches people out on a regular basis. Like many of the more irritating issues we come across, these don't always make themselves obvious when the image is being built, which makes the time wasted debugging these issues very frustrating. For this reason, it's worth keeping these settings in mind when supporting others who are using Docker images.

TECHNIQUE 27   **Stepping through layers with the image-stepper**

If you've built an image that has a number of steps, you can often find yourself in the position of wanting to know where a particular file was introduced, or what state it was in at a particular point in the build. Combing through each image layer can be laborious, because you'll have to determine the order of layers, retrieve each ID, and start each one up using that ID.

This technique shows you a one-liner that tags each layer of the build in order, meaning you only have to increment a number to work through the images and find out whatever it is you need to know.

PROBLEM

You want to easily refer to each step of your build.

SOLUTION

Use the docker-in-practice/image-stepper image to order the tags for your image.

To illustrate this technique, we'll first show you a script that achieves this result so you understand how it works. Then we'll give you a constructed image to make achieving the result easier.

Here's a simple script that tags every layer in a given image (myimage) in the order of creation.

The Dockerfile for myimage follows.

Listing 4.22   Dockerfile for image with multiple layers

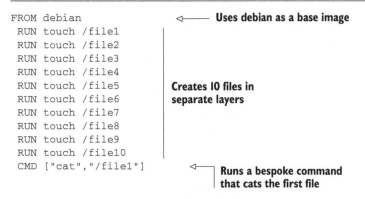

```
FROM debian              ⊲──── Uses debian as a base image
 RUN touch /file1
 RUN touch /file2
 RUN touch /file3
 RUN touch /file4
 RUN touch /file5          Creates 10 files in
 RUN touch /file6          separate layers
 RUN touch /file7
 RUN touch /file8
 RUN touch /file9
 RUN touch /file10
 CMD ["cat","/file1"]     ⊲──┐ Runs a bespoke command
                             │ that cats the first file
```

This is a simple enough Dockerfile, but it's one where it will be clear which stage you are at in the build.

Build this docker image with the following command.

Listing 4.23 Building the myimage image

**Builds the image with the quiet (-q)
flag, tagging it as myimage**

```
$ docker build -t myimage -q .     ⟵┘
  sha256:b21d1e1da994952d8e309281d6a3e3d14c376f9a02b0dd2ecbe6cabffea95288     ⟵
```

**The image identifier
is the only output.**

Once the image is built, you can run the following script.

Listing 4.24 Tagging each layer of myimage in numerical order

**Doesn't consider
the remotely built
layers, which are
marked as
missing (see the
note below)**

**Initializes the counter
variable (x) to 1**

**Runs a for loop to
retrieve the history
of the image**

```
#!/bin/bash
x=1     ⟵
 for id in $(docker history -q "myimage:latest" |     ⟵
⟹ grep -vw missing
⟹ | tac)     ⟵┐
 do
     docker tag "${id}" "myimage:latest_step_${x}"     ⟵
       ((x++))     ⟵
 done
```

**Uses the tac utility to reverse the order of image
IDs the docker history command outputs**

**In each iteration of the loop, tags
the image appropriately with the
incrementing number**

Increments the step counter

If you save the preceding file as tag.sh and run it, the image will be tagged in layer order.

NOTE This tagging method technique will only work on images built locally.
See the note in technique 16 for more information.

Listing 4.25 Tagging and showing the layers

Runs the script from listing 4.24

**Runs a docker images
command with a simple grep
to see the tagged layers**

```
$ ./tag.sh     ⟵
 $ docker images | grep latest_step     ⟵
myimage    latest_step_12    1bfca0ef799d    3 minutes ago    123.1 MB
myimage    latest_step_11    4d7f66939a4c    3 minutes ago    123.1 MB
myimage    latest_step_10    78d31766b5cb    3 minutes ago    123.1 MB
myimage    latest_step_9     f7b4dcbdd74f    3 minutes ago    123.1 MB
myimage    latest_step_8     69b2fa0ce520    3 minutes ago    123.1 MB
myimage    latest_step_7     b949d71fb58a    3 minutes ago    123.1 MB
myimage    latest_step_6     8af3bbf1e7a8    3 minutes ago    123.1 MB
myimage    latest_step_5     ce3dfbdfed74    3 minutes ago    123.1 MB
myimage    latest_step_4     598ed62cabb9    3 minutes ago    123.1 MB
myimage    latest_step_3     6b290f68d4d5    3 minutes ago    123.1 MB
myimage    latest_step_2     586da987f40f    3 minutes ago    123.1 MB
myimage    latest_step_1     19134a8202e7    7 days ago       123.1 MB
```

**The original (and older) base image has
also been tagged as latest_step_1.**

**The steps to build the
myimage image**

Now that you've seen the principle, we'll demonstrate how to dockerize this one-off script and make it work for the general case.

NOTE   The code for this technique is available at https://github.com/docker-in-practice/image-stepper.

First, turn the previous script into a script that can take arguments.

Listing 4.26   Generic tagging script for the image-stepper image

```bash
#!/bin/bash
IMAGE_NAME=$1
IMAGE_TAG=$2
if [[ $IMAGE_NAME = '' ]]
then
    echo "Usage: $0 IMAGE_NAME [ TAG ]"
    exit 1
fi
if [[ $IMAGE_TAG = '' ]]
then
    IMAGE_TAG=latest
fi
x=1
for id in $(docker history -q "${IMAGE_NAME}:${IMAGE_TAG}" |
➥ grep -vw missing | tac)
do
    docker tag "${id}" "${IMAGE_NAME}:${IMAGE_TAG}_step_$x"
    ((x++))
done
```

Defines a bash script that can take two arguments: the image name to process, and the tag you want to step up to

The script from listing 4.24, with the arguments substituted in

---

You can then embed the script in listing 4.26 into a Docker image that you place into a Dockerfile and run as the default `ENTRYPOINT`.

Listing 4.27   Dockerfile for image-stepper image

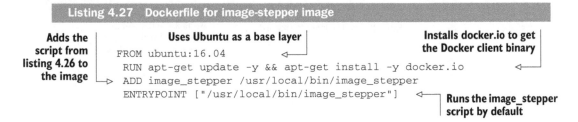

Adds the script from listing 4.26 to the image

Uses Ubuntu as a base layer

Installs docker.io to get the Docker client binary

```
FROM ubuntu:16.04
RUN apt-get update -y && apt-get install -y docker.io
ADD image_stepper /usr/local/bin/image_stepper
ENTRYPOINT ["/usr/local/bin/image_stepper"]
```

Runs the image_stepper script by default

The Dockerfile in listing 4.27 creates an image that runs the script in listing 4.26. The command in listing 4.28 runs this image, giving `myimage` as an argument.

This image, when run against another Docker image built on your host, will then create the tags for each step, allowing you to easily look at the layers in order.

The version of the client binary installed by the docker.io package must be compatible with the version of the Docker daemon on your host machine, typically meaning the client must not be newer.

Listing 4.28 Running image-stepper against another image

Runs the image-stepper image as a container, and removes the container when done

Mounts the host's docker socket, so you can use the Docker client installed in listing 4.27

Downloads the image-stepper image from the Docker Hub

```
$ docker run --rm
  -v /var/run/docker.sock:/var/run/docker.sock
  dockerinpractice/image-stepper
```

⟹ `myimage`   ⟵——— **Tags the myimage created previously**

```
Unable to find image 'dockerinpractice/image-stepper:latest' locally
latest: Pulling from dockerinpractice/image-stepper
b3e1c725a85f: Pull complete
4daad8bdde31: Pull complete
63fe8c0068a8: Pull complete
4a70713c436f: Pull complete
bd842a2105a8: Pull complete
1a3a96204b4b: Pull complete
d3959cd7b55e: Pull complete
Digest: sha256:
65e22f8a82f2221c846c92f72923927402766b3c1f7d0ca851ad418fb998a753
Status: Downloaded newer image for dockerinpractice/image-stepper:latest
$ docker images | grep myimage
```

The output of the docker run command

Runs docker images and greps out the images you've just tagged

```
myimage    latest          2c182dabe85c    24 minutes ago    123 MB
myimage    latest_step_12  2c182dabe85c    24 minutes ago    123 MB
myimage    latest_step_11  e0ff97533768    24 minutes ago    123 MB
myimage    latest_step_10  f46947065166    24 minutes ago    123 MB
myimage    latest_step_9   8a9805a19984    24 minutes ago    123 MB
myimage    latest_step_8   88e42bed92ce    24 minutes ago    123 MB
myimage    latest_step_7   5e638f955e4a    24 minutes ago    123 MB
myimage    latest_step_6   f66b1d9e9cbd    24 minutes ago    123 MB
myimage    latest_step_5   bd07d425bd0d    24 minutes ago    123 MB
myimage    latest_step_4   ba913e75a0b1    24 minutes ago    123 MB
myimage    latest_step_3   2ebcda8cd503    24 minutes ago    123 MB
myimage    latest_step_2   58f4ed4fe9dd    24 minutes ago    123 MB
myimage    latest_step_1   19134a8202e7    2 weeks ago       123 MB
$ docker run myimage:latest_step_8 ls / | grep file
file1
file2
file3
file4
file5
file6
file7
```

The images are tagged.

The files shown are those created up to that step.

Picks a step at random and lists the files in the root directory, grep-ing out the ones created in the Dockerfile from listing 4.27

NOTE On non-Linux OSs (such as Mac and Windows) you may need to specify the folder in which Docker runs in your Docker preferences as a file sharing setting.

This technique is useful for seeing where a particular file was added within a build, or what state a file was in at a particular point in the build. When debugging a build, this can be invaluable!

DISCUSSION

This technique is used in technique 52 to demonstrate that a deleted secret is accessible within a layer within an image.

TECHNIQUE 28   **Onbuild and golang**

The ONBUILD directive can cause a lot of confusion for new Docker users. This technique demonstrates its use in a real-world context by building and running a Go application with a two-line Dockerfile.

PROBLEM

You want to reduce the steps in building an image required for an application.

SOLUTION

Use the ONBUILD command to automate and encapsulate the building of an image.

First you'll run the process through, and then we'll explain what's going on. The example we'll use is the outyet project, which is an example in the golang GitHub repository. All it does is set up a web service that returns a page telling you whether Go 1.4 is available yet.

Build the image as follows.

> **Listing 4.29   Building the outyet image**

```
                  $ git clone https://github.com/golang/example   ◁── Clones the Git repository
Navigates to      $ cd example/outyet
the outyet   ▷
folder            $ docker build -t outyet .        ◁── Builds the outyet image
```

Run a container from the resulting image, and retrieve the served web page.

> **Listing 4.30   Running and validating the outyet image**

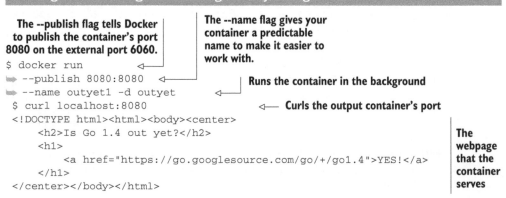

```
The --publish flag tells Docker          The --name flag gives your
to publish the container's port          container a predictable
8080 on the external port 6060.          name to make it easier to
                                         work with.
$ docker run              ◁─
▶ --publish 8080:8080     ◁─────
▶ --name outyet1 -d outyet      ◁─────  Runs the container in the background
 $ curl localhost:8080             ◁──  Curls the output container's port
<!DOCTYPE html><html><body><center>
    <h2>Is Go 1.4 out yet?</h2>                              The
    <h1>                                                     webpage
        <a href="https://go.googlesource.com/go/+/go1.4">YES!</a>    that the
    </h1>                                                    container
</center></body></html>                                      serves
```

That's it—a simple application that returns a web page that tells you whether Go 1.4 is out yet or not.

If you look around the cloned repository, you'll see the Dockerfile is just two lines!

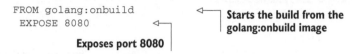

Listing 4.31 The onyet Dockerfile

```
FROM golang:onbuild          ←─┐  Starts the build from the
 EXPOSE 8080         ←──────┐  │  golang:onbuild image
                            │
        Exposes port 8080 ──┘
```

Confused yet? OK, it may make more sense when you look at the Dockerfile for the golang:onbuild image.

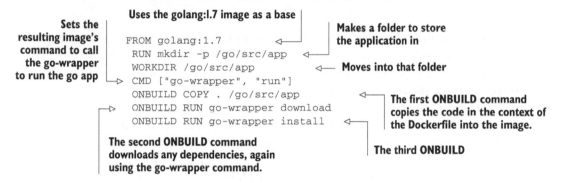

Listing 4.32 The golang:onbuild Dockerfile

```
                        Uses the golang:l.7 image as a base

   Sets the                                         Makes a folder to store
resulting image's    FROM golang:1.7         ←       the application in
command to call       RUN mkdir -p /go/src/app  ←─┐
the go-wrapper        WORKDIR /go/src/app          ←── Moves into that folder
to run the go app ─┐  CMD ["go-wrapper", "run"]
                   └→ ONBUILD COPY . /go/src/app
                     ONBUILD RUN go-wrapper download   ←─┐  The first ONBUILD command
                     ONBUILD RUN go-wrapper install  ←    │  copies the code in the context of
                                                          │  the Dockerfile into the image.
        The second ONBUILD command
        downloads any dependencies, again        The third ONBUILD
        using the go-wrapper command.
```

The golang:onbuild image defines what happens when the image is used in the `FROM` directive in any other Dockerfile. The result is that when a Dockerfile uses this image as a base, the `ONBUILD` commands will fire as soon as the `FROM` image is downloaded, and (if not overridden) the `CMD` will be run when the resulting image is run as a container.

Now the output of the `docker build` command in the next listing may make more sense.

```
                     Step 1 : FROM golang:onbuild
                      onbuild: Pulling from library/golang
                      6d827a3ef358: Pull complete
                      2726297beaf1: Pull complete
                      7d27bd3d7fec: Pull complete             The FROM directive
                      62ace0d726fe: Pull complete             is run, and the
                      af8d7704cf0d: Pull complete             golang:onbuild
                      6d8851391f39: Pull complete             image is
    The Docker        988b98d9451c: Pull complete
  build signals its   5bbc96f59ddc: Pull complete
intention to run      Digest: sha256:
   the ONBUILD     ➡ 886a63b8de95d5767e779dee4ce5ce3c0437fa48524aedd93199fb12526f15e0
    directives.       Status: Downloaded newer image for golang:onbuild
                   ┌→ # Executing 3 build triggers...
   The second     │  Step 1 : COPY . /go/src/app        ←    The first ONBUILD directive copies
    ONBUILD       │  Step 1 : RUN go-wrapper download        the Go code in the Dockerfile's
  directive is  ──┤    ---> Running in c51f9b0c4da8          context into the build.
  fired, which
  downloads.
```

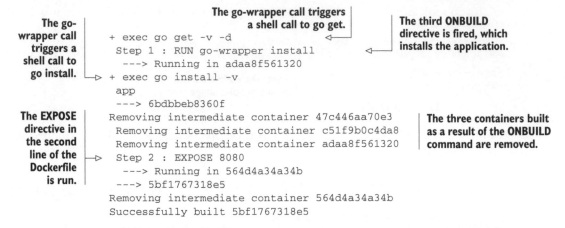

The result of this technique is that you have an easy way to build an image that only contains the code required to run it, and no more. Leaving the build tools lying around in the image not only makes it larger than it needs to be, but also increases the security attack surface of the running container.

DISCUSSION

Because Docker and Go are fashionable technologies currently often seen together, we've used this to demonstrate how ONBUILD can be used to build a Go binary.

Other examples of ONBUILD images exist. There are node:onbuild and python:onbuild images available on Docker Hub.

It's hoped that this might inspire you to construct your own ONBUILD image that could help your organization with common patterns of building. This standardization can help reduce impedance mismatch between different teams even further.

Summary

- You can insert files from your local machine and from the internet into images.
- The cache is a crucial part of building images, but it can be a fickle friend and occasionally needs prompting to do what you want.
- You can "bust" the cache using build arguments or using the ADD directive, or you can ignore the cache completely with the no-cache option.
- The ADD directive is generally used to inject local files and folders into the built image.
- System configuration may still be relevant inside Docker, and image build time is a great time to do it.
- You can debug your build process using the "image-stepper" technique (technique 27), which tags each stage of the build for you.
- The time zone setting is the most common "gotcha" when configuring containers, especially when you are a non-U.S. or multinational company.
- Images with ONBUILD are very easy to use, because you might not need to customize the build at all.

Running containers

You can't get very far without running containers when using Docker, and there's a lot to understand if you want to use the full power they make available.

This chapter will look at some of the details involved in running containers, examine some concrete use cases, and provide a thorough treatment of the possibilities enabled by volumes along the way.

5.1 Running containers

Although much of this book is about running containers, there are some practical techniques related to running containers on your host that may not be immediately obvious. We'll look at how you can get GUI applications working, start a container on a remote machine, inspect the state of containers and their source images, shut down containers, manage Docker daemons on remote machines, and use a wildcard DNS service to make testing easier.

TECHNIQUE 29   Running GUIs within Docker

You've already seen a GUI served from within a Docker container using a VNC server in technique 19. That's one way to view applications within your Docker container, and it's self-contained, requiring only a VNC client to use.

Fortunately there's a more lightweight and well-integrated way to run GUIs on your desktop, but it requires more setup on your part. It mounts the directory on the host that manages communications with the X server, so that it's accessible to the container.

PROBLEM

You want to run GUIs in a container as though they were normal desktop apps.

SOLUTION

Create an image with your user credentials and the program, and bind mount your X server to it.

Figure 5.1 shows how the final setup will work.

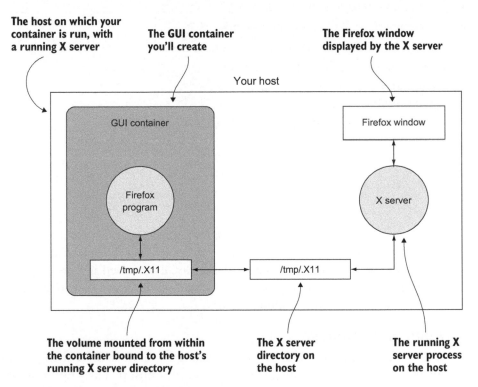

Figure 5.1   Communicating with the host's X server

The container is linked to the host via the mount of the host's /tmp/.X11 directory, and this is how the container can perform actions on the host's desktop.

First make a new directory somewhere convenient, and determine your user and group IDs with the `id` command, as shown in the following listing.

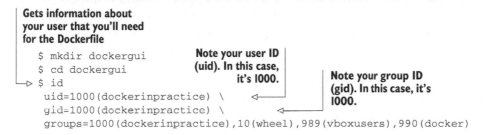

Listing 5.1 Setting up a directory and finding out your user details

Gets information about your user that you'll need for the Dockerfile

```
$ mkdir dockergui
$ cd dockergui
$ id
 uid=1000(dockerinpractice) \
 gid=1000(dockerinpractice) \
 groups=1000(dockerinpractice),10(wheel),989(vboxusers),990(docker)
```

Note your user ID (uid). In this case, it's 1000.

Note your group ID (gid). In this case, it's 1000.

Now create a file called Dockerfile as follows.

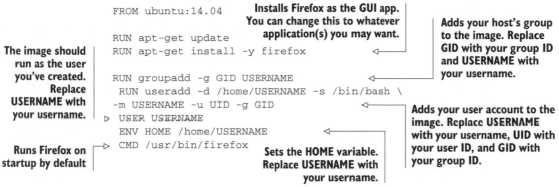

Listing 5.2 Firefox in a Dockerfile

```
FROM ubuntu:14.04

RUN apt-get update
RUN apt-get install -y firefox

RUN groupadd -g GID USERNAME
RUN useradd -d /home/USERNAME -s /bin/bash \
-m USERNAME -u UID -g GID
USER USERNAME
ENV HOME /home/USERNAME
CMD /usr/bin/firefox
```

Installs Firefox as the GUI app. You can change this to whatever application(s) you may want.

Adds your host's group to the image. Replace GID with your group ID and USERNAME with your username.

The image should run as the user you've created. Replace USERNAME with your username.

Adds your user account to the image. Replace USERNAME with your username, UID with your user ID, and GID with your group ID.

Runs Firefox on startup by default

Sets the HOME variable. Replace USERNAME with your username.

Now you can build from that Dockerfile and tag the result as "gui":

```
$ docker build -t gui .
```

Run it as follows:

Bind mounts the X server directory to the container

Sets the DISPLAY variable in the container to be the same as that used in the host, so the program knows which X server to talk to

```
docker run -v /tmp/.X11-unix:/tmp/.X11-unix \
 -h $HOSTNAME -v $HOME/.Xauthority:/home/$USER/.Xauthority \
 -e DISPLAY=$DISPLAY gui
```

Gives the container the appropriate credentials

You'll see a Firefox window pop up!

DISCUSSION

You can use this technique to avoid mixing up your desktop work with your development work. With Firefox, for example, you might want to see how your application behaves with no web cache, bookmarks, or search history in a repeatable way for testing purposes. If you see error messages about being unable to open a display when trying to start the image and run Firefox, see technique 65 for other ways to allow containers to start graphical applications that are displayed on the host.

We understand that some people run almost all their applications inside Docker, including games! Although we don't go quite that far, it's useful to know that somebody has probably already encountered any problems you see.

TECHNIQUE 30   Inspecting containers

Although the Docker commands give you access to information about images and containers, sometimes you'll want to know more about the internal metadata of these Docker objects.

PROBLEM

You want to find out a container's IP address.

SOLUTION

Use the docker inspect command.

The docker inspect command gives you access to Docker's internal metadata in JSON format, including the IP address. This command produces a lot of output, so only a brief snippet of an image's metadata is shown here.

Listing 5.3   Raw inspect output on an image

```
$ docker inspect ubuntu | head
[{
    "Architecture": "amd64",
    "Author": "",
    "Comment": "",
    "Config": {
        "AttachStderr": false,
        "AttachStdin": false,
        "AttachStdout": false,
        "Cmd": [
            "/bin/bash"
$
```

You can inspect images and containers by name or ID. Obviously, their metadata will differ—for example, a container will have runtime fields such as "State" that the image will lack (an image has no state).

In this case, you want to find out a container's IP address on your host. To do this, you can use the docker inspect command with the format flag.

Listing 5.4   Determining a container's IP address

The docker
inspect command

The format flag. This uses Go templates
(not covered here) to format the
output. Here, the IPAddress field is
taken from the NetworkSettings field
in the inspect output.

```
docker inspect \
 --format '{{.NetworkSettings.IPAddress}}' \
 0808ef13d450
```

The ID of the Docker item
you want to inspect

This technique can be useful for automation, as the interface is likely to be more stable than that of other Docker commands.

The following command gives you the IP addresses of all running containers and pings them.

Listing 5.5   Getting IP addresses of running containers and pinging each in turn

Gets the container IDs of
all running containers

Runs the inspect command against all
container IDs to get their IP addresses

```
$ docker ps -q | \
 xargs docker inspect --format='{{.NetworkSettings.IPAddress}}' | \
 xargs -l1 ping -c1
 PING 172.17.0.5 (172.17.0.5) 56(84) bytes of data.
64 bytes from 172.17.0.5: icmp_seq=1 ttl=64 time=0.095 ms

--- 172.17.0.5 ping statistics ---
1 packets transmitted, 1 received, 0% packet loss, time 0ms
rtt min/avg/max/mdev = 0.095/0.095/0.095/0.000 ms
```

Takes each IP address
and runs ping against
each in turn

Note that because ping only accepts one IP address, we had to pass an additional argument to xargs telling it to run the command for each individual line.

TIP If you have no running containers, run this command to get one going: `docker run -d ubuntu sleep 1000`.

DISCUSSION

Inspecting containers and the method of jumping into containers in technique 47 are likely the two most important tools in your inventory for debugging why containers aren't working. Inspect shines most when you believe you've started a container configured in a particular way but it behaves unexpectedly—your first step should be to inspect the container to verify that Docker agrees with your expectation of the port and volume mappings of the container, among other things.

TECHNIQUE 31   **Cleanly killing containers**

If the state of a container is important to you when it terminates, you may want to understand the distinction between `docker kill` and `docker stop`. This distinction can also be important if you need your applications to close gracefully in order to save data.

PROBLEM

You want to cleanly terminate a container.

SOLUTION

Use `docker stop` rather than `docker kill` to cleanly terminate the container.

The crucial point to understand is that `docker kill` doesn't behave in the same way as the standard command-line `kill` program.

The `kill` program works by sending a TERM (a.k.a. signal value 15) signal to the process specified, unless directed otherwise. This signal indicates to the program that it should terminate, but it doesn't force the program. Most programs will perform some kind of cleanup when this signal is handled, but the program can do what it likes—including ignoring the signal.

A KILL signal (a.k.a. signal value 9), by contrast, forces the specified program to terminate.

Confusingly, `docker kill` uses a KILL signal on the running process, giving the processes within it no chance to handle the termination. This means that stray files, such as files containing running process IDs, may be left in the filesystem. Depending on the application's ability to manage state, this may or may not cause problems for you if you start up the container again.

Even more confusingly, the `docker stop` command acts like the standard `kill` command, sending a TERM signal (see table 5.1), except it will wait for 10 seconds and then send the KILL signal if the container hasn't stopped.

Table 5.1   **Stopping and killing**

Command	Default signal	Default signal value
`kill`	TERM	15
`docker kill`	KILL	9
`docker stop`	TERM	15

In summary, don't use `docker kill` as you'd use `kill`. You're probably best off getting into the habit of using `docker stop`.

DISCUSSION

Although we recommend `docker stop` for everyday use, `docker kill` has some additional configurability that allows you to choose the signal sent to the container via the `--signal` argument. As discussed, the default is KILL, but you can also send TERM or one of the less common Unix signals.

If you're writing your own application that you'll start in a container, the USR1 signal may be of interest. This is explicitly reserved for applications to do whatever they want with it, and in some places it's used as an indication to print out progress information, or the equivalent—you could use it for whatever you see fit. HUP is another popular one, conventionally interpreted by servers and other long-running applications to trigger the reloading of configuration files and a "soft" restart. Of course, make sure you check the documentation of the application you're running before you start sending random signals to it!

Using Docker Machine to provision Docker hosts

Setting up Docker on your local machine was probably not too difficult—there's a script you can use for convenience, or you can use a few commands to add the appropriate sources for your package manager. But this can get tedious when you're trying to manage Docker installs on other hosts.

PROBLEM

You want to spin up containers on a separate Docker host from your machine.

SOLUTION

Docker Machine is the official solution for managing Docker installs on remote machines.

This technique will be useful if you need to run Docker containers on multiple external hosts. You may want this for a number of reasons: to test networking between Docker containers by provisioning a VM to run within your own physical host; to provision containers on a more powerful machine through a VPS provider; to risk trashing a host with some kind of crazy experiment; to have the choice of running on multiple cloud providers. Whatever the reason, Docker Machine is probably the answer for you. It's also the gateway to more sophisticated orchestration tools like Docker Swarm.

WHAT DOCKER MACHINE IS

Docker Machine is mainly a convenience program. It wraps a lot of potentially tortuous instructions around provisioning external hosts and turns them into a few easy-to-use commands. If you're familiar with Vagrant, it has a similar feel: provisioning and managing other machine environments is made simpler with a consistent interface. If you cast your mind back to our architecture overview in chapter 2, one way of viewing Docker Machine is to imagine that it's facilitating the management of different Docker daemons from one client (see figure 5.2).

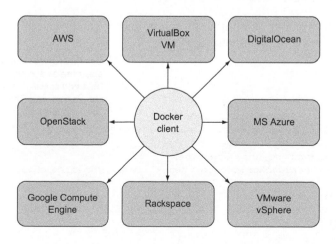

Figure 5.2 Docker Machine as a client of external hosts

The list of Docker host providers in figure 5.2 isn't exhaustive, and it's likely to grow. At the time of writing, the following drivers are available, which allow you to provision the given host provider:

- Amazon Web Services
- DigitalOcean
- Google Compute Engine
- IBM SoftLayer

- Microsoft Azure
- Microsoft Hyper-V
- OpenStack
- Oracle VirtualBox

- Rackspace
- VMware Fusion
- VMware vCloud Air
- VMware vSphere

The options that must be specified to provision a machine will vary greatly depending on the functionality provided by the driver. At one end, provisioning an Oracle VirtualBox VM on your machine has only 3 flags available to `create`, compared with OpenStack's 17.

> **NOTE** It's worth clarifying that Docker Machine is not any kind of clustering solution for Docker. Other tools, such as Docker Swarm, fulfill that function, and we'll look at them later.

INSTALLATION

Installation involves a straightforward binary. Download links and installation instructions for different architectures are available here: https://github.com/docker/machine/releases.

> **NOTE** You may want to move the binary to a standard location, like /usr/bin, and ensure it's renamed or symlinked to `docker-machine` before continuing, as the downloaded file may have a longer name suffixed with the binary's architecture.

USING DOCKER MACHINE

To demonstrate Docker Machine's use, you can start by creating a VM with a Docker daemon on it that you can work with.

> **NOTE** You'll need to have Oracle's VirtualBox installed for this to work. It's widely available in most package managers.

Use docker-machine's create subcommand to create a new host and specify its type with the --driver flag. The host has been named `host1`.

```
$ docker-machine create --driver virtualbox host1   ◁──┘
 INFO[0000] Creating CA: /home/imiell/.docker/machine/certs/ca.pem
INFO[0000] Creating client certificate:
➥ /home/imiell/.docker/machine/certs/cert.pem
INFO[0002] Downloading boot2docker.iso to /home/imiell/.docker/machine/cache/
➥ boot2docker.iso...
INFO[0011] Creating VirtualBox VM...
INFO[0023] Starting VirtualBox VM...
INFO[0025] Waiting for VM to start...
```

```
INFO[0043] "host1" has been created and is now the active machine.
 INFO[0043] To point your Docker client at it, run this in your shell:
```

Your machine is now created.

```
⇒ $(docker-machine env host1)
```

Run this command to set the DOCKER_HOST environment variable, which sets the default host that Docker commands will be run on

Vagrant users will feel right at home here. By running these commands, you've created a machine that you can now manage Docker on. If you follow the instructions given in the output, you can SSH directly to the new VM:

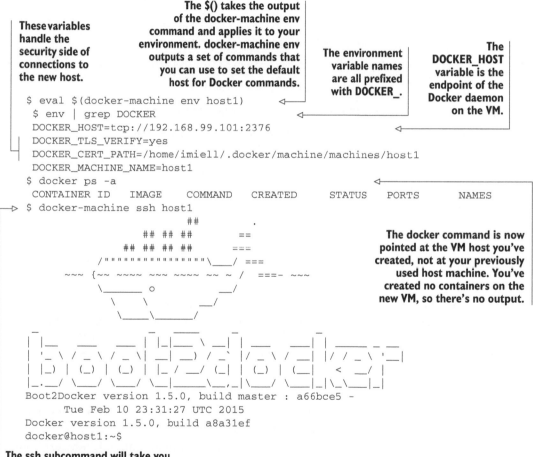

The $() takes the output of the docker-machine env command and applies it to your environment. docker-machine env outputs a set of commands that you can use to set the default host for Docker commands.

These variables handle the security side of connections to the new host.

The environment variable names are all prefixed with DOCKER_.

The DOCKER_HOST variable is the endpoint of the Docker daemon on the VM.

```
$ eval $(docker-machine env host1)
 $ env | grep DOCKER
DOCKER_HOST=tcp://192.168.99.101:2376
DOCKER_TLS_VERIFY=yes
DOCKER_CERT_PATH=/home/imiell/.docker/machine/machines/host1
DOCKER_MACHINE_NAME=host1
$ docker ps -a
 CONTAINER ID   IMAGE   COMMAND   CREATED   STATUS   PORTS   NAMES
$ docker-machine ssh host1
                    ##         .
              ## ## ##        ==
           ## ## ## ##        ===
       /"""""""""""""""""\___/ ===
  ~~~ {~~ ~~~~ ~~~ ~~~~ ~~ ~ /  ===- ~~~
       _____ o           __/
         \    \         __/
          _____/
 _                 _   ____     _            _
| |__   ___   ___ | |_|___ \ __| | ___   ___| | _____ _ __
| '_ \ / _ \ / _ \| __| __) / _` |/ _ \ / __| |/ / _ \ '__|
| |_) | (_) | (_) | |_ / __/ (_| | (_) | (__|   < __/ |
|_.__/ \___/ \___/ \__|_____,_|\___/ \___|_|\_\___|_|
Boot2Docker version 1.5.0, build master : a66bce5 -
     Tue Feb 10 23:31:27 UTC 2015
Docker version 1.5.0, build a8a31ef
docker@host1:~$
```

The docker command is now pointed at the VM host you've created, not at your previously used host machine. You've created no containers on the new VM, so there's no output.

The ssh subcommand will take you directly to the new VM itself.

MANAGING HOSTS

Managing multiple Docker hosts from one client machine can make it difficult to track what's going on. Docker Machine comes with various management commands to make this simpler, as shown in table 5.2.

Table 5.2   List of docker-machine commands

Subcommand	Action
create	Creates a new machine
ls	Lists the Docker host machines
stop	Stops the machine
start	Starts a machine
restart	Stops and starts a machine
rm	Destroys a machine
kill	Kills a machine off
inspect	Returns a JSON representation of the machine's metadata
config	Returns the configuration required to connect to the machine
ip	Returns the IP address of the machine
url	Returns a URL for the Docker daemon on the machine
upgrade	Upgrades the Docker version on the host to the latest

The following example lists two machines. The active machine is listed with an asterisk, and it has a state associated with it, analogous to the state of containers or processes:

```
$ docker-machine ls
NAME    ACTIVE  DRIVER      STATE    URL                           SWARM
host1           virtualbox  Running  tcp://192.168.99.102:2376
host2   *       virtualbox  Running  tcp://192.168.99.103:2376
```

> **TIP** You may be wondering how to switch back to your original host machine Docker instance. At the time of writing we haven't found a simple way to do this. You can either `docker-machine rm` all the machines, or if that's not an option you can manually unset the environment variables previously set with `unset DOCKER_HOST DOCKER_TLS_VERIFY DOCKER_CERT_PATH`.

DISCUSSION

You can look at this as turning machines into processes, much like Docker itself can be seen as turning environments into processes.

It may be tempting to use a Docker Machine setup to manually manage containers across multiple hosts, but if you find yourself manually taking down containers, rebuilding them, and starting them back up again on code changes, we encourage you to look at part 4 of this book. Tedious tasks like this can be done by computers perfectly well. Technique 87 covers the official solution from Docker Inc. for creating an automatic cluster of containers. Technique 84 may be appealing if you like the idea of the unified view of a cluster, but also prefer to retain ultimate control over where your containers end up running.

Wildcard DNS

When working with Docker, it's very common to have many containers running that need to refer to a central or external service. When testing or developing such systems, it's normal to use a static IP address for these services. But for many Docker-based systems, such as OpenShift, an IP address isn't sufficient. Such applications demand that there's a DNS lookup.

The usual solution to this is to edit your /etc/hosts file on the hosts you're running your services on. But this isn't always possible. For example, you might not have access to edit the file. Neither is it always practical. You might have too many hosts to maintain, or other bespoke DNS lookup caches might get in the way.

In these cases, there's a solution that uses "real" DNS servers.

PROBLEM

You need a DNS-resolvable URL for a specific IP address.

SOLUTION

Use the NIP.IO web service to resolve an IP address to a DNS-resolvable URL without any DNS setup.

This one is really simple. NIP.IO is a web-based service that turns an IP address into a URL automatically for you. You just need to replace the "IP" section of the URL "http://IP.nip.io" with your desired IP address.

Let's say the IP address you want a URL to resolve to is "10.0.0.1". Your URL could look like this,

http://myappname.10.0.0.1.nip.io

where myappname refers to your preferred name for your application, 10.0.0.1 refers to the IP address you want the URL to resolve to, and nip.io is the "real" domain on the internet that manages this DNS lookup service.

The myappname. part is optional, so this URL would resolve to the same IP address:

http://10.0.0.1.nip.io

DISCUSSION

This technique is handy in all sorts of contexts, not just when using Docker-based services.

It should be obvious that this technique isn't suitable for production or proper UAT environments, because it submits DNS requests to a third party and reveals information about your internal IP address layout. But it can be a very handy tool for development work.

If you're using this service with HTTPS, make sure that the URL (or a suitable wildcard) is baked into the certificate you use.

5.2   *Volumes—a persistent problem*

Containers are a powerful concept, but sometimes not everything you want to access is ready to be encapsulated. You may have a reference Oracle database stored on a large cluster that you want to connect to for testing. Or maybe you have a large legacy server already set up with binaries that can't easily be reproduced.

When you begin working with Docker, most of the things you'll want to access will likely be data and programs external to your container. We'll take you from the straightforward mounting of files from your host to more sophisticated container patterns: the data container and the dev tools container. We'll also demonstrate a pragmatic favorite of ours for remote mounting across a network that requires only an SSH connection to work, and we'll look at a means of sharing data with other users via the BitTorrent protocol.

Volumes are a core part of Docker, and the issue of external data reference is yet another fast-changing area of the Docker ecosystem.

TECHNIQUE 34   Docker volumes: Problems of persistence

Much of the power of containers comes from the fact that they encapsulate as much of the state of the environment's filesystem as is useful.

Sometimes, though, you don't want to put files into a container. You might have some large files that you want to share across containers or manage separately. The classic example is a large centralized database that you want your container to access, but you also want other (perhaps more traditional) clients to access alongside your newfangled containers.

The solution is *volumes*, Docker's mechanism for managing files outside the lifecycle of the container. Although this goes against the philosophy of containers being "deployed anywhere" (you won't be able to deploy your database-dependent container where there's no compatible database available to mount, for example), it's a useful feature for real-world Docker use.

PROBLEM

You want to access files on the host from within a container.

SOLUTION

Use Docker's volume flag to access host files from within the container. Figure 5.3 illustrates the use of a volume flag to interact with the host's filesystem.

The following command shows the host's /var/db/tables directory being mounted on /var/data1, and it could be run to start the container in figure 5.3.

```
$ docker run -v /var/db/tables:/var/data1 -it debian bash
```

The -v flag (--volume in longhand) indicates that a volume external to the container is required. The subsequent argument gives the volume specification in the form of two directories separated by a colon, instructing Docker to map the external /var/db/tables directory to the container's /var/data1 directory. Both the external and container directories will be created if they don't exist.

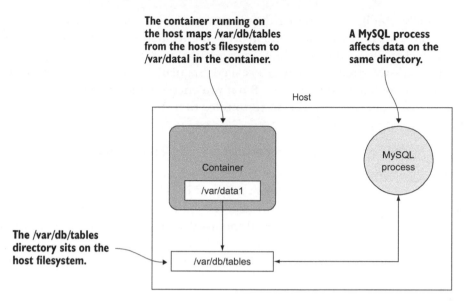

Figure 5.3   A volume inside a container

Beware of mapping over existing directories. The container's directory will be mapped even if it already exists in the image. This means that the directory you're mapping to within the container will effectively disappear. Fun things happen if you try to map a key directory! Try mounting an empty directory over /bin, for example.

Also note that volumes are assumed not to persist in Dockerfiles. If you add a volume and then make changes to that folder within a Dockerfile, the changes won't be persisted to the resulting image.

> **WARNING**   You may run into difficulties if your host runs SELinux. If SELinux policy is enforced, the container may not be able to write to the /var/db/tables directory. You'll see a "permission denied" error. If you need to work around this, you'll have to talk to your sysadmin (if you have one) or switch off SELinux (for development purposes only). See technique 113 for more on SELinux.

DISCUSSION

Exposing files from the host in a container is one of the most common operations we perform when experimenting with individual containers—containers are intended to be ephemeral, and it's all too easy to blow one away after spending a significant amount of time working on some files within one. Better to be confident that the files are safe, come what may.

There's also the advantage that the normal overhead of copying files into containers with the method in technique 114 is simply not present. Databases like the one in technique 77 are the obvious beneficiary if they grow large.

Finally, you'll see a number of techniques that use `-v /var/run/docker.sock:/var/run/docker.sock`, one of the many being technique 45. This exposes the special Unix socket file to the container and demonstrates an important capability of this technique—you aren't limited to so-called "regular" files—you can also permit more unusual filesystem-based use cases. But if you encounter permissions issues with device nodes (for example), you may need to refer to technique 93 to get a handle on what the `--privileged` flag does.

TECHNIQUE 35   Distributed volumes with Resilio Sync

When experimenting with Docker in a team, you may want to share large quantities of data among team members, but you may not be allocated the resources for a shared server with sufficient capacity. The lazy solution to this is copying the latest files from other team members when you need them—this quickly gets out of hand for a larger team.

The solution is to use a decentralized tool for sharing files—no dedicated resource required.

PROBLEM
You want to share volumes across hosts over the internet.

SOLUTION
Use a technology called Resilio to share volumes over the internet.

Figure 5.4 illustrates the setup you're aiming for.

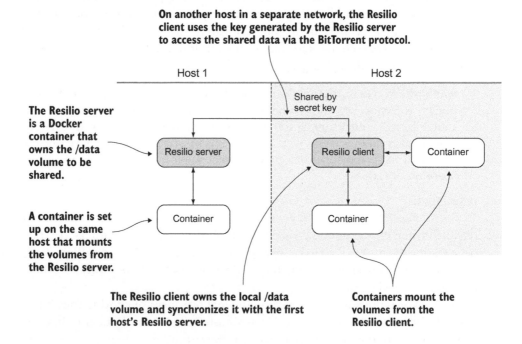

Figure 5.4   Using Resilio

The end result is a volume (/data) conveniently synchronized over the internet without requiring any complicated setup.

On your primary server, run the following commands to set up the containers on the first host:

> **Runs the published ctlc/btsync image as a daemon container, calls the btsync binary, and opens the required ports**

Make a note of this key—it will be different for your run.

```
[host1]$ docker run -d -p 8888:8888 -p 55555:55555 \
  --name resilio ctlc/btsync
$ docker logs resilio
  Starting btsync with secret: \
ALSVEUABQQ5ILRS2OQJKAOKCU5SIIP6A3
  By using this application, you agree to our Privacy Policy and Terms.
http://www.bittorrent.com/legal/privacy
http://www.bittorrent.com/legal/terms-of-use

total physical memory 536870912 max disk cache 2097152
Using IP address 172.17.4.121

[host1]$ docker run -i -t --volumes-from resilio \
  ubuntu /bin/bash
$ touch /data/shared_from_server_one
  $ ls /data
shared_from_server_one
```

> **Gets the output of the resilio container so you can make a note of the key**

> **Starts up an interactive container with the volumes from the resilio server**

Adds a file to the /data volume

On the second server, open up a terminal and run these commands to synchronize the volume:

Starts an interactive container that mounts the volumes from your client daemon

> **Starts a resilio client container as a daemon with the key generated by the daemon run on host1**

```
[host2]$ docker run -d --name resilio-client -p 8888:8888 \
-p 55555:55555 \
ctlc/btsync ALSVEUABQQ5ILRS2OQJKAOKCU5SIIP6A3
  [host2]$ docker run -i -t --volumes-from resilio-client \
ubuntu bash
  $ ls /data
shared_from_server_one
  $ touch /data/shared_from_server_two
  $ ls /data
shared_from_server_one  shared_from_server_two
```

> **The file created on host1 has been transferred to host2.**

> **Creates a second file on host2**

Back on host1's running container, you should see that the file has been synchronized between the hosts exactly as the first file was:

```
[host1]$ ls /data
shared_from_server_one  shared_from_server_two
```

DISCUSSION

The synchronization of files comes with no timing guarantees, so you may have to wait for the data to sync. This is particularly the case for larger files.

WARNING   Because the data may be sent over the internet and is processed by a protocol over which you have no control, you shouldn't rely on this technique if you have any meaningful security, scalability, or performance constraints.

We've only demonstrated that this technique works between two containers, as mentioned at the beginning, but it should also work across many members of a team. Aside from the obvious use case of large files that don't fit in version control, candidates for distribution include backups and possibly Docker images themselves, particularly if this technique is used in combination with an efficient compression mechanism like the one shown in technique 72. To avoid conflicts, make sure that images are always going in one direction (for example, from a build machine to many servers), or follow an agreed-upon process for performing updates.

TECHNIQUE 36   Retaining your container's bash history

Experimenting inside a container, knowing that you can wipe everything out when you're done, can be a liberating experience. But there are some conveniences that you lose when doing this. One that we've hit many times is forgetting a sequence of commands we've run inside a container.

PROBLEM

You want to share your container's bash history with your host's history.

SOLUTION

Use the -e flag, Docker mounts, and a bash alias to automatically share your container's bash history with the host's.

To understand this problem, we'll show you a simple scenario where losing this history is plain annoying.

Imagine you're experimenting in Docker containers, and in the midst of your work you do something interesting and reusable. We'll use a simple echo command for this example, but it could be a long and complex concatenation of programs that results in useful output:

```
$ docker run -ti --rm ubuntu /bin/bash
$ echo my amazing command
$ exit
```

After some time, you want to recall the incredible echo command you ran earlier. Unfortunately you can't remember it, and you no longer have the terminal session on your screen to scroll to. Out of habit, you try looking through your bash history on the host:

```
$ history | grep amazing
```

Nothing comes back, because the bash history is kept within the now-removed container and not the host you were returned to.

To share your bash history with the host, you can use a volume mount when running your Docker images. Here's an example:

```
$ docker run -e HIST_FILE=/root/.bash_history \
  -v=$HOME/.bash_history:/root/.bash_history \
  -ti ubuntu /bin/bash
```

Sets the environment variable picked up by bash. This ensures the bash history file used is the one you mount.

Maps the container's root's bash history file to the host's

TIP You may want to separate the container's bash history from your host's. One way to do this is to change the value for the first part of the preceding -v argument.

This is quite a handful to type every time, so to make this more user-friendly you can set up an alias by putting this into your ~/.bashrc file:

```
$ alias dockbash='docker run -e HIST_FILE=/root/.bash_history \
 -v=$HOME/.bash_history:/root/.bash_history
```

This still isn't seamless, because you have to remember to type dockbash if you want to perform a docker run command. For a more seamless experience, you can add these to your ~/.bashrc file:

Listing 5.6 Function alias to auto-mount host bash history

Determines whether the first argument to basher/docker is "run"

Creates a bash function called basher that will handle the docker command

Runs the docker run command you ran earlier, invoking the absolute path to the Docker runtime to avoid confusion with the following docker alias. The absolute path is discovered by running the "which docker" command on your host before implementing this solution.

Removes that argument from the list of arguments you've passed in

Runs the docker command with the original arguments intact

```
function basher() {
  if [[ $1 = 'run' ]]
  then
    shift
    /usr/bin/docker run \
      -e HIST_FILE=/root/.bash_history \
      -v $HOME/.bash_history:/root/.bash_history "$@"
  else
    /usr/bin/docker "$@"
  fi
}
alias docker=basher
```

Passes the arguments after "run" to the Docker runtime

Aliases the docker command when it's invoked on the command line to the basher function you've created. This ensures that the call to docker is caught before bash finds the docker binary on the path.

DISCUSSION

Now, when you next open a bash shell and run any docker run command, the commands that are run within that container will be added to your host's bash history. Make sure the path to Docker is correct. It might be located in /bin/docker, for example.

> **NOTE** You'll need to log out of your host's original bash session for the history file to be updated. This is due to a subtlety of bash and how it updates the bash history it keeps in memory. If in doubt, exit all bash sessions you're aware of, and then start one up to ensure your history is as up-to-date as possible.

A number of command-line tools with prompts also store history, SQLite being one example (storing history in a .sqlite_history file). If you don't want to use the integrated logging solutions available in Docker described in technique 102, you could use a similar practice to make your application write to a file that ends up outside the container. Be aware that the complexities of logging, such as log rotation, mean that it may be simpler to use a log directory volume rather than just a file.

TECHNIQUE 37 Data containers

If you use volumes a lot on a host, managing the container's startup can get tricky. You may also want the data to be managed by Docker exclusively, and not be generally accessible on the host. One way to manage these things more cleanly is to use the data-only container design pattern.

PROBLEM
You want to use an external volume within a container, but you only want Docker to access the files.

SOLUTION
Start up a data container and use the `--volumes-from` flag when running other containers.

Figure 5.5 shows the structure of the data container pattern and explains how it works. The key thing to note is that in the second host, the containers don't need to know where the data is located on disk. All they need to know is the name of the data container, and they're good to go. This can make the operation of containers more portable.

Another benefit of this approach over the straightforward mapping of host directories is that access to these files is managed by Docker, which means that a non-Docker process is less likely to affect the contents.

> **NOTE** People are commonly confused about whether the data-only container needs to run. It doesn't! It merely needs to exist, to have been run on the host, and not been deleted.

Let's go through a simple example so you can get a feel for how to use this technique.
First you run your data container:

```
$ docker run -v /shared-data --name dc busybox \
  touch /shared-data/somefile
```

The -v argument doesn't map the volume to a host directory, so it creates the directory within the scope of this container's responsibility. This directory is populated with a single file with `touch`, and the container immediately exists—a data container need

This host is running three containers, each pointed at the
host's /var/db/tables directory with the --volume/-v flag.
No data container exists here.

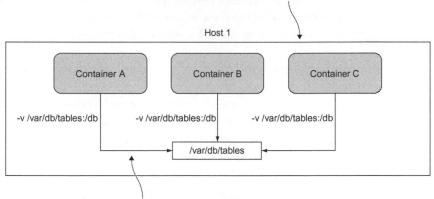

Host 1

Each container has mounted the directory separately, so if
the location of the folder changes or the mount needs to
be moved, each container has to be reconfigured.

This host is running four containers. The three containers
from the previous host are run with the --volumes-from
flags all pointing at the data container.

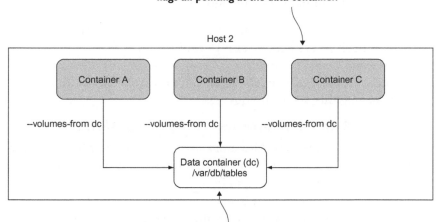

Host 2

This single data container mounts the host's
volume, creating a single point of responsibility
for data mounts on the host.

Figure 5.5 The data container pattern

not be running to be used. We've used the small but functional busybox image to
reduce the amount of extra baggage our data container needs.

Then you run up another container to access the file you just created:

```
docker run -t -i --volumes-from dc busybox /bin/sh
/ # ls /shared-data
somefile
```

DISCUSSION

The `--volumes-from` flag allows you to reference the files from the data container by mounting them in the current container—you just need to pass it the ID of a container with volumes defined. The busybox image doesn't have bash, so you need to start up a simpler shell to verify that the /shared-data folder from the dc container is available to you.

You can start up any number of containers, all reading from and writing to the specified data container's volumes.

You don't need to use this pattern in order to use volumes—you may find this approach harder to manage than a straightforward mount of a host directory. If, however, you like to cleanly delegate responsibility for managing data to a single point managed within Docker and uncontaminated by other host processes, data containers may be useful for you.

> **WARNING** If your application is logging from multiple containers to the same data container, it's important to ensure that each container log file writes to a unique file path. If you don't, different containers might overwrite or truncate the file, resulting in lost data, or they might write interleaved data, which is less easy to analyze. Similarly, if you invoke `--volumes-from` from a data container, you allow that container to potentially overlay directories over yours, so be careful of name clashes here.

It's important to understand that this pattern can result in heavy disk usage that can be relatively difficult to debug. Because Docker manages the volume within the data-only container and doesn't delete the volume when the last container referencing it has exited, any data on a volume will persist. This is to prevent undesired data loss. For advice on managing this, see technique 43.

TECHNIQUE 38   Remote volume mounting using SSHFS

We've discussed mounting local files, but soon the question of how to mount remote filesystems arises. Perhaps you want to share a reference database on a remote server and treat it as if it were local, for example.

Although it's theoretically possible to set up NFS on your host system and the server, and then access the filesystem by mounting that directory, there's a quicker and simpler way for most users that requires no setup on the server side (as long as there is SSH access).

> **NOTE** You'll need root privileges for this technique to work, and you'll need FUSE (Linux's "Filesystem in Userspace" kernel module) installed. You can determine whether you have the latter by running `ls /dev/fuse` in a terminal to see whether the file exists.

PROBLEM

You want to mount a remote filesystem without requiring any server-side configuration.

SOLUTION

Use a technology called SSHFS to mount the remote filesystem so that it appears to be local to your machine.

This technique works by using a FUSE kernel module with SSH to give you a standard interface to a filesystem, while in the background doing all communications via SSH. SSHFS also provides various behind-the-scenes features (such as remote file readahead) to facilitate the illusion that the files are local. The upshot is that once a user is logged into the remote server, they'll see the files as if they were local. Figure 5.6 helps explain this.

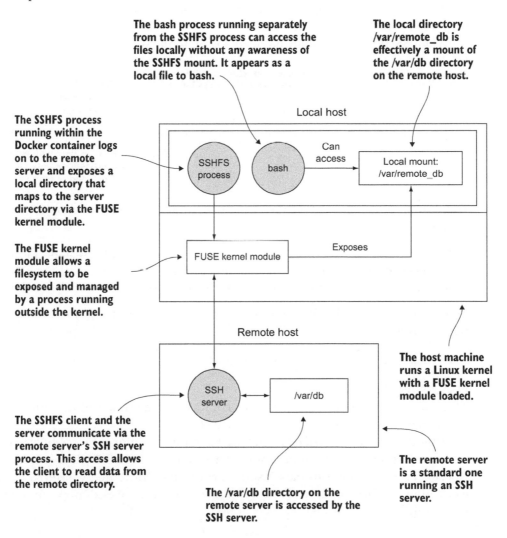

The bash process running separately from the SSHFS process can access the files locally without any awareness of the SSHFS mount. It appears as a local file to bash.

The local directory /var/remote_db is effectively a mount of the /var/db directory on the remote host.

The SSHFS process running within the Docker container logs on to the remote server and exposes a local directory that maps to the server directory via the FUSE kernel module.

The FUSE kernel module allows a filesystem to be exposed and managed by a process running outside the kernel.

Local host

SSHFS process

bash

Can access

Local mount: /var/remote_db

FUSE kernel module

Exposes

The host machine runs a Linux kernel with a FUSE kernel module loaded.

Remote host

SSH server

/var/db

The SSHFS client and the server communicate via the remote server's SSH server process. This access allows the client to read data from the remote directory.

The remote server is a standard one running an SSH server.

The /var/db directory on the remote server is accessed by the SSH server.

Figure 5.6   Mounting a remote filesystem with SSHFS

> **WARNING** Although this technique doesn't use the Docker volumes function-
> ality, and the files are visible through the filesystem, this technique doesn't
> give you any container-level persistence. Any changes made take place on the
> remote server's filesystem only.

You can get started by running the following commands, adjusted for your environment.

The first step is to start up a container with `--privileged` on your host machine:

```
$ docker run -t -i --privileged debian /bin/bash
```

Then, when it's started up, run `apt-get update && apt-get install sshfs` from
within the container to install SSHFS.

When SSHFS is successfully installed, log on to the remote host as follows:

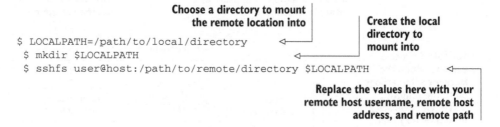

You'll now see the contents of the path on the remote server in the folder you've just
created.

> **TIP** It's simplest to mount to a directory that you've newly created, but it's
> also possible to mount a pre-existing directory with files already present if you
> use the `-o nonempty` option. See the SSHFS man page for more information.

To cleanly unmount the files, use the `fusermount` command as follows, replacing the
path as appropriate:

```
fusermount -u /path/to/local/directory
```

DISCUSSION
This is a great way to quickly get remote mounts working from within containers (and
on standard Linux machines) with minimal effort.

Although we've only talked about SSHFS in this technique, successfully managing
this opens up the wonderful (and sometimes weird) world of FUSE filesystems inside
Docker. From storing your data inside Gmail to the distributed GlusterFS filesystem
for storing petabytes of data across many machines, a number of opportunities open
up to you.

Sharing data over NFS

In a larger company, NFS shared directories will likely already be in use—NFS is a well-proven option for serving files out of a central location. For Docker to get traction, it's usually fairly important to be able to get access to these shared files.

Docker doesn't support NFS out of the box, and installing an NFS client on every container so you can mount the remote folders isn't considered a best practice. Instead, the suggested approach is to have one container act as a translator from NFS to a more Docker-friendly concept: volumes.

PROBLEM
You want seamless access to a remote filesystem over NFS.

SOLUTION
Use an infrastructure data container to broker access to your remote NFS filesystem.

This technique builds on technique 37, where we created a data container to manage data in a running system.

Figure 5.7 shows the idea of this technique in the abstract. The NFS server exposes the internal directory as the /export folder, which is bind-mounted on the host. The Docker host then mounts this folder using the NFS protocol to its /mnt folder. Then a so-called "infrastructure container" is created, which binds the mount folder.

This may seem a little over-engineered at first glance, but the benefit is that it provides a level of indirection as far as the Docker containers are concerned: all they need to do is mount the volumes from a pre-agreed infrastructure container, and whoever is responsible for the infrastructure can worry about the internal plumbing, availability, network, and so on.

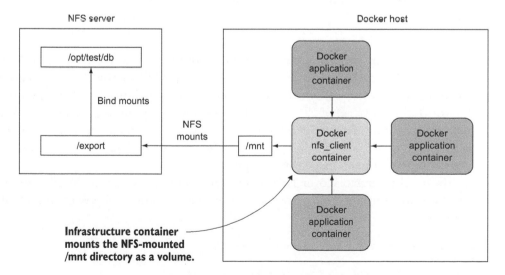

Figure 5.7 An infrastructure container that brokers NFS access

A thorough treatment of NFS is beyond the scope of this book. In this technique, we're just going to go through the steps of setting up such a share on a single host by having the NFS server's components on the same host as the Docker containers. This has been tested on Ubuntu 14.04.

Suppose you want to share the contents of your host's /opt/test/db folder, which contains the file mybigdb.db.

As root, install the NFS server and create an export directory with open permissions:

```
# apt-get install nfs-kernel-server
# mkdir /export
# chmod 777 /export
```

> **NOTE** We've created the NFS share with open permissions, which is not a secure way to proceed for a production system. We've taken this approach in the interest of simplifying this tutorial. NFS security is a complicated and varied topic, which is beyond the scope of this book. For more on Docker and security, see chapter 14.

Now bind mount the db directory to your export directory:

```
# mount --bind /opt/test/db /export
```

You should now be able to see the contents of the /opt/test/db directory in /export:

> **TIP** If you want this to persist following a reboot, add this line to your /etc/fstab file: /opt/test/db /export none bind 0 0

Now add this line to your /etc/exports file:

```
/export        127.0.0.1(ro,fsid=0,insecure,no_subtree_check,async)
```

For this proof of concept example, we're mounting locally on 127.0.0.1, which defeats the object a little. In a real-world scenario, you'd lock this down to a class of IP addresses such as 192.168.1.0/24. If you like playing with fire, you can open it up to the world with * instead of 127.0.0.1. For safety, we're mounting read-only (ro) here, but you can mount read-write by replacing ro with rw. Remember that if you do this, you'll need to add a no_root_squash flag after the async flag there, but think about security before going outside this sandpit.

Mount the directory over NFS to the /mnt directory, export the filesystems you specified previously in /etc/exports, and then restart the NFS service to pick up the changes:

```
# mount -t nfs 127.0.0.1:/export /mnt
# exportfs -a
# service nfs-kernel-server restart
```

Now you're ready to run your infrastructure container:

```
# docker run -ti --name nfs_client --privileged
➥ -v /mnt:/mnt busybox /bin/true
```

And now you can run—without privileges, or knowledge of the underlying implementation—the directory you want to access:

```
# docker run -ti --volumes-from nfs_client debian /bin/bash
root@079d70f79d84:/# ls /mnt
myb
root@079d70f79d84:/# cd /mnt
root@079d70f79d84:/mnt# touch asd
touch: cannot touch `asd': Read-only file system
```

DISCUSSION

This pattern of centrally mounting a shared resource with privileged access for use by others in multiple containers is a powerful one that can make development workflows much simpler.

> **TIP** If you have a lot of these containers to manage, you can make this easier to manage by having a naming convention such as `--name nfs_client_opt _database_live` for a container that exposes the /opt/database/live path.

> **TIP** Remember that this technique only provides security through obscurity (which is no security at all). As you'll see later, anyone who can run the Docker executable effectively has root privileges on the host.

Infrastructure containers for brokering access and abstracting away details are in some ways an equivalent of service-discovery tools for networking—the precise details of how the service runs or where it lives aren't important. You just need to know its name.

   As it happens, you've seen `--volumes-from` being used before in technique 35. The details are a little different because the access is being brokered to infrastructure running *inside* the container rather than on the host, but the principle of using names to refer to available volumes remains. You could even swap out that container for the one in this technique and, if configured correctly, applications wouldn't notice a difference in where they look to retrieve their files.

TECHNIQUE 40 **Dev tools container**

If you're an engineer who often finds yourself on others' machines, struggling without the programs or configuration you have on your beautiful unique-as-a-snowflake development environment, this technique may be for you. Similarly, if you want to share your pimped-up dev environment with others, Docker can make this easy.

PROBLEM

You want to access your development environment on others' machines.

SOLUTION

Create a Docker image with your setup on it, and place it on a registry.

As a demonstration, we're going to use one of our dev tools images. You can download it by running `docker pull dockerinpractice/docker-dev-tools-image`. The repo is available at https://github.com/docker-in-practice/docker-dev-tools-image if you want to inspect the Dockerfile.

Running up the container is simple—a straightforward `docker run -t -i docker-inpractice/docker-dev-tools-image` will give you a shell in our dev environment. You can root around our dotfiles and maybe send us some advice about the setup.

The real power of this technique can be seen when it's combined with others. In the following listing you can see a dev tools container used to display a GUI on the host's network and IPDC stacks and to mount the host's code.

Listing 5.7   Running dev-tools image with a GUI

Mounts the Docker socket to give access to the host's Docker daemon

Mounts the X server Unix domain socket to allow you to start up GUI-based applications (see technique 29)

Sets an environment variable instructing the container to use the host display

These arguments bypass the container's network bridge and allow you access to the host's interprocess communication files (see technique 109).

Mounts the work area to the container's home directory

```
docker run -t -i \
-v /var/run/docker.sock:/var/run/docker.sock \
-v /tmp/.X11-unix:/tmp/.X11-unix \
-e DISPLAY=$DISPLAY \
--net=host --ipc=host \
-v /opt/workspace:/home/dockerinpractice \
dockerinpractice/docker-dev-tools-image
```

The preceding command gives you an environment with access to the host's resources:

- Network
- Docker daemon (to run normal Docker commands as though on the host)
- Interprocess communication (IPC) files
- X server to start GUI-based apps, if needed

NOTE   As always when mounting host directories, be careful not to mount any vital directories, as you could do damage. Mounting any host directory under root is generally best avoided.

DISCUSSION

We mentioned that you have access to the X server, so it's worth looking at technique 29 for a reminder of some of the possibilities.

For some more invasive dev tools, perhaps for inspecting processes on the host, you may need to look at technique 109 to understand how to grant permission to view some (by default) restricted parts of your system. Technique 93 is also an important read—just because a container can see parts of your system doesn't necessarily mean it has permission to alter them.

Summary

- You should reach for volumes if you need to get at external data from inside a container.
- SSHFS is a simple way to access data on other machines with no extra setup.
- Running GUI applications in Docker requires only a small amount of preparation of your image.
- You can use data containers to abstract away the location of your data.

Day-to-day Docker

This chapter covers

- Keeping a handle on your container and volume space usage
- Detaching from containers without stopping them
- Visualizing your Docker image lineage in a graph
- Running commands directly on your containers from the host

As with any moderately complex software project, Docker has a lot of nooks and crannies that are important to know about if you want to keep your experience as smooth as possible.

This chapter's techniques will show you some of the more important of these, as well as introduce some external tools built by third parties to scratch their own itches. Think of it as your Docker toolbox.

6.1 Staying ship-shape

If you're anything like us (and if you're following this book studiously), your growing Docker addiction will mean that you start up numerous containers on, and download a variety of images to, your chosen host.

As time goes on, Docker will take up more and more resources, and some house-keeping of containers and volumes will be required. We'll show you the how and why of this. We'll also introduce some visual tools for keeping your Docker environment clean and tidy, in case you want an escape from the command line.

Running containers is all very well, but you'll fairly quickly find yourself wanting to do more than just start a single command in the foreground. We'll take a look at escaping a running container without killing it, and at executing commands inside a running container.

TECHNIQUE 41 Running Docker without sudo

The Docker daemon runs in the background of your machine as the root user, giving it a significant amount of power, which it exposes to you, the user. Needing to use sudo is a result of this, but it can be inconvenient and make some third-party Docker tools impossible to use.

PROBLEM

You want to be able to run the docker command without having to use sudo.

SOLUTION

The official solution is to add yourself to the docker group.

Docker manages permissions around the Docker Unix domain socket through a user group. For security reasons, distributions don't make you part of that group by default, as it effectively grants full root access to the system.

By adding yourself to this group, you'll be able to use the docker command as yourself:

```
$ sudo addgroup -a username docker
```

Restart Docker and fully log out and in again, or reboot your machine if that's easier. Now you don't need to remember to type sudo or set up an alias to run Docker as yourself.

DISCUSSION

This is an extremely important technique for a number of tools used later in the book. In general, anything that wants to talk to Docker (without being started in a container) will need access to the Docker socket, requiring either sudo or the setup described in this technique. Docker Compose, introduced in technique 76, is an official tool from Docker Inc. and is an example of such a tool.

TECHNIQUE 42 Housekeeping containers

A frequent gripe of new Docker users is that in a short space of time you can end up with many containers on your system in various states, and there are no standard tools for managing this on the command line.

PROBLEM

You want to prune the containers on your system.

SOLUTION

Set up aliases to run the commands that tidy up old containers.

The simplest approach here is to delete all containers. Obviously, this is something of a nuclear option that should only be used if you're certain it's what you want.

The following command will remove all containers on your host machine.

Get a list of all container IDs, both running and stopped, and pass them to...

```
$ docker ps -a -q | \
  xargs --no-run-if-empty docker rm -f
```

...the `docker rm -f` command, which will remove any containers passed, even if they're running.

To briefly explain `xargs`, it takes each line of the input and passes them all as arguments to the subsequent command. We've passed an additional argument here, `--no-run-if-empty`, which avoids running the command at all if there's no output from the previous command, in order to avoid an error.

If you have containers running that you may want to keep, but you want to remove all those that have exited, you can filter the items returned by the `docker ps` command:

The --filter flag tells the docker ps command which containers you want returned. In this case you're restricting it to containers that have exited. Other options are running and restarting.

```
docker ps -a -q --filter status=exited | \
  xargs --no-run-if-empty docker rm
```

This time you don't force the removal of containers because they shouldn't be running, based on the filter you've given.

In fact, removing all stopped containers is such a common use case that Docker added a command specifically for it: `docker container prune`. However, this command is limited to just that use case, and you'll need to refer back to the commands in this technique for any more complex manipulation of containers.

As an example of a more advanced use case, the following command will list all containers with a nonzero error code. You may need this if you have many containers on your system and you want to automate the examination and removal of any containers that exited unexpectedly:

Runs the comm command to compare the contents of two files. The -3 argument suppresses lines that appear in both files (in this example, those with a zero exit code) and outputs any others.

Finds exited container IDs, sorts them, and passes them as a file to comm

Finds containers with an exit code of 0, sorts them, and passes them as a file to comm

```
comm -3 \
  <(docker ps -a -q --filter=status=exited | sort) \
  <(docker ps -a -q --filter=exited=0 | sort) | \
  xargs --no-run-if-empty docker inspect > error_containers
```

Runs docker inspect against containers with a nonzero exit code (as piped in by comm) and saves the output to the error_containers file

TIP If you've not seen it before, the <(command) syntax is called *process substitution*. It allows you to treat the output of a command as a file and pass it to another command, which can be useful where piping output isn't possible.

The preceding example is rather complicated, but it shows the power you can get from combining different utilities. It outputs all stopped container IDs, and then picks just those that have a nonzero exit code (those that exited in an unexpected way). If you're struggling to follow this, running each command separately and understanding them that way first can be helpful in learning the building blocks.

Such a command could be useful for gathering container information on production. You may want to adapt it to run a cron to clear out containers that exited in expected ways.

Make these one-liners available as commands

You can add commands as aliases so that they're more easily run whenever you log in to your host. To do this, add lines like the following to the end of your ~/.bashrc file:

```
alias dockernuke='docker ps -a -q | \
xargs --no-run-if-empty docker rm -f'
```

When you next log in, running dockernuke from the command line will delete any Docker containers found on your system.

We've found that this saves a surprising amount of time. But be careful! It's all too easy to remove production containers this way, as we can attest. And even if you're careful enough not to remove running containers, you still might remove non-running but still useful data-only containers.

DISCUSSION

Many of the techniques in this book end up creating containers, particularly when introducing Docker Compose in technique 76 and in the chapters devoted to orchestration—after all, orchestration is all about managing multiple containers. You may find the commands discussed here useful for cleaning up your machines (local or remote) to get a fresh start when you finish each technique.

TECHNIQUE 43 **Housekeeping volumes**

Although volumes are a powerful feature of Docker, they come with a significant operational downside. Because volumes can be shared between different containers, they can't be deleted when a container that mounted them is deleted. Imagine the scenario outlined in figure 6.1.

"Easy!" you might think. "Delete the volume when the last-referencing container is removed!" Indeed, Docker could have taken that option, and this approach is the one

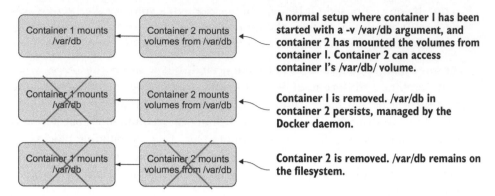

Figure 6.1   What happens to /var/db when containers are removed?

that garbage-collected programming languages take when they remove objects from memory: when no other object references it, it can be deleted.

But Docker judged that this could leave people open to losing valuable data accidentally and preferred to make it a user decision as to whether a volume should be deleted on removal of the container. An unfortunate side effect of this is that, by default, volumes remain on your Docker daemon's host disk until they're removed manually. If these volumes are full of data, your disk can fill up, so it's useful to be aware of ways to manage these orphaned volumes.

PROBLEM

You're using too much disk space because orphaned Docker mounts exist in your host.

SOLUTION

Use the -v flag when calling `docker rm`, or use the `docker volume` subcommands to destroy them if you forget.

In the scenario in figure 6.1, you can ensure that /var/db is deleted if you always call `docker rm` with the -v flag. The -v flag removes any associated volumes if no other container still has it mounted. Fortunately, Docker is smart enough to know whether any other container has the volume mounted, so there are no nasty surprises.

The simplest approach is to get into the habit of typing -v whenever you remove a container. That way you retain control of whether volumes are removed. But the problem with this approach is that you might not want to always delete volumes. If you're writing a lot of data to these volumes, it's quite likely that you won't want to lose the data. Additionally, if you get into such a habit, it's likely to become automatic, and you'll only realize you've deleted something important when it's too late.

In these scenarios you can use a command that was added to Docker after much griping and many third-party solutions: `docker volume prune`. This will remove any unused volumes:

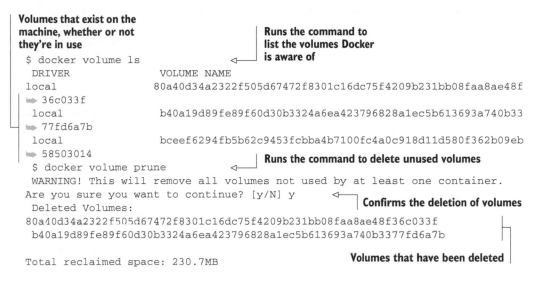

Volumes that exist on the machine, whether or not they're in use

Runs the command to list the volumes Docker is aware of

```
$ docker volume ls
 DRIVER              VOLUME NAME
local               80a40d34a2322f505d67472f8301c16dc75f4209b231bb08faa8ae48f
36c033f
 local               b40a19d89fe89f60d30b3324a6ea423796828a1ec5b613693a740b33
77fd6a7b
 local               bceef6294fb5b62c9453fcbba4b7100fc4a0c918d11d580f362b09eb
58503014
$ docker volume prune
 WARNING! This will remove all volumes not used by at least one container.
Are you sure you want to continue? [y/N] y
 Deleted Volumes:
80a40d34a2322f505d67472f8301c16dc75f4209b231bb08faa8ae48f36c033f
 b40a19d89fe89f60d30b3324a6ea423796828a1ec5b613693a740b3377fd6a7b

Total reclaimed space: 230.7MB
```

Runs the command to delete unused volumes

Confirms the deletion of volumes

Volumes that have been deleted

If you want to skip the confirmation prompt, perhaps for an automated script, you can pass -f to docker volume prune to skip it.

> **TIP** If you want to recover data from an undeleted volume that's no longer referenced by any containers, you can use docker volume inspect to discover the directory a volume lives in (likely under /var/lib/docker/volumes/). You can then browse it as the root user.

DISCUSSION

Deleting volumes is likely not something you'll need to do very often, as large files in a container are usually mounted from the host machine and don't get stored in the Docker data directory. But it's worth doing a cleanup every week or so, to avoid them piling up, particularly if you're using data containers from technique 37.

TECHNIQUE 44 Detaching containers without stopping them

When working with Docker, you'll often find yourself in a position where you have an interactive shell, but exiting from the shell would terminate the container, as it's the container's principal process. Fortunately there's a way to detach from a container (and, if you want, you can use docker attach to connect to the container again).

PROBLEM

You want to detach from a container interaction without stopping it.

SOLUTION

Use the built-in key combination in Docker to escape from the container.

Docker has helpfully implemented a key sequence that's unlikely to be needed by any other application and that's also unlikely to be pressed by accident.

Let's say you started up a container with docker run -t -i -p 9005:80 ubuntu /bin/bash, and then apt-get installed an Nginx web server. You want to test that it's accessible from your host with a quick curl command to localhost:9005.

Press Ctrl-P and then Ctrl-Q. Note that it's not all three keys pressed at once.

NOTE If you're running with --rm and detach, the container will still be removed once it terminates, either because the command finishes or you stop it manually.

DISCUSSION

This technique is useful if you've started a container but perhaps forgot to start it in the background, as shown in technique 2. It also allows you to freely attach and detach from containers if you want to check how they're doing or provide some input.

TECHNIQUE 45   Using Portainer to manage your Docker daemon

When demonstrating Docker, it can be difficult to demonstrate how containers and images differ—lines on a terminal aren't visual. In addition, the Docker command-line tools can be unfriendly if you want to kill and remove specific containers out of many. This problem has been solved with the creation of a point-and-click tool for managing the images and containers on your host.

PROBLEM

You want to manage containers and images on your host without using the CLI.

SOLUTION

Use Portainer, a tool created by one of the core contributors to Docker.

Portainer started out life as DockerUI, and you can read about it and find the source at https://github.com/portainer/portainer. Because there are no prerequisites, you can jump straight to running it:

```
$ docker run -d -p 9000:9000 \
-v /var/run/docker.sock:/var/run/docker.sock \
portainer/portainer -H unix:///var/run/docker.sock
```

This will start the portainer container in the background. If you now visit http://localhost:9000, you'll see the dashboard giving you at-a-glance information for Docker on your computer.

Container management functionality is probably one of the most useful pieces of functionality here—go to the Containers page, and you'll see your running containers listed (including the portainer container), with an option to display all containers. From here you can perform bulk operations on containers (such as killing them) or click on a container name to dive into more detail about the container and perform individual operations relevant to that container. For example, you'll be shown the option to remove a running container.

The Images page looks fairly similar to the Containers page and also allows you to select multiple images and perform bulk operations on them. Clicking on the image ID offers some interesting options, such as creating a container from the image and tagging the image.

Remember that Portainer may lag behind official Docker functionality—if you want to use the latest and greatest functionality, you may be forced to resort to the command line.

DISCUSSION

Portainer is one of many interfaces available for Docker, and it's one of the most popular, with many features and active development. As one example, you can use it to manage remote machines, perhaps after starting containers on them with technique 32.

TECHNIQUE 46 **Generating a dependency graph of your Docker images**

The file-layering system in Docker is an immensely powerful idea that can save space and make building software much quicker. But once you start using a lot of images, it can be difficult to understand how your images are related. The `docker images -a` command will return a list of all the layers on your system, but this isn't a user-friendly way to comprehend these relationships—it's much easier to visualize the relationships between your images by creating a tree of them as an image using Graphviz.

This is also a demonstration of Docker's power to make complicated tasks simpler. Installing all the components to produce the image on a host machine would previously have involved a long series of error-prone steps, but with Docker it can be turned into a single portable command that's far less likely to fail.

PROBLEM

You want to visualize a tree of the images stored on your host.

SOLUTION

Use an image that we've created (based on one by CenturyLink Labs) with this functionality to output a PNG or get a web view. This image contains scripts that use Graphviz to generate the PNG image file.

This technique uses the Docker image at `dockerinpractice/docker-image-graph`. This image may go out of date over time and stop working, so you may want to run the following commands to ensure it's up to date.

Listing 6.1 Building an up-to-date docker-image-graph image (optional)

```
$ git clone https://github.com/docker-in-practice/docker-image-graph
$ cd docker-image-graph
$ docker build -t dockerinpractice/docker-image-graph
```

All you need to do in your `run` command is mount the Docker server socket and you're good to go, as the next listing shows.

Listing 6.2 Generating an image of your layer tree

Removes the container when
the image is produced

Mounts the Docker server's Unix domain socket so
you can access the Docker server from within the
container. If you've changed the default for the Docker
daemon, this won't work.

Specifies an
image and
produces a PNG
as an artifact

```
$ docker run --rm \
  -v /var/run/docker.sock:/var/run/docker.sock \
  dockerinpractice/docker-image-graph > docker_images.png
```

Figure 6.2 shows a PNG of an image tree from one of our machines. You can see from this figure that the node and golang:1.3 images share a common root, and that the golang:runtime only shares the global root with the golang:1.3 image. Similarly, the mesosphere image is built from the same root as the ubuntu-upstart image.

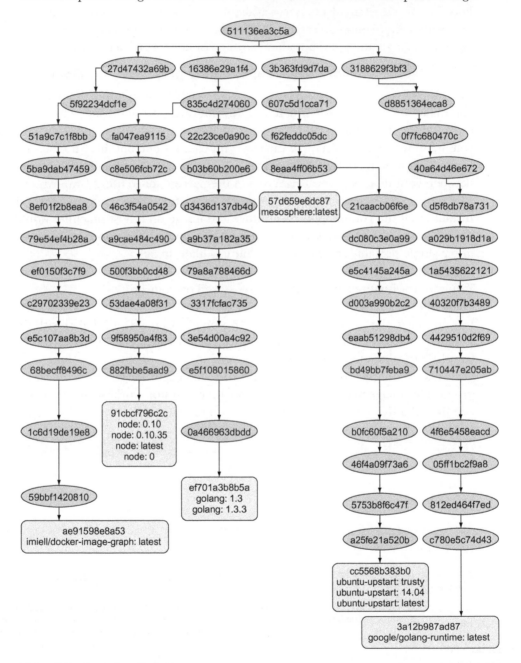

Figure 6.2   Image tree diagram

You may be wondering what the global root node on the tree is. This is the *scratch* pseudo-image, which is exactly 0 bytes in size.

DISCUSSION

When you start building more Docker images, perhaps as part of continuous delivery in chapter 9, it can be overwhelming to keep track of the history of an image and what it's built on. This can be particularly important if you're trying to speed up your delivery by sharing more layers to optimize for size. Periodically pulling all your images and generating a graph can be a great way to keep track.

TECHNIQUE 47 **Direct action: Executing commands on your container**

In the early days of Docker, many users added SSH servers to their images so that they could access them with a shell from outside. This was frowned upon by Docker, as it treated the container as a VM (and we know that containers aren't VMs) and added process overhead to a system that shouldn't need it. Many objected that once started, there was no easy way to get into a container. As a result, Docker introduced the `exec` command, which was a much neater solution to the problem of affecting and inspecting the internals of containers once started. It's this command that we'll discuss here.

PROBLEM

You want to perform commands on a running container.

SOLUTION

Use the `docker exec` command.

The following command starts a container in the background (with -d) and tells it to sleep forever (do nothing). We'll name this command `sleeper`.

```
docker run -d --name sleeper debian sleep infinity
```

Now that you've started a container, you can perform various actions on it using Docker's `exec` command. The command can be viewed as having three basic modes, listed in table 6.1.

Table 6.1 Docker `exec` modes

Mode	Description
Basic	Runs the command in the container synchronously on the command line
Daemon	Runs the command in the background on the container
Interactive	Runs the command and allows the user to interact with it

First we'll cover the basic mode. The following command runs an `echo` command inside our `sleeper` container.

```
$ docker exec sleeper echo "hello host from container"
hello host from container
```

Note that the structure of this command is very similar to the `docker run` command, but instead of the ID of an image, we give it the ID of a running container. The `echo` command refers to the echo binary within the container, not outside.

Daemon mode runs the command in the background; you won't see the output in your terminal. This might be useful for regular housekeeping tasks, where you want to fire the command and forget, such as cleaning up log files:

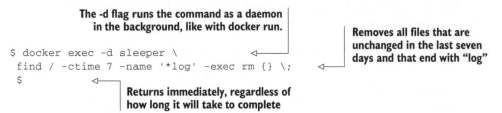

```
$ docker exec -d sleeper \
  find / -ctime 7 -name '*log' -exec rm {} \;
  $
```

The -d flag runs the command as a daemon in the background, like with docker run.

Removes all files that are unchanged in the last seven days and that end with "log"

Returns immediately, regardless of how long it will take to complete

Finally, we have interactive mode. This allows you to run whatever commands you like from within the container. To enable this, you'll usually want to specify that the shell should run interactively, which in the following code is bash:

```
$ docker exec -i -t sleeper /bin/bash
root@d46dc042480f:/#
```

The `-i` and `-t` arguments do the same thing you're familiar with from `docker run`— they make the command interactive and set up a TTY device so shells will function correctly. After running this, you'll have a prompt running inside the container.

DISCUSSION

Jumping into a container is an essential debugging step when something is going wrong, or if you want to figure out what a container is doing. It's often not possible to use the attach and detach method enabled by technique 44 because processes in containers are typically run in the foreground, making it impossible to get access to a shell prompt. Because `exec` allows you to specify the binary you want to run, this isn't an issue … as long as the container filesystem actually has the binary you want to run.

In particular, if you've used technique 58 to create a container with a single binary, you won't be able to start a shell. In this case you may want to stick with technique 57 as a low-overhead way to permit `exec`.

TECHNIQUE 48   Are you in a Docker container?

When creating containers, it's common to put logic inside shell scripts rather than trying to directly write the script in a Dockerfile. Or you may have assorted scripts for use while the container is running. Either way, the tasks these perform are often carefully customized for use inside a container and can be damaging to run on a "normal" machine. In situations like this, it's useful to have some safety rails to prevent accidental execution outside a container.

PROBLEM

Your code needs to know whether you're operating from within a Docker container.

SOLUTION

Check for the existence of the /.dockerenv file. If it exists, you're likely in a Docker container.

Note that this isn't a cast-iron guarantee—if anyone, or anything, removed the /.dockerenv file, this check could give misleading results. These scenarios are unlikely, but at worst you'll get a false positive with no ill effects; you'll think you're not in a Docker container and at worst *won't* run a potentially destructive piece of code.

A more realistic scenario is that this undocumented behavior of Docker has been altered or removed in a newer version of Docker (or you're using a version from before the behavior was first implemented).

The code might be part of a startup bash script, as in the following listing, followed by the remainder of your startup script code.

> **Listing 6.3   Shell script fails if it's run outside a container**

```bash
#!/bin/bash
if ! [ -f /.dockerenv ]
then
    echo 'Not in a Docker container, exiting.'
    exit 1
fi
```

Of course, the opposite logic could be used to determine that you are *not* running within a container, if that's your need:

> **Listing 6.4   Shell script fails if it's run inside a container**

```bash
#!/bin/bash
if [ -f /.dockerenv ]
then
    echo 'In a Docker container, exiting.'
    exit 1
fi
```

This example uses bash to determine the existence of the file, but the vast majority of programming languages will have their own ways to determine the existence of files on the container (or host) filesystem.

DISCUSSION

You may be wondering how often this situation arises. It happens often enough for it to be a regular discussion point on Docker forums, where somewhat religious arguments flare up about whether this is a valid use case, or whether something else in your application's design is amiss.

Leaving these discussions aside, you can easily end up in a situation where you need to switch your code path depending on whether you're in a Docker container or not. One such example we've experienced is when using a Makefile to build a container.

Summary

- You can configure your machine to let you run Docker without `sudo`.
- Use the built-in Docker commands to clean up unused containers and volumes.
- External tools can be used to expose information about your containers in new ways.
- The `docker exec` command is the correct way to get inside a running container—resist installing SSH.

Configuration management: Getting your house in order

This chapter covers

- Managing the building of images using Dockerfiles
- Building images using traditional configuration management tools
- Managing the secret information required to build images
- Reducing the size of your images for faster, lighter, and safer delivery

Configuration management is the art of managing your environments so that they're stable and predictable. Tools such as Chef and Puppet have attempted to alleviate the sysadmin burden of managing multiple machines. To an extent, Docker also reduces this burden by making the software environment isolated and portable. Even so, configuration management techniques are required to produce Docker images, and it's an important topic to recognize.

By the end of the chapter, you'll know how to integrate your existing tools with Docker, solve some Docker-specific problems like removing secrets from layers, and follow the best practice of minimizing your final image. As you get more experience with Docker, these techniques will give you the ability to build images for whatever configuration needs you're trying to satisfy.

7.1 Configuration management and Dockerfiles

Dockerfiles are considered to be the standard way of building Docker images. Dockerfiles are often confusing in terms of what they mean for configuration management. You may have many questions (particularly if you have experience with other configuration management tools), such as

- What happens if the base image changes?
- What happens if the packages I'm installing change and I rebuild?
- Does this replace Chef/Puppet/Ansible?

In fact, Dockerfiles are quite simple: starting from a given image, a Dockerfile specifies a series of shell commands and meta-instructions to Docker, which will produce the desired final image.

Dockerfiles provide a common, simple, and universal language for provisioning Docker images. Within them, you can use anything you like to reach the desired end state. You could call out to Puppet, copy in another script, or copy in an entire filesystem!

First we'll consider how you can deal with some minor challenges that Dockerfiles bring with them. Then we'll move on to the meatier issues we just outlined.

TECHNIQUE 49　Creating reliable bespoke tools with ENTRYPOINT

Docker's potential for allowing you to run commands *anywhere* means that complex bespoke instructions or scripts that are run on the command line can be preconfigured and wrapped up into a packaged tool.

The easily misunderstood ENTRYPOINT instruction is a vital part of this. You're going to see how it enables you to create Docker images as tools that are well-encapsulated, clearly defined, and flexible enough to be useful.

PROBLEM

You want to define the command the container will run, but leave the command's arguments up to the user.

SOLUTION

Use the Dockerfile ENTRYPOINT instruction.

As a demonstration, we'll imagine a simple scenario in a corporation where a regular admin task is to clean up old log files. Often this is prone to error, and people accidentally delete the wrong things, so we're going to use a Docker image to reduce the risk of problems arising.

The following script (which you should name "clean_log" when you save it) deletes logs over a certain number of days old, where the number of days is passed in as a command-line option. Create a new folder anywhere with any name you like, move into it, and place clean_log within it.

Listing 7.1   clean_log shell script

```
#!/bin/bash
echo "Cleaning logs over $1 days old"
find /log_dir -ctime "$1" -name '*log' -exec rm {} \;
```

Note that the log cleaning takes place on the /log_dir folder. This folder will only exist when you mount it at runtime. You may have also noticed that there's no check for whether an argument has been passed in to the script. The reason for this will be revealed as we go through the technique.

Now let's create a Dockerfile in the same directory to create an image, with the script running as the defined command, or *entrypoint.*

Listing 7.2   Creating an image with the clean_log script

```
FROM ubuntu:17.04
ADD clean_log /usr/bin/clean_log          Adds the previous corporate
 RUN chmod +x /usr/bin/clean_log          clean_log script to the image
ENTRYPOINT ["/usr/bin/clean_log"]    ⊲     Defines the entrypoint for this image
 CMD ["7"]                    ⊲             as being the clean_log script

  Defines the default argument for
  the entrypoint command (7 days)
```

> **TIP** You'll observe that we generally prefer the array form for CMD and ENTRYPOINT (for example, CMD ["/usr/bin/command"]) over the shell form (CMD /usr/bin/command). This is because the shell form automatically prepends a /bin/bash -c command to the command you supply, which can result in unexpected behavior. Sometimes, however, the shell form is more useful (see technique 55).

The difference between ENTRYPOINT and CMD often confuses people. The key point to understand is that an entrypoint will always be run when the image is started, even if a command is supplied to the docker run invocation. If you try to supply a command, it will add that as an argument to the entrypoint, replacing the default defined in the CMD instruction. You can only override the entrypoint if you explicitly pass in an --entrypoint flag to the docker run command. This means that running the image with a /bin/bash command won't give you a shell; rather, it will supply /bin/bash as an argument to the clean_log script.

The fact that a default argument is defined by the CMD instruction means that the argument supplied need not be checked. Here's how you might build and invoke this tool:

```
docker build -t log-cleaner .
docker run -v /var/log/myapplogs:/log_dir log-cleaner 365
```

After building the image, the image is invoked by mounting `/var/log/myapplogs` into the directory the script will use and passing 365 to remove log files over a year old, rather than a week.

If someone tries to use the image incorrectly by not specifying a number of days, they'll be given an error message:

```
$ docker run -ti log-cleaner /bin/bash
Cleaning logs over /bin/bash days old
find: invalid argument `-name' to `-ctime'
```

DISCUSSION

This example was quite trivial, but you can imagine that a corporation could apply it to centrally manage scripts used across its estate, such that they could be maintained and distributed safely with a private registry.

You can view and use the image we created in this technique at dockerinpractice/log-cleaner on the Docker Hub.

TECHNIQUE 50   Avoiding package drift by specifying versions

Dockerfiles have simple syntax and limited functionality, they can help greatly to clarify your build's requirements, and they can aid the stability of image production, but they can't guarantee repeatable builds. We're going to explore one of the numerous approaches to solving this problem and reducing the risk of nasty surprises when the underlying package management dependencies change.

This technique is helpful for avoiding those "it worked yesterday" moments, and it may be familiar if you've used classic configuration management tools. Building Docker images is fundamentally quite different from maintaining a server, but some hard-learned lessons are still applicable.

> **NOTE** This technique will only work for Debian-based images, such as Ubuntu. Yum users could find analogous techniques to make it work under their package manager.

PROBLEM

You want to ensure that your deb packages are the versions you expect.

SOLUTION

Run a script to capture the versions of all dependent packages on a system that's set up as you desire. Then install the specific versions in your Dockerfile, to ensure the versions are exactly as you expect.

A basic check for versions can be performed with an `apt-cache` call on a system you've verified as OK:

```
$ apt-cache show nginx | grep ^Version:
Version: 1.4.6-1ubuntu3
```

You can then specify the version in your Dockerfile like this:

```
RUN apt-get -y install nginx=1.4.6-1ubuntu3
```

This may be enough for your needs. What this doesn't do is guarantee that all dependencies from this version of nginx have the same versions that you originally verified.

You can get information about all of those dependencies by adding a `--recurse` flag to the argument:

```
apt-cache --recurse depends nginx
```

The output of this command is intimidatingly large, so getting a list of version requirements is tricky. Fortunately, we maintain a Docker image (what else?) to make this easier for you. It outputs the RUN line you need to put into your Dockerfile to ensure that the versions of all the dependencies are correct.

```
$ docker run -ti dockerinpractice/get-versions vim
RUN apt-get install -y \
vim=2:7.4.052-1ubuntu3 vim-common=2:7.4.052-1ubuntu3 \
vim-runtime=2:7.4.052-1ubuntu3 libacl1:amd64=2.2.52-1 \
libc6:amd64=2.19-0ubuntu6.5 libc6:amd64=2.19-0ubuntu6.5 \
libgpm2:amd64=1.20.4-6.1 libpython2.7:amd64=2.7.6-8 \
libselinux1:amd64=2.2.2-1ubuntu0.1 libselinux1:amd64=2.2.2-1ubuntu0.1 \
libtinfo5:amd64=5.9+20140118-1ubuntu1 libattr1:amd64=1:2.4.47-1ubuntu1 \
libgcc1:amd64=1:4.9.1-0ubuntu1 libgcc1:amd64=1:4.9.1-0ubuntu1 \
libpython2.7-stdlib:amd64=2.7.6-8 zlib1g:amd64=1:1.2.8.dfsg-1ubuntu1 \
libpcre3:amd64=1:8.31-2ubuntu2 gcc-4.9-base:amd64=4.9.1-0ubuntu1 \
gcc-4.9-base:amd64=4.9.1-0ubuntu1 libpython2.7-minimal:amd64=2.7.6-8 \
mime-support=3.54ubuntu1.1 mime-support=3.54ubuntu1.1 \
libbz2-1.0:amd64=1.0.6-5 libdb5.3:amd64=5.3.28-3ubuntu3 \
libexpat1:amd64=2.1.0-4ubuntu1 libffi6:amd64=3.1~rc1+r3.0.13-12 \
libncursesw5:amd64=5.9+20140118-1ubuntu1 libreadline6:amd64=6.3-4ubuntu2 \
libsqlite3-0:amd64=3.8.2-1ubuntu2 libssl1.0.0:amd64=1.0.1f-1ubuntu2.8 \
libssl1.0.0:amd64=1.0.1f-1ubuntu2.8 readline-common=6.3-4ubuntu2 \
debconf-1.5.51ubuntu2 dpkg-1.17.5ubuntu5.3 dpkg-1.17.5ubuntu5.3 \
libnewt0.52:amd64=0.52.15-2ubuntu5 libslang2:amd64=2.2.4-15ubuntu1 \
vim=2:7.4.052-1ubuntu3
```

At some point your build will fail because a version is no longer available. When this happens, you'll be able to see which package has changed and review the change to determine whether it's OK for your particular image's needs.

This example assumes that you're using ubuntu:14.04. If you're using a different flavor of Debian, fork the repo and change the Dockerfile's FROM instruction and build it. The repo is available here: https://github.com/docker-in-practice/get-versions.git.

Although this technique can help you with the stability of your build, it does nothing in terms of security, because you're still downloading packages from a repository you have no direct control over.

DISCUSSION

This technique may seem like a lot of effort to ensure that a text editor is exactly as you expect it to be. In the field, though, package drift can result in bugs that are incredibly difficult to pin down. Libraries and applications can move in subtle ways in builds from one day to the next, and figuring out what happened can ruin your day.

By pinning down the versions as tightly as possible within your Dockerfile, you ensure that one of two things happens. Either the build succeeds and your software will behave the same way as it did yesterday, or it fails to build because a piece of software has changed, and you'll need to retest your development pipeline. In the second case, you're aware of what's changed, and you can narrow down any failures that ensue to that specific change.

The point is that when you're doing continuing builds and integrations, reducing the number of variables that change reduces the time spent debugging. That translates to money for your business.

TECHNIQUE 51 Replacing text with perl -p -i -e

It's not uncommon when building images with Dockerfiles that you'll need to replace specific items of text across multiple files. Numerous solutions for this exist, but we'll introduce a somewhat unusual favorite that's particularly handy in Dockerfiles.

PROBLEM

You want to alter specific lines in files during a build.

SOLUTION

Use the perl -p -i -e command.

We recommend this command for a few reasons:

- Unlike sed -i (a command with a similar syntax and effect), this command works on multiple files out of the box, even if it encounters a problem with one of the files. This means you can run it across a directory with a '*' glob pattern without fear that it will suddenly break when a directory is added in a later revision of the package.
- As with sed, you can replace the forward slashes in the search and replace commands with other characters.
- It's easy to remember (we refer to it as the "perl pie" command).

NOTE This technique assumes an understanding of regular expressions. If you're not familiar with regular expressions, there are plenty of websites available to help you.

Here's a typical example of this command's use:

```
perl -p -i -e 's/127\.0\.0\.1/0.0.0.0/g' *
```

In this command, the -p flag asks Perl to assume a loop while it processes all the lines seen. The -i flag asks Perl to update the matched lines in place, and the -e flag asks Perl to treat the supplied string as a Perl program. The s is an instruction to Perl to search and replace strings as they're matched in the input. Here 127.0.0.1 is replaced with 0.0.0.0. The g modifier ensures that all matches are updated, not just the first on any given line. Finally, the asterisk (*) applies the update to all files in this directory.

The preceding command performs a fairly common action for Docker containers. It replaces the standard localhost IP address (127.0.0.1) with one that indicates "any" IPv4 address (0.0.0.0) when used as an address to listen on. Many applications restrict access to the localhost IP by only listening on that address, and frequently you'll want to change this in their config files to the "any" address because you'll be accessing the application from your host, which appears to the container to be an external machine.

> **TIP** If an application within a Docker container appears not to be accessible to you from the host machine, despite the port being open, it can be worth trying to update the addresses to listen on to 0.0.0.0 in the application config file and restarting. It may be that the application is rejecting you because you're not coming from its localhost. Using --net=host (covered later in technique 109) when running your image can help confirm this hypothesis.

Another nice feature of perl -p -i -e (and sed) is that you can use other characters to replace the forward slashes if escaping the slashes gets awkward. Here's a real-world example from one of our scripts that adds some directives to the default Apache site file. This awkward command,

```
perl -p -i -e 's/\/usr\/share\/www\/\/var\/www\/html/g' /etc/apache2/*
```

becomes this:

```
perl -p -i -e 's@/usr/share/www@/var/www/html/@g' /etc/apache2/*
```

In the rare cases that you want to match or replace both the / and @ characters, you can try other characters such as | or #.

DISCUSSION

This is one of those tips that applies beyond the world of Docker as much as within it. It's a useful tool to have in your armory.

We find this technique particularly useful because of its broad application beyond use in Dockerfiles, combined with the ease with which it's remembered: it's "easy as pie," if you'll forgive the pun.

TECHNIQUE 52 **Flattening images**

A consequence of the design of Dockerfiles and their production of Docker images is that the final image contains the data state at each step in the Dockerfile. In the course of building your images, secrets may need to be copied in to ensure the build can work. These secrets may be SSH keys, certificates, or password files. Deleting these secrets before committing your image doesn't provide you with any real protection, as they'll be present in higher layers of the final image. A malicious user could easily extract them from the image.

One way of handling this problem is to flatten the resulting image.

PROBLEM

You want to remove secret information from the layer history of your image.

SOLUTION

Instantiate a container with the image, export it, import it, and then tag it with the original image ID.

To demonstrate a scenario where this could be useful, let's create a simple Dockerfile in a new directory that contains a Big Secret. Run `mkdir secrets && cd secrets` and then create a Dockerfile in that folder with the following contents.

Listing 7.3   A Dockerfile that copies in and deletes a secret

```
FROM debian                                          Place a file with some secret
RUN echo "My Big Secret" >> /tmp/secret_key    ◀──┘ information within your build.
 RUN cat /tmp/secret_key        ◀─┐
 RUN rm /tmp/secret_key    ◀──┐   │  Do something with the secret file. This Dockerfile
        Remove the secret file. │  │  only cats the file, but yours might SSH to another
                                   │  server or encrypt that secret within the image.
```

Now run `docker build -t mysecret .` to build and tag that Dockerfile.

Once it's built, you can examine the layers of the resulting Docker image with the `docker history` command:

```
                Runs the docker history command against              The layer where you
                  the name of the image you created                removed the secret key
$ docker history mysecret    ◀──┘
  IMAGE           CREATED        CREATED BY                          SIZE
 55f3c131a35d 3 days ago /bin/sh -c rm /tmp/secret_key        ◀──┘
   5b376ff3d7cd 3 days ago /bin/sh -c cat /tmp/secret_key          0 B
▶ 5e39caf7560f 3 days ago /bin/sh -c echo "My Big Secret" >> /tmp/se 14 B
   c90d655b99b2 6 days ago /bin/sh -c #(nop) CMD [/bin/bash]       0 B
 30d39e59ffe2 6 days ago /bin/sh -c #(nop) ADD file:3f1a40df75bc567 85.01 MB ◀─┐
   511136ea3c5a 20 months ago                                      0 B    ◀─┘
 The layer where you                                      The scratch (empty) layer
 added the secret key
                                The layer that added the Debian filesystem. Note
                                 that this layer is the largest one in the history.
```

Now imagine that you've downloaded this image from a public registry. You could inspect the layer history and then run the following command to reveal the secret information:

```
$ docker run 5b376ff3d7cd cat /tmp/secret_key
My Big Secret
```

Here we've run a specific layer and instructed it to `cat` the secret key we removed at a higher layer. As you can see, the file is accessible.

Now you have a "dangerous" container with a secret inside that you've seen can be hacked to reveal its secrets. To make this image safe, you'll need to *flatten* it. This means you'll keep the same data in the image but remove the intermediate layering information. To achieve this, you need to export the image as a trivially run container and then re-import and tag the resulting image:

Runs a trivial command to allow the container to exit quickly, because you don't need it to be running

```
$ docker run -d mysecret /bin/true          <─
28cde380f0195b24b33e19e132e81a4f58d2f055a42fa8406e755b2ef283630f
$ docker export 28cde380f | docker import - mysecret   <─
$ docker history mysecret
IMAGE              CREATED          CREATED BY   SIZE
fdbeae08751b   13 seconds ago                85.01 MB   <─
```

The docker history output now shows only one layer with the final set of files.

Runs docker export, taking a container ID as an argument and outputting a TAR file of the filesystem contents. This is piped to docker import, which takes a TAR file and creates an image from the contents.

The - argument to the docker import command indicates that you wish to read the TAR file from the command's standard input. The final argument to docker import indicates how the imported image should be tagged. In this case you're overwriting the previous tag.

Because there's now only one layer in the image, there's no record of the layers that contained the secrets. No secrets can now be extracted from the image.

DISCUSSION

This technique is useful enough to be re-used at various points throughout this book, such as in section 7.3.

One point to consider if you're thinking of using this technique is that the benefits of multilayered images on layer caching and download times can be lost. If your organization plans carefully around this, this technique can play a role in these images' real-world use.

TECHNIQUE 53 **Managing foreign packages with Alien**

Although most Dockerfile examples in this book (and on the internet) use a Debian-based image, the reality of software development means that many people won't be dealing with them exclusively.

Fortunately tools exist to help you with this.

PROBLEM

You want to install a package from a foreign distribution.

SOLUTION

Use a tool called Alien to convert the package. Alien is embedded into a Docker image we'll use as part of the technique.

Alien is a command-line utility designed to convert package files between the various formats listed in table 7.1. On more than one occasion, we've been required to make packages from foreign package management systems work, such as .deb files in CentOS, and .rpm files in non-Red Hat-based systems.

Table 7.1   Package formats supported by Alien

Extension	Description
.deb	Debian package
.rpm	Red Hat package management
.tgz	Slackware gzipped TAR file
.pkg	Solaris PKG package
.slp	Stampede package

NOTE For the purposes of this technique, Solaris and Stampede packages aren't fully covered. Solaris requires software peculiar to Solaris, and Stampede is an abandoned project.

Researching this book, we discovered that it could be a little fiddly to install Alien on non-Debian-based distributions. This being a Docker book, we've naturally decided to provide a conversion tool in the format of a Docker image. As a bonus, this tool uses the ENTRYPOINT command from technique 49 to make using the tools simpler.

As an example, let's download and convert (with Alien) the eatmydata package, which will be used in technique 62.

Retrieves the package files you want to convert

Creates an empty directory to work in

Runs the dockerinpractice/alienate image, mounting the current directory to the container's /io path. The container will examine that directory and try to convert any valid files it finds.

```
$ mkdir tmp && cd tmp
 $ wget \
http://mirrors.kernel.org/ubuntu/pool/main/libe/libeatmydata
 ➥ /eatmydata_26-2_i386.deb
 $ docker run -v $(pwd):/io dockerinpractice/alienate
 Examining eatmydata_26-2_i386.deb from /io
eatmydata_26-2_i386.deb appears to be a Debian package
 eatmydata-26-3.i386.rpm generated
eatmydata-26.slp generated
eatmydata-26.tgz generated
===============================================
/io now contains:
eatmydata-26-3.i386.rpm
eatmydata-26.slp
eatmydata-26.tgz
eatmydata_26-2_i386.deb
===============================================
$ ls -1
 eatmydata_26-2_i386.deb
eatmydata-26-3.i386.rpm
eatmydata-26.slp
eatmydata-26.tgz
```

The container informs you of its actions as it runs its Alien wrapper script.

The files have been converted to RPM, Slackware TGZ, and Stampede files.

Alternatively, you can pass the URL of a package to be downloaded and converted directly to the docker run command:

```
$ mkdir tmp && cd tmp
$ docker run -v $(pwd):/io dockerinpractice/alienate \
http://mirrors.kernel.org/ubuntu/pool/main/libe/libeatmydata
➥ /eatmydata_26-2_i386.deb
wgetting http://mirrors.kernel.org/ubuntu/pool/main/libe/libeatmydata
➥ /eatmydata_26-2_i386.deb
--2015-02-26 10:57:28--  http://mirrors.kernel.org/ubuntu/pool/main/libe
➥ /libeatmydata/eatmydata_26-2_i386.deb
Resolving mirrors.kernel.org (mirrors.kernel.org)... 198.145.20.143,
➥ 149.20.37.36, 2001:4f8:4:6f:0:1994:3:14, ...
Connecting to mirrors.kernel.org (mirrors.kernel.org)|198.145.20.143|:80...
➥ connected.
HTTP request sent, awaiting response... 200 OK
Length: 7782 (7.6K) [application/octet-stream]
Saving to: 'eatmydata_26-2_i386.deb'

   OK .......                             100% 2.58M=0.003s

2015-02-26 10:57:28 (2.58 MB/s) - 'eatmydata_26-2_i386.deb' saved
➥ [7782/7782]


Examining eatmydata_26-2_i386.deb from /io
eatmydata_26-2_i386.deb appears to be a Debian package
eatmydata-26-3.i386.rpm generated
eatmydata-26.slp generated
eatmydata-26.tgz generated
=========================================================
/io now contains:
eatmydata-26-3.i386.rpm
eatmydata-26.slp
eatmydata-26.tgz
eatmydata_26-2_i386.deb
=========================================================
$ ls -1
eatmydata_26-2_i386.deb
eatmydata-26-3.i386.rpm
eatmydata-26.slp
eatmydata-26.tgz
```

If you want to run Alien in a container yourself, you can start up the container with this:

```
docker run -ti --entrypoint /bin/bash dockerinpractice/alienate
```

> **WARNING** Alien is a best-effort tool, and it's not guaranteed to work with the packages you give it.

DISCUSSION

Docker use has brought into sharp focus the "distro wars" that lay dormant for some time. Most organizations had settled into simply being Red Hat or Debian shops that didn't need to be concerned with other packaging systems. Now, it's not uncommon to receive requests for the introduction of Docker images that are based on "alien" distributions within an organization.

That's where this technique can help, as "foreign" packages can be converted to a more friendly format. This topic will be revisited in chapter 14, where we'll discuss security.

7.2   *Traditional configuration management tools with Docker*

Now we'll move on to how Dockerfiles can work alongside more traditional configuration management tools.

We'll look here at traditional configuration management with make, show you how you can use your existing Chef scripts to provision your images with Chef Solo, and look at a shell script framework built to help non-Docker experts build images.

TECHNIQUE 54   Traditional: Using make with Docker

At some point you might find that having a bunch of Dockerfiles is limiting your build process. For example, it's impossible to produce any output *files* if you limit yourself to running docker build, and there's no way to have variables in Dockerfiles.

This requirement for additional tooling can be addressed by a number of tools (including plain shell scripts). In this technique we'll look at how you can twist the venerable make tool to work with Docker.

PROBLEM

You want to add additional tasks around docker build execution.

SOLUTION

Use an ancient (in computing terms) tool called make.

In case you haven't used it before, make is a tool that takes one or more input files and produces an output file, but it can also be used as a task runner. Here's a simple example (note that all indents must be tabs):

Listing 7.4   A simple Makefile

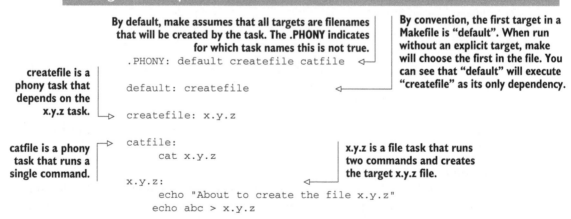

By default, make assumes that all targets are filenames that will be created by the task. The .PHONY indicates for which task names this is not true.

By convention, the first target in a Makefile is "default". When run without an explicit target, make will choose the first in the file. You can see that "default" will execute "createfile" as its only dependency.

createfile is a phony task that depends on the x.y.z task.

catfile is a phony task that runs a single command.

x.y.z is a file task that runs two commands and creates the target x.y.z file.

```
.PHONY: default createfile catfile

default: createfile

createfile: x.y.z

catfile:
	cat x.y.z

x.y.z:
	echo "About to create the file x.y.z"
	echo abc > x.y.z
```

WARNING   All indents in a Makefile must be tabs, and each command in a target is run in a different shell (so environment variables won't be carried across).

Once you have the preceding content in a file called Makefile, you can invoke any target with a command like `make createfile`.

Now let's look at some useful patterns in a Makefile—the rest of the targets we'll talk about will be phony, as it's difficult (although possible) to use file-change tracking to trigger Docker builds automatically. Dockerfiles use a cache of layers, so builds tend to be fast.

The first step is to run a Dockerfile. Because a Makefile consists of shell commands, this is easy.

Listing 7.5 Makefile for building an image

```
base:
    docker build -t corp/base .
```

Normal variations of this work as you'd expect (such as piping the file to `docker build` to remove the context, or using `-f` to use a differently named Dockerfile), and you can use the dependencies feature of `make` to automatically build base images (used in `FROM`) where necessary. For example, if you checked out a number of repositories into a subdirectory called repos (also easily doable with `make`), you could add a target, as in the following listing.

Listing 7.6 Makefile for building an image in a subdirectory

```
app1: base
    cd repos/app1 && docker build -t corp/app1 .
```

The downside of this is that every time your base image needs rebuilding, Docker will upload a build context that includes all of your repos. You can fix this by explicitly passing a build context TAR file to Docker.

Listing 7.7 Makefile for building an image with a specific set of files

```
base:
    tar -cvf - file1 file2 Dockerfile | docker build -t corp/base -
```

This explicit statement of dependencies will provide a significant speed increase if your directory contains a large number of files that are irrelevant to the build. You can slightly modify this target if you want to keep all your build dependencies in a different directory.

Listing 7.8 Makefile for building an image with a specific set of files with renamed paths

```
base:
    tar --transform 's/^deps\///' -cf - deps/* Dockerfile | \
        docker build -t corp/base -
```

Here you add everything in the deps directory to the build context, and use the --transform option of tar (available in recent tar versions on Linux) to strip any leading "deps/" from filenames. In this particular case, a better approach would have been to put the deps and Dockerfile in a directory of their own to permit a normal docker build, but it's useful to be aware of this advanced use as it can come in handy in the most unlikely places. Always think carefully before using it, though, as it adds complexity to your build process.

Simple variable substitution is a relatively simple matter, but (as with --transform previously) think carefully before you use it—Dockerfiles deliberately don't support variables in order to keep builds easily reproducible.

Here we're going to use variables passed to make and substitute using sed, but you can pass and substitute however you like.

Listing 7.9 Makefile for building an image with basic Dockerfile variable substitution

```
VAR1 ?= defaultvalue
base:
    cp Dockerfile.in Dockerfile
    sed -i 's/{VAR1}/$(VAR1)/' Dockerfile
    docker build -t corp/base .
```

The Dockerfile will be regenerated every time the base target is run, and you can add more variable substitutions by adding more sed -i lines. To override the default value of VAR1, you run make VAR1=newvalue base. If your variables include slashes, you may need to choose a different sed separator, like sed -i 's#{VAR1}#$(VAR1)#' Dockerfile.

Finally, if you've been using Docker as a build tool, you need to know how to get files back out of Docker. We'll present a couple of different possibilities, depending on your use case.

Listing 7.10 Makefile for copying files out of an image

```
singlefile: base
    docker run --rm corp/base cat /path/to/myfile > outfile
multifile: base
    docker run --rm -v $(pwd)/outdir:/out corp/base sh \
        -c "cp -r /path/to/dir/* /out/"
```

Here, singlefile runs cat on a file and pipes the output to a new file. This approach has the advantage of automatically setting the correct owner of the file, but it becomes cumbersome for more than one file. The multifile approach mounts a volume in the container and copies all files from a directory to the volume. You can follow this up with a chown command to set the correct owner on the files, but bear in mind that you'll probably need to invoke it with sudo.

The Docker project itself uses the volume-mounting approach when building Docker from source.

DISCUSSION

It might seem a little odd for a tool as old as make to appear within a book about a relatively new technology like Docker. Why not use a newer build technology like Ant, or Maven, or any of the many other general build tools available.

The answer is that, for all its faults, make is a tool that is

- Unlikely to go away any time soon
- Well-documented
- Highly flexible
- Widely available

Having spent many hours fighting bugs or poorly documented (or undocumented) limitations of new build technologies, or trying to install dependencies of these systems, make's features have saved us many times. It's also more likely that make will be available in five years' time when other tools are gone, or have fallen out of maintenance by their owners.

TECHNIQUE 55 Building images with Chef Solo

One of the things that confuses newcomers to Docker is whether Dockerfiles are the only supported configuration management tool, and whether existing configuration management tools should be ported to Dockerfiles. Neither of these is true.

Although Dockerfiles are designed to be a simple and portable means of provisioning images, they're also flexible enough to allow any other configuration management tool to take over. In short, if you can run it in a terminal, you can run it in a Dockerfile.

As a demonstration of this, we'll show you how to get up and running with Chef, arguably the most established configuration management tool, in a Dockerfile. Using a tool like Chef can reduce the amount of work required for you to configure images.

> **NOTE** Although familiarity with Chef isn't required to follow this technique, some familiarity will be required to follow it the first time with ease. Covering a whole configuration management tool is a book in itself. With careful study and some research, this technique can be used to get a good understanding of Chef basics.

PROBLEM

You want to reduce configuration effort by using Chef.

SOLUTION

Install Chef in your container, and run recipes using Chef Solo within that container to provision it, all within your Dockerfile.

What you're going to provision is a simple Hello World Apache website. This will give you a taste of what Chef can do for your configuration.

Chef Solo requires no external Chef server setup. If you're already familiar with Chef, this example can easily be adapted to enable your pre-existing scripts to contact your Chef server if you wish.

We're going to walk through the creation of this Chef example, but if you want to download the working code, it's available as a Git repository. To download it, run this command:

```
git clone https://github.com/docker-in-practice/docker-chef-solo-example.git
```

We'll begin with the simple aim of setting up a web server with Apache that outputs "Hello World!" (what else?) when you hit it. The site will be served from mysite.com, and a `mysiteuser` user will be set up on the image.

To begin, create a directory and set it up with the files you'll need for Chef configuration.

Listing 7.11   Creating the necessary files for a Chef configuration

The Chef attributes file, which defines the variables for this image (or node, in Chef parlance), will contain the recipes in the run-list for this image, and other information.

The Dockerfile that will build the image

The Chef config file, which sets some base variables for the Chef configuration

Creates the templates for the dynamically configured content

```
$ mkdir chef_example
$ cd chef_example
$ touch attributes.json
 $ touch config.rb
 $ touch Dockerfile
 $ mkdir -p cookbooks/mysite/recipes
  $ touch cookbooks/mysite/recipes/default.rb
$ mkdir -p cookbooks/mysite/templates/default
  $ touch cookbooks/mysite/templates/default/message.erb
```

Creates the default recipe folder, which stores the Chef instructions for building the image

---

First we'll fill out attributes.json.

Listing 7.12   attributes.json

```
{
        "run_list": [
                "recipe[apache2::default]",
                "recipe[mysite::default]"
        ]
}
```

This file sets out the recipes you're going to run. The apache2 recipes will be retrieved from a public repository; the mysite recipes will be written here.

Next, populate your config.rb with some basic information, as shown in the next listing.

Listing 7.13   config.rb

```
base_dir        "/chef/"
file_cache_path base_dir + "cache/"
```

```
cookbook_path   base_dir + "cookbooks/"
verify_api_cert true
```

This file sets up basic information about the location and adds the configuration setting `verify_api_cert` to suppress an irrelevant error.

   Now we get to the meat of the work: the image's Chef recipe. Each stanza termi-
nated by an `end` in the code block defines a Chef resource.

Listing 7.14   cookbooks/mysite/recipes/default.rb

```
user "mysiteuser" do              ◁──── Creates a user
    comment "mysite user"
    home "/home/mysiteuser"
    shell "/bin/bash"
end

directory "/var/www/html/mysite" do      ◁──── Creates a directory
    owner "mysiteuser"                          for the web content
    group "mysiteuser"
    mode 0755
    action :create
end

template "/var/www/html/mysite/index.html" do    ◁──── Defines a file that will be placed
    source "message.erb"                                in the web folder. This file will be
    variables(                                          created from a template defined
        :message => "Hello World!"                      in the "source" attribute.
    )
    user "mysiteuser"
    group "mysiteuser"
    mode 0755
end

web_app "mysite" do              ◁──── Defines a web app for apache2
    server_name "mysite.com"
    server_aliases ["www.mysite.com","mysite.com"] ◁──── In a real scenario you'd have to
    docroot "/var/www/html/mysite"                       change references from mysite
    cookbook 'apache2'                                   to your website's name. If
end                                                      you're accessing or testing from
                                                         your host, this doesn't matter.
```

The content of the website is contained within the template file. It contains one line,
which Chef will read, substituting in the "Hello World!" message from config.rb. Chef
will then write the substituted file out to the template target (/var/www/html/mysite/
index.html). This uses a templating language that we're not going to cover here.

Listing 7.15   cookbooks/mysite/templates/default/message.erb

```
<%= @message %>
```

Finally, you put everything together with the Dockerfile, which sets up the Chef prerequisites and runs Chef to configure the image, as shown in the following listing.

Listing 7.16 Dockerfile

Downloads and installs Chef. If this download doesn't work for you, check the latest code in docker-chef-solo-example mentioned earlier in this discussion, as a later version of Chef may now be required.

```
FROM ubuntu:14.04

RUN apt-get update && apt-get install -y git curl

RUN curl -L \
https://opscode-omnibus-packages.s3.amazonaws.com/ubuntu/12.04/x86_64
➥ /chefdk_0.3.5-1_amd64.deb \
-o chef.deb
RUN dpkg -i chef.deb && rm chef.deb

COPY . /chef

WORKDIR /chef/cookbooks
  RUN knife cookbook site download apache2
  RUN knife cookbook site download iptables
  RUN knife cookbook site download logrotate

RUN /bin/bash -c 'for f in $(ls *gz); do tar -zxf $f; rm $f; done'

RUN chef-solo -c /chef/config.rb -j /chef/attributes.json

CMD /usr/sbin/service apache2 start && sleep infinity
```

Copies the contents of the working folder into the /chef folder on the image

Moves to the cookbooks folder and downloads the apache2 cookbook and its dependencies as tarballs using Chef's knife utility

Extracts the downloaded tarballs and removes them

Runs the chef command to configure your image. Supplies it with the attributes and config files you already created.

Defines the default command for the image. The sleep infinity command ensures that the container doesn't exit as soon as the service command has finished its work.

You're now ready to build and run the \image:

```
docker build -t chef-example .
docker run -ti -p 8080:80 chef-example
```

If you now navigate to http://localhost:8080, you should see your "Hello World!" message.

> **WARNING** If your Chef build takes a long time and you're using the Docker Hub workflow, the build can time out. If this happens, you can perform the build on a machine you control, pay for a supported service, or break the build steps into smaller chunks so that each individual step in the Dockerfile takes less time to return.

Although this is a trivial example, the benefits of using this approach should be clear. With relatively straightforward configuration files, the details of getting the image into a desired state are taken care of by the configuration management tool. This doesn't mean that you can forget about the details of configuration; changing the values will require you to understand the semantics to ensure you don't break anything. But this approach can save you much time and effort, particularly in projects where you don't need to get into the details too much.

DISCUSSION

The purpose of this technique is to correct a common confusion about the Dockerfile concept, specifically that it's a competitor to other configuration management tools like Chef and Ansible.

What Docker really is (as we say elsewhere in the book) is a *packaging* tool. It allows you to present the results of a build process in a predictable and packaged way. How you choose to build it is up to you. You can use Chef, Puppet, Ansible, Makefiles, shell scripts, or sculpt them by hand.

The reason most people don't use Chef, Puppet, and the like to build images is primarily because Docker images tend to be built as single-purpose and single-process tools. But if you already have configuration scripts to hand, why not re-use them?

7.3   *Small is beautiful*

If you're creating lots of images and sending them hither and thither, the issue of image size will be more likely to arise. Although Docker's use of image layering can help with this, you may have such a panoply of images on your estate that this isn't practical to manage.

In these cases, it can be helpful to have some best practices in your organization related to reducing images to as small a size as possible. In this section we'll show you some of these, and even how a standard utility image can be reduced by an order of magnitude—a much smaller object to fling around your network.

TECHNIQUE 56   Tricks for making an image smaller

Let's say you've been given an image by a third party, and you want to make the image smaller. The simplest approach is to start with an image that works and remove the unnecessary files.

Classic configuration management tools tend not to remove things unless explicitly instructed to do so—instead, they start from a non-working state and add new configurations and files. This leads to *snowflake* systems crafted for a particular purpose, which may look very different from what you'd get if you ran your configuration management tool against a fresh server, especially if the configuration has evolved over time. Courtesy of layering and lightweight images in Docker, you can perform the reverse of this process and experiment with removing things.

PROBLEM

You want to make your images smaller.

SOLUTION

Follow these steps to reduce the size of an image by removing unnecessary packages and doc files:

1 Run the image.
2 Enter the container.
3 Remove unnecessary files.
4 Commit the container as a new image (see technique 15).
5 Flatten the image (see technique 52).

The last two steps have been covered earlier in the book, so we're only going to cover the first three here.

To illustrate how to do this, we're going to take the image created in technique 49 and try to make that image smaller.

First, run up the image as a container:

```
docker run -ti --name smaller --entrypoint /bin/bash \
dockerinpractice/log-cleaner
```

Because this is a Debian-based image, you can start by seeing which packages you might not need and removing them. Run dpkg -l | awk '{print $2}' and you'll get a list of installed packages on the system.

You can then go through those packages running apt-get purge -y package_name on them. If there's a scary message warning you that "You are about to do something potentially harmful," press Return to continue.

Once you've removed all the packages that can safely be removed, you can run these commands to clean up the apt cache:

```
apt-get autoremove
apt-get clean
```

This is a relatively safe way to reduce space in your images.

Further significant savings can be made by removing docs. For example, running rm -rf /usr/share/doc/* /usr/share/man/* /usr/share/info/* will often remove sizable files you'll probably never need. You can take this to the next level by manually running rm on binaries and libraries you don't need.

Another area for rich pickings is the /var folder, which should contain temporary data, or data not essential to the running of programs.

This command will get rid of all files with the .log suffix:

```
find /var | grep '\.log$' | xargs rm -v
```

Now you'll have a much smaller image than you previously had, ready to commit.

DISCUSSION

Using this somewhat manual process, you can get the original dockerinpractice/log-cleaner image down to a few dozen MB quite easily, and even make it smaller if you have the motivation. Remember that due to Docker's layering, you'll need to export and import the image as explained in technique 52; otherwise the image's overall size will include the deleted files.

Technique 59 will show you a much more effective (but risky) way to significantly reduce the size of your images.

> **TIP** An example of the commands described here is maintained at https://github.com/docker-in-practice/log-cleaner-purged, and it can be pulled with Docker from dockerinpractice/log-cleaner-purged.

TECHNIQUE 57 Tiny Docker images with BusyBox and Alpine

Small, usable OSs that can be embedded onto a low-power or cheap computer have existed since Linux began. Fortunately, the efforts of these projects have been repurposed to produce small Docker images for use where image size is important.

PROBLEM
You want a small, functional image.

SOLUTION
Use a small base image, like BusyBox or Alpine, when building your own images.

This is another area where the state of the art is fast changing. The two popular choices for minimal Linux base images are BusyBox and Alpine, and each has different characteristics.

If lean but useful is your aim, BusyBox may fit the bill. If you start up a BusyBox image with the following command, something surprising happens:

```
$ docker run -ti busybox /bin/bash
exec: "/bin/bash": stat /bin/bash: no such file or directory2015/02/23 >
09:55:38 Error response from daemon: Cannot start container >
73f45e34145647cd1996ae29d8028e7b06d514d0d32dec9a68ce9428446faa19: exec: >
"/bin/bash": stat /bin/bash: no such file or directory
```

BusyBox is so lean it has no bash! Instead it uses ash, which is a posix-compliant shell—effectively a limited version of more advanced shells such as bash and ksh.

```
$ docker run -ti busybox /bin/ash
/ #
```

As the result of many decisions like this, the BusyBox image weighs in at under 2.5 MB.

> **WARNING** BusyBox can contain some other nasty surprises. The tar version, for example, will have difficulty untarring TAR files created with GNU tar.

This is great if you want to write a small script that only requires simple tools, but if you want to run anything else you'll have to install it yourself. BusyBox comes with no package management.

Other maintainers have added package management functionality to BusyBox. For example, progrium/busybox might not be the smallest BusyBox container (it's currently a little under 5 MB), but it has opkg, which means you can easily install other common packages while keeping the image size to an absolute minimum. If you're missing bash, for example, you can install it like this:

```
$ docker run -ti progrium/busybox /bin/ash
/ # opkg-install bash > /dev/null
/ # bash
bash-4.3#
```

When committed, this results in a 6 MB image.

Another interesting Docker image (which has become a Docker standard for small images) is gliderlabs/alpine. It's similar to BusyBox but has a more extensive range of packages that you can browse at https://pkgs.alpinelinux.org/packages.

The packages are designed to be lean on install. To take a concrete example, here's a Dockerfile that results in an image that's just over a quarter of a gigabyte.

Listing 7.17   Ubuntu plus mysql-client

```
FROM ubuntu:14.04
RUN apt-get update -q \
&& DEBIAN_FRONTEND=noninteractive apt-get install -qy mysql-client \
&& apt-get clean && rm -rf /var/lib/apt
ENTRYPOINT ["mysql"]
```

> **TIP**   The DEBIAN_FRONTEND=noninteractive before the apt-get install ensures that the install doesn't prompt for any input during the install. As you can't easily engineer responses to questions when running commands, this is often useful in Dockerfiles.

By contrast, the following listing results in an image that's a little over 36 MB.

Listing 7.18   Alpine plus `mysql-client`

```
FROM gliderlabs/alpine:3.6
RUN apk-install mysql-client
ENTRYPOINT ["mysql"]
```

DISCUSSION

This is an area in which there's been much development over the past couple of years. The Alpine base image has edged out BusyBox to become something of a Docker standard, with the help of some backing from Docker Inc. itself.

In addition, the other more "standard" base images have been on diets themselves. The Debian image stands at roughly 100 MB as we prepare the second edition of this book—much less than it originally was.

One point worth referring to here is that there's a lot of discussion around reducing the size of images, or using smaller base images, when this is not something that needs to be addressed. Remember that it's often best to spend time and effort overcoming existing bottlenecks than achieving theoretical benefits that may turn out to give little bang for your buck.

TECHNIQUE 58   **The Go model of minimal containers**

Although it can be illuminating to winnow down your working containers by removing redundant files, there's another option—compiling minimal binaries without dependencies.

Doing this radically simplifies the task of configuration management—if there's only one file to deploy and no packages are required, a significant amount of configuration management tooling becomes redundant.

PROBLEM

You want to build binary Docker images with no external dependencies.

SOLUTION

Build a statically linked binary—one that will not try to load any system libraries when it starts running.

To demonstrate how this can be useful, we'll first create a small Hello World image with a small C program. Then we'll go on to show you how to do something equivalent for a more useful application.

A MINIMAL HELLO WORLD BINARY

To create the minimal Hello World binary, first create a new directory and a Dockerfile, as shown in the following listing.

Listing 7.19   Hello Dockerfile

The gcc image is an image designed for compiling.

Creates a simple one-line C program

```
FROM gcc
 RUN echo 'int main() { puts("Hello world!"); }' > hi.c
 RUN gcc -static hi.c -w -o hi
```

Compiles the program with the -static flag, and suppresses warnings with -w

The preceding Dockerfile compiles a simple Hello World program without dependencies. You can now build it and extract that binary from the container, as shown in the next listing.

Listing 7.20   Extracting the binary from the image

Copies the "hi" binary using the docker cp command

Builds the image containing the statically linked "hi" binary

Runs the image with a trivial command in order to copy out the binary

```
$ docker build -t hello_build .
 $ docker run --name hello hello_build /bin/true
 $ docker cp hello:/hi hi
 $ docker rm hello
 hello
 $ docker rmi hello_build
 Deleted: 6afcbf3a650d9d3a67c8d67c05a383e7602baecc9986854ef3e5b9c0069ae9f2
 $ mkdir -p new_folder
```

Cleanup: you don't need these anymore

Makes a new folder called "new_folder"

```
$ mv hi new_folder
$ cd new_folder
```

Moves the "hi" binary into this folder

Changes directory into this new folder

You now have a statically built binary in a fresh directory and have moved into it.

Now create another Dockerfile, as shown in the next listing.

Listing 7.21   Minimal Hello Dockerfile

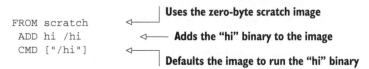

```
FROM scratch
 ADD hi /hi
 CMD ["/hi"]
```

Uses the zero-byte scratch image

Adds the "hi" binary to the image

Defaults the image to run the "hi" binary

Build and run it as shown in the following listing.

Listing 7.22   Creating the minimal container

```
$ docker build -t hello_world .
Sending build context to Docker daemon 931.3 kB
Sending build context to Docker daemon
Step 0 : FROM scratch
 --->
Step 1 : ADD hi /hi
 ---> 2fe834f724f8
Removing intermediate container 01f73ea277fb
Step 2 : ENTRYPOINT /hi
 ---> Running in 045e32673c7f
 ---> 5f8802ae5443
Removing intermediate container 045e32673c7f
Successfully built 5f8802ae5443
$ docker run hello_world
Hello world!
$ docker images | grep hello_world
hello_world     latest     5f8802ae5443    24 seconds ago   928.3 kB
```

The image builds, runs, and weighs in at under 1 MB.

A MINIMAL GO WEB SERVER IMAGE

That was a relatively trivial example, but you can apply the same principle to programs built in Go. An interesting feature of the Go language is that it's relatively easy to build such static binaries.

To demonstrate this ability, we created a simple web server in Go whose code is available at https://github.com/docker-in-practice/go-web-server.

The Dockerfile for building this simple web server is shown in the following listing.

Listing 7.23   Dockerfile to statically compile a Go web server

This build is known to work against this version number of the golang image; if the build fails, it may be that this version is no longer available.

"go get" retrieves the source code from the URL provided and compiles it locally. The CGO_ENABLED environment variable is set to 0 to prevent cross-compilation.

```
FROM golang:1.4.2
 RUN CGO_ENABLED=0 go get \
 -a -ldflags '-s' –installsuffix cgo \
 github.com/docker-in-practice/go-web-server \
 CMD ["cat","/go/bin/go-web-server"]
```

Defaults the resulting image to output the executable

The Go web server source code repository

Sets a number of miscellaneous flags to the Go compiler to ensure static compilation and reduce size

If you save this Dockerfile into an empty directory and build it, you'll now have an image containing the program. Because you specified the default command of the image to output the executable content, you now just need to run the image and send the output to a file on your host, as the following listing shows.

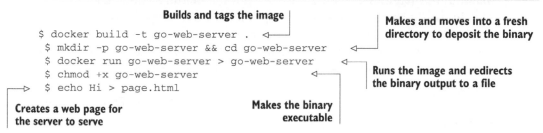

Listing 7.24   Getting the Go web server from the image

Builds and tags the image

Makes and moves into a fresh directory to deposit the binary

```
$ docker build -t go-web-server .
 $ mkdir -p go-web-server && cd go-web-server
 $ docker run go-web-server > go-web-server
 $ chmod +x go-web-server
 $ echo Hi > page.html
```

Creates a web page for the server to serve

Makes the binary executable

Runs the image and redirects the binary output to a file

Now, as with the "hi" binary, you have a binary with no library dependencies or need to access the filesystem. We're therefore going to create a Dockerfile from the zero-byte scratch image and add the binary to it, as before.

Listing 7.25   Go web server Dockerfile

Adds the static binary to the image

Adds a page to serve from the web server

```
FROM scratch
ADD go-web-server /go-web-server
 ADD page.html /page.html
 ENTRYPOINT ["/go-web-server"]
```

Makes the binary the default program run by the image

Now build it and run the image. The resulting image is a little over 4 MB in size.

Listing 7.26   Building and running the Go web server image

```
$ docker build -t go-web-server .
$ docker images | grep go-web-server
go-web-server    latest    de1187ee87f3   3 seconds ago    4.156 MB
$ docker run -p 8080:8080 go-web-server -port 8080
```

You can access it on http://localhost:8080. If the port is already in use, you can replace the 8080s in the preceding code with a port of your choice.

DISCUSSION

If you can bundle applications into one binary, why bother with Docker at all? You can move the binary around, run multiple copies, and so on.

You can do so if you want, but you'd lose the following:

- All the container management tools in the Docker ecosystem
- The metadata within the Docker images that document significant application information, such as ports, volumes, and labels
- The isolation that gives Docker its operational power

As a concrete example, etcd is a static binary by default, but when we examine it in technique 74 we'll demonstrate it inside a container to make it easier to see how the same process would work across multiple machines and ease deployment.

TECHNIQUE 59   **Using inotifywait to slim containers**

We're now going to take slimming our containers to the next level by using a nifty tool that tells us what files are being referenced when we run a container.

This could be called the nuclear option, as it can be quite risky to implement on production. But it can be an instructive means of learning about your system, even if you don't follow through with using it for real—a crucial part of configuration management is understanding what your application requires to operate correctly.

PROBLEM

You want to reduce your container to the smallest possible set of files and permissions.

SOLUTION

Monitor which files are accessed by your program with inotify, and then remove any that seem unused.

At a high level, you need to know what files are being accessed when you run a command in a container. If you remove all the other files on the container filesystem, you'll theoretically still have everything you need.

In this walkthrough, we're going to use the log-cleaner-purged image from technique 56. You'll install inotify-tools, and then run `inotifywait` to get a report on which files were accessed. You'll then run a simulation of the image's entrypoint (the log_clean script). Then, using the file report generated, you'll remove any file that hasn't been accessed.

Listing 7.27   Performing manual install steps while monitoring with inotifywait

Overrides the default entrypoint for this image

Gives the container a name you can refer to later

```
[host]$ docker run -ti --entrypoint /bin/bash \
  --name reduce dockerinpractice/log-cleaner-purged
  $ apt-get update && apt-get install -y inotify-tools
  $ inotifywait -r -d -o /tmp/inotifywaitout.txt \
```

Installs the inotify-tools package

Runs inotifywait in recursive (-r) and daemon (-d) modes to get a list of accessed files in the outfile (specified with the -o flag)

Specifies the folders you're interested in watching. Note that you don't watch /tmp because /tmp/inotifywaitout.txt would cause an infinite loop if it were itself watched.

Calls inotifywait again on subfolders of the /usr folder. There are too many files in the /usr folder for inotifywait to handle, so you need to specify each one separately.

```
/bin /etc /lib /sbin /var
inotifywait[115]: Setting up watches.  Beware: since -r was given, this >
may take a while!
inotifywait[115]: Watches established.
$ inotifywait -r -d -o /tmp/inotifywaitout.txt /usr/bin /usr/games \
  /usr/include /usr/lib /usr/local /usr/sbin /usr/share /usr/src
inotifywait[118]: Setting up watches.  Beware: since -r was given, this >
may take a while!
inotifywait[118]: Watches established.
$ sleep 5
$ cp /usr/bin/clean_log /tmp/clean_log
$ rm /tmp/clean_log
$ bash
$ echo "Cleaning logs over 0 days old"
$ find /log_dir -ctime "0" -name '*log' -exec rm {} \;
$ awk '{print $1$3}' /tmp/inotifywaitout.txt | sort -u > \
/tmp/inotify.txt
$ comm -2 -3 \
<(find /bin /etc /lib /sbin /var /usr -type f | sort) \
<(cat /tmp/inotify.txt) > /tmp/candidates.txt
$ cat /tmp/candidates.txt | xargs rm
$ exit
$ exit
```

Sleeps to give inotifywait a decent amount of time to start up

Accesses the script file you'll need to use, as well as the rm command, to make sure they're marked as being used.

Starts a bash shell, as the script does, and runs the commands the script would. Note that this will fail, because we didn't mount any actual log folder from the host.

Uses the awk utility to generate a list of filenames from the output of the inotifywait log, and turns it into a unique and sorted list

Removes all files not accessed

Uses the comm utility to output a list of files on the filesystem that were not accessed

Exits the bash shell you started and then the container itself

At this point you've

- Placed a watch on files to see what files are being accessed
- Run all the commands to simulate the running of the script
- Run commands to ensure you access the script you'll definitely need, and the rm utility
- Gained a list of all files not accessed during the run
- Removed all the non-accessed files

Now you can flatten this container (see technique 52) to create a new image and test that it still works.

Listing 7.28 Flattening the image and running it

```
$ ID=$(docker export reduce | docker import -)
$ docker tag $ID smaller
$ docker images | grep smaller
```

Flattens the image and puts the ID into the variable "ID"

Tags the newly flattened image as "smaller"

The image is now less than 10% of its previous size.

```
smaller  latest  2af3bde3836a  18 minutes ago  6.378 MB
 $ mkdir -p /tmp/tmp
 $ touch /tmp/tmp/a.log
 $ docker run -v /tmp/tmp:/log_dir smaller \
/usr/bin/clean_log 0
Cleaning logs over 0 days old
 $ ls /tmp/tmp/a.log
  ls: cannot access /tmp/tmp/a.log: No such file or directory
```

Creates a new folder and file to simulate a log directory for testing

Runs the newly created image over the test directory and checks that the file created has been removed

We reduced the size of this image from 96 MB to around 6.5 MB, and it still appears to work. Quite a saving!

> **WARNING**   This technique, like overclocking your CPU, is not an optimization for the unwary. This particular example works well because it's an application that's quite limited in scope, but your mission-critical business application is likely to be more complex and dynamic in how it accesses files. You could easily remove a file that wasn't accessed on your run, but that is needed at some other point.

If you're a little nervous of potentially breaking your image by removing files you'll need later, you can use the /tmp/candidates.txt file to get a list of the biggest files that were untouched, like this:

```
cat /tmp/candidates.txt | xargs wc -c | sort -n | tail
```

You can then remove the larger files that you're sure won't be needed by your application. There can be big wins here too.

DISCUSSION

Although this technique has been presented as a Docker technique, it falls into the category of "generally useful" techniques that can be applied in other contexts. It's particularly useful when debugging processes where you don't know quite what's happening, and you want to see which files are being referenced. strace is another option for doing this, but inotifywait is in some ways an easier tool to use for this purpose.

   This general approach is also used as one avenue of attack in technique 97 in the context of reducing the attack surface of a container.

TECHNIQUE 60   **Big can be beautiful**

Although this section is about keeping images small, it's worth remembering that small is not necessarily better. As we'll discuss, a relatively large monolithic image can be more efficient than a small one.

PROBLEM

You want to reduce disk space use and network bandwidth due to Docker images.

SOLUTION

Create a universal, large, monolithic base image for your organization.

It's paradoxical, but a large monolithic image could save you disk space and network bandwidth.

Recall that Docker uses a copy-on-write mechanism when its containers are running. This means that you could have hundreds of Ubuntu containers running, but only a small amount of additional disk space is used for each container started.

If you have lots of different, smaller images on your Docker server, as in figure 7.1, more disk space may be used than if you have one larger monolithic image with everything you need in it.

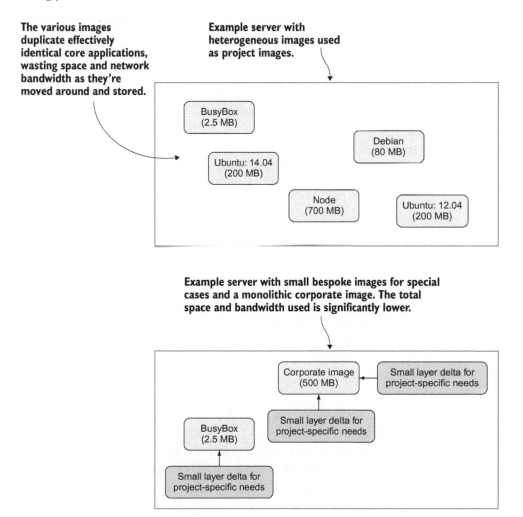

The various images duplicate effectively identical core applications, wasting space and network bandwidth as they're moved around and stored.

Example server with heterogeneous images used as project images.

BusyBox (2.5 MB)

Debian (80 MB)

Ubuntu: 14.04 (200 MB)

Node (700 MB)

Ubuntu: 12.04 (200 MB)

Example server with small bespoke images for special cases and a monolithic corporate image. The total space and bandwidth used is significantly lower.

Corporate image (500 MB)

Small layer delta for project-specific needs

Small layer delta for project-specific needs

BusyBox (2.5 MB)

Small layer delta for project-specific needs

Figure 7.1   Many small base images vs. fewer large base images

You may be reminded of the principle of a shared library. A shared library can be loaded by multiple applications at once, reducing the amount of disk and memory needed to run the required programs. In the same way, a shared base image for your organization can save space, as it only needs to be downloaded once and should contain everything you need. Programs and libraries previously required in multiple images are now only required once.

In addition, there can be other benefits of sharing a monolithic, centrally managed image across teams. The maintenance of this image can be centralized, improvements can be shared, and issues with the build need only be solved once.

If you're going to adopt this technique, here are some things to watch out for:

- The base image should be reliable first. If it doesn't behave consistently, the users will avoid using it.
- Changes to the base image must be tracked somewhere that's visible so that users can debug problems themselves.
- Regression tests are essential to reduce confusion when updating the vanilla image.
- Be careful about what you add to the base—once it's in the base image, it's hard to remove, and the image can bloat fast.

DISCUSSION

We used this technique to great effect in our 600-strong development company. A monthly build of core applications was bundled into a large image and published on the internal Docker registry. Teams would build on the so-called "vanilla" corporate image by default, and create bespoke layers if necessary on top of that.

It's worth taking a look at technique 12 for some additional details on monolithic containers—particularly for the mention of the phusion/base image Docker image, an image designed with running multiple processes in mind.

Summary

- ENTRYPOINT is another way to start Docker containers that allows runtime parameters to be configured.
- Flattening images can be used to prevent the leakage of secrets from your build via your image's layers.
- Packages foreign to your chosen base image's distribution can be integrated using Alien.
- Traditional build tools such as make, as well as modern ones like Chef, still have their place in the Docker world.
- Docker images can be reduced using smaller base images, using languages appropriate to the task, or removing unnecessary files.
- It's worth considering whether the size of your image is the most important challenge to tackle.

Part 3

Docker and DevOps

Now you're ready to take Docker beyond your development environment and start using it in other phases of software delivery. Build and testing automation are cornerstones of the DevOps movement. We'll demonstrate Docker's power through automation of the software delivery lifecycle, deployments, and realistic environment testing.

Chapter 8 will show various techniques for delivering and improving continuous integration, making your software deliveries both more reliable and scalable.

Chapter 9 focuses on continuous delivery. We'll explain what continuous delivery is, and look at ways in which Docker can be used to improve this aspect of your development pipeline.

Chapter 10 shows how you can harness Docker's networking model to full effect, creating multicontainer services, simulating realistic networks, and creating networks on demand.

This part takes you from development all the way to the point where you can think about running Docker in production.

Continuous integration: Speeding up your development pipeline

8

This chapter covers

- Using the Docker Hub workflow as a CI tool
- Speeding up your I/O-heavy builds
- Using Selenium for automated testing
- Running Jenkins within Docker
- Using Docker as a Jenkins slave
- Scaling your available compute with your dev team

In this chapter we're going to look at various techniques that will use Docker to enable and improve your continuous integration (CI) efforts.

By now you should understand how Docker is well suited to being used for automation. Its lightweight nature, and the power it gives you to port environments from one place to another, can make it a key enabler of CI. We've found the techniques in this chapter to be invaluable in making a CI process feasible within a business.

By the end of this chapter you'll understand how Docker can make the process of CI faster, more stable, and reproducible. By using test tools such as Selenium, and expanding your build capacity with the Jenkins Swarm plugin, you'll see how Docker can help you get even more out of your CI process.

> **NOTE** In case you don't know, *continuous integration* is a software lifecycle strategy used to speed up the development pipeline. By automatically rerunning tests every time a significant change is made to the codebase, you get faster and more stable deliveries because there's a base level of stability in the software being delivered.

8.1 *Docker Hub automated builds*

The Docker Hub automated build feature was mentioned in technique 10, though we didn't go into any detail on it. In short, if you point to a Git repository containing a Dockerfile, the Docker Hub will handle the process of building the image and making it available to download. An image rebuild will be triggered on any changes in the Git repository, making this quite useful as part of a CI process.

TECHNIQUE 61   Using the Docker Hub workflow

This technique will introduce you to the Docker Hub workflow, which enables you to trigger rebuilds of your images

> **NOTE** For this section, you'll need an account on docker.com linked to either a GitHub or a Bitbucket account. If you don't already have these set up and linked, instructions are available from the homepages of github.com and bitbucket.org.

PROBLEM

You want to automatically test and push changes to your image when the code changes.

SOLUTION

Set up a Docker Hub repository and link it to your code.

Although the Docker Hub build isn't complicated, a number of steps are required:

1 Create your repository on GitHub or BitBucket.
2 Clone the new Git repository.
3 Add code to your Git repository.
4 Commit the source.
5 Push the Git repository.
6 Create a new repository on the Docker Hub.
7 Link the Docker Hub repository to the Git repository.
8 Wait for the Docker Hub build to complete.
9 Commit and push a change to the source.
10 Wait for the second Docker Hub build to complete.

NOTE Both Git and Docker use the term "repository" to refer to a project. This can confuse people. A Git repository and a Docker repository are not the same thing, even though here we're linking the two types of repositories.

CREATE YOUR REPOSITORY ON GITHUB OR BITBUCKET

Create a new repository on GitHub or Bitbucket. You can give it any name you want.

CLONE THE NEW GIT REPOSITORY

Clone your new Git repository to your host machine. The command for this will be available from the Git project's homepage.

Change directory into this repository.

ADD CODE TO YOUR GIT REPOSITORY

Now you need to add code to the project.

You can add any Dockerfile you like, but the following listing shows an example known to work. It consists of two files representing a simple dev tools environment. It installs some preferred utilities and outputs the bash version you have.

Listing 8.1   Dockerfile—simple dev tools container Dockerfile

```
FROM ubuntu:14.04
ENV DEBIAN_FRONTEND noninteractive
RUN apt-get update
RUN apt-get install -y curl
 RUN apt-get install -y nmap
 RUN apt-get install -y socat
 RUN apt-get install -y openssh-client
 RUN apt-get install -y openssl
 RUN apt-get install -y iotop                    Installs useful
 RUN apt-get install -y strace                   packages
 RUN apt-get install -y tcpdump
 RUN apt-get install -y lsof
 RUN apt-get install -y inotify-tools
 RUN apt-get install -y sysstat
 RUN apt-get install -y build-essential          Adds a line to the
                                                 root's bashrc to
 RUN echo "source /root/bash_extra" >> /root/.bashrc    source bash_extra
ADD bash_extra /root/bash_extra
CMD ["/bin/bash"]        Adds bash_extra from the
                         source to the container
```

Now you'll need to add the bash_extra file you referenced and give it the following content:

```
bash --version
```

This file is just for illustration. It shows that you can create a bash file that's sourced on startup. In this case it displays the version of bash you're using in your shell, but it could contain all manner of things that set up your shell to your preferred state.

COMMIT THE SOURCE

To commit your source code source, use this command:

```
git commit -am "Initial commit"
```

PUSH THE GIT REPOSITORY

Now you can push the source to the Git server with this command:

```
git push origin master
```

CREATE A NEW REPOSITORY ON THE DOCKER HUB

Next you need to create a repository for this project on the Docker Hub. Go to https://hub.docker.com and ensure you're logged in. Then click on Create and choose Create Automated Build.

For the first time only, you'll need to go through the account-linking process. You'll see a prompt to link your account to a hosted Git service. Select your service and follow the instructions to link your account. You may be offered the choice to give full or more limited access to Docker Inc. for the integration. If you opt for the more limited access, you should read the official documentation for your specific service to identify what extra work you might need to do during the rest of the steps.

LINK THE DOCKER HUB REPOSITORY TO THE GIT REPOSITORY

You'll see a screen with a choice of Git services. Pick the source code service you use (GitHub or Bitbucket) and select your new repository from the provided list.

You'll see a page with options for the build configuration. You can leave the defaults and click Create Repository at the bottom.

WAIT FOR THE DOCKER HUB BUILD TO COMPLETE

You'll see a page with a message explaining that the link worked. Click on the Build Details link.

Next, you'll see a page that shows the details of the builds. Under Builds History, there will be an entry for this first build. If you don't see anything listed, you may need to click the button to trigger the build manually. The Status field next to the build ID will show Pending, Finished, Building, or Error. If all is well, you'll see one of the first three. If you see Error, something has gone wrong and you'll need to click on the build ID to see what the error was.

> **NOTE**   It can take a while for the build to start, so seeing Pending for some time while waiting is perfectly normal.

Click Refresh periodically until you see that the build has completed. Once it's complete, you can pull the image with the `docker pull` command listed on the top of the same page.

COMMIT AND PUSH A CHANGE TO THE SOURCE

Now you decide that you want more information about your environment when you log in, so you want to output the details of the distribution you're running in. To achieve this, add these lines to your bash_extra file so that it now looks like this:

```
bash --version
cat /etc/issue
```

Then commit and push as in steps 4 and 5.

WAIT FOR THE SECOND DOCKER HUB BUILD TO COMPLETE

If you return to the build page, a new line should show up under the Builds History section, and you can follow this build as in step 8.

> TIP   You'll be emailed if there's an error with your build (no email if all is OK), so once you're used to this workflow, you'll only need to check up on it if you receive an email.

You can now use the Docker Hub workflow. You'll quickly get used to this framework and find it invaluable for keeping your builds up to date and reducing the cognitive load of rebuilding Dockerfiles by hand.

DISCUSSION

Because the Docker Hub is the canonical source of images, pushing there during your CI process can make some things more straightforward (distributing images to third parties, for one). Not having to run the build process yourself is easier and gives you some additional benefits, like a checkmark against the listing on the Docker Hub indicating that the build was performed on a trusted server.

Having this additional confidence in your builds helps you comply with the *Docker contract* in technique 70—in technique 113 we'll look at how specific machines can sometimes affect Docker builds, so using a completely independent system is good for increasing confidence in the final results.

8.2   *More efficient builds*

CI implies a more frequent rebuilding of your software and tests. Although Docker makes delivering CI easier, the next problem you may bump into is the resulting increased load on your compute resources.

We'll look at ways to alleviate this pressure in terms of disk I/O, network bandwidth, and automated testing.

TECHNIQUE 62   Speeding up I/O-intensive builds with eatmydata

Because Docker is a great fit for automated building, you'll likely perform a lot of disk-I/O-intensive builds as time goes on. Jenkins jobs, database rebuild scripts, and large code checkouts will all hit your disks hard. In these cases, you'll be grateful for any speed increases you can get, both to save time and to minimize the many overheads that result from resource contention.

This technique has been shown to give up to a 1:3 speed increase, and our experience backs this up. This is not to be sniffed at!

PROBLEM

You want to speed up your I/O-intensive builds.

SOLUTION

eatmydata is a program that takes your system calls to write data and makes them super-fast by bypassing work required to persist those changes. This entails some lack of safety, so it's not recommended for normal use, but it's quite useful for environments not designed to persist, such as in testing.

INSTALLING EATMYDATA

To install eatmydata in your container, you have a number of options:

- If you're running a deb-based distribution, you can `apt-get install` it.
- If you're running an rpm-based distribution, you'll be able to `rpm --install` it by searching for it on the web and downloading it. Websites such as rpmfind.net are a good place to start.
- As a last resort, and if you have a compiler installed, you can download and compile it directly as shown in the next listing.

Listing 8.2   Compiling and installing eatmydata

If this version doesn't download, check on the website to see whether it's been updated to a number later than 105.

Flamingspork.com is the website of the maintainer.

```
$ url=https://www.flamingspork.com/projects/libeatmydata
  /libeatmydata-105.tar.gz
$ wget -qO- $url | tar -zxf - && cd libeatmydata-105
$ ./configure --prefix=/usr
$ make
$ sudo make install
```

Builds the eatmydata executable

Change the prefix directory if you want the eatmydata executable to be installed somewhere other than /usr/bin.

Installs the software; this step requires root privileges

USING EATMYDATA

Once libeatmydata is installed on your image (either from a package or from source), run the eatmydata wrapper script before any command, to take advantage of it:

```
docker run -d mybuildautomation eatmydata /run_tests.sh
```

Figure 8.1 shows at a high level how eatmydata saves you processing time.

> **WARNING**   eatmydata skips the steps to guarantee that data is safely written to disk, so there's a risk that data will not yet be on disk when the program thinks it is. For test runs, this usually doesn't matter, because the data is disposable, but don't use eatmydata to speed up any kind of environment where the data matters!

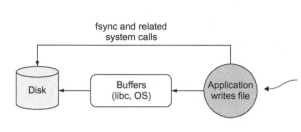

Normally there are two ways to ensure a file written by an application is stored on the disk. First, tell the OS that a write has to be made; it will cache the data until it's ready to write to disk. Second, force the write to disk using various system call combinations; the command won't return until the file is stored. Applications that care about data integrity tend to use the forcing system calls.

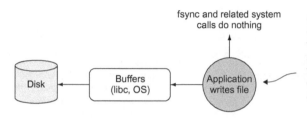

eatmydata ensures that forcing system calls do nothing. Applications that use these calls will then run more quickly, as they don't have to stop and wait for the write to disk. If there's a crash, data may be in an inconsistent state and unrecoverable.

Figure 8.1 Application writes to disk without (top) and with (bottom) eatmydata

Be aware that running eatmydata docker run … to start a Docker container, perhaps after installing eatmydata on your host or mounting the Docker socket, will not have the effect you may expect due to the Docker client/server architecture outlined in chapter 2. Instead, you need to install eatmydata inside each individual container you want to use it in.

DISCUSSION

Although precise use cases will vary, one place you should immediately be able to apply this is in technique 68. It's very rare for the data integrity on a CI job to matter—you're usually just interested in success or failure, and the logs in the case of failure.

One other relevant technique is technique 77. A database is one place where data integrity really does matter a lot (any popular one will be designed to not lose data in the case of machine power loss), but if you're just running some tests or experiments, it's overhead that you don't need.

TECHNIQUE 63 **Setting up a package cache for faster builds**

As Docker lends itself to frequent rebuilding of services for development, testing, and production, you can quickly get to a point where you're repeatedly hitting the network a lot. One major cause is downloading package files from the internet. This can be a slow (and costly) overhead, even on a single machine. This technique shows you how to set up a local cache for your package downloads, covering apt and yum.

PROBLEM

You want to speed up your builds by reducing network I/O.

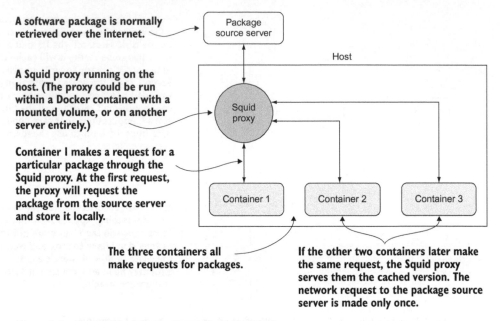

A software package is normally retrieved over the internet.

Package source server

Host

A Squid proxy running on the host. (The proxy could be run within a Docker container with a mounted volume, or on another server entirely.)

Squid proxy

Container 1 makes a request for a particular package through the Squid proxy. At the first request, the proxy will request the package from the source server and store it locally.

Container 1   Container 2   Container 3

The three containers all make requests for packages.

If the other two containers later make the same request, the Squid proxy serves them the cached version. The network request to the package source server is made only once.

Figure 8.2   Using a Squid proxy to cache packages

SOLUTION

Install a Squid proxy for your package manager. Figure 8.2 illustrates how this technique works.

Because the calls for packages go to the local Squid proxy first, and are only requested over the internet the first time, there should only be one request over the internet for each package. If you have hundreds of containers all pulling down the same large packages from the internet, this can save you a lot of time and money.

> **NOTE** You may have network configuration issues when setting this up on your host. Advice is given in the following sections to determine whether this is the case, but if you're unsure how to proceed, you may need to seek help from a friendly network admin.

DEBIAN

For Debian (otherwise known as apt or .deb) packages, the setup is simpler because there is a prepackaged version.

On your Debian-based host run this command:

```
sudo apt-get install squid-deb-proxy
```

Ensure that the service is started by telneting to port 8000:

```
$ telnet localhost 8000
Trying ::1...
Connected to localhost.
Escape character is '^]'.
```

Press Ctrl-] followed by Ctrl-d to quit if you see the preceding output. If you don't see this output, then Squid has either not installed properly or it has installed on a non-standard port.

To set up your container to use this proxy, we've provided the following example Dockerfile. Bear in mind that the IP address of the host, from the point of view of the container, may change from run to run. For this reason, you may want to convert this Dockerfile to a script to be run from within the container before installing new software.

Listing 8.3 Configuring a Debian image to use an apt proxy

> To determine the host's IP address from the point of view of the container, runs the route command and uses awk to extract the relevant IP address from the output (see technique 67).

Ensures the route tool is installed

```
FROM debian
RUN apt-get update -y && apt-get install net-tools
RUN echo "Acquire::http::Proxy \"http://$( \
route -n | awk '/^0.0.0.0/ {print $2}' \
):8000\";" \
> /etc/apt/apt.conf.d/30proxy
RUN echo "Acquire::http::Proxy::ppa.launchpad.net  DIRECT;" >> \
    /etc/apt/apt.conf.d/30proxy
CMD ["/bin/bash"]
```

Port 8000 is used to connect to the Squid proxy on the host machine.

> The echoed lines with the appropriate IP address and configuration are added to apt's proxy configuration file.

YUM

On the host, ensure Squid is installed by installing the squid package with your package manager.

Then you'll need to change the Squid configuration to create a larger cache space. Open up the /etc/squid/squid.conf file and replace the commented line beginning with #cache_dir ufs /var/spool/squid with this: cache_dir ufs /var/spool/squid 10000 16 256. This creates a space of 10,000 MB, which should be sufficient.

Ensure the service is started by telneting to port 3128:

```
$ telnet localhost 3128
Trying ::1...
Connected to localhost.
Escape character is '^]'.
```

Press Ctrl-] followed by Ctrl-d to quit if you see the preceding output. If you don't see this output, then Squid has either not installed properly or has installed on a nonstandard port.

To set up your container to use this proxy, we've provided the following example Dockerfile. Bear in mind that the IP address of the host, from the point of view of the container, may change from run to run. You may want to convert this Dockerfile to a script to be run from within the container before installing new software.

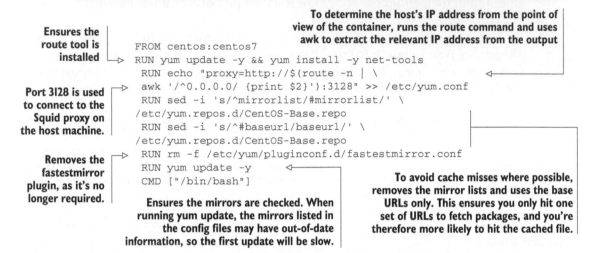

Listing 8.4   Configuring a CentOS image to use a yum proxy

To determine the host's IP address from the point of view of the container, runs the route command and uses awk to extract the relevant IP address from the output

Ensures the route tool is installed

```
FROM centos:centos7
RUN yum update -y && yum install -y net-tools
RUN echo "proxy=http://$(route -n | \
awk '/^0.0.0.0/ {print $2}'):3128" >> /etc/yum.conf
RUN sed -i 's/^mirrorlist/#mirrorlist/' \
/etc/yum.repos.d/CentOS-Base.repo
RUN sed -i 's/^#baseurl/baseurl/' \
/etc/yum.repos.d/CentOS-Base.repo
RUN rm -f /etc/yum/pluginconf.d/fastestmirror.conf
RUN yum update -y
CMD ["/bin/bash"]
```

Port 3128 is used to connect to the Squid proxy on the host machine.

Removes the fastestmirror plugin, as it's no longer required.

Ensures the mirrors are checked. When running yum update, the mirrors listed in the config files may have out-of-date information, so the first update will be slow.

To avoid cache misses where possible, removes the mirror lists and uses the base URLs only. This ensures you only hit one set of URLs to fetch packages, and you're therefore more likely to hit the cached file.

If you set up two containers this way and install the same large package on both, one after the other, you should notice that the second installation downloads its prerequisites much quicker than the first.

DISCUSSION

You may have observed that you can run the Squid proxy on a container rather than on the host. That option wasn't shown here to keep the explanation simple (in some cases, more steps are required to make Squid work within a container). You can read more about this, along with how to make containers automatically use the proxy, at https://github.com/jpetazzo/squid-in-a-can.

TECHNIQUE 64   Headless Chrome in a container

Running tests is a crucial part of CI, and most unit test frameworks will run within Docker without any issues. But sometimes more involved testing is called for, from making sure multiple microservices cooperate correctly to ensuring that website frontend functionality still works. Visiting a website frontend requires a browser of some kind, so to solve this problem we need a way to start a browser inside a container, and then to control it programmatically.

PROBLEM

You want to test against the Chrome browser within a container, without needing a GUI.

SOLUTION

Use the Puppeteer Node.js library in an image to automate Chrome actions.

This library is maintained by the Google Chrome development team, and it allows you to write scripts against Chrome for testing purposes. It's "headless," which means you don't need a GUI to work against it.

NOTE This image is also maintained by us on GitHub at https://github.com/ docker-in-practice/docker-puppeteer. It's also accessible as a Docker image with `docker pull dockerinpractice/docker-puppeteer`.

The following listing shows a Dockerfile that will create an image containing all you need to get started with Puppeteer.

Listing 8.5 Puppeteer Dockerfile

```
FROM ubuntu:16.04                                              ◁── Starts with an
 RUN apt-get update -y && apt-get install -y \                      Ubuntu base image
    npm python-software-properties curl git \
    libpangocairo-1.0-0 libx11-xcb1 \
    libxcomposite1 libxcursor1 libxdamage1 \
    libxi6 libxtst6 libnss3 libcups2 libxss1 \              Installs all the software required.
    libxrandr2 libgconf-2-4 libasound2 \                    This is most of the display
    libatk1.0-0 libgtk-3-0 vim gconf-service \              libraries required to get Chrome
    libappindicator1 libc6 libcairo2 libcups2 \             to operate within a container.
    libdbus-1-3 libexpat1 libfontconfig1 libgcc1 \
    libgdk-pixbuf2.0-0 libglib2.0-0 libnspr4 \
    libpango-1.0-0 libstdc++6 libx11-6 libxcb1 \            Installs the Ubuntu
    libxext6 libxfixes3  libxrender1 libxtst6 \             nodejs package
    ca-certificates fonts-liberation lsb-release \
    xdg-utils wget
    RUN curl -sL https://deb.nodesource.com/setup_8.x | bash -
    RUN apt-get install -y nodejs                ◁──         Creates a non-root
    RUN useradd -m puser                      ◁──            user, "puser"
    USER puser                                               (which the library
    RUN mkdir -p /home/puser/node_modules       ◁──         requires to run)
    ENV NODE_PATH /home/puppeteer/node_modules   ◁──
    WORKDIR /home/puser/node_modules                        Sets the NODE_PATH
    RUN npm i webpack            Goes to the Puppeteer code folder   environment
    RUN git clone https://github.com/GoogleChrome/puppeteer  ◁──   variable to the
    WORKDIR /home/puser/node_modules/puppeteer                     node_module folder
    RUN npm i .                ◁── Goes to the Puppeteer examples folder
    WORKDIR /home/puser/node_modules/puppeteer/examples     Sets the current
    RUN perl -p -i -e \                                     working directory to
        "s/puppeteer.launch\(\)/puppeteer.launch({args: ['--no-sandbox']})/" *    the node module path
    CMD echo 'eg: node pdf.js' && bash              ◁──
```

Annotations (left): Sets up the latest nodejs version · Installs webpack (a dependency of Puppeteer) · Clones the Puppeteer module code · Installs the Puppeteer NodeJS library

Annotations (right): Creates a node modules folder · Starts the container with bash, adding a helpful echo command · Adds a no-sandbox argument to the Puppeteer launch arguments, to overcome a security setting when running within a container

---

Build and run this Dockerfile with this command:

```
$ docker build -t puppeteer .
```

Then run it:

```
$ docker run -ti puppeteer
eg: node pdf.js
puser@03b9be05e81d:~/node_modules/puppeteer/examples$
```

You'll be presented with a terminal and the suggestion to run `node pdf.js`.

The pdf.js file contains a simple script that serves as an example of what can be done with the Puppeteer library.

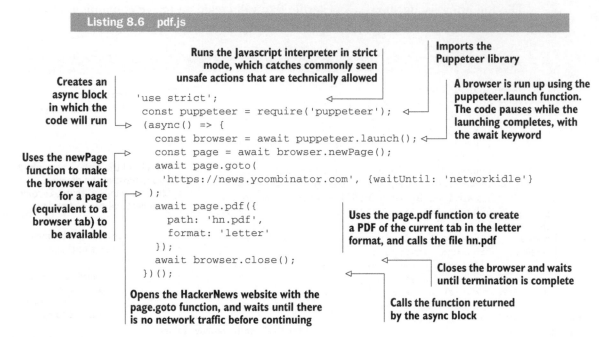

Listing 8.6   pdf.js

Runs the Javascript interpreter in strict mode, which catches commonly seen unsafe actions that are technically allowed

Imports the Puppeteer library

Creates an async block in which the code will run

A browser is run up using the puppeteer.launch function. The code pauses while the launching completes, with the await keyword

Uses the newPage function to make the browser wait for a page (equivalent to a browser tab) to be available

```
'use strict';
const puppeteer = require('puppeteer');
(async() => {
  const browser = await puppeteer.launch();
  const page = await browser.newPage();
  await page.goto(
    'https://news.ycombinator.com', {waitUntil: 'networkidle'}
  );
  await page.pdf({
    path: 'hn.pdf',
    format: 'letter'
  });
  await browser.close();
})();
```

Uses the page.pdf function to create a PDF of the current tab in the letter format, and calls the file hn.pdf

Closes the browser and waits until termination is complete

Opens the HackerNews website with the page.goto function, and waits until there is no network traffic before continuing

Calls the function returned by the async block

A host of options are available to the Puppeteer user beyond this simple example. It's beyond the scope of this technique to explain the Puppeteer API in detail. If you want to look in more depth at the API and adapt this technique, take a look at the Puppeteer API documentation on GitHub: https://github.com/GoogleChrome/puppeteer/blob/master/docs/api.md.

DISCUSSION

This technique shows you how Docker can be used to test against a specific browser.

The next technique broadens this one in two ways: by using Selenium, a popular testing tool that can work against multiple browsers, and combining this with some exploration of X11 to allow you to see a browser running in an graphical window rather than in the headless fashion used in this technique.

TECHNIQUE 65   Running Selenium tests inside Docker

One Docker use case we haven't yet examined in much detail is running graphical applications. In chapter 3, VNC was used to connect to containers during the "save game" approach to development (technique 19), but this can be clunky—windows are contained inside the VNC viewer window, and desktop interaction can be a little limited. We'll explore an alternative to this by demonstrating how you can write graphical tests using Selenium. We'll also show you how this image can be used to run the tests as part of your CI workflow.

PROBLEM

You want to be able to run graphical programs in your CI process while having the option to display those same graphical programs on your own screen.

SOLUTION

Share your X11 server socket to view the programs on your own screen, and use xvfb in your CI process.

No matter what other things you need to do to start your container, you must have the Unix socket that X11 uses to display your windows mounted as a volume inside the container, and you need to indicate which display your windows should be shown on. You can double-check whether these two things are set to their defaults by running the following commands on your host:

```
~ $ ls /tmp/.X11-unix/
X0
~ $ echo $DISPLAY
:0
```

The first command checks that the X11 server Unix socket is running in the location assumed for the rest of the technique. The second command checks the environment variable applications use to find the X11 socket. If your output for these commands doesn't match the output here, you may need to alter some arguments to the commands in this technique.

Now that you've checked your machine setup, you need to get the applications running inside a container to be seamlessly displayed outside the container. The main problem you need to overcome is the security that your computer puts in place to prevent other people from connecting to your machine, taking over your display, and potentially recording your keystrokes. In technique 29 you briefly saw how to do this, but we didn't talk about how it worked or look at any alternatives.

X11 has multiple ways of authenticating a container to use your X socket. First we'll look at the .Xauthority file—it should be present in your home directory. It contains hostnames along with the "secret cookie" each host must use to connect. By giving your Docker container the same hostname as your machine and using the same username as outside the container, you can use your existing .Xauthority file.

Listing 8.7   Starting a container with an Xauthority-enabled display

```
$ ls $HOME/.Xauthority
/home/myuser/.Xauthority
$ docker run -e DISPLAY=$DISPLAY -v /tmp/.X11-unix:/tmp/.X11-unix \
    --hostname=$HOSTNAME -v $HOME/.Xauthority:$HOME/.Xauthority \
    -it -e EXTUSER=$USER ubuntu:16.04 bash -c 'useradd $USER && exec bash'
```

The second method of allowing Docker to access the socket is a much blunter instrument and it has security issues, because it disables all the protection X gives you. If nobody has access to your computer, this may be an acceptable solution, but you should always try to use the .Xauthority file first. You can secure yourself again after you try the following steps by running xhost - (though this will lock out your Docker container):

> **Listing 8.8 Starting a container with xhost-enabled display**

```
$ xhost +
access control disabled, clients can connect from any host
$ docker run -e DISPLAY=$DISPLAY -v /tmp/.X11-unix:/tmp/.X11-unix \
    -it ubuntu:16.04 bash
```

The first line in the preceding listing disables all access control to X, and the second runs the container. Note that you don't have to set the hostname or mount anything apart from the X socket.

Once you've started up your container, it's time to check that it works. You can do this by running the following commands if going the .Xauthority route:

```
root@myhost:/# apt-get update && apt-get install -y x11-apps
[...]
root@myhost:/# su - $EXTUSER -c "xeyes"
```

Alternatively you can use these slightly different commands if you're going the xhost route, because you don't need to run the command as a specific user:

```
root@ef351febcee4:/# apt-get update && apt-get install -y x11-apps
[...]
root@ef351febcee4:/# xeyes
```

This will start up a classic application that tests whether X is working—xeyes. You should see the eyes follow your cursor as you move it around the screen. Note that (unlike VNC) the application is integrated into your desktop—if you were to start xeyes multiple times, you'd see multiple windows.

It's time to get started with Selenium. If you've never used it before, it's a tool with the ability to automate browser actions, and it's commonly used to test website code—it needs a graphical display for the browser to run in. Although it's most commonly used with Java, we're going to use Python to allow more interactivity.

The following listing first installs Python, Firefox, and a Python package manager, and then it uses the Python package manager to install the Selenium Python package. It also downloads the "driver" binary that Selenium uses to control Firefox. A Python REPL is then started, and the Selenium library is used to create a Firefox instance.

For simplicity, this will only cover the xhost route—to go the Xauthority route, you'll need to create a home directory for the user so Firefox has somewhere to save its profile settings.

Listing 8.9 Installing the Selenium requirements and starting a browser

```
root@myhost:/# apt-get install -y python2.7 python-pip firefox wget
[...]
root@myhost:/# pip install selenium
Collecting selenium
[...]
Successfully installed selenium-3.5.0
root@myhost:/# url=https://github.com/mozilla/geckodriver/releases/download
➥ /v0.18.0/geckodriver-v0.18.0-linux64.tar.gz
root@myhost:/# wget -qO- $url | tar -C /usr/bin -zxf -
root@myhost:/# python
Python 2.7.6 (default, Mar 22 2014, 22:59:56)
[GCC 4.8.2] on linux2
Type "help", "copyright", "credits" or "license" for more information.
>>> from selenium import webdriver
>>> b = webdriver.Firefox()
```

As you may have noticed, Firefox has launched and appeared on your screen.

You can now experiment with Selenium. An example session running against GitHub follows—you'll need a basic understanding of CSS selectors to understand what's going on here. Note that websites frequently change, so this particular snippet may need modifying to work correctly:

```
>>> b.get('https://github.com/search')
>>> searchselector = '#search_form input[type="text"]'
>>> searchbox = b.find_element_by_css_selector(searchselector)
>>> searchbox.send_keys('docker-in-practice')
>>> searchbox.submit()
>>> import time
>>> time.sleep(2) # wait for page JS to run
>>> usersxpath = '//nav//a[contains(text(), "Users")]'
>>> userslink = b.find_element_by_xpath(usersxpath)
>>> userslink.click()
>>> dlinkselector = '.user-list-info a'
>>> dlink = b.find_elements_by_css_selector(dlinkselector)[0]
>>> dlink.click()
>>> mlinkselector = '.meta-item a'
>>> mlink = b.find_element_by_css_selector(mlinkselector)
>>> mlink.click()
```

The details here aren't important, though you can get an idea of what's going on by switching to Firefox between commands—we're navigating to the docker-in-practice organization on GitHub, and clicking the organization link. The main takeaway is that we're writing commands in Python in our container and seeing them take effect in the Firefox window running inside the container, but visible on the desktop.

This is great for debugging tests you write, but how would you integrate them into a CI pipeline with the same Docker image? A CI server typically doesn't have a graphical display, so you need to make this work without mounting your own X server socket. But Firefox still needs an X server to run on.

There's a useful tool created for situations like this called xvfb, which pretends to have an X server running for applications to use, but it doesn't require a monitor.

To see how this works, we'll install xvfb, commit the container, tag it as selenium, and create a test script:

> **Listing 8.10   Creating a Selenium test script**

```
>>> exit()
root@myhost:/# apt-get install -y xvfb
[...]
root@myhost:/# exit
$ docker commit ef351febcee4 selenium
d1cbfbc76790cae5f4ae95805a8ca4fc4cd1353c72d7a90b90ccfb79de4f2f9b
$ cat > myscript.py << EOF
from selenium import webdriver
b = webdriver.Firefox()
print 'Visiting github'
b.get('https://github.com/search')
print 'Performing search'
searchselector = '#search_form input[type="text"]'
searchbox = b.find_element_by_css_selector(searchselector)
searchbox.send_keys('docker-in-practice')
searchbox.submit()
print 'Switching to user search'
import time
time.sleep(2) # wait for page JS to run
usersxpath = '//nav//a[contains(text(), "Users")]'
userslink = b.find_element_by_xpath(usersxpath)
userslink.click()
print 'Opening docker in practice user page'
dlinkselector = '.user-list-info a'
dlink = b.find_elements_by_css_selector(dlinkselector)[99]
dlink.click()
print 'Visiting docker in practice site'
mlinkselector = '.meta-item a'
mlink = b.find_element_by_css_selector(mlinkselector)
mlink.click()
print 'Done!'
EOF
```

Note the subtle difference in the assignment of the dlink variable (indexing to position 99 rather than 0). By attempting to get the hundredth result containing the text "Docker in Practice", you'll trigger an error, which will cause the Docker container to exit with a nonzero status and trigger failures in the CI pipeline.

Time to try it out:

```
$ docker run --rm -v $(pwd):/mnt selenium sh -c \
"xvfb-run -s '-screen 0 1024x768x24 -extension RANDR'\
python /mnt/myscript.py"
Visiting github
Performing search
Switching to user search
```

```
Opening docker in practice user page
Traceback (most recent call last):
  File "myscript.py", line 15, in <module>
      dlink = b.find_elements_by_css_selector(dlinkselector)[99]
      IndexError: list index out of range
$ echo $?
1
```

You've run a self-removing container that executes the Python test script running under a virtual X server. As expected, it failed and returned a nonzero exit code.

> **NOTE** The sh -c "command string here" is an unfortunate result of how Docker treats CMD values by default. If you built this image with a Dockerfile, you'd be able to remove the sh -c and make xvfb-run -s '-screen 0 1024x768x24 -extension RANDR' the entrypoint, allowing you to pass the test command as image arguments.

DISCUSSION

Docker is a flexible tool and can be put to some initially surprising uses (graphical apps in this case). Some people run *all* of their graphical apps inside Docker, including games!

We wouldn't go that far (technique 40 does look at doing this for at least your developer tools) but we've found that re-examining assumptions about Docker can lead to some surprising use cases. For example, appendix A talks about running graphical Linux applications on Windows after installing Docker for Windows.

8.3   *Containerizing your CI process*

Once you have a consistent development process across teams, it's important to also have a consistent build process. Randomly failing builds defeat the point of Docker.

As a result, it makes sense to *containerize* your entire CI process. This not only makes sure your builds are repeatable, it allows you to move your CI process anywhere without fear of leaving some vital piece of configuration behind (likely discovered with much frustration later).

In these techniques, we'll use Jenkins (as this is the most widely used CI tool), but the same techniques should apply to other CI tools. We don't assume a great deal of familiarity with Jenkins here, but we won't cover setting up standard tests and builds. That information isn't essential to the techniques here.

TECHNIQUE 66   **Running the Jenkins master within a Docker container**

Putting the Jenkins master inside a container doesn't have as many benefits as doing the same for a slave (see the next technique), but it does give you the normal Docker win of immutable images. We've found that being able to commit known-good master configurations and plugins eases the burden of experimentation significantly.

PROBLEM

You want a portable Jenkins server.

SOLUTION

Use the official Jenkins Docker image to run your server.

Running Jenkins within a Docker container gives you some advantages over a straightforward host install. Cries of "Don't touch my Jenkins server configuration!" or, even worse, "Who touched my Jenkins server?" aren't unheard of in our office, and being able to clone the state of a Jenkins server with a docker export of the running container to experiment with upgrades and changes helps silence these complaints. Similarly, backups and porting become easier.

In this technique, we'll take the official Jenkins Docker image and make a few changes to facilitate some later techniques that require the ability to access the Docker socket, like doing a Docker build from Jenkins.

> **NOTE**   The Jenkins-related examples from this book are available on GitHub: git clone https://github.com/docker-in-practice/jenkins.git.

> **NOTE**   This Jenkins image and its run command will be used as the server in Jenkins-related techniques in this book.

BUILDING THE SERVER

We'll first prepare a list of plugins we want for the server and place it in a file called jenkins_plugins.txt:

```
swarm:3.4
```

This very short list consists of the Jenkins' Swarm plugin (no relation to Docker Swarm), which we'll use in a later technique.

The following listing shows the Dockerfile for building the Jenkins server.

Listing 8.11   Jenkins server build

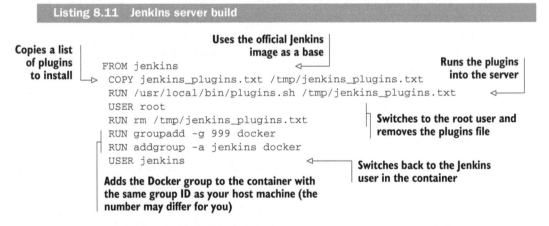

No CMD or ENTRYPOINT instruction is given because we want to inherit the startup command defined in the official Jenkins image.

The group ID for Docker may be different on your host machine. To see what the ID is for you, run this command to see the local group ID:

```
$ grep -w ^docker /etc/group
docker:x:999:imiell
```

Replace the value if it differs from 999.

> **WARNING** The group ID must match on the Jenkins server environment and your slave environment if you plan to run Docker from within the Jenkins Docker container. There will also be a potential portability issue if you choose to move the server (you'd encounter the same issue on a native server install). Environment variables won't help here by themselves, as the group needs to be set up at build time rather than being dynamically configured.

To build the image in this scenario, run this command:

```
docker build -t jenkins_server .
```

RUNNING THE SERVER

Now you can run the server under Docker with this command:

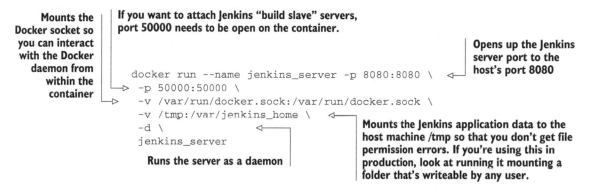

If you access http://localhost:8080, you'll see the Jenkins configuration interface—follow the process to your linking, probably using `docker exec` (described in technique 12) to retrieve the password you'll be prompted for at the first step.

Once complete, your Jenkins server will be ready to go, with your plugins already installed (along with some others, depending on the options you selected during the setup process). To check this, go to Manage Jenkins > Manage Plugins > Installed, and look for Swarm to verify that it's installed.

DISCUSSION

You'll see that we've mounted the Docker socket with this Jenkins master as we did in technique 45, providing access to the Docker daemon. This allows you to perform Docker builds with the built-in master slave by running the containers on the host.

> **NOTE** The code for this technique and related ones is available on GitHub at https://github.com/docker-in-practice/jenkins.

Docker's portability and lightweight nature make it an obvious choice for a CI slave (a machine the CI master connects to in order to carry out builds). A Docker CI slave is a step change from a VM slave (and is even more of a leap from bare-metal build machines). It allows you to perform builds on a multitude of environments with a single host, to quickly tear down and bring up clean environments to ensure uncontaminated builds, and to use all your familiar Docker tooling to manage your build environments.

Being able to treat the CI slave as just another Docker container is particularly interesting. Do you have mysterious build failures on one of your Docker CI slaves? Pull the image and try the build yourself.

PROBLEM

You want to scale and modify your Jenkins slave.

SOLUTION

Use Docker to encapsulate the configuration of your slave in a Docker image, and deploy.

Many organizations set up a heavyweight Jenkins slave (often on the same host as the server), maintained by a central IT function, that serves a useful purpose for a time. As time goes on, and teams grow their codebases and diverge, requirements grow for more and more software to be installed, updated, or altered so that the jobs will run.

Figure 8.3 shows a simplified version of this scenario. Imagine hundreds of software packages and multiple new requests all giving an overworked infrastructure team headaches.

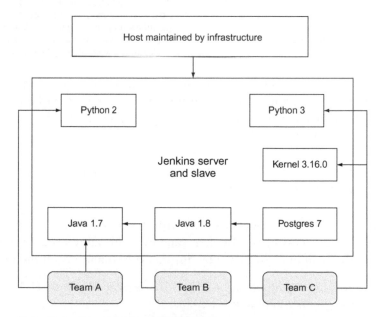

Figure 8.3 An overloaded Jenkins server

> **NOTE** This technique has been constructed to show you the essentials of running a Jenkins slave in a container. This makes the result less portable but the lesson easier to grasp. Once you understand all the techniques in this chapter, you'll be able to make a more portable setup.

Stalemate has been known to ensue, because sysadmins may be reluctant to update their configuration management scripts for one group of people as they fear breaking another's build, and teams get increasingly frustrated over the slowness of change.

Docker (naturally) offers a solution by allowing multiple teams to use a base image for their own personal Jenkins slave, while using the same hardware as before. You can create an image with the required shared tooling on it, and allow teams to alter it to meet their own needs.

Some contributors have uploaded their own reference slaves on the Docker Hub; you can find them by searching for "jenkins slave" on the Docker Hub. The following listing is a minimal Jenkins slave Dockerfile.

Listing 8.12 Bare-bones Jenkins slave Dockerfile

Sets the Jenkins user password to "jpass". In a more sophisticated setup, you'd likely want to use other authentication methods.

```
FROM ubuntu:16.04
ENV DEBIAN_FRONTEND noninteractive
RUN groupadd -g 1000 jenkins_slave
 RUN useradd -d /home/jenkins_slave -s /bin/bash \
-m jenkins_slave -u 1000 -g jenkins_slave
 RUN echo jenkins_slave:jpass | chpasswd
 RUN apt-get update && apt-get install -y \
openssh-server openjdk-8-jre wget iproute2
 RUN mkdir -p /var/run/sshd
 CMD ip route | grep "default via" \
 | awk '{print $3}' && /usr/sbin/sshd -D
```

Creates the Jenkins slave user and group

Installs the required software to function as a Jenkins slave.

On startup, outputs the IP address of the host machine from the point of view of the container, and starts the SSH server

---

Build the slave image, tagging it as `jenkins_slave`:

```
$ docker build -t jenkins_slave .
```

Run it with this command:

```
$ docker run --name jenkins_slave -ti -p 2222:22 jenkins_slave
172.17.0.1
```

> ### Jenkins server needs to be running
> If you don't have a Jenkins server already running on your host, set one up using the previous technique. If you're in a hurry, run this command:

(continued)

```
$ docker run --name jenkins_server -p 8080:8080 -p 50000:50000 \
dockerinpractice/jenkins:server
```

This will make the Jenkins server available at http://localhost:8080 if you've run it on your local machine. You'll need to go through the setup process before using it.

If you navigate to the Jenkins server, you'll be greeted with the page in figure 8.4.

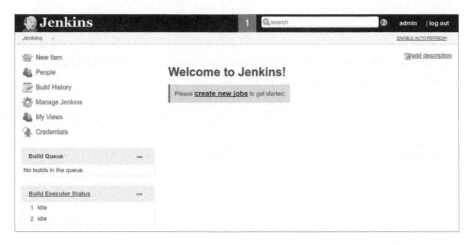

Figure 8.4   The Jenkins homepage

You can add a slave by clicking on Build Executor Status > New Node and adding the node name as a Permanent Agent, as shown in figure 8.5. Call it `mydockerslave`.

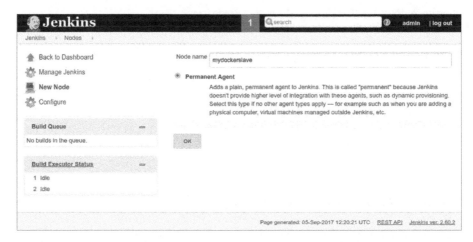

Figure 8.5   Naming a new node page

Click OK and configure it with these settings, as shown in figure 8.6:

- Set Remote Root Directory to /home/jenkins_slave.
- Give it a Label of "dockerslave".
- Make sure the Launch Slave Agents Via SSH option is selected.
- Set the host to the route IP address seen from within the container (output with the `docker run` command earlier).
- Click Add to add credentials, and set the username to "jenkins_slave" and the password to "jpass". Now select those credentials from the drop-down list.
- Set Host Key Verification Strategy to either Manually Trusted Key Verification Strategy, which will accept the SSH key on first connect, or Non Verifying Verification Strategy, which will perform no SSH host key checking.
- Click Advanced to expose the Port field, and set it to 2222.
- Click Save.

Now click through to the new slave, and click Launch Slave Agent (assuming this doesn't happen automatically). After a minute you should see that the slave agent is marked as online.

Go back to the homepage by clicking on Jenkins at the top left, and click on New Item. Create a Freestyle Project called "test", and under the Build section, click Add Build Step > Execute Shell, with the command `echo done`. Scroll up, and select Restrict Where Project Can Be Run and enter the Label Expression "dockerslave". You should see that Slaves In Label is set as 1, meaning the job is now linked to the Docker slave. Click Save to create the job.

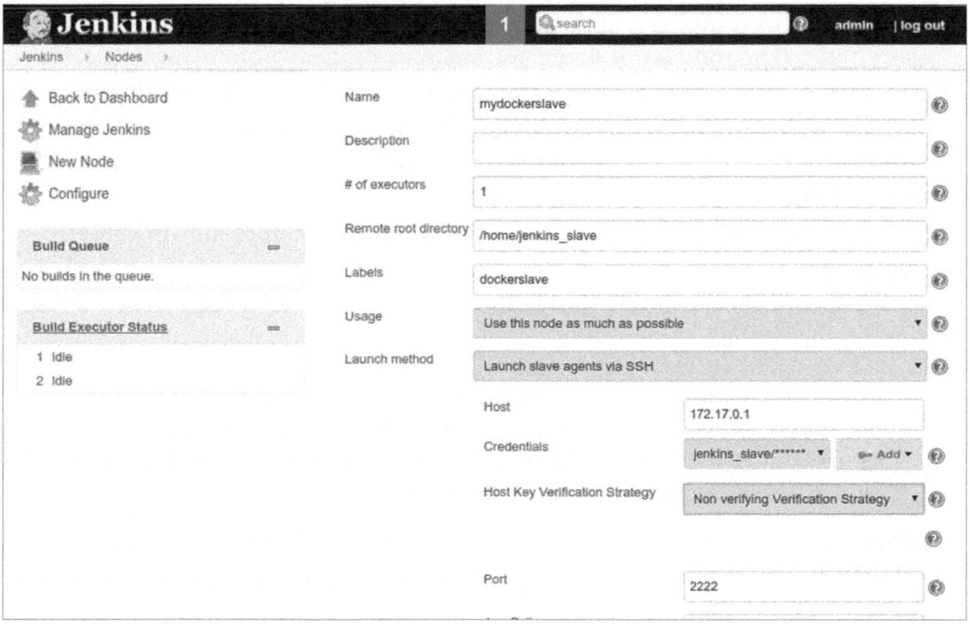

Figure 8.6   The Jenkins node settings page

Click Build Now, and then click the build "#1" link that appears below on the left. Then click Console Output, and you should see output like this in the main window:

```
Started by user admin
Building remotely on mydockerslave (dockerslave)
⇒ in workspace /home/jenkins_slave/workspace/test
[test] $ /bin/sh -xe /tmp/jenkins5620917016462917386.sh
+ echo done
done
Finished: SUCCESS
```

Well done! You've successfully created your own Jenkins slave.

Now if you want to create your own bespoke slave, all you need to do is alter the slave image's Dockerfile to your taste, and run that instead of the example one.

> **NOTE** The code for this technique and related ones is available on GitHub at https://github.com/docker-in-practice/jenkins.

DISCUSSION

This technique walks you down the road of creating a container to act like a virtual machine, much like technique 12 but with the added complexity of Jenkins integration. One particularly useful strategy is to also mount the Docker socket inside the container and install the Docker client binary so you can perform Docker builds. See technique 45 for information on mounting the Docker socket (for a different purpose) and appendix A for installation details.

TECHNIQUE 68   **Scaling your CI with Jenkins' Swarm plugin**

Being able to reproduce environments is a big win, but your build capacity is still constrained by the number of dedicated build machines you have available. If you want to do experiments on different environments with the newfound flexibility of Docker slaves, this may become frustrating. Capacity can also become a problem for more mundane reasons—the growth of your team!

PROBLEM

You want your CI compute to scale up with your development work rate.

SOLUTION

Use Jenkins' Swarm plugin and a Docker Swarm slave to dynamically provision Jenkins slaves.

> **NOTE** It's been mentioned before, but it's worth repeating here: the Jenkins' Swarm plugin is not at all related to Docker's Swarm technology. They are two entirely unrelated things that happen to use the same word. The fact that they can be used together here is pure coincidence.

Many small- to medium-sized businesses have a model for CI where one or more Jenkins servers are devoted to supplying the resources required to run Jenkins jobs. This is illustrated in figure 8.7.

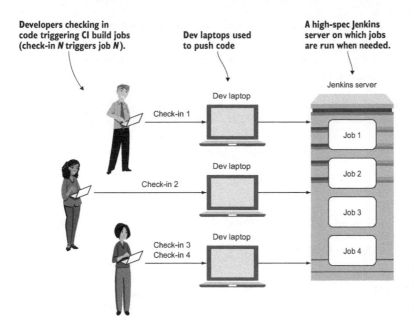

Figure 8.7 Before: Jenkins server—OK with one dev, but doesn't scale

This works fine for a time, but as the CI processes become more embedded, capacity limits are often reached. Most Jenkins workloads are triggered by check-ins to source control, so as more developers check in, the workload increases. The number of complaints to the ops team then explodes as busy developers impatiently wait for their build results.

One neat solution is to have as many Jenkins slaves as there are people checking in code, as illustrated in figure 8.8.

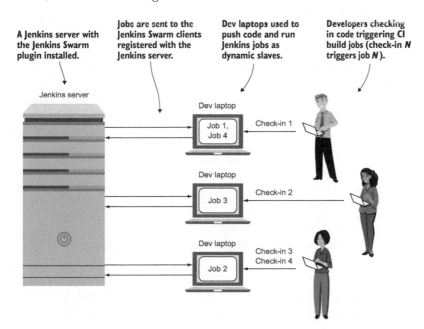

Figure 8.8 After: compute scales with team

The Dockerfile shown in listing 8.13 creates an image with the Jenkins Swarm client plugin installed, allowing a Jenkins master with the appropriate Jenkins Swarm server plugin to connect and run jobs. It begins in the same way as the normal Jenkins slave Dockerfile in the last technique.

Listing 8.13   Dockerfile

```
FROM ubuntu:16.04
ENV DEBIAN_FRONTEND noninteractive
RUN groupadd -g 1000 jenkins_slave
RUN useradd -d /home/jenkins_slave -s /bin/bash \
-m jenkins_slave -u 1000 -g jenkins_slave
RUN echo jenkins_slave:jpass | chpasswd
RUN apt-get update && apt-get install -y \
openssh-server openjdk-8-jre wget iproute2
RUN wget -O /home/jenkins_slave/swarm-client-3.4.jar \       <──  Retrieves the Jenkins
 https://repo.jenkins-ci.org/releases/org/jenkins-ci/plugins/swarm-client      Swarm plugin
 /3.4/swarm-client-3.4.jar
COPY startup.sh /usr/bin/startup.sh
 RUN chmod +x /usr/bin/startup.sh              <──  Copies the startup
 ENTRYPOINT ["/usr/bin/startup.sh"]    <──       script to the container

Makes the startup script the          Marks the startup script as executable
default command run
```

The following listing is the startup script copied into the preceding Dockerfile.

Listing 8.14   startup.sh

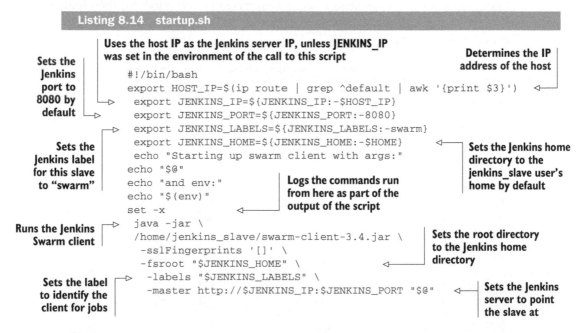

Most of the preceding script sets up and outputs the environment for the Java call at the end. The Java call runs the Swarm client, which turns the machine on which it's run into a dynamic Jenkins slave rooted in the directory specified in the `-fsroot` flag, running jobs labeled with the `-labels` flag and pointed at the Jenkins server specified with the `-master` flag. The lines with `echo` just provide some debugging information about the arguments and environment setup.

Building and running the container is a simple matter of running what should be the now-familiar pattern:

```
$ docker build -t jenkins_swarm_slave .
$ docker run -d --name \
jenkins_swarm_slave jenkins_swarm_slave \
-username admin -password adminpassword
```

The `username` and `password` should be an account on your Jenkins instance with permission to create slaves—the `admin` account will work, but you can also create another account for this purpose.

Now that you have a slave set up on this machine, you can run Jenkins jobs on it. Set up a Jenkins job as normal, but add `swarm` as a label expression in the Restrict Where This Project Can Be Run section (see technique 67).

> **WARNING** Jenkins jobs can be onerous processes, and it's quite possible that their running will negatively affect the laptop. If the job is a heavy one, you can set the labels on jobs and Swarm clients appropriately. For example, you might set a label on a job as 4CPU8G and match it to Swarm containers run on 4CPU machines with 8 GB of memory.

This technique gives some indication of the Docker concept. A predictable and portable environment can be placed on multiple hosts, reducing the load on an expensive server and reducing the configuration required to a minimum.

Although this isn't a technique that can be rolled out without considering performance, we think there's a lot of scope here to turn contributing developers' computer resources into a form of game, increasing efficiency in a development organization without needing expensive new hardware.

DISCUSSION

You can automate this process by setting it up as a supervised system service on all of your estate's PCs (see technique 82).

> **NOTE** The code for this technique and related ones is available on GitHub at https://github.com/docker-in-practice/jenkins.

TECHNIQUE 69 Upgrading your containerized Jenkins server safely

If you've used Jenkins for a while in production, you'll be aware that Jenkins frequently publishes updates to its server for security and functionality changes.

On a dedicated, non-dockerized host, this is generally managed for you through package management. With Docker, it can get slightly more complicated to reason about upgrades, as you've likely separated out the context of the server from its data.

PROBLEM

You want to reliably upgrade your Jenkins server.

SOLUTION

Run a Jenkins updater image that will handle the upgrade of a Jenkins server.

This technique is delivered as a Docker image composed of a number of parts.

First we'll outline the Dockerfile that builds the image. This Dockerfile draws from the library Docker image (which contains a Docker client) and adds a script that manages the upgrade.

The image is run in a Docker command that mounts the Docker items on the host, giving it the ability to manage any required Jenkins upgrade.

DOCKERFILE

We start with the Dockerfile.

Listing 8.15   Dockerfile for Jenkins updater

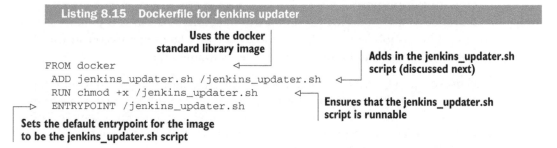

The preceding Dockerfile encapsulates the requirements to back up Jenkins in a runnable Docker image. It uses the `docker` standard library image to get a Docker client to run within a container. This container will run the script in listing 8.16 to manage any required upgrade of Jenkins on the host.

NOTE   If your docker daemon version differs from the version in the `docker` Docker image, you may run into problems. Try to use the same version.

JENKINS_UPDATER.SH

This is the shell script that manages the upgrade within the container.

Listing 8.16   Shell script to back up and restart Jenkins

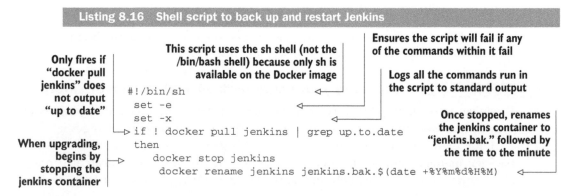

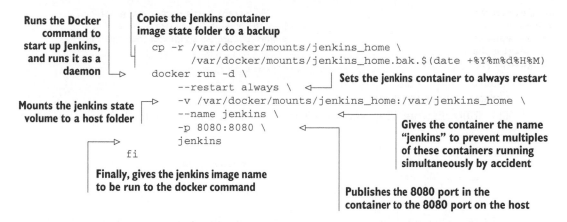

Runs the Docker command to start up Jenkins, and runs it as a daemon

Copies the Jenkins container image state folder to a backup

```
cp -r /var/docker/mounts/jenkins_home \
      /var/docker/mounts/jenkins_home.bak.$(date +%Y%m%d%H%M)
docker run -d \
      --restart always \
      -v /var/docker/mounts/jenkins_home:/var/jenkins_home \
      --name jenkins \
      -p 8080:8080 \
      jenkins
fi
```

Mounts the jenkins state volume to a host folder

Sets the jenkins container to always restart

Gives the container the name "jenkins" to prevent multiples of these containers running simultaneously by accident

Finally, gives the jenkins image name to be run to the docker command

Publishes the 8080 port in the container to the 8080 port on the host

The preceding script tries to pull `jenkins` from the Docker Hub with the `docker pull` command. If the output contains the phrase "up to date", the `docker pull | grep ...` command returns `true`. But you only want to upgrade when you don't see "up to date" in the output. This is why the `if` statement is negated with a `!` sign after the `if`.

The result is that the code in the `if` block is only fired if you downloaded a new version of the "latest" Jenkins image. Within this block, the running Jenkins container is stopped and renamed. You rename it rather than delete it in case the upgrade doesn't work and you need to reinstate the previous version. Further to this rollback strategy, the mount folder on the host containing Jenkins' state is also backed up.

Finally, the latest-downloaded Jenkins image is started up using the `docker run` command.

> **NOTE** You may want to change the host mount folder or the name of the running Jenkins container based on personal preference.

You might be wondering how this Jenkins image is connected to the host's Docker daemon. To achieve this, the image is run using the method seen in technique 66.

THE JENKINS-UPDATER IMAGE INVOCATION

The following command will perform a Jenkins upgrade, using the image (with shell script inside it) that was created earlier:

Listing 8.17 Docker command to run the Jenkins updater

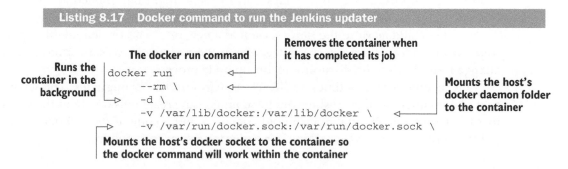

Runs the container in the background

The docker run command

Removes the container when it has completed its job

```
docker run
      --rm \
      -d \
      -v /var/lib/docker:/var/lib/docker \
      -v /var/run/docker.sock:/var/run/docker.sock \
```

Mounts the host's docker daemon folder to the container

Mounts the host's docker socket to the container so the docker command will work within the container

Specifies that the dockerinpractice/ jenkins-updater image is the image to be run

Mounts the host's docker mount folder where the Jenkins data is stored, so that the jenkins_updater.sh script can copy the files

```
-v /var/docker/mounts:/var/docker/mounts
      dockerinpractice/jenkins-updater
```

AUTOMATING THE UPGRADE

The following one-liner makes it easy to run within a crontab. We run this on our home servers.

```
0 * * * * docker run --rm -d -v /var/lib/docker:/var/lib/docker -v
➥ /var/run/docker.sock:/var/run/docker.sock -v
➥ /var/docker/mounts:/var/docker/mounts dockerinpractice/jenkins-updater
```

> **NOTE** The preceding command is all on one line because crontab does not ignore newlines if there is a backslash in front in the way that shell scripts do.

The end result is that a single crontab entry can safely manage the upgrade of your Jenkins instance without you having to worry about it.

The task of automating the cleanup of old backed-up containers and volume mounts is left as an exercise for the reader.

DISCUSSION

This technique exemplifies a few things we come across throughout the book, which can be applied in similar contexts to situations other than Jenkins.

First, it uses the core `docker` image to communicate with the Docker daemon on the host. Other portable scripts might be written to manage Docker daemons in other ways. For example, you might want to write scripts to remove old volumes, or to report on the activity on your daemon.

More specifically, the `if` block pattern could be used to update and restart other images when a new one is available. It's not uncommon for images to be updated for security reasons or to make minor upgrades.

If you're concerned with difficulties in upgrading versions, it's also worth pointing out that you need not take the "latest" image tag (which this technique does). Many images have different tags that track different version numbers. For example, your image `exampleimage` might have an `exampleimage:latest` tag, as well as `example-image:v1.1` and `exampleimage:v1` tags. Any of these might be updated at any time, but the `:v1.1` tag is less likely to move to a new version than the `:latest` tag. The `:latest` tag could move to the same version as a new `:v1.2` tag (which might require steps to upgrade) or even a `:v2.1` tag, where the new major version 2 indicates a change more likely to be disruptive to any upgrade process.

This technique also outlines a rollback strategy for Docker upgrades. The separation of container and data (using volume mounts) can create tension about the stability of any upgrade. By retaining the old container and a copy of the old data at the point where the service was working, it's easier to recover from failure.

DATABASE UPGRADES AND DOCKER

Database upgrades are a particular context in which stability concerns are germane. If you want to upgrade your database to a new version, you have to consider whether the upgrade requires a change to the data structures and storage of the database's data. It's not enough to run the new version's image as a container and expect it to work. It gets a bit more complicated if the database is smart enough to know which version of the data it's seeing and can perform the upgrade itself accordingly. In these cases, you might be more comfortable upgrading.

Many factors feed into your upgrade strategy. Your app might tolerate an optimistic approach (as you see here in the Jenkins example) that assumes everything will be OK, and prepares for failure when (not if) it occurs. On the other hand, you might demand 100% uptime and not tolerate failure of any kind. In such cases, a fully tested upgrade plan and a deeper knowledge of the platform than running `docker pull` is generally desired (with or without the involvement of Docker).

Although Docker doesn't eliminate the upgrade problem, the immutability of versioned images can make it simpler to reason about them. Docker can also help you prepare for failure in two ways: backing up state in host volumes, and making testing predictable state easier. The hit you take in managing and understanding what Docker is doing can give you more control over and certainty about the upgrade process.

Summary

- You can use the Docker Hub workflow to automatically trigger builds on code changes.
- Builds can be sped up significantly by using eatmydata and package caches.
- Builds can also be sped up by using proxy caches for external artifacts such as system packages.
- You can run GUI tests (like Selenium) inside Docker.
- Your CI platform (such as Jenkins) can itself be run from a container.
- A Docker CI slave lets you keep complete control over your environment.
- You can farm out build processes to your whole team using Docker and Jenkins' Swarm plugin.

Continuous delivery: A perfect fit for Docker principles

9

This chapter covers

- The Docker contract between dev and ops
- Taking manual control over build availability across environments
- Moving builds between environments over low-bandwidth connections
- Centrally configuring all containers in an environment
- Achieving zero-downtime deployment with Docker

Once you're confident that all of your builds are being quality-checked with a consistent CI process, the logical next step is to start looking at deploying every good build to your users. This goal is known as continuous delivery (CD).

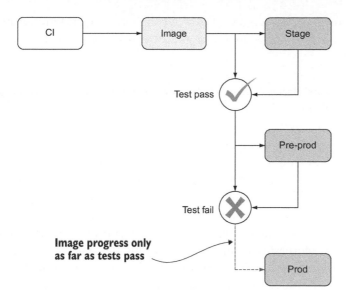

Figure 9.1   A typical CD pipeline

In this chapter we'll refer to your "CD pipeline"—the process your build goes through after it comes out of your "CI pipeline." The dividing line can sometimes be blurred, but think of the CD pipeline as starting when you have a final image that has passed your initial tests during the build process. Figure 9.1 demonstrates how the image might progress through a CD pipeline until it (hopefully) reaches production.

It's worth repeating that last point—the image that comes out of CI should be final and unmodified throughout your CD process! Docker makes this easy to enforce with immutable images and encapsulation of state, so using Docker takes you one step down the CD road already.

When this chapter is done, you'll fully understand why Docker's immutability makes it a perfect partner for your CD strategy. In this way, Docker can be a key enabler for any DevOps strategy in any organization.

9.1   Interacting with other teams in the CD pipeline

First we're going to take a little step back and look at how Docker changes the relationship between development and operations.

Some of the biggest challenges in software development aren't technical—splitting people up into teams based on their roles and expertise is a common practice, yet this can result in communication barriers and insularity. Having a successful CD pipeline requires involvement from the teams at all stages of the process, from development to testing to production. Having a single reference point for all teams can help ease this interaction by providing structure.

TECHNIQUE 70   The Docker contract: Reducing friction

One of Docker's aims is to allow easy expression of inputs and outputs as they relate to a container that contains a single application. This can provide clarity when working with other people—communication is a vital part of collaboration, and understanding how Docker can ease things by providing a single reference point can help you win over Docker unbelievers.

PROBLEM

You want cooperating teams' deliverables to be clean and unambiguous, reducing friction in your delivery pipeline.

SOLUTION

Use the *Docker contract* to facilitate clean deliverables between teams.

As companies scale, they frequently find that the flat, lean organization they once had, in which key individuals "knew the whole system," gives way to a more structured organization within which different teams have different responsibilities and competencies. We've seen this firsthand in the organizations we've worked at.

If technical investment isn't made, friction can arise as growing teams deliver to each other. Complaints of increasing complexity, "throwing the release over the wall," and buggy upgrades all become familiar. Cries of "Well, it works on our machine!" will increasingly be heard, to the frustration of all concerned. Figure 9.2 gives a simplified but representative view of this scenario.

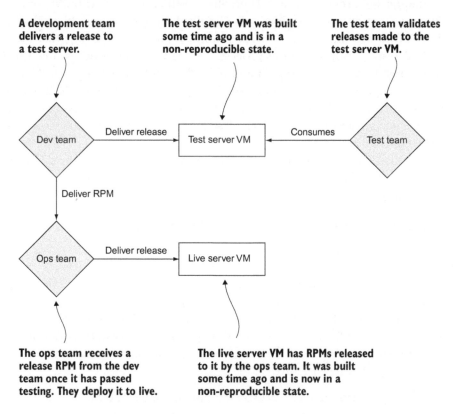

Figure 9.2   Before: a typical software workflow

The workflow in figure 9.2 has a number of problems that may well look familiar to you. They all boil down to the difficulties of managing state. The test team might test something on a machine that differs from what the operations team has set up. In theory, changes to all environments should be carefully documented, rolled back when problems are seen, and kept consistent. Unfortunately, the realities of commercial pressure and human behavior routinely conspire against this goal, and environmental drift is seen.

Existing solutions to this problem include VMs and RPMs. VMs can be used to reduce the surface area of environmental risk by delivering complete machine representations to other teams. The downside is that VMs are relatively monolithic entities that are difficult for teams to manipulate efficiently. At the other end, RPMs offer a standard way of packaging applications that helps define dependencies when rolling out software. This doesn't eliminate configuration management issues, though, and rolling out RPMs created by fellow teams is far more error-prone than using RPMs that have been battle-tested across the internet.

THE DOCKER CONTRACT

What Docker can do is give you a clean line of separation between teams, where the Docker image is both the borderline and the unit of exchange. We call this the *Docker contract*, illustrated in figure 9.3.

With Docker, the reference point for all teams becomes much cleaner. Rather than dealing with sprawling monolithic virtual (or real) machines in unreproducible states, all teams are talking about the same code, whether it's on test, live, or development. In addition, there's a clean separation of data from code, which makes it easier to reason about whether problems are caused by variations in data or code.

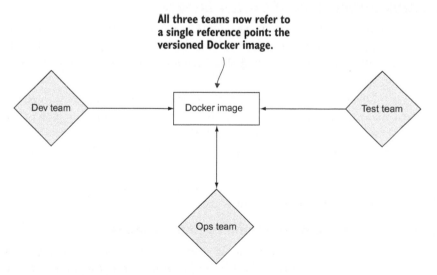

Figure 9.3 After: the Docker contract

Because Docker uses the remarkably stable Linux API as its environment, teams that deliver software have far more freedom to build software and services in whatever fashion they like, safe in the knowledge that it will run predictably in various environments. This doesn't mean that you can ignore the context in which it runs, but it does reduce the risk of environmental differences causing issues.

Various operational efficiencies result from having this single reference touchpoint. Bug reproduction becomes much easier, as all teams are able to describe and reproduce issues from a known starting point. Upgrades become the responsibility of the team delivering the change. In short, state is managed by those making the change. All these benefits greatly reduce the communications overhead and allow teams to get on with their jobs. This reduced communications overhead can also help encourage moves toward a microservices architecture.

This is no merely theoretical benefit: we've seen this improvement firsthand in a company of over 500 developers, and it's a frequent topic of discussion at Docker technical meetups.

DISCUSSION

This technique outlines a strategy, useful to keep in mind as you continue throughout the book, to identify how other techniques fit into this new world. For example, technique 76 describes a way to run a microservices-based application in the same cross-container way it would be run on production systems, eliminating a source of configuration file tweaking. When you do find yourself with external URLs or other unchanging factors on different environments, technique 85 will step up with information about service discovery—a good way to turn a sprawl of configuration files into a single source of truth.

9.2   *Facilitating deployment of Docker images*

The first problem when trying to implement CD is moving the outputs of your build process to the appropriate location. If you're able to use a single registry for all stages of your CD pipeline, it may seem like this problem has been solved. But it doesn't cover a key aspect of CD.

One of the key ideas behind CD is *build promotion*: each stage of a pipeline (user acceptance tests, integration tests, and performance tests) can only trigger the next stage if the previous one has been successful. With multiple registries you can ensure that only *promoted* builds are used by only making them available in the next registry when a build stage passes.

We'll look at a few ways of moving your images between registries, and even at a way of sharing Docker objects without a registry.

TECHNIQUE 71   **Manually mirroring registry images**

The simplest image-mirroring scenario is when you have a machine with a high-bandwidth connection to both registries. This permits the use of normal Docker functionality to perform the image copy.

PROBLEM

You want to copy an image between two registries.

SOLUTION

Manually use the standard pulling and pushing commands in Docker to transfer the image.

The solution for this involves:

- Pulling the image from the registry
- Retagging the image
- Pushing the retagged image

If you have an image at test-registry.company.com and you want to move it to stage-registry.company.com, the process is simple.

Listing 9.1   Transferring an image from a test to a staging registry

```
$ IMAGE=mygroup/myimage:mytag
$ OLDREG=test-registry.company.com
$ NEWREG=stage-registry.company.com
$ docker pull $OLDREG/$MYIMAGE
[...]
$ docker tag -f $OLDREG/$MYIMAGE $NEWREG/$MYIMAGE
$ docker push $NEWREG/$MYIMAGE
$ docker rmi $OLDREG/$MYIMAGE
$ docker image prune -f
```

There are three important points to note about this process:

1. The new image has been force tagged. This means that any older image with the same name on the machine (left there for layer-caching purposes) will lose the image name, so the new image can be tagged with the desired name.
2. All dangling images have been removed. Although layer caching is extremely useful for speeding up deployment, leaving unused image layers around can quickly use up disk space. In general, old layers are less likely to be used as time passes and they become more out-of-date.
3. You may need to log into your new registry with `docker login`.

The image is now available in the new registry for use in subsequent stages of your CD pipeline.

DISCUSSION

This technique illustrates a simple point about Docker tagging: the tag itself contains information about the registry it belongs to.

Most of the time this is hidden from users because they normally pull from the default registry (the Docker Hub at docker.io). When you're starting to work with registries, this issue comes to the fore because you have to explicitly tag the registry with the registry location in order to push it to the correct endpoint.

TECHNIQUE 72   Delivering images over constrained connections

Even with layering, pushing and pulling Docker images can be a bandwidth-hungry process. In a world of free large-bandwidth connections, this wouldn't be a problem, but sometimes reality forces us to deal with low-bandwidth connections or costly bandwidth metering between data centers. In this situation you need to find a more efficient way of transferring differences, or the CD ideal of being able to run your pipeline multiple times a day will remain out of reach.

The ideal solution is a tool that will reduce the average size of an image so it's even smaller than classic compression methods can manage.

PROBLEM

You want to copy an image between two machines with a low-bandwidth connection between them.

SOLUTION

Export the image, split it up, transfer the chunks, and import the recombined image on the other end.

To do all this, we must first introduce a new tool: bup. It was created as a backup tool with extremely efficient deduplication—*deduplication* being the ability to recognize where data is used repeatedly and only store it once. It works particularly well on archives containing a number of similar files, which is conveniently a format Docker allows you to export images as.

For this technique we've created an image called dbup (short for "Docker bup"), which makes it easier to use bup to deduplicate images. You can find the code behind it at https://github.com/docker-in-practice/dbup.

As a demonstration, let's see how much bandwidth we could save when upgrading from the ubuntu:14.04.1 image to ubuntu:14.04.2. Bear in mind that in practice you'd have a number of layers on top of each of these, which Docker would want to completely retransfer after a lower layer change. By contrast, this technique would recognize the significant similarities and give you much greater savings than you'll see in the following example.

The first step is to pull both of those images so we can see how much is transferred over the network.

Listing 9.2   Examining and saving two Ubuntu images

```
$ docker pull ubuntu:14.04.1 && docker pull ubuntu:14.04.2
[...]
$ docker history ubuntu:14.04.1
IMAGE           CREATED      CREATED BY                                      SIZE
ab1bd63e0321 2 years ago /bin/sh -c #(nop) CMD [/bin/bash]              0B
<missing>      2 years ago /bin/sh -c sed -i 's/^#\s*\(deb.*universe\... 1.9kB
<missing>      2 years ago /bin/sh -c echo '#!/bin/sh' > /usr/sbin/po... 195kB
<missing>      2 years ago /bin/sh -c #(nop) ADD file:62400a49cced0d7... 188MB
<missing>      4 years ago                                                 0B
$ docker history ubuntu:14.04.2
```

```
IMAGE           CREATED     CREATED BY                                 SIZE
44ae5d2a191e 2 years ago /bin/sh -c #(nop) CMD ["/bin/bash"]           0B
<missing>    2 years ago /bin/sh -c sed -i 's/^#\s*\(deb.*universe\...  1.9kB
<missing>    2 years ago /bin/sh -c echo '#!/bin/sh' > /usr/sbin/po...  195kB
<missing>    2 years ago /bin/sh -c #(nop) ADD file:0a5fd3a659be172...  188MB
$ docker save ubuntu:14.04.1 | gzip | wc -c
65973497
$ docker save ubuntu:14.04.2 | gzip | wc -c
65994838
```

The bottom layer on each image (the ADD) is the majority of the size, and you can see that the file being added is different, so you can treat the whole image size as the amount that would be transferred when pushing the new image. Also note that the Docker registry uses gzip compression to transfer layers, so we've included that in our measurement (instead of taking the size from docker history). About 65 MB is being transferred in both the initial deployment and the subsequent deployment.

In order to get started, you'll need two things—a directory to store the pool of data bup uses as storage, and the dockerinpractice/dbup image. You can then go ahead and add your image to the bup data pool.

Listing 9.3   Saving two Ubuntu images into the bup data pool

```
$ mkdir bup_pool
$ alias dbup="docker run --rm \
    -v $(pwd)/bup_pool:/pool -v /var/run/docker.sock:/var/run/docker.sock \
    dockerinpractice/dbup"
$ dbup save ubuntu:14.04.1
Saving image!
Done!
$ du -sh bup_pool
74M     bup_pool
$ dbup save ubuntu:14.04.2
Saving image!
Done!
$ du -sh bup_pool
96M     bup_pool
```

Adding the second image to the bup data pool has only increased the size by about 20 MB. Assuming you synced the folder to another machine (possibly with rsync) after adding ubuntu:14.04.1, syncing the folder again will only transfer 20 MB (as opposed to the 65 MB before).

You then need to load the image at the other end.

Listing 9.4   Loading an image from the bup data pool

```
$ dbup load ubuntu:14.04.1
Loading image!
Done!
```

The process for transferring between registries would look something like this:

1 `docker pull` on host1
2 `dbup save` on host1
3 `rsync` from host1 to host2
4 `dbup load` on host2
5 `docker push` on host2

This technique opens up a number of possibilities that may not have been possible previously. For example, you can now rearrange and consolidate layers without having to worry about how long it will take to transfer all of the new layers over the low-bandwidth connection.

DISCUSSION

Even when following best practices and adding your application code as the last stage, bup may be able to help—it will recognize that most of the code is unchanged and only add the difference to the data pool.

The data pools can be very large, such as database files, and bup will likely perform very well (which is useful if you've decided to use technique 77 with the database inside the container, meaning there's no volume). This is actually somewhat unusual—database exports and backups are typically very efficient to incrementally transfer, but the actual on-disk storage of databases can vary significantly and occasionally defeat tools like rsync. On top of this, dbup puts a full history of your images at your fingertips—there's no need to store three full copies of images to roll back to. You can pull them out of the pool at your leisure. Unfortunately there's currently no way to clean the pool of images you don't want any more, so you'll probably need to clear the pool every now and again.

Although you may not see an immediate need for dbup, keep it in mind, in case your bandwidth bills start growing.

TECHNIQUE 73   Sharing Docker objects as TAR files

TAR files are a classic method of moving files around on Linux. Docker allows you to create TAR files and ship them around manually when there's no registry available and no possibility of setting one up. Here we're going to show you the ins and outs of these commands.

PROBLEM

You want to share images and containers with others, with no available registry.

SOLUTION

Use `docker export` or `docker save` to create TAR file artifacts, and then consume them with `docker import` or `docker load` over SSH.

The distinctions between the commands can be difficult to grasp if you're using them casually, so let's take a moment to quickly go over what they do. Table 9.1 outlines the inputs and outputs of the commands.

Table 9.1 Export and import vs. save and load

Command	Creates?	Of what?	From what?
export	TAR file	Container filesystem	Container
import	Docker image	Flat filesystem	TAR file
save	TAR file	Docker image (with history)	Image
load	Docker image	Docker image (with history)	TAR file

The first two commands work with flat filesystems. The command docker export outputs a TAR file of the files that make up the state of the container. As always with Docker, the state of running processes isn't stored—only the files. The command docker import creates a Docker image—with no history or metadata—from a TAR file.

These commands aren't symmetrical—you can't create a container from an existing container using only import and export. This asymmetry can be useful because it allows you to docker export an image to a TAR file, and then docker import it to "lose" all the layer history and metadata. This is the image-flattening approach described in technique 52.

If you're exporting or saving to a TAR file, the file is sent to stdout by default, so make sure you save it to a file like this:

```
docker pull debian:7:3
[...]
docker save debian:7.3 > debian7_3.tar
```

A TAR file like the one just created can be flung around the network safely (though you may want to compress it with gzip first), and other people can use them to import images intact. They can be sent by email or scp if you have access:

```
$ scp debian7_3.tar example.com:/tmp/debian7_3.tar
```

You can take this one step further and deliver images to other users' Docker daemons directly—assuming you have the permission.

Listing 9.5 Sending an image directly over SSH

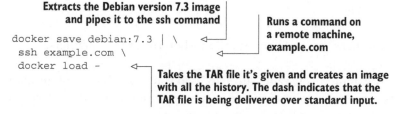

Extracts the Debian version 7.3 image and pipes it to the ssh command

Runs a command on a remote machine, example.com

```
docker save debian:7.3 | \
  ssh example.com \
  docker load -
```

Takes the TAR file it's given and creates an image with all the history. The dash indicates that the TAR file is being delivered over standard input.

If you want to discard the history of the image, you can use import instead of load.

Listing 9.6   Transferring a Docker image directly over SSH, discarding layers

```
docker export $(docker run -d debian:7.3 true) | \
    ssh example.com docker import
```

> **NOTE** Unlike `docker import`, `docker load` doesn't require a dash at the end to indicate that the TAR file is being delivered through standard input.

DISCUSSION

You may remember the export and import process from technique 52, where you saw how flattening images can be used to remove secrets that may be hidden in lower layers. The fact that secrets may be accessible in lower layers is worth bearing in mind if you're transferring images to other people—realizing that you deleted your public key on the top image layer but that it's available lower down can be a real hassle, because you should then treat it as compromised and change it everywhere.

If you find yourself doing the image transfer in this technique a lot, it may be worth putting a little time into technique 9 to set up your own registry and make things less ad hoc.

9.3   *Configuring your images for environments*

As mentioned in the introduction to this chapter, one of the keystones of CD is the concept of "doing the same thing everywhere." Without Docker, this would mean building a deployment artifact once and using the same one everywhere. In a Docker-ized world, this means using the same image everywhere.

But environments aren't all the same—there may be different URLs for external services, for example. For "normal" applications you'd be able to use environment variables to solve this problem (with the caveat that they're not easy to apply to numerous machines). The same solution can work for Docker (explicitly passing the variables in), but there's a better way of doing it with Docker that comes with some additional benefits.

TECHNIQUE 74   **Informing your containers with etcd**

Docker images are designed so they can be deployed anywhere, but you'll often want to add some extra information after deployment to affect the behavior of the application while it's running. In addition, machines running Docker may need to remain unaltered, so you may need an external source of information (making environment variables less suitable).

PROBLEM

You need an external source of configuration when running containers.

SOLUTION

Set up etcd, a distributed key/value store, to hold your container configuration.

etcd holds pieces of information and can be part of a multinode cluster for resiliency. In this technique you'll create an etcd cluster to hold your configuration and use an etcd proxy to access it.

> **NOTE** Each value held by etcd should be kept small—under 512 KB is a good rule of thumb; past this point you should consider doing benchmarking to verify that etcd is still performing as you'd expect. This limit is not unique to etcd. You should bear it in mind for other key/value stores like Zookeeper and Consul.

Because etcd cluster nodes need to talk to each other, the first step is to identify your external IP address. If you were going to run the nodes on different machines, you'd need the external IP for each of them.

Listing 9.7 Identifying IP addresses of the local machine

```
$ ip addr | grep 'inet ' | grep -v 'lo$\|docker0$'
    inet 192.168.1.123/24 brd 192.168.1.255 scope global dynamic wlp3s0
    inet 172.18.0.1/16 scope global br-0c3386c9db5b
```

Here we've looked for all IPv4 interfaces and excluded LoopBack and Docker. The top line (the first IP address on that line) is the one you need, and it represents the machine on the local network—try pinging it from another machine if you're not sure.

We can now get started with the three-node cluster, all running on the same machine. Be careful with the following arguments—the ports being exposed and advertised change on each line, as do the names of the cluster nodes and containers.

Listing 9.8 Setting up a three-node etcd cluster

The external IP address of your machine

Uses the external IP address of the machine in the cluster definition, giving the nodes a way to communicate with others. Because all nodes will be on the same host, the cluster ports (for connecting to other nodes) must be different.

```
$ IMG=quay.io/coreos/etcd:v3.2.7
$ docker pull $IMG
[...]
$ HTTPIP=http://192.168.1.123
$ CLUSTER="etcd0=$HTTPIP:2380,etcd1=$HTTPIP:2480,etcd2=$HTTPIP:2580"
$ ARGS="etcd"
$ ARGS="$ARGS -listen-client-urls http://0.0.0.0:2379"
$ ARGS="$ARGS -listen-peer-urls http://0.0.0.0:2380"
$ ARGS="$ARGS -initial-cluster-state new"
$ ARGS="$ARGS -initial-cluster $CLUSTER"
$ docker run -d -p 2379:2379 -p 2380:2380 --name etcd0 $IMG \
    $ARGS -name etcd0 -advertise-client-urls $HTTPIP:2379 \
    -initial-advertise-peer-urls $HTTPIP:2380
912390c041f8e9e71cf4cc1e51fba2a02d3cd4857d9ccd90149e21d9a5d3685b
$ docker run -d -p 2479:2379 -p 2480:2380 --name etcd1 $IMG \
    $ARGS -name etcd1 -advertise-client-urls $HTTPIP:2479 \
    -initial-advertise-peer-urls $HTTPIP:2480
446b7584a4ec747e960fe2555a9aaa2b3e2c7870097b5babe65d65cffa175dec
$ docker run -d -p 2579:2379 -p 2580:2380 --name etcd2 $IMG \
    $ARGS -name etcd2 -advertise-client-urls $HTTPIP:2579 \
    -initial-advertise-peer-urls $HTTPIP:2580
3089063b6b2ba0868e0f903a3d5b22e617a240cec22ad080dd1b497ddf4736be
```

The port for handling requests from clients

The port to listen on for talking to other nodes in the cluster, corresponding to the ports specified in $CLUSTER

```
$ curl -L $HTTPIP:2579/version
{"etcdserver":"3.2.7","etcdcluster":"3.2.0"}
$ curl -sSL $HTTPIP:2579/v2/members | python -m json.tool | grep etcd
          "name": "etcd0",
          "name": "etcd1",           Currently connected
          "name": "etcd2",           nodes in the cluster
```

You've now started up the cluster and have a response from one node. In the preceding commands, anything referring to "peer" is controlling how the etcd nodes find and talk to each other, and anything referring to "client" defines how other applications can connect to etcd.

Let's see the distributed nature of etcd in action.

Listing 9.9   Testing the resilience of an etcd cluster

```
$ curl -L $HTTPIP:2579/v2/keys/mykey -XPUT -d value="test key"
{"action":"set","node": >
{"key":"/mykey","value":"test key","modifiedIndex":7,"createdIndex":7}}
$ sleep 5
$ docker kill etcd2
etcd2
$ curl -L $HTTPIP:2579/v2/keys/mykey
curl: (7) couldn't connect to host
$ curl -L $HTTPIP:2379/v2/keys/mykey
{"action":"get","node": >
{"key":"/mykey","value":"test key","modifiedIndex":7,"createdIndex":7}}
```

In the preceding code, you add a key to your etcd2 node and then kill it. But etcd has automatically replicated the information to the other nodes and is able to provide you with the information anyway. Although the preceding code paused for five seconds, etcd will typically replicate in under a second (even across different machines). Feel free to docker start etcd2 now to make it available again—any changes you've made in the meantime will replicate back to it.

You can see that the data is still available, but it's a little unfriendly to have to manually choose another node to connect to. Fortunately etcd has a solution for this—you can start a node in "proxy" mode, which means it doesn't replicate any data; rather, it forwards the requests to the other nodes.

Listing 9.10   Using an etcd proxy

```
$ docker run -d -p 8080:8080 --restart always --name etcd-proxy $IMG \
    etcd -proxy on -listen-client-urls http://0.0.0.0:8080 \
    -initial-cluster $CLUSTER
037c3c3dba04826a76c1d4506c922267885edbfa690e3de6188ac6b6380717ef
$ curl -L $HTTPIP:8080/v2/keys/mykey2 -XPUT -d value="t"
{"action":"set","node": >
{"key":"/mykey2","value":"t","modifiedIndex":12,"createdIndex":12}}
$ docker kill etcd1 etcd2
$ curl -L $HTTPIP:8080/v2/keys/mykey2
```

```
{"action":"get","node": >
{"key":"/mykey2","value":"t","modifiedIndex":12,"createdIndex":12}}
```

This now gives you some freedom to experiment with how etcd behaves when over half the nodes are offline.

Listing 9.11 Using etcd with more than half the nodes down

```
$ curl -L $HTTPIP:8080/v2/keys/mykey3 -XPUT -d value="t"
{"errorCode":300,"message":"Raft Internal Error", >
"cause":"etcdserver: request timed out","index":0}
$ docker start etcd2
etcd2
$ curl -L $HTTPIP:8080/v2/keys/mykey3 -XPUT -d value="t"
{"action":"set","node": >
{"key":"/mykey3","value":"t","modifiedIndex":16,"createdIndex":16}}
```

Etcd permits reading but prevents writing when half or more of the nodes are not available.

You can now see that it would be possible to start an etcd proxy on each node in a cluster to act as an "ambassador container" for retrieving centralized configuration, as follows.

Listing 9.12 Using an etcd proxy inside an ambassador container

```
$ docker run -it --rm --link etcd-proxy:etcd ubuntu:14.04.2 bash
root@8df11eaae71e:/# apt-get install -y wget
root@8df11eaae71e:/# wget -q -O- http://etcd:8080/v2/keys/mykey3
{"action":"get","node": >
{"key":"/mykey3","value":"t","modifiedIndex":16,"createdIndex":16}}
```

> **TIP** An ambassador is a so-called "Docker pattern" that has some currency among Docker users. An ambassador container is placed between your application container and some external service and handles the request. It's similar to a proxy, but it has some intelligence baked into it to handle the specific requirements of the situation—much like a real-life ambassador.

Once you have an etcd running in all environments, creating a machine in an environment is just a matter of starting it up with a link to an etcd-proxy container—all CD builds to the machine will then use the correct configuration for the environment. The next technique shows how to use etcd-provided configuration to drive zero-downtime upgrades.

DISCUSSION

The ambassador container shown in the previous section draws on the link flag introduced in technique 8. As noted there, linking has fallen somewhat out of favor in the Docker world, and a more idiomatic way to achieve the same thing now is with named containers on a virtual network, covered in technique 80.

Having a cluster of key/value servers providing a consistent view of the world is a big step forward from managing configuration files on many machines, and it helps you push toward fulfilling the Docker contract described in technique 70.

9.4   *Upgrading running containers*

In order to achieve the ideal of multiple deployments to production every day, it's important to reduce downtime during the final step of the deployment process—turning off the old applications and starting up the new ones. There's no point deploying four times a day if the switchover is an hour-long process each time!

Because containers provide an isolated environment, a number of problems are already mitigated. For example, you don't need to worry about two versions of an application using the same working directory and conflicting with each other, or about rereading some configuration files and picking up new values without restarting using the new code.

Unfortunately there are some downsides to this—it's no longer simple to change files in-place, so soft-restarts (required to pick up configuration file changes) become harder to achieve. As a result, we've found it a best practice to always perform the same upgrade process regardless of whether you're changing a few configuration files or thousands of lines of code.

Let's look at an upgrade process that will achieve the gold standard of zero-downtime deployment for web-facing applications.

TECHNIQUE 75   Using confd to enable zero-downtime switchovers

Because containers can exist side by side on a host, the simple switchover approach of removing a container and starting a new one can be performed in as little as a few seconds (and it permits a similarly fast rollback).

For most applications, this may well be fast enough, but applications with a long startup time or high availability requirements need an alternative approach. Sometimes this is an unavoidably complex process requiring special handling with the application itself, but web-facing applications have an option you may wish to consider first.

PROBLEM

You need to be able to upgrade web-facing applications with zero downtime.

SOLUTION

Use confd with nginx on your host to perform a two-stage switchover.

Nginx is an extremely popular web server with a crucial built-in ability—it can reload configuration files without dropping connections to the server. By combining this with confd, a tool that can retrieve information from a central datastore (like etcd) and alter configuration files accordingly, you can update etcd with the latest settings and watch everything else be handled for you.

> **NOTE**   The Apache HTTP server and HAProxy both also offer zero-downtime reloading and can be used instead of nginx if you have existing configuration expertise.

The first step is to start an application that will serve as an old application that you'll eventually update. Python comes with Ubuntu and has a built-in web server, so we'll use it as an example.

Listing 9.13   Starting a simple fileserver in a container

```
$ ip addr | grep 'inet ' | grep -v 'lo$\|docker0$'
    inet 10.194.12.221/20 brd 10.194.15.255 scope global eth0
$ HTTPIP=http://10.194.12.221
$ docker run -d --name py1 -p 80 ubuntu:14.04.2 \
  sh -c 'cd / && python3 -m http.server 80'
e6b769ec3efa563a959ce771164de8337140d910de67e1df54d4960fdff74544
$ docker inspect -f '{{.NetworkSettings.Ports}}' py1
map[80/tcp:[{0.0.0.0 32768}]]
$ curl -s localhost:32768 | tail | head -n 5
<li><a href="sbin/">sbin/</a></li>
<li><a href="srv/">srv/</a></li>
<li><a href="sys/">sys/</a></li>
<li><a href="tmp/">tmp/</a></li>
<li><a href="usr/">usr/</a></li>
```

The HTTP server has started successfully, and we used the filter option of the `inspect` command to pull out information about what port on the host is mapped to point inside the container.

Now make sure you have etcd running—this technique assumes you're still in the same working environment as the previous technique. This time you're going to use etcdctl (short for "etcd controller") to interact with etcd (rather than `curl`ing etcd directly) for simplicity.

Listing 9.14   Download and use the etcdctl Docker image

```
$ IMG=dockerinpractice/etcdctl
$ docker pull dockerinpractice/etcdctl
[...]
$ alias etcdctl="docker run --rm $IMG -C \"$HTTPIP:8080\""
$ etcdctl set /test value
value
$ etcdctl ls
/test
```

This has downloaded an etcdctl Docker image that we prepared, and it has set up an alias to always connect the etcd cluster set up previously. Now start up nginx.

Listing 9.15   Start an nginx + confd container

```
$ IMG=dockerinpractice/confd-nginx
$ docker pull $IMG
[...]
$ docker run -d --name nginx -p 8000:80 $IMG $HTTPIP:8080
ebdf3faa1979f729327fa3e00d2c8158b35a49acdc4f764f0492032fa5241b29
```

This is an image we prepared earlier, which uses confd to retrieve information from etcd and automatically update configuration files. The parameter that we pass tells the container where it can connect to the etcd cluster. Unfortunately we haven't told it where it can find our apps yet, so the logs are filled with errors.

Let's add the appropriate information to etcd.

Listing 9.16   Demonstrating the auto-configuration of the nginx container

```
$ docker logs nginx
Using http://10.194.12.221:8080 as backend
2015-05-18T13:09:56Z ebdf3faa1979 confd[14]: >
ERROR 100: Key not found (/app) [14]
2015-05-18T13:10:06Z ebdf3faa1979 confd[14]: >
ERROR 100: Key not found (/app) [14]
$ echo $HTTPIP
http://10.194.12.221
$ etcdctl set /app/upstream/py1 10.194.12.221:32768
10.194.12.221:32768
$ sleep 10
$ docker logs nginx
Using http://10.194.12.221:8080 as backend
2015-05-18T13:09:56Z ebdf3faa1979 confd[14]: >
ERROR 100: Key not found (/app) [14]
2015-05-18T13:10:06Z ebdf3faa1979 confd[14]: >
ERROR 100: Key not found (/app) [14]
2015-05-18T13:10:16Z ebdf3faa1979 confd[14]: >
ERROR 100: Key not found (/app) [14]
2015-05-18T13:10:26Z ebdf3faa1979 confd[14]: >
INFO Target config /etc/nginx/conf.d/app.conf out of sync
2015-05-18T13:10:26Z ebdf3faa1979 confd[14]: >
INFO Target config /etc/nginx/conf.d/app.conf has been updated
$ curl -s localhost:8000 | tail | head -n5
<li><a href="sbin/">sbin/</a></li>
<li><a href="srv/">srv/</a></li>
<li><a href="sys/">sys/</a></li>
<li><a href="tmp/">tmp/</a></li>
<li><a href="usr/">usr/</a></li>
```

The update to etcd has been read by confd and applied to the nginx configuration file, allowing you to visit your simple file server. The sleep command is included because confd has been configured to check for updates every 10 seconds. Behind the scenes, a confd daemon running in the confd-nginx container polls for changes in the etcd cluster, using a template within the container to regenerate the nginx configuration only when changes are detected.

Let's say we've decided we want to serve /etc rather than /. We'll now start up our second application and add it to etcd. Because we'll then have two backends, we'll end up getting responses from each of them.

Listing 9.17 Using confd to set up two backend web services for nginx

```
$ docker run -d --name py2 -p 80 ubuntu:14.04.2 \
  sh -c 'cd /etc && python3 -m http.server 80'
9b5355b9b188427abaf367a51a88c1afa2186e6179ab46830715a20eacc33660
$ docker inspect -f '{{.NetworkSettings.Ports}}' py2
map[80/tcp:[{0.0.0.0 32769}]]
$ curl -s $HTTPIP:32769 | tail | head -n 5
<li><a href="udev/">udev/</a></li>
<li><a href="update-motd.d/">update-motd.d/</a></li>
<li><a href="upstart-xsessions">upstart-xsessions</a></li>
<li><a href="vim/">vim/</a></li>
<li><a href="vtrgb">vtrgb@</a></li>
$ echo $HTTPIP
http://10.194.12.221
$ etcdctl set /app/upstream/py2 10.194.12.221:32769
10.194.12.221:32769
$ etcdctl ls /app/upstream
/app/upstream/py1
/app/upstream/py2
$ curl -s localhost:8000 | tail | head -n 5
<li><a href="sbin/">sbin/</a></li>
<li><a href="srv/">srv/</a></li>
<li><a href="sys/">sys/</a></li>
<li><a href="tmp/">tmp/</a></li>
<li><a href="usr/">usr/</a></li>
$ curl -s localhost:8000 | tail | head -n 5
<li><a href="udev/">udev/</a></li>
<li><a href="update-motd.d/">update-motd.d/</a></li>
<li><a href="upstart-xsessions">upstart-xsessions</a></li>
<li><a href="vim/">vim/</a></li>
<li><a href="vtrgb">vtrgb@</a></li>
```

In the preceding process, we checked that the new container came up correctly before adding it to etcd (see figure 9.4). We could have performed the process in one step by overwriting the /app/upstream/py1 key in etcd—this is also useful if you need only one backend to be accessible at a time.

With the two-stage switchover, the second stage is to remove the old backend and container.

Listing 9.18 Removing the old upstream address

```
$ etcdctl rm /app/upstream/py1
PrevNode.Value: 192.168.1.123:32768
$ etcdctl ls /app/upstream
/app/upstream/py2
$ docker rm -f py1
py1
```

The new application is up and running by itself! At no point has the application been inaccessible to users, and there has been no need to manually connect to web server machines to reload nginx.

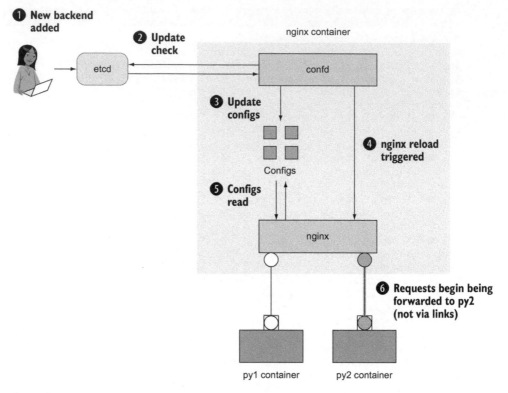

Figure 9.4   Adding the py2 container to etcd

DISCUSSION

The uses of confd extend to more than configuring web servers: if you have any file containing text that needs updating based on external values, confd is there to step in—a useful connector between configuration files stored on disk and a single-point-of-truth etcd cluster.

As noted in the previous technique, etcd is not designed for storing large values. There's also no reason you must use etcd with confd—there are a number of integrations available for the most popular key/value stores, so you might not need to add another moving part if you've already got something that works for you.

Later on, in technique 86, when we look at using Docker in production, you'll see a method that avoids having to manually alter etcd at all if you want to update the backend servers for a service.

Summary

- Docker provides a great basis for a contract between development and operations teams.
- Moving images between registries can be a good way to control how far builds progress through your CD pipeline.

- Bup is good at squeezing image transfers even more than layers can.
- Docker images can be moved and shared as TAR files.
- etcd can act as a central configuration store for an environment.
- Zero-downtime deployment can be achieved by combining etcd, confd, and nginx.

Network simulation: Realistic environment testing without the pain

This chapter covers

- Coming to grips with Docker Compose
- Testing your applications on troublesome networks
- Taking a first look at Docker network drivers
- Creating a substrate network for seamless communications across Docker hosts

As part of your DevOps workflow, you'll likely need to use the network in some way. Whether you're trying to find out where the local memcache container is, connecting to the outside world, or plumbing together Docker containers running on different hosts, you're likely to want to reach out to the wider network sooner or later.

After reading this chapter you'll know how to manage containers as a unit using Docker Compose, and simulate and manage networks by using Docker's virtual network tooling. This chapter is a small first step toward orchestration and service discovery—subjects we'll take a deeper dive into in part 4 of this book.

10.1 Container communication: Beyond manual linking

In technique 8 you saw how to connect containers with links, and we mentioned the advantages provided by a clear statement of container dependencies. Unfortunately, links have a number of disadvantages. Links have to be manually specified when starting each container, containers have to be started in the correct order, loops in links are forbidden, and there's no way to replace a link (if a container dies, every dependent container must be restarted to recreate the links). On top of everything else, they're deprecated!

Docker Compose is currently the most popular replacement for anything that previously involved a complex links setup, and we'll take a look at it now.

TECHNIQUE 76 A simple Docker Compose cluster

Docker Compose started life as *fig*, a now-deprecated independent effort to ease the pain of starting multiple containers with appropriate arguments for linking, volumes, and ports. Docker Inc. liked this so much that they acquired it, gave it a makeover, and released it with a new name.

This technique introduces you to Docker Compose using a simple example of Docker container orchestration.

PROBLEM
You want to coordinate connected containers on your host machine.

SOLUTION
Use Docker Compose, a tool for defining and running multicontainer Docker applications.

The central idea is that rather than wiring up container startup commands with complex shell scripts or Makefiles, you declare the application's startup configuration, and then bring the application up with a single, simple command.

> **NOTE** We assume you have Docker Compose installed—refer to the official instructions (http://docs.docker.com/compose/install) for the latest advice.

In this technique we're going to keep things as simple as possible with an echo server and client. The client sends the familiar "Hello world!" message every five seconds to the echo server, and then receives the message back.

> **TIP** The source code for this technique is available at https://github.com/ docker-in-practice/docker-compose-echo.

The following commands create a directory for you to work in while creating the server image:

```
$ mkdir server
$ cd server
```

Create the server Dockerfile with the code shown in the following listing.

Listing 10.1   Dockerfile—a simple echo server

Installs the nmap package, which provides the ncat program used here

```
.FROM debian
RUN apt-get update && apt-get install -y nmap
 CMD ncat -l 2000 -k --exec /bin/cat
```

Runs the ncat program by default when starting the image

The `-l 2000` arguments instruct ncat to listen on port 2000, and `-k` tells it to accept multiple client connections simultaneously and to continue running after clients close their connections so more clients can connect. The final arguments, `--exec /bin/cat`, will make ncat run `/bin/cat` for any incoming connections and forward any data coming over the connection to the running program.

Next, build the Dockerfile with this command:

```
$ docker build -t server .
```

Now you can set up the client image that sends messages to the server. Create a new directory and place the client.py file and Dockerfile in there:

```
$ cd ..
$ mkdir client
$ cd client
```

We'll use a simple Python program as the echo server client in the next listing.

Listing 10.2   client.py—a simple echo client

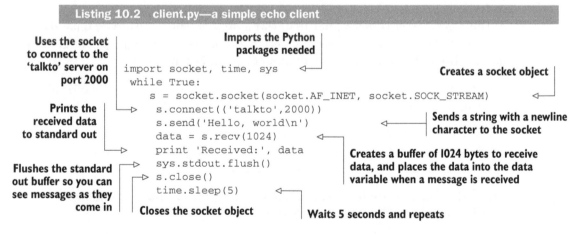

Uses the socket to connect to the 'talkto' server on port 2000

Imports the Python packages needed

Creates a socket object

```
import socket, time, sys
 while True:
    s = socket.socket(socket.AF_INET, socket.SOCK_STREAM)
    s.connect(('talkto',2000))
    s.send('Hello, world\n')
    data = s.recv(1024)
    print 'Received:', data
    sys.stdout.flush()
    s.close()
    time.sleep(5)
```

Prints the received data to standard out

Sends a string with a newline character to the socket

Creates a buffer of 1024 bytes to receive data, and places the data into the data variable when a message is received

Flushes the standard out buffer so you can see messages as they come in

Closes the socket object

Waits 5 seconds and repeats

The Dockerfile for the client is straightforward. It installs Python, adds the client.py file, and then defaults it to run on startup, as shown in the following listing.

Listing 10.3   Dockerfile—a simple echo client

```
FROM debian
RUN apt-get update && apt-get install -y python
ADD client.py /client.py
CMD ["/usr/bin/python","/client.py"]
```

Build the client with this command:

```
docker build -t client .
```

To demonstrate the value of Docker Compose, we'll first run these containers by hand:

```
docker run --name echo-server -d server
docker run --name client --link echo-server:talkto client
```

When you're finished, Ctrl-C out of the client, and remove the containers:

```
docker rm -f client echo-server
```

Many things can go wrong even in this trivial example: starting the client first will result in the failure of the application to start; forgetting to remove the containers will result in problems when you try to restart; and naming containers incorrectly will result in failure. These kinds of orchestration problems will only increase as your containers and their architecture get more sophisticated.

Compose helps with this by encapsulating the orchestration of these containers' startup and configuration within a simple text file, managing the nuts and bolts of the startup and shutdown commands for you.

Compose takes a YAML file. You create this in a new directory:

```
cd ..
mkdir docker-compose
cd docker-compose
```

The YAML file's contents are shown in the following listing.

Listing 10.4   docker-compose.yml—Docker Compose echo server and client YAML file

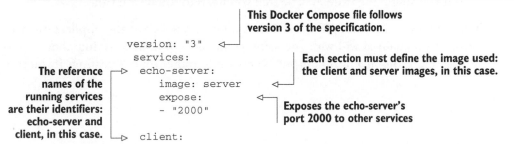

This Docker Compose file follows
version 3 of the specification.

The reference
names of the
running services
are their identifiers:
echo-server and
client, in this case.

Each section must define the image used:
the client and server images, in this case.

Exposes the echo-server's
port 2000 to other services

```
version: "3"
services:
  echo-server:
    image: server
    expose:
    - "2000"
  client:
```

Each section must define the image used:
the client and server images, in this case.

```
image: client
links:
- echo-server:talkto
```

Defines a link to the echo-server. References to
"talkto" within the client will be sent to the echo
server. The mapping is done by setting up the
/etc/hosts file dynamically in the running container.

The syntax of docker-compose.yml is fairly easy to grasp: each service is named under the `services` key, and configuration is stated in an indented section underneath. Each item of configuration has a colon after its name, and attributes of these items are stated either on the same line or on the following lines, beginning with dashes at the same level of indentation.

The key item of configuration to understand here is `links` within the client definition. This is created in the same way as the `docker run` command sets up links, except Compose handles startup order for you. In fact, most of the Docker command-line arguments have direct analogues in the docker-compose.yml syntax.

We used the `image:` statement in this example to define the image used for each service, but you can also get docker-compose to rebuild the required image dynamically by defining the path to the Dockerfile in a `build:` statement. Docker Compose will perform the build for you.

> **TIP** A YAML file is a text configuration file with a straightforward syntax. You can read more about it at http://yaml.org.

Now that all the infrastructure is set up, running the application is easy:

```
$ docker-compose up
Creating dockercompose_server_1...
Creating dockercompose_client_1...
Attaching to dockercompose_server_1, dockercompose_client_1
client_1 | Received: Hello, world
client_1 |
client_1 | Received: Hello, world
client_1 |
```

> **TIP** If you get an error when starting docker-compose that looks like "Couldn't connect to Docker daemon at http+unix://var/run/docker.sock— is it running?" the issue may be that you need to run it with sudo.

When you've seen enough, press Ctrl-C a few times to exit the application. You can bring it up again at will with the same command, without worrying about removing containers. Note that it will output "Recreating" rather than "Creating" if you rerun it.

DISCUSSION

We mentioned a possible need for sudo in the previous section—you may want to revisit technique 41 if this applies to you, as it makes using tools that interact with the Docker daemon significantly easier.

Docker Inc. advertises Docker Compose as ready for use in production, either on a single machine as shown here, or deploying it across multiple machines with swarm mode—you'll see how to do this in technique 87.

Now that you've come to grips with Docker Compose, we'll move on to a more complex and real-world scenario for docker-compose: using socat, volumes, and the replacement for links to add server-like functionality to a SQLite instance running on the host machine.

TECHNIQUE 77   A SQLite server using Docker Compose

SQLite doesn't come with any concept of a TCP server by default. By building on previous techniques, this technique provides you with a means of achieving TCP server functionality using Docker Compose.

Specifically, it builds on these previously covered tools and concepts:

- Volumes
- Proxying with socat
- Docker Compose

We'll also introduce the replacement for links—networks.

> **NOTE** This technique requires SQLite version 3 to be installed on your host. We also suggest that you install rlwrap to make line editing friendlier when interacting with your SQLite server (this is optional). These packages are freely available from standard package managers.

The code for this technique is available for download here: https://github.com/docker-in-practice/docker-compose-sqlite.

PROBLEM

You want to efficiently develop a complex application referencing external data on your host using Docker.

SOLUTION

Use Docker Compose.

Figure 10.1 gives an overview of this technique's architecture. At a high level there are two running Docker containers: one responsible for executing SQLite clients, and the other for proxying separate TCP connections to these clients. Note that the container executing SQLite isn't exposed to the host; the proxy container achieves that. This kind of separation of responsibility into discrete units is a common feature of microservices architectures.

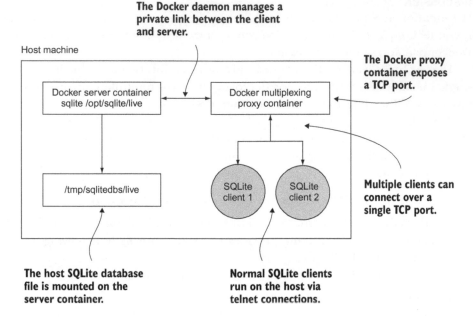

Figure 10.1   How the SQLite server works

We're going to use the same image for all our nodes. Set up the Dockerfile in the next listing.

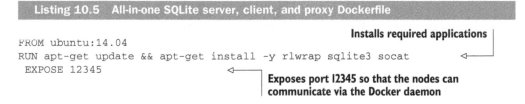

Listing 10.5   All-in-one SQLite server, client, and proxy Dockerfile

Installs required applications

```
FROM ubuntu:14.04
RUN apt-get update && apt-get install -y rlwrap sqlite3 socat
 EXPOSE 12345
```

Exposes port 12345 so that the nodes can communicate via the Docker daemon

The following listing shows docker-compose.yml, which defines how the containers should be started up.

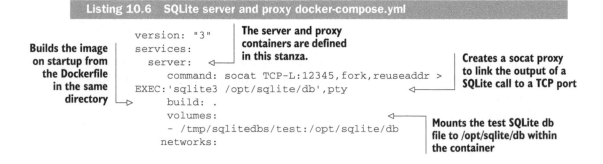

Listing 10.6   SQLite server and proxy docker-compose.yml

Builds the image on startup from the Dockerfile in the same directory

The server and proxy containers are defined in this stanza.

```
version: "3"
services:
  server:
    command: socat TCP-L:12345,fork,reuseaddr >
EXEC:'sqlite3 /opt/sqlite/db',pty
    build: .
    volumes:
    - /tmp/sqlitedbs/test:/opt/sqlite/db
    networks:
```

Creates a socat proxy to link the output of a SQLite call to a TCP port

Mounts the test SQLite db file to /opt/sqlite/db within the container

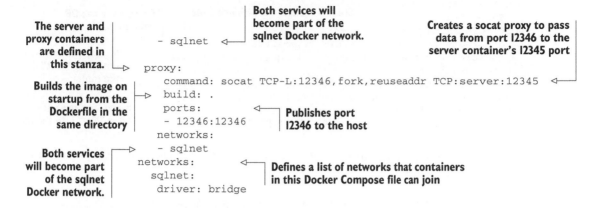

The socat process in the server container will listen on port 12345 and permit multiple connections, as specified by the `TCP-L:12345,fork,reuseaddr` argument. The part following `EXEC:` tells `socat` to run SQLite on the /opt/sqlite/db file for every connection, assigning a pseudo-terminal to the process. The socat process in the client container has the same listening behavior as the server container (except on a different port), but instead of running something in response to an incoming connection, it will establish a TCP connection to the SQLite server.

One notable difference from the previous technique is the use of networks rather than links—networks present a way to create new virtual networks inside Docker. Docker Compose will always use a new "bridge" virtual network by default; it's just been named explicitly in the preceding Compose configuration. Because any new bridge network allows access to containers using their service names, there's no need to use links (though you still can if you want aliases for services).

Although this functionality could be achieved in one container, the server/proxy container setup allows the architecture of this system to grow more easily, as each container is responsible for one job. The server is responsible for opening SQLite connections, and the proxy is responsible for exposing the service to the host machine.

The following listing (simplified from the original in the repository, https://github.com/docker-in-practice/docker-compose-sqlite) creates two minimal SQLite databases, test and live, on your host machine.

Listing 10.7 setup_dbs.sh

```
#!/bin/bash
echo "Creating directory"          Removes any directory
SQLITEDIR=/tmp/sqlitedbs           from a previous run
rm -rf $SQLITEDIR
 if [ -a $SQLITEDIR ]              Throws an error if the
 then                             directory still exists
    echo "Failed to remove $SQLITEDIR"
    exit 1
fi
```

```
mkdir -p $SQLITEDIR
cd $SQLITEDIR
echo "Creating DBs"
echo 'create table t1(c1 text);' | sqlite3 test
 echo 'create table t1(c1 text);' | sqlite3 live
 echo "Inserting data"
echo 'insert into t1 values ("test");' | sqlite3 test
 echo 'insert into t1 values ("live");' | sqlite3 live
 cd - > /dev/null 2>&1
 echo "All done OK"
```

Creates the test DB with one table

Creates the live DB with one table

Inserts one row with the string "test" into the table

Inserts one row with the string "live" into the table

Returns to the previous directory

To run this example, set up the databases and call docker-compose up, as shown in the following listing.

Listing 10.8   Run up the Docker Compose cluster

```
$ chmod +x setup_dbs.sh
$ ./setup_dbs.sh
$ docker-compose up
Creating network "tmpnwxqlnjvdn_sqlnet" with driver "bridge"
Building proxy
Step 1/3 : FROM ubuntu:14.04
14.04: Pulling from library/ubuntu
[...]
Successfully built bb347070723c
Successfully tagged tmpnwxqlnjvdn_proxy:latest
[...]
Successfully tagged tmpnwxqlnjvdn_server:latest
[...]
Creating tmpnwxqlnjvdn_server_1
Creating tmpnwxqlnjvdn_proxy_1 ... done
Attaching to tmpnwxqlnjvdn_server_1, tmpnwxqlnjvdn_proxy_1
```

Then, in one or more other terminals, you can run Telnet to create multiple sessions against one SQLite database.

Listing 10.9   Connecting to the SQLite server

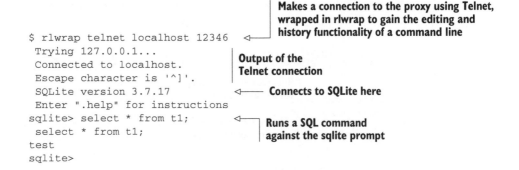

Makes a connection to the proxy using Telnet, wrapped in rlwrap to gain the editing and history functionality of a command line

```
$ rlwrap telnet localhost 12346
 Trying 127.0.0.1...
 Connected to localhost.
 Escape character is '^]'.
 SQLite version 3.7.17
 Enter ".help" for instructions
sqlite> select * from t1;
 select * from t1;
test
sqlite>
```

Output of the Telnet connection

Connects to SQLite here

Runs a SQL command against the sqlite prompt

If you want to switch the server to live, you can change the configuration by changing the volumes line in docker-compose.yml from this,

```
- /tmp/sqlitedbs/test:/opt/sqlite/db
```

to this:

```
- /tmp/sqlitedbs/live:/opt/sqlite/db
```

Then rerun this command:

```
$ docker-compose up
```

> **WARNING** Although we did some basic tests with this multiplexing of SQLite clients, we make no guarantees about the data integrity or performance of this server under any kind of load. The SQLite client wasn't designed to work in this way. The purpose of this technique is to demonstrate the general approach of exposing a binary in this way.

This technique demonstrates how Docker Compose can take something relatively tricky and complicated, and make it robust and straightforward. Here we've taken SQLite and given it extra server-like functionality by wiring up containers to proxy SQLite invocations to the data on the host. Managing the container complexity is made significantly easier with Docker Compose's YAML configuration, which turns the tricky matter of orchestrating containers correctly from a manual, error-prone process to a safer, automated one that can be put under source control. This is the beginning of our journey into orchestration, which you'll be hearing much more about in part 4 of the book.

DISCUSSION

Using networks with the depends_on feature of Docker Compose allows you to effectively emulate the functionality of links by controlling startup order. For a full treatment of all possible options available to Docker Compose, we recommend you read the official documentation at https://docs.docker.com/compose/compose-file/.

To find out more about Docker virtual networks, take a look at technique 80—it goes into the details of what Docker Compose is doing behind the scenes to set up your virtual networks.

10.2 *Using Docker to simulate real-world networking*

Most people who use the internet treat it as a black box that somehow retrieves information from other places around the world and puts it on their screens. Sometimes they experience slowness or connection drops, and it's not uncommon to observe cursing of the ISP as a result.

When you build images containing applications that need to be connected, you likely have a much firmer grasp of which components need to connect to where, and how the overall setup looks. But one thing remains constant: you can still experience slowness and connection drops. Even large companies, with data centers they own and operate, have observed unreliable networking and the issues it causes with applications.

We'll look at a couple of ways you can experiment with flaky networks to help determine what problems you may be facing in the real world.

TECHNIQUE 78   Simulating troublesome networks with Comcast

As much as we might wish for perfect network conditions when we distribute applications across many machines, the reality is much uglier—tales of packet loss, connection drops, and network partitions abound, particularly on commodity cloud providers.

It's prudent to test your stack before it encounters these situations in the real world to see how it behaves—an application designed for high availability shouldn't grind to a halt if an external service starts experiencing significant additional latency.

PROBLEM

You want to be able to apply varying network conditions to individual containers.

SOLUTION

Use Comcast (the networking tool, not the ISP).

Comcast (https://github.com/tylertreat/Comcast) is a humorously named tool for altering network interfaces on your Linux machine in order to apply unusual (or, if you're unfortunate, typical!) conditions to them.

Whenever Docker creates a container, it also creates virtual network interfaces—this is how all your containers have different IP addresses and can ping each other. Because these are standard network interfaces, you can use Comcast on them, as long as you can find the network interface name. This is easier said than done.

The following listing shows a Docker image containing Comcast, all its prerequisites, and some tweaks.

Listing 10.10   Preparing to run the comcast image

```
$ IMG=dockerinpractice/comcast
$ docker pull $IMG
latest: Pulling from dockerinpractice/comcast
[...]
Status: Downloaded newer image for dockerinpractice/comcast:latest
$ alias comcast="docker run --rm --pid=host --privileged \
-v /var/run/docker.sock:/var/run/docker.sock $IMG"
$ comcast -help
Usage of comcast:
  -cont string
        Container ID or name to get virtual interface of
  -default-bw int
        Default bandwidth limit in kbit/s (fast-lane) (default -1)
  -device string
        Interface (device) to use (defaults to eth0 where applicable)
  -dry-run
        Specifies whether or not to actually commit the rule changes
  -latency int
        Latency to add in ms (default -1)
```

```
-packet-loss string
      Packet loss percentage (e.g. 0.1%)
-stop
      Stop packet controls
-target-addr string
      Target addresses, (e.g. 10.0.0.1 or 10.0.0.0/24 or >
10.0.0.1,192.168.0.0/24 or 2001:db8:a::123)
-target-bw int
      Target bandwidth limit in kbit/s (slow-lane) (default -1)
-target-port string
      Target port(s) (e.g. 80 or 1:65535 or 22,80,443,1000:1010)
-target-proto string
      Target protocol TCP/UDP (e.g. tcp or tcp,udp or icmp) (default >
"tcp,udp,icmp")
-version
      Print Comcast's version
```

The tweaks we added here provide the -cont option, which allows you to refer to a container rather than having to find the name of a virtual interface. Note that we've had to add some special flags to the docker run command in order to give the container more permissions—this is so Comcast is freely able to examine and apply changes to network interfaces.

To see the difference Comcast can make, we'll first find out what a normal network connection looks like. Open a new terminal and run the following commands to set your expectations for baseline network performance:

The connection between this machine and www.example.com seems to be reliable, with no packets lost.

```
$ docker run -it --name c1 ubuntu:14.04.2 bash
root@0749a2e74a68:/# apt-get update && apt-get install -y wget
[...]
root@0749a2e74a68:/# ping -q -c 5 www.example.com
PING www.example.com (93.184.216.34) 56(84) bytes of data.

--- www.example.com ping statistics ---
5 packets transmitted, 5 received, 0% packet loss, >
time 4006ms
  rtt min/avg/max/mdev = 86.397/86.804/88.229/0.805 ms
  root@0749a2e74a68:/# time wget -o /dev/null https://www.example.com
```

The average round trip time is about 100 ms for www.example.com.

```
real    0m0.379s
 user    0m0.008s
sys     0m0.008s
root@0749a2e74a68:/#
```

The total time taken to download the HTML homepage of www.example.com is about 0.7 s.

Once you've done this, leave the container running and you can apply some network conditions to it:

```
$ comcast -cont c1 -default-bw 50 -latency 100 -packet-loss 20%
Found interface veth62cc8bf for container 'c1'
sudo tc qdisc show | grep "netem"
sudo tc qdisc add dev veth62cc8bf handle 10: root htb default 1
```

```
sudo tc class add dev veth62cc8bf parent 10: classid 10:1 htb rate 50kbit
sudo tc class add dev veth62cc8bf parent 10: classid 10:10 htb rate 1000000kb
➥ it
sudo tc qdisc add dev veth62cc8bf parent 10:10 handle 100: netem delay 100ms
➥ loss 20.00%
sudo iptables -A POSTROUTING -t mangle -j CLASSIFY --set-class 10:10 -p tcp
sudo iptables -A POSTROUTING -t mangle -j CLASSIFY --set-class 10:10 -p udp
sudo iptables -A POSTROUTING -t mangle -j CLASSIFY --set-class 10:10 -p icmp
sudo ip6tables -A POSTROUTING -t mangle -j CLASSIFY --set-class 10:10 -p tcp
sudo ip6tables -A POSTROUTING -t mangle -j CLASSIFY --set-class 10:10 -p udp
sudo ip6tables -A POSTROUTING -t mangle -j CLASSIFY --set-class 10:10 -p icmp
Packet rules setup...
Run `sudo tc -s qdisc` to double check
Run `comcast --device veth62cc8bf --stop` to reset
```

The preceding command applies three different conditions: 50 KBps bandwidth cap for all destinations (to bring back memories of dial-up), an added latency of 100 ms (on top of any inherent delay), and a packet loss percentage of 20%.

Comcast first identifies the appropriate virtual network interface for the container and then invokes a number of standard Linux command-line networking utilities to apply the traffic rules, listing what it's doing as it goes along. Let's see how our container reacts to this:

```
root@0749a2e74a68:/# ping -q -c 5 www.example.com
PING www.example.com (93.184.216.34) 56(84) bytes of data.

--- www.example.com ping statistics ---
5 packets transmitted, 2 received, 60% packet loss, time 4001ms
rtt min/avg/max/mdev = 186.425/189.429/195.008/3.509 ms
root@0749a2e74a68:/# time wget -o /dev/null https://www.example.com

real    0m1.993s
user    0m0.011s
sys     0m0.011s
```

Success! An additional 100 ms of latency is reported by ping, and the timing from wget shows a slightly greater than 5x slowdown, approximately as expected (the bandwidth cap, latency addition, and packet loss will all impact on this time). But there's something odd about the packet loss—it seems to be three times greater than expected. It's important to bear in mind that the ping is sending a few packets, and that packet loss isn't a precise "one in five" counter—if you increase the ping count to 50, you'll find that the resulting loss is much closer to what's expected.

Note that the rules we've applied apply to *all* network connections via this network interface. This includes connections to the host and other containers.

Let's now instruct Comcast to remove the rules. Comcast is sadly not yet able to add and remove individual conditions, so altering anything on a network interface means completely removing and re-adding rules on the interface. You also need to remove the rules if you want to get your normal container network operation back.

Don't worry about removing them if you exit the container, though—they'll be automatically deleted when Docker deletes the virtual network interface.

```
$ comcast -cont c1 -stop
Found interface veth62cc8bf for container 'c1'
[...]
Packet rules stopped...
Run `sudo tc -s qdisc` to double check
Run `comcast` to start
```

If you want to get your hands dirty, you can dig into Linux traffic control tools, possibly using Comcast with -dry-run to generate example sets of commands to use. A full treatment of the possibilities is outside the scope of the technique, but remember, if you can put it in a container, and it hits the network, you can toy with it.

DISCUSSION

With some implementation effort, there's no reason you can't use Comcast for more than just manual control of container bandwidth. For example, imagine you were using a tool like btsync (technique 35) but wanted to limit the available bandwidth so it doesn't saturate your connection—download Comcast, put it in the container, and use ENTRYPOINT (technique 49) to set up the bandwidth limits as part of container startup.

To do this, you'll need to install the dependencies of Comcast (listed for the alpine image in our Dockerfile at https://github.com/docker-in-practice/docker-comcast/blob/master/Dockerfile) and likely give at least network admin capabilities to the container—you can read more about capabilities in technique 93.

TECHNIQUE 79   **Simulating troublesome networks with Blockade**

Comcast is an excellent tool with a number of applications, but there's an important use case it doesn't solve—how can you apply network conditions to containers en masse? Manually running Comcast against tens of containers would be painful, and hundreds would be unthinkable! This is a particularly relevant problem for containers, because they're so cheap to spin up—if you're trying to run a large network simulation on a single machine with hundreds of VMs rather than containers, you may find you have bigger problems, like a lack of memory!

On the subject of simulating a network with many machines, there's a particular kind of network failure that becomes interesting at this scale—a network partition. This is when a group of networked machines splits into two or more parts, such that all machines in the same part can talk to each other, but different parts can't communicate. Research indicates that this happens more than you might think, particularly on consumer-grade clouds!

Going down the classic Docker microservices route brings these problems into sharp relief, and having the tools to do experiments is crucial for understanding how your service will deal with it.

PROBLEM

You want to orchestrate setting network conditions for large numbers of containers, including creating network partitions.

SOLUTION

Use Blockade (https://github.com/worstcase/blockade)—an open source piece of software originally from a team at Dell, created for "testing network failures and partitions."

Blockade works by reading a configuration file (blockade.yml) in your current directory that defines how to start containers and what conditions to apply to them. In order to apply conditions, it may download other images with required utilities installed. The full configuration details are available in the Blockade documentation, so we'll only cover the essentials.

First you need to create a blockade.yml file.

Listing 10.11   The blockade.yml file

```
containers:
  server:
    container_name: server
    image: ubuntu:14.04.2
    command: /bin/sleep infinity

  client1:
    image: ubuntu:14.04.2
    command: sh -c "sleep 5 && ping server"

  client2:
    image: ubuntu:14.04.2
    command: sh -c "sleep 5 && ping server"

network:
  flaky: 50%
  slow: 100ms
  driver: udn
```

The containers in the preceding configuration are set up to represent a server being connected to by two clients. In practice, this could be something like a database server with client applications, and there's no inherent reason you have to limit the number of components you want to model. Chances are, if you can represent it in a compose .yml file (see technique 76), you can probably model it in Blockade.

We've specified the network driver as udn here—this makes Blockade mimic the behavior of Docker Compose in technique 77, creating a new virtual network so containers can ping each other by container name. To this end, we've had to explicitly specify container_name for the server, as Blockade generates one itself by default. The sleep 5 commands are to make sure the server is running before starting the clients—if you prefer to use links with Blockade, they will ensure the containers are started up in the correct order. Don't worry about the network section for now; we'll come back to it shortly.

As usual, the first step in using Blockade is to pull the image:

```
$ IMG=dockerinpractice/blockade
$ docker pull $IMG
latest: Pulling from dockerinpractice/blockade
[...]
Status: Downloaded newer image for dockerinpractice/blockade:latest
$ alias blockade="docker run --rm -v \$PWD:/blockade \
-v /var/run/docker.sock:/var/run/docker.sock $IMG"
```

You'll notice that we're missing a few arguments to docker run, compared to the previous technique (like --privileged and --pid=host). Blockade uses other containers to perform the network manipulation, so it doesn't need permissions itself. Also note the argument to mount the current directory into the container, so that Blockade is able to access blockade.yml and store state in a hidden folder.

NOTE If you're running on a networked filesystem, you may encounter strange permission issues when you start Blockade for the first time—this is likely because Docker is trying to create the hidden state folder as root, but the networked filesystem isn't cooperating. The solution is to use a local disk.

Finally we come to the moment of truth—running Blockade. Make sure you're in the directory you've saved blockade.yml into:

```
$ blockade up
NODE       CONTAINER ID   STATUS   IP           NETWORK   PARTITION
client1    613b5b1cdb7d   UP       172.17.0.4   NORMAL
client2    2aeb2ed0dd45   UP       172.17.0.5   NORMAL
server     53a7fa4ce884   UP       172.17.0.3   NORMAL
```

NOTE On startup, Blockade may sometimes give cryptic errors about files in /proc not existing. The first thing to check is whether a container has immediately exited on startup, preventing Blockade from checking its network status. Additionally, try to resist any temptation to use the Blockade -c option to specify a custom path to the config file—only subdirectories of the current directory are available inside the container.

All of the containers defined in our config file have been started, and we've been given a bunch of helpful information about the started containers. Let's now apply some basic network conditions. Tail the logs of client1 in a new terminal (with docker logs -f 613b5b1cdb7d) so you can see what happens as you change things:

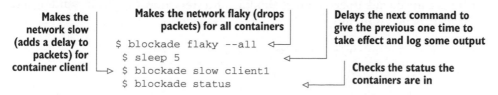

```
                    NODE      CONTAINER ID    STATUS   IP            NETWORK   PARTITION
Reverts all the     client1   613b5b1cdb7d    UP       172.17.0.4    SLOW
containers to       client2   2aeb2ed0dd45    UP       172.17.0.5    FLAKY
normal              server    53a7fa4ce884    UP       172.17.0.3    FLAKY
operation  ─────▷   $ blockade fast --all
```

The `flaky` and `slow` commands use the values defined in the `network` section of the preceding configuration file (listing 10.11)—there's no way to specify a limit on the command line. If you want, it's possible to edit blockade.yml while containers are running and then selectively apply the new limits to containers. Be aware that a container can either be on a slow *or* flaky network, not both. These limitations aside, the convenience of running this against hundreds of containers is fairly significant.

If you look back at your logs from `client1`, you should now be able to see when the different commands took effect:

`icmp_seq` starts skipping numbers—the `flaky` command has taken effect.

`icmp_seq` is sequential (no packets being dropped) and `time` is low (a small delay).

```
   64 bytes from 172.17.0.3: icmp_seq=638 ttl=64 time=0.054 ms
    64 bytes from 172.17.0.3: icmp_seq=639 ttl=64 time=0.098 ms
   64 bytes from 172.17.0.3: icmp_seq=640 ttl=64 time=0.112 ms
─▷ 64 bytes from 172.17.0.3: icmp_seq=645 ttl=64 time=0.112 ms
    64 bytes from 172.17.0.3: icmp_seq=652 ttl=64 time=0.113 ms
   64 bytes from 172.17.0.3: icmp_seq=654 ttl=64 time=0.115 ms
   64 bytes from 172.17.0.3: icmp_seq=660 ttl=64 time=100 ms
    64 bytes from 172.17.0.3: icmp_seq=661 ttl=64 time=100 ms
   64 bytes from 172.17.0.3: icmp_seq=662 ttl=64 time=100 ms
   64 bytes from 172.17.0.3: icmp_seq=663 ttl=64 time=100 ms
```

`time` has taken a big jump—the `slow` command has taken effect.

All this is useful, but it's nothing we couldn't have done already with some (likely painful) scripting on top of Comcast, so let's take a look at the killer feature of Blockade—network partitions:

```
$ blockade partition server client1,client2
$ blockade status
NODE       CONTAINER ID    STATUS   IP            NETWORK   PARTITION
client1    613b5b1cdb7d    UP       172.17.0.4    NORMAL    2
client2    2aeb2ed0dd45    UP       172.17.0.5    NORMAL    2
server     53a7fa4ce884    UP       172.17.0.3    NORMAL    1
```

This has put our three nodes in two boxes—the server in one and clients in the other—with no way of communicating between them. You'll see that the log for `client1` has stopped doing anything because all of the ping packets are being lost. The clients can still talk to each other, though, and you can verify this by sending a few ping packets between them:

```
$ docker exec 613b5b1cdb7d ping -qc 3 172.17.0.5
PING 172.17.0.5 (172.17.0.5) 56(84) bytes of data.
```

```
--- 172.17.0.5 ping statistics ---
3 packets transmitted, 3 received, 0% packet loss, time 2030ms
rtt min/avg/max/mdev = 0.109/0.124/0.150/0.018 ms
```

No packet loss, low delay … looks like a good connection. Partitions and other network conditions operate independently, so you can play with packet loss while your apps are partitioned. There's no limit to the number of partitions you can define, so you can play with complex scenarios to your heart's content.

DISCUSSION

If you need more power than Blockade and Comcast can individually provide, you can combine the two. Blockade is excellent at creating partitions and doing the heavy lifting of starting up containers; adding Comcast to the mix gives you fine-grained control over the network connections of each and every container.

It's also worth looking into the complete help for Blockade—it offers other things you may find useful, like "chaos" functionality to impact random containers with assorted conditions and a `--random` argument to commands so you could (for example) see how your application reacts when containers are killed at random. If you've heard of Netflix's Chaos Monkey, this is a way to mimic it on a smaller scale.

10.3 *Docker and virtual networks*

Docker's core functionality is all about isolation. Previous chapters have shown some of the benefits of process and filesystem isolation, and in this chapter you've seen network isolation.

You could think of there being two aspects to network isolation:

- *Individual sandbox*—Each container has its own IP address and set of ports to listen on without stepping on the toes of other containers (or the host).
- *Group sandbox*—This is a logical extension of the individual sandbox—all of the isolated containers are grouped together in a private network, allowing you to play around without interfering with the network your machine lives on (and incurring the wrath of your company network administrator!).

The previous two techniques provide some practical examples of these two aspects of network isolation—Comcast manipulated individual sandboxes to apply rules to each container, whereas partitioning in Blockade relied on the ability to have complete oversight of the private container network to split it into pieces. Behind the scenes, it looks a bit like figure 10.2.

The exact details of how the bridge works aren't important. Suffice it to say that the bridge creates a flat network between containers (it allows direct communication with no intermediate steps) and it forwards requests to the outside world to your external connection.

Docker Inc. then altered this model based on feedback from users to allow you to create your own virtual networks with *network drivers*, a plugin system to extend the networking capabilities of Docker. These plugins are either built-in or provided by third

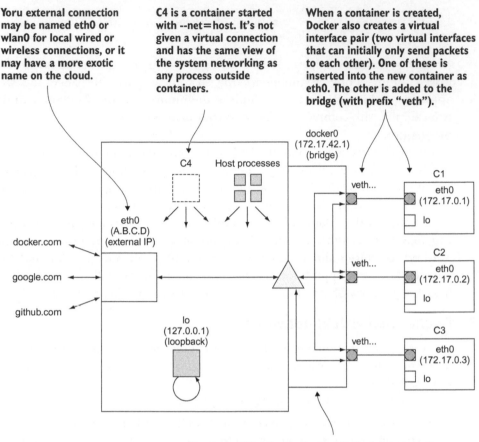

Yoru external connection may be named eth0 or wlan0 for local wired or wireless connections, or it may have a more exotic name on the cloud.

C4 is a container started with --net=host. It's not given a virtual connection and has the same view of the system networking as any process outside containers.

When a container is created, Docker also creates a virtual interface pair (two virtual interfaces that can initially only send packets to each other). One of these is inserted into the new container as eth0. The other is added to the bridge (with prefix "veth").

The docker0 bridge (created when Docker is stared) provides a place for container connections to route through. If it's taken down, containers will be unable to access the network.

Figure 10.2 **Internal Docker networking on a host machine**

parties and should do all the necessary work to wire up the network, letting you get on with using it.

New networks you create can be thought of as additional group sandboxes, typically providing access within the sandbox but not allowing cross-sandbox communication (though the precise details of the network behavior depend on the driver).

TECHNIQUE 80 Creating another Docker virtual network

When people first learn about the ability to create their own virtual networks, one common response is to ask how they can create a copy of the default Docker bridge, to allow sets of containers to communicate but be isolated from other containers.

Docker Inc. realized this would be a popular request, so it was implemented as one of the first features of virtual networks in the initial experimental release.

PROBLEM

You want a solution supported by Docker Inc. for creating virtual networks.

SOLUTION

Use the set of Docker subcommands nested under docker network to create your own virtual network.

The built-in "bridge" driver is probably the most commonly used driver—it's officially supported and allows you to create fresh copies of the default built-in bridge. There's one important difference we'll look at later in this technique, though—in non-default bridges, you can ping containers by name.

You can see the list of built-in networks with the docker network ls command:

```
$ docker network ls
NETWORK ID          NAME                DRIVER              SCOPE
100ce06cd9a8        bridge              bridge              local
d53919a3bfa1        host                host                local
2d7fcd86306c        none                null                local
```

Here you can see the three networks that are always available for containers to join on my machine. The bridge network is where containers end up by default, with the ability to talk to other containers on the bridge. The host network specifies what happens when you use --net=host when starting a container (the container sees the network as any normal program running on your machine would), and none corresponds to --net=none, a container that only has the loopback interface.

Let's add a new bridge network, providing a new flat network for containers to freely communicate in:

```
$ docker network create --driver=bridge mynet
770ffbc81166d54811ecf9839331ab10c586329e72cea2eb53a0229e53e8a37f
$ docker network ls | grep mynet
770ffbc81166        mynet               bridge              local
$ ip addr | grep br-
522: br-91b29e0d29d5: <NO-
    CARRIER,BROADCAST,MULTICAST,UP> mtu 1500 qdisc noqueue state DOWN group
⮡ default
    inet 172.18.0.1/16 scope global br-91b29e0d29d5
$ ip addr | grep docker
5: docker0: <NO-
    CARRIER,BROADCAST,MULTICAST,UP> mtu 1500 qdisc noqueue state DOWN group
⮡ default
    inet 172.17.0.1/16 scope global docker0
```

This has created a new network interface that will use a different IP address range than the normal Docker bridge. For bridges, the new network interface name will currently begin with br-, but this may change in future.

Let's now start up two containers attached to the network:

Starts a container with name
c1 (on the default bridge)

Connects
container c1 with
the mynet network

```
$ docker run -it -d --name c1 ubuntu:14.04.2 bash
 87c67f4fb376f559976e4a975e3661148d622ae635fae4695747170c00513165
$ docker network connect mynet c1
 $ docker run -it -d --name c2 \
--net=mynet ubuntu:14.04.2 bash
 0ee74a3e3444f27df9c2aa973a156f2827bcdd0852c6fd4ecfd5b152846dea5b
 $ docker run -it -d --name c3 ubuntu:14.04.2 bash
```

Starts a container with name c3
(on the default bridge)

Creates a container named c2
inside the mynet network

The preceding commands demonstrate two different ways of connecting a container to a network—starting the container and then attaching the service, and creating and attaching in one step.

There's a difference between these two. The first will join the default network on startup (usually the Docker bridge, but this is customizable with an argument to the Docker daemon), and then will add a new interface so it can access mynet as well. The second will *just* join mynet—any containers on the normal Docker bridge will be unable to access it.

Let's do some connectivity checks. First we should take a look at the IP addresses of our container:

Lists the interfaces and IP
addresses for c1—one on the
default bridge, one in mynet

```
$ docker exec c1 ip addr | grep 'inet.*eth'
    inet 172.17.0.2/16 scope global eth0
    inet 172.18.0.2/16 scope global eth1
$ docker exec c2 ip addr | grep 'inet.*eth'
    inet 172.18.0.3/16 scope global eth0
$ docker exec c3 ip addr | grep 'inet.*eth'
    inet 172.17.0.3/16 scope global eth0
```

Lists the interface and IP
address for c2, inside mynet

Lists the interface and IP address
for c3, on the default bridge

Now we can do some connectivity tests:

Attempts to ping the name for container
1 from container 2 (success)

```
$ docker exec c2 ping -qc1 c1
 PING c1 (172.18.0.2) 56(84) bytes of data.

--- c1 ping statistics ---
1 packets transmitted, 1 received, 0% packet loss, time 0ms
rtt min/avg/max/mdev = 0.041/0.041/0.041/0.000 ms
$ docker exec c2 ping -qc1 c3
 ping: unknown host c3
$ docker exec c2 ping -qc1 172.17.0.3
 PING 172.17.0.3 (172.17.0.3) 56(84) bytes of data.

--- 172.17.0.3 ping statistics ---
1 packets transmitted, 0 received, 100% packet loss, time 0ms
$ docker exec c1 ping -qc1 c2
 PING c2 (172.18.0.3) 56(84) bytes of data.
```

Attempts to ping the name
and IP address for container 3
from container 2 (failure)

Attempts to
ping the name
for container 2
from container 1
(success)

```
--- c2 ping statistics ---
1 packets transmitted, 1 received, 0% packet loss, time 0ms
rtt min/avg/max/mdev = 0.047/0.047/0.047/0.000 ms
$ docker exec c1 ping -qc1 c3
 ping: unknown host c3
$ docker exec c1 ping -qc1 172.17.0.3
 PING 172.17.0.3 (172.17.0.3) 56(84) bytes of data.

--- 172.17.0.3 ping statistics ---
1 packets transmitted, 1 received, 0% packet loss, time 0ms
rtt min/avg/max/mdev = 0.095/0.095/0.095/0.000 ms
```

> **Attempts to ping the name and IP address for container 3 from container I (failure, success)**

There's a lot going on here! These are the key takeaways:

- On the new bridge, containers can ping each other with IP address and name.
- On the default bridge, containers can only ping each other by IP address.
- Containers straddling multiple bridges can access containers from any network they're a member of.
- Containers can't access each other at all across bridges, even with an IP address.

DISCUSSION
This new bridge creation functionality was used in technique 77 with Docker Compose and technique 79 with Blockade to provide the ability for containers to ping each other by name. But you've also seen that this is a highly flexible piece of functionality with the potential to model reasonably complex networks.

For example, you might want to experiment with a *bastion host*, a single locked-down machine that provides access to another higher-value network. By putting your application services in a new bridge and then only exposing services via a container connected to both the default and new bridges, you can start running somewhat realistic penetration tests while staying isolated on your own machine.

TECHNIQUE 81 Setting up a substrate network with Weave

A substrate network is a software-level network layer built on top of another network. In effect, you end up with a network that appears to be local, but under the hood it's communicating across other networks. This means that performance-wise, the network will behave less reliably than a local network, but from a usability point of view it can be a great convenience: you can communicate with nodes in completely different locations as though they were in the same room.

This is particularly interesting for Docker containers—containers can be seamlessly connected across hosts in the same way as connecting hosts across networks. Doing this removes any urgent need to plan how many containers you can fit on a single host.

PROBLEM
You want to seamlessly communicate between containers across hosts.

SOLUTION

Use Weave Net (referred to as just "Weave" for the rest of this technique) to set up a network that lets containers talk to each other as if they're on a local network together.

We're going to demonstrate the principle of a substrate network with Weave (https://www.weave.works/oss/net/), a tool designed for this purpose. Figure 10.3 shows an overview of a typical Weave network.

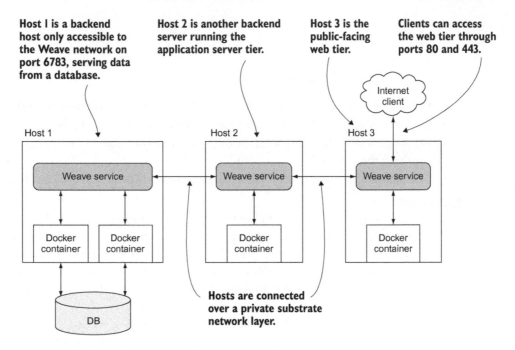

Figure 10.3   A typical Weave network

In figure 10.3, host 1 has no access to host 3, but they can talk to each other over the Weave network as though they were locally connected. The Weave network isn't open to the public—only to those containers started up under Weave. This makes the development, testing, and deployment of code across different environments relatively straightforward, because the network topology can be made the same in each case.

INSTALLING WEAVE

Weave is a single binary. You can find installation instructions at https://www.weave .works/docs/net/latest/install/installing-weave/.

The instructions in the preceding link (and listed below for convenience) worked for us. Weave needs to be installed on every host that you want to be part of your Weave network:

```
$ sudo curl -L git.io/weave -o /usr/local/bin/weave
$ sudo chmod +x /usr/local/bin/weave
```

WARNING If you experience problems with this technique, there may already
be a Weave binary on your machine that's part of another software package.

SETTING UP WEAVE

To follow this example, you'll need two hosts. We'll call them host1 and host2. Make
sure they can talk to each other by using ping. You'll need the IP address of the first
host you start Weave on.

A quick way to get a host's public IP address is by accessing https://ifconfig.co/
with a browser, or by running curl https://ifconfig.co, but be aware that you'll
probably need to open firewalls for the two hosts to connect across the open internet.
You can also run Weave on a local network if you select the correct IP address.

TIP If you experience problems with this technique, it's likely that the network is firewalled in some way. If you're not sure, talk to your network administrator. Specifically, you'll need to have port 6783 open for both TCP and
UDP, and 6784 for UDP.

On the first host, you can run the first Weave router:

Determines host1's
IP address

Launches the Weave service on host1. This needs to be
done once on each host, and it will download and run
some Docker containers to run in the background to
manage the substrate network.

```
host1$ curl https://ifconfig.co
1.2.3.4
host1$ weave launch
[...]
host1$ eval $(weave env)
  host1$ docker run -it --name a1 ubuntu:14.04 bash
  root@34fdd53a01ab:/# ip addr show ethwe
  43: ethwe@if44: <BROADCAST,MULTICAST,UP,LOWER_UP> mtu 1376 qdisc noqueue
    state UP group default
     link/ether 72:94:41:e3:00:df brd ff:ff:ff:ff:ff:ff
     inet 10.32.0.1/12 scope global ethwe
       valid_lft forever preferred_lft forever
```

Sets up the docker command in this shell to use
Weave. If you close your shell or open a new
one, you'll need to run this command again.

Starts the container

Retrieves the IP address of the
container on the Weave network

Weave takes care of inserting an additional interface into the container, ethwe, which
provides an IP address on the Weave network.

You can perform similar steps on host2, but telling Weave about the location of
host1:

Launches the Weave service on host2 as root.
This time you add the first host's public IP
address so it can attach to the other host.

Sets up your environment
appropriately for Weave's service

```
host2$ sudo weave launch 1.2.3.4
 host2$ eval $(weave env)
 host2$ docker run -it --name a2 ubuntu:14.04 bash
 root@a2:/# ip addr show ethwe
 553: ethwe@if554: <BROADCAST,MULTICAST,UP,LOWER_UP> mtu 1376 qdisc noqueue
   state UP group default
```

Continues as with host1

```
link/ether fe:39:ca:74:8a:ca brd ff:ff:ff:ff:ff:ff
inet 10.44.0.0/12 scope global ethwe
    valid_lft forever preferred_lft forever
```

The only difference on host2 is that you tell Weave that it should peer with the Weave on host1 (specified with the IP address or hostname, and optional :port, by which host2 can reach it).

TESTING YOUR CONNECTION

Now that you've got everything set up, you can test whether your containers can talk to each other. Let's take the container on host2:

```
root@a2:/# ping -qc1 10.32.0.1                    ◁─── Pings the other server's
 PING 10.32.0.1 (10.32.0.1) 56(84) bytes of data.       assigned IP address

--- 10.32.0.1 ping statistics ---                      ◁─┐ A successful
1 packets transmitted, 1 received, 0% packet loss, time 0ms  ├─ ping response
 rtt min/avg/max/mdev = 1.373/1.373/1.373/0.000 ms
```

If you get a successful ping, you've proven connectivity within your self-assigned private network spanning two hosts. You're also able to ping by container name, as with a custom bridge.

> **TIP** It's possible that this won't work due to ICMP protocol (used by ping) messages being blocked by a firewall. If this doesn't work, try telnetting to port 6783 on the other host to test whether connections can be made.

DISCUSSION

A substrate network is a powerful tool for imposing some order on the occasionally chaotic world of networks and firewalls. Weave even claims to intelligently route your traffic across partially partitioned networks, where some host B can see A and C, but A and C can't talk—this may be familiar from technique 80. That said, bear in mind that sometimes these complex network setups exist for a reason—the whole point of bastion hosts is isolation for the sake of security.

All of this power comes at a cost—there are reports of Weave networks sometimes being significantly slower than "raw" networks, and you have to run additional management machinery in the background (because the plugins model for networks doesn't cover all use cases).

The Weave network has many additional pieces of functionality, from visualization to integration with Kubernetes (we'll introduce Kubernetes as an orchestrator in technique 88). We recommend you look at the Weave Net overview to find out more and get the most out of your network—https://www.weave.works/docs/net/latest/overview/.

One thing we haven't covered here is the built-in overlay network plugin. Depending on your use case, this may be worth some research as a possible replacement for Weave, though it requires either use of Swarm mode (technique 87) or setting up a globally accessible key/value store (perhaps etcd, from technique 74).

Summary

- Docker Compose can be used to set up clusters of containers.
- Comcast and Blockade are both useful tools for testing containers in bad networks.
- Docker virtual networks are an alternative to linking.
- You can manually model networks in Docker with virtual networks.
- Weave Net is useful for stringing containers together across hosts.

Part 4

Orchestration from a single machine to the cloud

Part 4 covers the essential area of orchestration. As soon as you run any number of containers in the same environment, you'll need to think about how they're managed in a consistent and reliable way, so we'll look at some of the most popular tools currently available.

Chapter 11 explains the significance of orchestration, and builds up from managing Docker based on a single host with systemd to using service discovery on a network with Consul and Registrator.

Chapter 12 moves into clustered Docker environments, where we'll briefly cover Docker Swarm before going over Kubernetes, the most popular orchestrator around. Then we'll reverse things by showing you how to use Docker to simulate AWS services locally. Finally, we'll cover the building of a Docker framework on Mesos.

Chapter 13 is an extended discussion of the factors that might be considered in choosing a Docker-based platform. The choices can be bewildering, but this might help you structure your thoughts and make a better decision, should you need to.

11

A primer on
container orchestration

This chapter covers

- Managing simple Docker services with systemd
- Managing multi-host Docker services with Helios
- Using Hashicorp's Consul for service discovery
- Service registration using Registrator

The technology Docker is built on has existed for a while in different forms, but Docker is the solution that's managed to grab the interest of the technology industry. This puts Docker in an enviable position—Docker's mindshare did the initial job of kickstarting an ecosystem of tools, which became a self-perpetuating cycle of people being drawn into the ecosystem and contributing back to it.

This is particularly evident when it comes to orchestration. After seeing a list of company names with offerings in this space, you'd be forgiven for thinking that everyone has their own opinion on how to do things and has developed their own tool.

Although the ecosystem is a huge strength of Docker (and is why we've been drawing from it so much in this book), the sheer quantity of possible orchestration tools can be overwhelming to novices and veterans alike. This chapter will tour some of the most notable tools and give you a feel for the high-level offerings, so you're better informed when it comes to evaluating what you want a framework to do for you.

There are many ways of arranging family trees of the orchestration tools. Figure 11.1 shows some of the tools we're familiar with. At the root of the tree is `docker run`, the most common way to start a container. Everything inspired by Docker is an offshoot of this. On the left side are tools that treat groups of containers as a single entity. The middle shows the tools focused on managing containers under the umbrella of systemd and service files. Finally, the right side treats individual containers as just that. As you move down the branches, the tools end up doing more for you, be it working across multiple hosts or taking the tedium of manual container deployment away from you.

You'll note two seemingly isolated areas on the diagram—Mesos and the Consul/etcd/Zookeeper group. Mesos is an interesting case—it existed before Docker, and the support it has for Docker is an added feature rather than core functionality. It works very well, though, and should be evaluated carefully, if only to see what features from it you might want in other tools. By contrast, Consul, etcd, and Zookeeper aren't orchestration tools at all. Instead, they provide the important complement to orchestration: service discovery.

This chapter and the next will navigate this orchestration ecosystem. In this chapter we'll introduce tools that give you more fine-grained control and may feel like less of a jump coming from managing containers manually. We'll look at managing Docker containers on a single host and across multiple hosts, and then at saving and

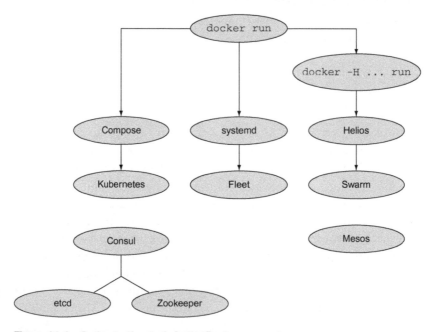

Figure 11.1   Orchestration tools in the Docker ecosystem

retrieving information about where containers have been deployed. Then, in the next chapter, we'll look at more complete solutions that abstract away a lot of the detail.

As you read these two chapters, it might be helpful to take a step back as you come to each orchestration tool and try to come up with a scenario the tool would be useful in. This will help clarify whether a particular tool is relevant for you. We'll offer some examples along the way to get you started.

We'll start slow by turning our gaze inward to a single computer.

11.1 Simple single-host Docker

Managing the containers on your local machine can be a painful experience. The features provided by Docker for managing long-running containers are relatively primitive, and starting up containers with links and shared volumes can be a frustratingly manual process.

In chapter 10 we looked at using Docker Compose to make managing links easier, so we'll deal with the other pain point now and see how the management of long-running containers on a single machine can be made more robust.

TECHNIQUE 82   Managing your host's containers with systemd

In this technique we'll take you through setting up a simple Docker service with systemd. If you're already familiar with systemd, this chapter will be relatively easy to follow, but we assume no prior knowledge of the tool.

Using systemd to control Docker can be useful for a mature company with an operations team that prefers to stick to proven technologies that they already understand and have the tooling for.

PROBLEM

You want to manage the running of Docker container services on your host.

SOLUTION

Use systemd to manage your container services.

systemd is a system-management daemon that replaced SysV init scripts in Fedora some time ago. It manages services on your system—everything from mount points to processes to one-shot scripts—as individual "units." It's growing in popularity as it spreads to other distributions and operating systems, though some systems (Gentoo being an example at the time of writing) may have problems installing and enabling it. It's worth looking around for experiences other people have had with systemd on a setup similar to yours.

In this technique we'll demonstrate how the startup of your containers can be managed by systemd by running the to-do app from chapter 1.

INSTALLING SYSTEMD

If you don't have systemd on your host system (you can check by running `systemctl status` and seeing whether you get a coherent response), you can install it directly on your host OS using your standard package manager.

If you're not comfortable interfering with your host system in this way, the recommended way to play with it is to use Vagrant to provision a systemd-ready VM, as shown in the following listing. We'll cover it briefly here, but see appendix C for more advice on installing Vagrant.

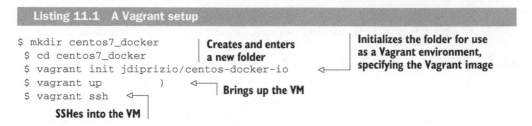

```
$ mkdir centos7_docker                              Creates and enters    Initializes the folder for use
 $ cd centos7_docker                                a new folder          as a Vagrant environment,
 $ vagrant init jdiprizio/centos-docker-io                                specifying the Vagrant image
 $ vagrant up            )
 $ vagrant ssh                                       Brings up the VM
     SSHes into the VM
```

NOTE   At the time of writing, jdiprizio/centos-docker-io is a suitable and available VM image. If it's no longer available when you're reading this, you can replace that string in the preceding listing with another image name. You can search for one on HashiCorp's "Discover Vagrant Boxes" page: https://app .vagrantup.com/boxes/search ("box" is the terminology Vagrant uses to refer to a VM image). To find this image, we searched for "docker centos". You may need to look up help for the command-line `vagrant box add` command to figure out how to download your new VM before attempting to start it.

SETTING UP A SIMPLE DOCKER APPLICATION UNDER SYSTEMD

Now that you have a machine with systemd and Docker on it, we'll use it to run the to-do application from chapter 1.

Systemd works by reading configuration files in the simple INI file format.

TIP   INI files are simple text files with a basic structure composed of sections, properties, and values.

First you need to create a service file as root in /etc/systemd/system/todo.service, as shown in the next listing. In this file you tell systemd to run the Docker container with the name "todo" on port 8000 on this host.

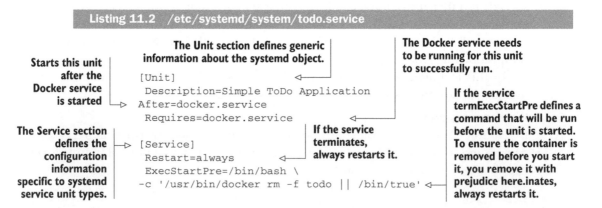

```
[Unit]
 Description=Simple ToDo Application
After=docker.service
 Requires=docker.service

[Service]
 Restart=always
 ExecStartPre=/bin/bash \
-c '/usr/bin/docker rm -f todo || /bin/true'
```

The Unit section defines generic information about the systemd object.

Starts this unit after the Docker service is started

The Docker service needs to be running for this unit to successfully run.

If the service termExecStartPre defines a command that will be run before the unit is started. To ensure the container is removed before you start it, you remove it with prejudice here.inates, always restarts it.

The Service section defines the configuration information specific to systemd service unit types.

If the service terminates, always restarts it.

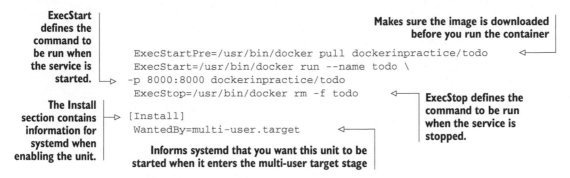

This configuration file should make it clear that systemd offers a simple declarative schema for managing processes, leaving the details of dependency management up to the systemd service. This doesn't mean that you can ignore the details, but it does put a lot of tools at your disposal for managing Docker (and other) processes.

> **NOTE** Docker doesn't set any container restart policies by default, but be aware that any you set will conflict with most process managers. Don't set restart policies if you're using a process manager.

Enabling a new unit is just a matter of invoking the `systemctl enable` command. If you want this unit to start automatically when the system boots, you can also create a symlink in the multi-user.target.wants systemd directory. Once done, you can start the unit with `systemctl start`.

```
$ systemctl enable /etc/systemd/system/todo.service
$ ln -s '/etc/systemd/system/todo.service' \
'/etc/systemd/system/multi-user.target.wants/todo.service'
$ systemctl start todo.service
```

Then just wait for it to start. If there's a problem, you'll be informed.

To check that all is OK, use the `systemctl status` command. It will print out some general information about the unit, such as how long it's been running and the process ID, followed by a number of log lines from the process. In this case, seeing `Swarm server started port 8000` is a good sign:

```
[root@centos system]# systemctl status todo.service
todo.service - Simple ToDo Application
   Loaded: loaded (/etc/systemd/system/todo.service; enabled)
   Active: active (running) since Wed 2015-03-04 19:57:19 UTC; 2min 13s ago
  Process: 21266 ExecStartPre=/usr/bin/docker pull dockerinpractice/todo \
(code=exited, status=0/SUCCESS)
  Process: 21255 ExecStartPre=/bin/bash -c /usr/bin/docker rm -f todo || \
/bin/true (code=exited, status=0/SUCCESS)
  Process: 21246 ExecStartPre=/bin/bash -c /usr/bin/docker kill todo || \
/bin/true (code=exited, status=0/SUCCESS)
 Main PID: 21275 (docker)
   CGroup: /system.slice/todo.service
           ??21275 /usr/bin/docker run --name todo
➥ -p 8000:8000 dockerinpractice/todo
```

```
Mar 04 19:57:24 centos docker[21275]: TodoApp.js:117:          \
// TODO scroll into view
Mar 04 19:57:24 centos docker[21275]: TodoApp.js:176:          \
if (i>=list.length()) { i=list.length()-1; } // TODO .length
Mar 04 19:57:24 centos docker[21275]: local.html:30:     \
<!-- TODO 2-split, 3-split -->
Mar 04 19:57:24 centos docker[21275]: model/TodoList.js:29:         \
// TODO one op - repeated spec? long spec?
Mar 04 19:57:24 centos docker[21275]: view/Footer.jsx:61:         \
// TODO: show the entry's metadata
Mar 04 19:57:24 centos docker[21275]: view/Footer.jsx:80:         \
todoList.addObject(new TodoItem()); // TODO create default
Mar 04 19:57:24 centos docker[21275]: view/Header.jsx:25:         \
// TODO list some meaningful header (apart from the id)
Mar 04 19:57:24 centos docker[21275]: > todomvc-swarm@0.0.1 start /todo
Mar 04 19:57:24 centos docker[21275]: > node TodoAppServer.js
Mar 04 19:57:25 centos docker[21275]: Swarm server started port 8000
```

You can now visit the server on port 8000.

DISCUSSION

The principles in this technique can be applied to more than just systemd—most process managers, including other init systems, can be configured in a similar way. If you're interested, you could leverage this to replace existing services running on your system (perhaps a PostgreSQL database) with dockerized ones.

In the next technique, we'll take this further by implementing in systemd the SQLite server we created in technique 77.

TECHNIQUE 83   **Orchestrating the startup of your host's containers**

Unlike docker-compose (at the time of writing), systemd is a mature technology ready for production. In this technique we'll show you how to achieve local orchestration functionality that's similar to docker-compose using systemd.

> **NOTE**   If you run into trouble with this technique, you may need to upgrade your version of Docker. Version 1.7.0 or greater should work fine.

PROBLEM

You want to manage more complex container orchestration on one host in production.

SOLUTION

Use systemd with dependent services to manage your containers.

To demonstrate the use of systemd for a more complex scenario, we're going to re-implement the SQLite TCP server example from technique 77 in systemd. Figure 11.2 illustrates the dependencies for our planned systemd service unit configuration.

This is a similar schema to what you saw with the Docker Compose example in technique 77. A key difference here is that rather than the SQLite service being treated as a single monolithic entity, each container is a discrete entity. In this scenario, the SQLite proxy can be stopped independently of the SQLite server.

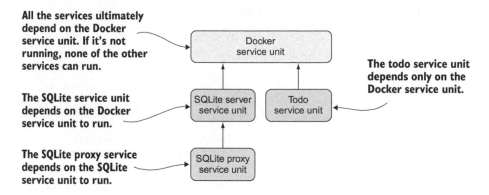

All the services ultimately depend on the Docker service unit. If it's not running, none of the other services can run.

The SQLite service unit depends on the Docker service unit to run.

The SQLite proxy service depends on the SQLite service unit to run.

The todo service unit depends only on the Docker service unit.

Figure 11.2 systemd unit dependency graph

Here's the listing for the SQLite server service. As before, it depends on the Docker service, but it has a couple of differences from the to-do example in the previous technique.

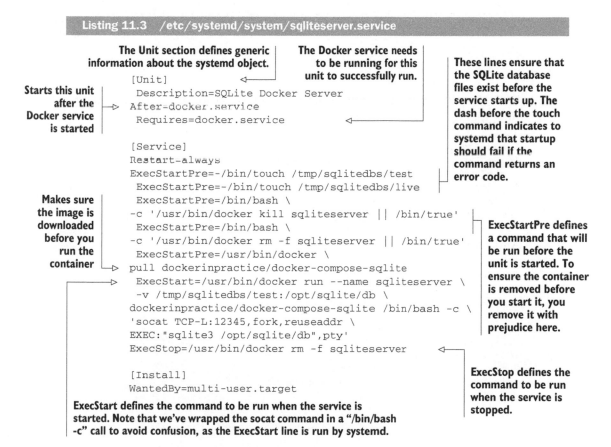

Listing 11.3 /etc/systemd/system/sqliteserver.service

The Unit section defines generic information about the systemd object.

The Docker service needs to be running for this unit to successfully run.

These lines ensure that the SQLite database files exist before the service starts up. The dash before the touch command indicates to systemd that startup should fail if the command returns an error code.

Starts this unit after the Docker service is started

Makes sure the image is downloaded before you run the container

```
[Unit]
  Description=SQLite Docker Server
After=docker.service
  Requires=docker.service

[Service]
Restart=always
ExecStartPre=-/bin/touch /tmp/sqlitedbs/test
  ExecStartPre=-/bin/touch /tmp/sqlitedbs/live
  ExecStartPre=/bin/bash \
-c '/usr/bin/docker kill sqliteserver || /bin/true'
  ExecStartPre=/bin/bash \
-c '/usr/bin/docker rm -f sqliteserver || /bin/true'
  ExecStartPre=/usr/bin/docker \
pull dockerinpractice/docker-compose-sqlite
  ExecStart=/usr/bin/docker run --name sqliteserver \
  -v /tmp/sqlitedbs/test:/opt/sqlite/db \
dockerinpractice/docker-compose-sqlite /bin/bash -c \
'socat TCP-L:12345,fork,reuseaddr \
EXEC:"sqlite3 /opt/sqlite/db",pty'
ExecStop=/usr/bin/docker rm -f sqliteserver

[Install]
WantedBy=multi-user.target
```

ExecStartPre defines a command that will be run before the unit is started. To ensure the container is removed before you start it, you remove it with prejudice here.

ExecStop defines the command to be run when the service is stopped.

ExecStart defines the command to be run when the service is started. Note that we've wrapped the socat command in a "/bin/bash -c" call to avoid confusion, as the ExecStart line is run by systemd.

> **TIP**   Paths must be absolute in systemd.

Now comes the listing for the SQLite proxy service. The key difference here is that the proxy service depends on the server process you just defined, which in turn depends on the Docker service.

Listing 11.4   /etc/systemd/system/sqliteproxy.service

```
[Unit]
Description=SQLite Docker Proxy
After=sqliteserver.service            ◄─── The proxy unit must run after the
 Requires=sqliteserver.service        ◄─── sqliteserver service defined previously.

                                            The proxy requires that the server instance
                                            be running before you start it up.
[Service]
Restart=always
ExecStartPre=/bin/bash -c '/usr/bin/docker kill sqliteproxy || /bin/true'
ExecStartPre=/bin/bash -c '/usr/bin/docker rm -f sqliteproxy || /bin/true'
ExecStartPre=/usr/bin/docker pull dockerinpractice/docker-compose-sqlite
ExecStart=/usr/bin/docker run --name sqliteproxy \
-p 12346:12346 --link sqliteserver:sqliteserver \
dockerinpractice/docker-compose-sqlite /bin/bash \
-c 'socat TCP-L:12346,fork,reuseaddr TCP:sqliteserver:12345'   ◄─── Runs the
 ExecStop=/usr/bin/docker rm -f sqliteproxy                         container

[Install]
WantedBy=multi-user.target
```

With these two configuration files, we've laid the groundwork for installing and running the SQLite service under systemd's control. Now we can enable these services:

```
$ sudo systemctl enable /etc/systemd/system/sqliteserver.service
ln -s '/etc/systemd/system/sqliteserver.service' \
'/etc/systemd/system/multi-user.target.wants/sqliteserver.service'
$ sudo systemctl enable /etc/systemd/system/sqliteproxy.service
ln -s '/etc/systemd/system/sqliteproxy.service' \
'/etc/systemd/system/multi-user.target.wants/sqliteproxy.service'
```

And start them up:

```
$ sudo systemctl start sqliteproxy
$ telnet localhost 12346
[vagrant@centos ~]$ telnet localhost 12346
Trying ::1...
Connected to localhost.
Escape character is '^]'.
SQLite version 3.8.2 2013-12-06 14:53:30
Enter ".help" for instructions
Enter SQL statements terminated with a ";"
sqlite> select * from t1;
select * from t1;
test
```

Note that because the SQLite proxy service depends on the SQLite server service to run, you only need to start the proxy—the dependencies get started automatically.

DISCUSSION

One of the challenges when administering a long-running application on a local machine is the management of dependency services. For example, a web application might expect to be running in the background as a service but might also depend on a database and a web server. This may sound familiar—you covered a web-app-db structure in technique 13.

Technique 76 showed how to set up this kind of structure with dependencies and so on, but tools like systemd have been working on this problem for a while and may offer flexibility that Docker Compose doesn't. For example, once you've written your service files, you can start any of them you want, and systemd will handle starting up any dependent services, even starting the Docker daemon itself if necessary.

11.2 *Manual multi-host Docker*

Now that you're comfortable with some fairly complicated arrangements of Docker containers on a machine, it's time to think bigger—let's move on to the world of multiple hosts to enable us to use Docker on a larger scale.

In the rest of this chapter, you're going to manually run a multi-host environment with Helios to introduce you to multi-host Docker concepts. In the next chapter, you'll see more automated and sophisticated ways to achieve the same result and more.

TECHNIQUE 84   Manual multi-host Docker with Helios

It can be intimidating to hand over all control of provisioning a group of machines to an application, so it doesn't hurt to ease yourself in with a more manual approach.

Helios is ideal for companies that have mostly static infrastructures and are interested in using Docker for their critical services but (understandably) want human oversight in the process.

PROBLEM

You want to be able to provision multiple Docker hosts with containers but retain manual control over what runs where.

SOLUTION

Use the Helios tool from Spotify to precisely manage containers on other hosts.

Helios is the tool Spotify currently uses to manage their servers in production, and it has the pleasing property of being both easy to get started with and stable (as you'd hope). Helios allows you to manage the deployment of Docker containers across multiple hosts. It gives you a single command-line interface that you can use to specify what you want to run and where to run it, as well as the ability to take a look at the current state of play.

Because we're just introducing Helios, we're going to run everything on a single node inside Docker for simplicity—don't worry, anything relevant to running on multiple hosts will be clearly highlighted. The high-level architecture of Helios is outlined in figure 11.3.

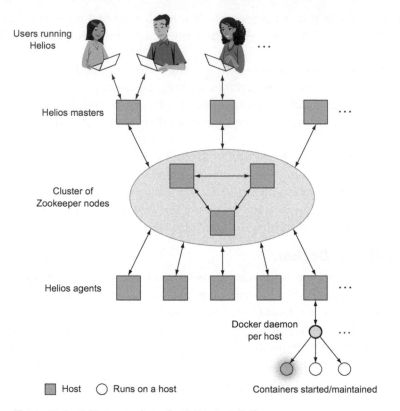

Figure 11.3 A birds-eye view of a Helios installation

As you can see, there's only one additional service required when running Helios: Zookeeper. Helios uses Zookeeper to track the state of all of your hosts and as a communication channel between the masters and agents.

> **TIP** Zookeeper is a lightweight distributed database written in Java that's optimized for storing configuration information. It's part of the Apache suite of open source software products. It's similar in functionality to etcd (which you learned about in chapter 9, and which you'll see again in this chapter).

All you need to know for this technique is that Zookeeper stores data such that it can be distributed across multiple nodes (for both scalability and reliability) by running multiple Zookeeper instances. This may sound familiar to our description of etcd in chapter 9—these two tools have significant overlap.

To start the single Zookeeper instance we'll use in this technique, run the following command:

```
$ docker run --name zookeeper -d jplock/zookeeper:3.4.6
cd0964d2ba18baac58b29081b227f15e05f11644adfa785c6e9fc5dd15b85910
$ docker inspect -f '{{.NetworkSettings.IPAddress}}' zookeeper
172.17.0.9
```

NOTE When starting a Zookeeper instance on its own node, you'll want to expose ports to make it accessible to other hosts and use volumes to persist data. Take a look at the Dockerfile on the Docker Hub for details about which ports and folders you should use (https://hub.docker.com/r/jplock/zookeeper/~/ dockerfile/). It's also likely you'll want to run Zookeeper on multiple nodes, but configuring a Zookeeper cluster is beyond the scope of this technique.

You can inspect the data Zookeeper has stored by using the zkCli.sh tool, either interactively or by piping input to it. The initial startup is quite chatty, but it'll drop you into an interactive prompt where you can run commands against the file-tree-like structure Zookeeper stores data in.

```
$ docker exec -it zookeeper bin/zkCli.sh
Connecting to localhost:2181
2015-03-07 02:56:05,076 [myid:] - INFO  [main:Environment@100] - Client >
environment:zookeeper.version=3.4.6-1569965, built on 02/20/2014 09:09 GMT
2015-03-07 02:56:05,079 [myid:] - INFO  [main:Environment@100] - Client >
environment:host.name=917d0f8ac077
2015-03-07 02:56:05,079 [myid:] - INFO  [main:Environment@100] - Client >
environment:java.version=1.7.0_65
2015-03-07 02:56:05,081 [myid:] - INFO  [main:Environment@100] - Client >
environment:java.vendor=Oracle Corporation
[...]
2015-03-07 03:00:59,043 [myid:] - INFO
➥ [main-SendThread(localhost:2181):ClientCnxn$SendThread@1235] -
➥ Session establishment complete on server localhost/0:0:0:0:0:0:0:1:2181,
➥ sessionid = 0x14bf223e159000d, negotiated timeout = 30000

WATCHER::

WatchedEvent state:SyncConnected type:None path:null
[zk: localhost:2181(CONNECTED) 0] ls /
[zookeeper]
```

Nothing's running against Zookeeper yet, so the only thing currently being stored is some internal Zookeeper information. Leave this prompt open, and we'll revisit it as we progress.

Helios itself is split into three parts:

- *The master*—This is used as an interface for making changes in Zookeeper.
- *The agent*—This runs on every Docker host, starts and stops containers based on Zookeeper, and reports state back.
- *The command-line tools*—These are used to make requests to the master.

Figure 11.4 shows how the final system is strung together when we perform an operation against it (the arrows indicate data flow).

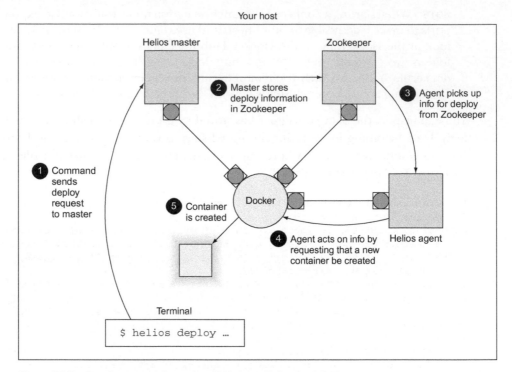

Figure 11.4   Starting a container on a single-host Helios installation

Now that Zookeeper is running, it's time to start Helios. We need to run the master while specifying the IP address of the Zookeeper node we started earlier:

```
$ IMG=dockerinpractice/docker-helios
$ docker run -d --name hmaster $IMG helios-master --zk 172.17.0.9
896bc963d899154436938e260b1d4e6fdb0a81e4a082df50043290569e5921ff
$ docker logs --tail=3 hmaster
03:20:14.460 helios[1]: INFO  [MasterService STARTING] ContextHandler: >
Started i.d.j.MutableServletContextHandler@7b48d370{/,null,AVAILABLE}
03:20:14.465 helios[1]: INFO  [MasterService STARTING] ServerConnector: >
Started application@2192bcac{HTTP/1.1}{0.0.0.0:5801}
03:20:14.466 helios[1]: INFO  [MasterService STARTING] ServerConnector: >
Started admin@28a0d16c{HTTP/1.1}{0.0.0.0:5802}
$ docker inspect -f '{{.NetworkSettings.IPAddress}}' hmaster
172.17.0.11
```

Now let's see what's new in Zookeeper:

```
[zk: localhost:2181(CONNECTED) 1] ls /
[history, config, status, zookeeper]
[zk: localhost:2181(CONNECTED) 2] ls /status/masters
[896bc963d899]
[zk: localhost:2181(CONNECTED) 3] ls /status/hosts
[]
```

It looks like the Helios master has created a bunch of new pieces of configuration, including registering itself as a master. Unfortunately we don't have any hosts yet.

Let's solve this by starting up an agent that will use the current host's Docker socket to start containers on:

```
$ docker run -v /var/run/docker.sock:/var/run/docker.sock -d --name hagent \
dockerinpractice/docker-helios helios-agent --zk 172.17.0.9
5a4abcb271070d0171ca809ff2beafac5798e86131b72aeb201fe27df64b2698
$ docker logs --tail=3 hagent
03:30:53.344 helios[1]: INFO  [AgentService STARTING] ContextHandler: >
Started i.d.j.MutableServletContextHandler@774c71b1{/,null,AVAILABLE}
03:30:53.375 helios[1]: INFO  [AgentService STARTING] ServerConnector: >
Started application@7d9e6c27{HTTP/1.1}{0.0.0.0:5803}
03:30:53.376 helios[1]: INFO  [AgentService STARTING] ServerConnector: >
Started admin@2bceb4df{HTTP/1.1}{0.0.0.0:5804}
$ docker inspect -f '{{.NetworkSettings.IPAddress}}' hagent
172.17.0.12
```

Again, let's check back in Zookeeper:

```
[zk: localhost:2181(CONNECTED) 4] ls /status/hosts
[5a4abcb27107]
[zk: localhost:2181(CONNECTED) 5] ls /status/hosts/5a4abcb27107
[agentinfo, jobs, environment, hostinfo, up]
[zk: localhost:2181(CONNECTED) 6] get /status/hosts/5a4abcb27107/agentinfo
{"inputArguments":["-Dcom.sun.management.jmxremote.port=9203", [...]
[...]
```

You can see here that /status/hosts now contains one item. Descending into the Zookeeper directory for the host reveals the internal information Helios stores about the host.

> **NOTE** When running on multiple hosts, you'll want to pass --name $(host-
> name -f) as an argument to both the Helios master and agent. You'll also
> need to expose ports 5801 and 5802 for the master and 5803 and 5804 for the
> agent.

Let's make it a bit easier to interact with Helios:

```
$ alias helios="docker run -i --rm dockerinpractice/docker-helios \
helios -z http://172.17.0.11:5801"
```

The preceding alias means that invoking helios will start a throwaway container to perform the action you want, pointing at the correct Helios cluster to begin with. Note that the command-line interface needs to be pointed at the Helios master rather than Zookeeper.

Everything is now set up. We're able to easily interact with our Helios cluster, so it's time to try an example.

```
$ helios create -p nc=8080:8080 netcat:v1 ubuntu:14.04.2 -- \
sh -c 'echo hello | nc -l 8080'
Creating job: {"command":["sh","-c","echo hello | nc -l 8080"], >
"creatingUser":null,"env":{},"expires":null,"gracePeriod":null, >
"healthCheck":null,"id": >
"netcat:v1:2067d43fc2c6f004ea27d7bb7412aff502e3cdac", >
"image":"ubuntu:14.04.2","ports":{"nc":{"externalPort":8080, >
"internalPort":8080,"protocol":"tcp"}},"registration":{}, >
"registrationDomain":"","resources":null,"token":"","volumes":{}}
Done.
netcat:v1:2067d43fc2c6f004ea27d7bb7412aff502e3cdac
$ helios jobs
JOB ID           NAME   VERSION HOSTS COMMAND              ENVIRONMENT
netcat:v1:2067d43 netcat v1       0     sh -c "echo hello | nc -l 8080"
```

Helios is built around the concept of *jobs*—everything to be executed must be expressed as a job before it can be sent to a host to be executed. At a minimum, you need an image with the basics Helios needs to know to start the container: a command to execute and any port, volume, or environment options. You may also want a number of other advanced options, including health checks, expiry dates, and service registration.

The previous command creates a job that will listen on port 8080, print "hello" to the first thing that connects to the port, and then terminate.

You can use `helios hosts` to list hosts available for job deployment, and then actually perform the deployment with `helios deploy`. The `helios status` command then shows us that the job has successfully started:

```
$ helios hosts
HOST           STATUS          DEPLOYED RUNNING CPUS MEM  LOAD AVG MEM USAGE >
OS                             HELIOS  DOCKER
5a4abcb27107.Up 19 minutes 0        0       4    7 gb 0.61      0.84      >
Linux 3.13.0-46-generic 0.8.213 1.3.1 (1.15)
$ helios deploy netcat:v1 5a4abcb27107
Deploying Deployment{jobId=netcat:v1: >
2067d43fc2c6f004ea27d7bb7412aff502e3cdac, goal=START, deployerUser=null} >
on [5a4abcb27107]
5a4abcb27107: done
$ helios status
JOB ID           HOST         GOAL   STATE    CONTAINER ID PORTS
netcat:v1:2067d43 5a4abcb27107.START RUNNING b1225bc      nc=8080:8080
```

Of course, we now want to verify that the service works:

```
$ curl localhost:8080
hello
$ helios status
JOB ID           HOST         GOAL   STATE         CONTAINER ID PORTS
netcat:v1:2067d43 5a4abcb27107.START PULLING_IMAGE b1225bc      nc=8080:8080
```

The result of `curl` clearly tells us that the service is working, but `helios status` is now showing something interesting. When defining the job, we noted that after serving "hello", the job would terminate, but the preceding output shows a `PULLING_IMAGE` status. This is down to how Helios manages jobs—once you've deployed to a host, Helios will do its best to keep the job running. The status you can see here is Helios going through the complete job startup process, which happens to involve ensuring the image is pulled.

Finally, we need to clear up after ourselves.

```
$ helios undeploy -a --yes netcat:v1
Undeploying netcat:v1:2067d43fc2c6f004ea27d7bb7412aff502e3cdac from >
[5a4abcb27107]
5a4abcb27107: done
$ helios remove --yes netcat:v1
Removing job netcat:v1:2067d43fc2c6f004ea27d7bb7412aff502e3cdac
netcat:v1:2067d43fc2c6f004ea27d7bb7412aff502e3cdac: done
```

We asked for the job to be removed from all nodes (terminating it if necessary, and stopping any more automatic restarts), and then we deleted the job itself, meaning it can't be deployed to any more nodes.

DISCUSSION

Helios is a simple and reliable way of deploying your containers to multiple hosts. Unlike a number of techniques we'll come to later on, there's no magic going on behind the scenes to determine appropriate locations—Helios starts containers exactly where you want them with minimal fuss.

But this simplicity comes at a cost once you move to more advanced deployment scenarios—features like resource limits, dynamic scaling, and so on are currently missing, so you may find yourself reinventing parts of tools like Kubernetes (technique 88) to achieve the behavior you want in your deployment.

11.3 *Service discovery: What have we here?*

This chapter's introduction referred to service discovery as the flip side of orchestration—being able to deploy your applications to hundreds of different machines is fine, but if you can't then find out which applications are located where, you won't be able to actually *use* them.

Although it's not nearly as saturated an area as orchestration, the service-discovery field still has a number of competitors. It doesn't help that they all offer slightly different feature sets.

There are two pieces of functionality that are typically desirable when it comes to service discovery: a generic key/value store and a way of retrieving service endpoints via some convenient interface (likely DNS). etcd and Zookeeper are examples of the former, whereas SkyDNS (a tool we won't go into) is an example of the latter. In fact, SkyDNS uses etcd to store the information it needs.

TECHNIQUE 85   Using Consul to discover services

etcd is a highly popular tool, but it does have one particular competitor that gets mentioned alongside it a lot: Consul. This is a little strange, because there are other tools more similar to etcd (Zookeeper has a similar feature set to etcd but is implemented in a different language), whereas Consul differentiates itself with some interesting additional features, like service discovery and health checks. In fact, if you squint, Consul might look a bit like etcd, SkyDNS, and Nagios all in one.

PROBLEM

You need to be able to distribute information to, discover services within, and monitor a collection of containers.

SOLUTION

Start a container with Consul on each Docker host to provide a service directory and configuration communication system.

Consul tries to be a generic tool for doing some important tasks required when you need to coordinate a number of independent services. These tasks can be performed by other tools, but configuring them in one place can be useful. From a high level, Consul provides the following:

- *Service configuration*—A key/value store for storing and sharing small values, like etcd and Zookeeper
- *Service discovery*—An API for registering services and a DNS endpoint for discovering them, like SkyDNS
- *Service monitoring*—An API for registering health checks, like Nagios

You can use all, some, or one of these features, as there's no tie-in. If you have existing monitoring infrastructure, there's no need to replace that with Consul.

This technique will cover the service-discovery and service-monitoring aspects of Consul, but not key/value storage. The strong similarities between etcd and Consul in this aspect make the two final techniques in chapter 9 (techniques 74 and 75) transferrable with some perusal of the Consul documentation.

Figure 11.5 shows a typical Consul setup.

The data stored in Consul is the responsibility of *server* agents. These are responsible for forming a *consensus* on the information stored—this concept is present in most distributed data-storage systems. In short, if you lose under half of your server agents, you're guaranteed to be able to recover your data (see an example of this with etcd in technique 74). Because these servers are so important and have greater resource requirements, keeping them on dedicated machines is a typical choice.

> **NOTE** Although the commands in this technique will leave the Consul data directory (/data) inside the container, it's generally a good idea to specify this directory as a volume for at least the servers, so you can keep backups.

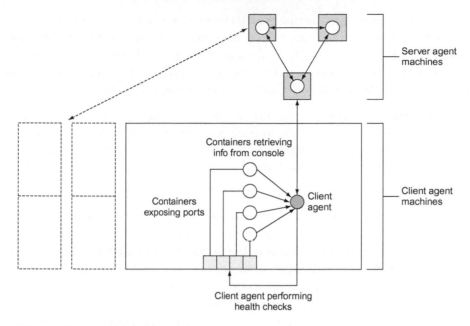

Figure 11.5 A typical Consul setup

It's recommended that all machines under your control that may want to interact with Consul should run a client agent. These agents forward requests on to the servers and run health checks.

The first step in getting Consul running is to start a server agent:

```
c1 $ IMG=dockerinpractice/consul-server
c1 $ docker pull $IMG
[...]
c1 $ ip addr | grep 'inet ' | grep -v 'lo$\|docker0$\|vbox.*$'
    inet 192.168.1.87/24 brd 192.168.1.255 scope global wlan0
c1 $ EXTIP1=192.168.1.87
c1 $ echo '{"ports": {"dns": 53}}' > dns.json
c1 $ docker run -d --name consul --net host \
-v $(pwd)/dns.json:/config/dns.json $IMG -bind $EXTIP1 -client $EXTIP1 \
-recursor 8.8.8.8 -recursor 8.8.4.4 -bootstrap-expect 1
88d5cb48b8b1ef9ada754f97f024a9ba691279e1a863fa95fa196539555310c1
c1 $ docker logs consul
[...]
     Client Addr: 192.168.1.87 (HTTP: 8500, HTTPS: -1, DNS: 53, RPC: 8400)
    Cluster Addr: 192.168.1.87 (LAN: 8301, WAN: 8302)
[...]
==> Log data will now stream in as it occurs:

  2015/08/14 12:35:41 [INFO] serf: EventMemberJoin: mylaptop 192.168.1.87
[...]
  2015/08/14 12:35:43 [INFO] consul: member 'mylaptop' joined, marking >
health alive
  2015/08/14 12:35:43 [INFO] agent: Synced service 'consul'
```

Because we want to use Consul as a DNS server, we've inserted a file into the folder Consul reads the configuration from to request it listen on port 53 (the registered port for the DNS protocol). We've then used a command sequence you may recognize from earlier techniques to try to find the external-facing IP address of the machine for both communicating with other agents and listening for client requests.

> **NOTE** The IP address 0.0.0.0 is typically used to indicate that an application should listen on all available interfaces on the machine. We've deliberately not done this, because some Linux distributions have a DNS-caching daemon listening on 127.0.0.1, which disallows listening on 0.0.0.0:53.

There are three items of note in the preceding docker run command:

- We've used --net host. Although this can be seen as a faux pas in the Docker world, the alternative is to expose up to eight ports on the command line—it's a matter of personal preference, but we feel it's justified here. It also helps bypass a potential issue with UDP communication. If you were to go the manual route, there'd be no need to set the DNS port—you could expose the default Consul DNS port (8600) as port 53 on the host.
- The two recursor arguments tell Consul what DNS servers to look at if a requested address is unknown by Consul itself.
- The -bootstrap-expect 1 argument means the Consul cluster will start operating with only one agent, which is not robust. A typical setup would set this to 3 (or more) to make sure the cluster doesn't start until the required number of servers has joined. To start the additional server agents, add a -join argument, as we'll discuss when we start a client.

Now let's go to a second machine, start a client agent, and add it to our cluster.

> **WARNING** Because Consul expects to be able to listen on a particular set of ports when communicating with other agents, it's tricky to set up multiple agents on a single machine while still demonstrating how it would work in the real world. We'll use a different host now—if you decide to use an IP alias, ensure you pass a -node newAgent, because by default the hostname will be used, which will conflict.

```
c2 $ IMG=dockerinpractice/consul-agent
c2 $ docker pull $IMG
[...]
c2 $ EXTIP1=192.168.1.87
c2 $ ip addr | grep docker0 | grep inet
    inet 172.17.42.1/16 scope global docker0
c2 $ BRIDGEIP=172.17.42.1
c2 $ ip addr | grep 'inet ' | grep -v 'lo$\|docker0$'
    inet 192.168.1.80/24 brd 192.168.1.255 scope global wlan0
c2 $ EXTIP2=192.168.1.80
c2 $ echo '{"ports": {"dns": 53}}' > dns.json
c2 $ docker run -d --name consul-client --net host \
```

```
-v $(pwd)/dns.json:/config/dns.json $IMG -client $BRIDGEIP -bind $EXTIP2 \
-join $EXTIP1 -recursor 8.8.8.8 -recursor 8.8.4.4
5454029b139cd28e8500922d1167286f7e4fb4b7220985ac932f8fd5b1cdef25
c2 $ docker logs consul-client
[...]
    2015/08/14 19:40:20 [INFO] serf: EventMemberJoin: mylaptop2 192.168.1.80
[...]
    2015/08/14 13:24:37 [INFO] consul: adding server mylaptop >
(Addr: 192.168.1.87:8300) (DC: dc1)
```

NOTE The images we've used are based on gliderlabs/consul-server:0.5 and gliderlabs/consul-agent:0.5, and they come with a newer version of Consul to avoid possible problems with UDP communication, indicated by the constant logging of lines like "Refuting a suspect message." When version 0.6 of the images is released, you can switch back to the images from gliderlabs.

All client services (HTTP, DNS, and so on) have been configured to listen on the Docker bridge IP address. This gives containers a known location from which they can retrieve information from Consul, and it only exposes Consul internally on the machine, forcing other machines to directly access the server agents rather than taking a slower route via a client agent to a server agent. To ensure the bridge IP address is consistent across all your hosts, you can look at the `--bip` argument to the Docker daemon.

As before, we've found the external IP address and bound cluster communication to it. The `-join` argument tells Consul where to initially look to find the cluster. Don't worry about micromanaging the cluster formation—when two agents initially meet each other, they'll *gossip*, transferring information about finding the other agents in the cluster. The final `-recursor` arguments tell Consul what upstream DNS servers to use for DNS requests that aren't trying to look up registered services.

Let's verify that the agent has connected to the server with the HTTP API on the client machine. The API call we'll use will return a list of members the client agent currently thinks are in the cluster. In large, quickly changing clusters, this may not always match the members of the cluster—there's another (slower) API call for that.

```
c2 $ curl -sSL $BRIDGEIP:8500/v1/agent/members | tr ',' '\n' | grep Name
[{"Name":"mylaptop2"
{"Name":"mylaptop"
```

Now that the Consul infrastructure is set up, it's time to see how you can register and discover services. The typical process for registration is to get your app to make an API call against the local client agent after initializing, which prompts the client agent to distribute the information to the server agents. For demonstration purposes, we'll perform the registration step manually.

```
c2 $ docker run -d --name files -p 8000:80 ubuntu:14.04.2 \
python3 -m http.server 80
96ee81148154a75bc5c8a83e3b3d11b73d738417974eed4e019b26027787e9d1
c2 $ docker inspect -f '{{.NetworkSettings.IPAddress}}' files
```

```
172.17.0.16
c2 $ /bin/echo -e 'GET / HTTP/1.0\r\n\r\n' | nc -i1 172.17.0.16 80 \
| head -n 1
HTTP/1.0 200 OK
c2 $ curl -X PUT --data-binary '{"Name": "files", "Port": 8000}' \
$BRIDGEIP:8500/v1/agent/service/register
c2 $ docker logs consul-client | tail -n 1
    2015/08/15 03:44:30 [INFO] agent: Synced service 'files'
```

Here we've set up a simple HTTP server in a container, exposing it on port 8000 on the host, and checked that it works. Then we used curl and the Consul HTTP API to register a service definition. The only thing absolutely necessary here is the name of the service—the port, along with the other fields listed in the Consul documentation, are all optional. The ID field is worth a mention—it defaults to the name of the service but must be unique across all services. If you want multiple instances of a service, you'll need to specify it.

The log line from Consul has told us that the service is synced, so we should be able to retrieve the information about it from the service DNS interface. This information comes from the server agents, so it acts as validation that the service has been accepted into the Consul catalog. You can use the dig command to query service DNS information and check that it's present:

Looks up the IP address of the files service from the server agent DNS. This DNS service is available to arbitrary machines not in your Consul cluster, allowing them to benefit from service discovery as well.

Looks up the IP address of the files service from the client agent DNS. If using $BRIDGEIP fails, you may wish to try with $EXTIP!.

Requests the SRV record of the files service from the client agent DNS

Starts a container configured to use the local client agent as the only DNS server

Verifies that service lookup works automatically inside the container

```
c2 $ EXTIP1=192.168.1.87
c2 $ dig @$EXTIP1 files.service.consul +short
  192.168.1.80
c2 $ BRIDGEIP=172.17.42.1
c2 $ dig @$BRIDGEIP files.service.consul +short
  192.168.1.80
c2 $ dig @$BRIDGEIP files.service.consul srv +short
  1 1 8000 mylaptop2.node.dc1.consul.
c2 $ docker run -it --dns $BRIDGEIP ubuntu:14.04.2 bash
  root@934e9c26bc7e:/# ping -c1 -q www.google.com
  PING www.google.com (216.58.210.4) 56(84) bytes of data.

--- www.google.com ping statistics ---
1 packets transmitted, 1 received, 0% packet loss, time 0ms
rtt min/avg/max/mdev = 25.358/25.358/25.358/0.000 ms
root@934e9c26bc7e:/# ping -c1 -q files.service.consul
  PING files.service.consul (192.168.1.80) 56(84) bytes of data.

--- files.service.consul ping statistics ---
1 packets transmitted, 1 received, 0% packet loss, time 0ms
rtt min/avg/max/mdev = 0.062/0.062/0.062/0.000 ms
```

Verifies that lookup of external addresses still works

NOTE SRV records are a way of communicating service information by DNS, including protocol, port, and other entries. In the preceding case, you can see the port number in the response, and you've been given the canonical hostname of the machine providing the service rather than the IP address.

Advanced users may want to avoid manually setting the --dns argument by configuring the –dns and –bip arguments for the Docker daemon itself, but remember to override the defaults for the Consul agent, or you may end up with unexpected behavior.

The similarities between the Consul DNS service and the Docker virtual networks in technique 80 are interesting—both allow you to discover containers by a human-readable name, and Docker has the built-in ability to make this work across multiple nodes with overlay networks. The key difference is that Consul exists outside Docker and so may be easier to integrate into existing systems.

However, as mentioned at the beginning of this technique, Consul has another interesting feature we'll take a look at: health checks.

Health checking is a big topic, so we'll leave the minutiae for the comprehensive Consul documentation and look at one of the options for monitoring—a script check. This runs a command and sets the health based on the return value, with 0 for success, 1 for warning, and any other value for critical. You can register a health check when initially defining the service, or in a separate API call, as we'll do here.

```
c2 $ cat >check <<'EOF'          ◁───   Creates a check script verifying that the HTTP
 #!/bin/sh                               status code from the service is "200 OK". The
set -o errexit                           service port is looked up from the service ID
set -o pipefail                          passed to the script as an argument.

SVC_ID="$1"
SVC_PORT=\
"$(wget -qO - 172.17.42.1:8500/v1/agent/services | jq ".$SVC_ID.Port")"
wget -qsO - "localhost:$SVC_PORT"
echo "Success!"
EOF
c2 $ cat check | docker exec -i consul-client sh -c \    Copies the check script into
'cat > /check && chmod +x /check'          ◁───          the Consul agent container
 c2 $ cat >health.json <<'EOF'   ◁───
 {                                        Creates a health check definition to send to the Consul
  "Name": "filescheck",                   HTTP API. The service ID has to be specified in both
  "ServiceID": "files",                   the ServiceID field and the script command line.
  "Script": "/check files",
  "Interval": "10s"            Submits the health check
}                             JSON to the Consul agent
EOF                                                       Waits for the check output
c2 $ curl -X PUT --data-binary @health.json \            to be communicated to the
172.17.42.1:8500/v1/agent/check/register   ◁───          server agents
 c2 $ sleep 300
 c2 $ curl -sSL 172.17.42.1:8500/v1/health/service/files | \
python -m json.tool | head -n 13           ◁───
 [                                         Retrieves health check information
    {                                      for the check you've registered
        "Checks": [
```

```
            {
                "CheckID": "filescheck",
                "Name": "filescheck",
                "Node": "mylaptop2",
                "Notes": "",
                "Output": "/check: line 6: jq: not \
found\nConnecting to 172.17.42.1:8500 (172.17.42.1:8500)\n",
                "ServiceID": "files",
                "ServiceName": "files",
                "Status": "critical"
            },
c2 $ dig @$BRIDGEIP files.service.consul srv +short
 c2 $
```

Attempts to look up the files service, with no results

> **NOTE** Because output from health checks can change on every execution (if
> it includes timestamps, for example), Consul only synchronizes check output
> with the server on a status change, or every five minutes (though this interval
> is configurable). Because statuses start as critical, there's no initial status
> change in this case, so you'll need to wait out the interval to get output.

We added a health check for the files service to be run every 10 seconds, but checking
it shows the service as having a critical status. Because of this, Consul has automatically
taken the failing endpoint out of the entries returned by DNS, leaving us with no servers. This is particularly helpful for automatically removing servers from a multiple-
backend service in production.

The root cause of the error we've hit is an important one to be aware of when running Consul inside a container. All checks are also run inside the container, so, as the
check script had to be copied into the container, you also need to make sure any commands you need are installed in the container. In this particular case, we're missing
the jq command (a helpful utility for extracting information from JSON), which we
can install manually, though the correct approach for production would be to add layers to the image.

```
c2 $ docker exec consul-client sh -c 'apk update && apk add jq'
fetch http://dl-4.alpinelinux.org/alpine/v3.2/main/x86_64/APKINDEX.tar.gz
v3.2.3 [http://dl-4.alpinelinux.org/alpine/v3.2/main]
OK: 5289 distinct packages available
(1/1) Installing jq (1.4-r0)
Executing busybox-1.23.2-r0.trigger
OK: 14 MiB in 28 packages
c2 $ docker exec consul-client sh -c \
'wget -qO - 172.17.42.1:8500/v1/agent/services | jq ".files.Port"'
8000
c2 $ sleep 15
c2 $ curl -sSL 172.17.42.1:8500/v1/health/service/files | \
python -m json.tool | head -n 13
[
    {
        "Checks": [
            {
```

```
              "CheckID": "filescheck",
              "Name": "filescheck",
              "Node": "mylaptop2",
              "Notes": "",
              "Output": "Success!\n",
              "ServiceID": "files",
              "ServiceName": "files",
              "Status": "passing"
          },
```

We've now installed jq onto the image using the Alpine Linux (see technique 57) package manager, verified that it works by manually executing the line that was previously failing in the script, and then waited for the check to rerun. It's now successful!

With script health checks, you now have a vital building block for constructing monitoring around your application. If you can express a health check as a series of commands you'd run in a terminal, you can get Consul to automatically run it—this isn't limited to HTTP status. If you find yourself wanting to check the status code returned by an HTTP endpoint, you're in luck, as this is such a common task that one of the three types of health checking in Consul is dedicated to it, and you don't need to use a script health check (we did so above for illustrative purposes).

The final type of health check, time to live, requires a deeper integration with your application. The status must be periodically set to healthy, or the check will automatically be set to failing. Combining these three types of health check gives you the power to build comprehensive monitoring on top of your system.

To round off this technique, we'll look at the optional Consul web interface that comes with the server agent image. It provides a helpful insight into the current state of your cluster. You can visit this by going to port 8500 on the external IP address of a server agent. In this case you'd want to visit $EXTIP1:8500. Remember that even if you're on a server agent host, localhost or 127.0.0.1 won't work.

DISCUSSION

We've covered a lot in this technique—Consul is a big topic! Fortunately, just as the knowledge you gained about utilizing key/value stores with etcd in technique 74 is transferable to other key/value stores (like Consul), this service-discovery knowledge is transferable to other tools offering DNS interfaces (SkyDNS being one you may come across).

The subtleties we covered related to using the host network stack and using external IP addresses are also transferable. Most containerized distributed tools requiring discovery across multiple nodes may have similar problems, and it's worth being aware of these potential issues.

TECHNIQUE 86　**Automatic service registration with Registrator**

The obvious downside of Consul (and any service discovery tool) so far is the overhead of having to manage the creation and deletion of service entries. If you integrate this into your applications, you'll have multiple implementations and multiple places it could go wrong.

Integration also doesn't work for applications you don't have complete control over, so you'll end up having to write wrapper scripts when starting up your database and the like.

PROBLEM

You don't want to manually manage service entries and health checks in Consul.

SOLUTION

Use Registrator.

This technique will build on top of the previous one and will assume you have a two-part Consul cluster available, as described previously. We'll also assume there are no services in it, so you may want to recreate your containers to start from scratch.

Registrator (http://gliderlabs.com/registrator/latest/) takes away much of the complexity of managing Consul services—it watches for containers to start and stop, registering services based on exposed ports and container environment variables. The easiest way to see this in action is to jump in.

Everything we do will be on the machine with the client agent. As discussed previously, no containers except the server agent should be running on the other machine.

The following commands are all you need to start up Registrator:

```
$ IMG=gliderlabs/registrator:v6
$ docker pull $IMG
[...]
$ ip addr | grep 'inet ' | grep -v 'lo$\|docker0$'
    inet 192.168.1.80/24 brd 192.168.1.255 scope global wlan0
$ EXTIP=192.168.1.80
$ ip addr | grep docker0 | grep inet
    inet 172.17.42.1/16 scope global docker0
$ BRIDGEIP=172.17.42.1
$ docker run -d --name registrator -h $(hostname)-reg \
-v /var/run/docker.sock:/tmp/docker.sock $IMG -ip $EXTIP -resync \
60 consul://$BRIDGEIP:8500 # if this fails, $EXTIP is an alternative
b3c8a04b9dfaf588e46a255ddf4e35f14a9d51199fc6f39d47340df31b019b90
$ docker logs registrator
2015/08/14 20:05:57 Starting registrator v6 ...
2015/08/14 20:05:57 Forcing host IP to 192.168.1.80
2015/08/14 20:05:58 consul: current leader  192.168.1.87:8300
2015/08/14 20:05:58 Using consul adapter: consul://172.17.42.1:8500
2015/08/14 20:05:58 Listening for Docker events ...
2015/08/14 20:05:58 Syncing services on 2 containers
2015/08/14 20:05:58 ignored: b3c8a04b9dfa no published ports
2015/08/14 20:05:58 ignored: a633e58c66b3 no published ports
```

The first couple of commands here, for pulling the image and finding the external IP address, should look familiar. This IP address is given to Registrator so it knows what IP address to advertise for the services. The Docker socket is mounted to allow Registrator to be automatically notified of container starts and stops as they happen. We've also told Registrator how it can connect to a Consul agent, and that we want all containers to be refreshed every 60 seconds. Because Registrator should automatically be notified of container changes, this final setting is helpful in mitigating the impact of Registrator possibly missing updates.

Now that Registrator is running, it's extremely easy to register a first service.

```
$ curl -sSL 172.17.42.1:8500/v1/catalog/services | python -m json.tool
{
    "consul": []
}
$ docker run -d -e "SERVICE_NAME=files" -p 8000:80 ubuntu:14.04.2 python3 \
-m http.server 80
3126a8668d7a058333d613f7995954f1919b314705589a9cd8b4e367d4092c9b
$ docker inspect 3126a8668d7a | grep 'Name.*/'
    "Name": "/evil_hopper",
$ curl -sSL 172.17.42.1:8500/v1/catalog/services | python -m json.tool
{
    "consul": [],
    "files": []
}
$ curl -sSL 172.17.42.1:8500/v1/catalog/service/files | python -m json.tool
[
    {
        "Address": "192.168.1.80",
        "Node": "mylaptop2",
        "ServiceAddress": "192.168.1.80",
        "ServiceID": "mylaptop2-reg:evil_hopper:80",
        "ServiceName": "files",
        "ServicePort": 8000,
        "ServiceTags": null
    }
]
```

The only effort we've had to put in when registering the service is passing an environment variable to tell Registrator what service name to use. By default, Registrator uses a name based on the container name component after the slash and before the tag: "mycorp.com/myteam/myimage:0.5" would have the name "myimage". Whether this is useful or you want to specify something manually will depend on your naming conventions.

The rest of the values are pretty much as you'd hope. Registrator has discovered the port being listened on, added it to Consul, and set a service ID that tries to give a hint about where you can find the container (which is why the hostname was set in the Registrator container).

DISCUSSION

Registrator is excellent at giving you a handle on a swiftly changing environment with a high churn of containers, making sure you don't need to worry about your service-creation checks being created.

In addition to service details, Registrator will pick up a number of pieces of information from environments if they're present, including tags, service names per port (if multiple), and using health checks (if you're using Consul as the data storage). All three types of Consul health checks can be enabled by specifying the check details in the environment in JSON—you can read more about this in the Consul section of the "Registrator Backends" documentation at http://gliderlabs.com/registrator/latest/ user/backends/#consul, or revisit the previous technique to get a brief introduction to Consul health checks themselves.

Summary

- systemd units are useful for controlling container execution on a single machine.
- Dependencies can be expressed in systemd units to provide startup orchestration.
- Helios is a production-quality, simple, multi-host orchestration solution.
- Consul can hold information about your services, allowing dynamic service discovery.
- Registrator can automatically register container-based services into Consul.

The data center
as an OS with Docker

This chapter covers

- How to use the official Docker solution for orchestration
- The different ways Mesos can be used to manage Docker containers
- Two heavyweights in the Docker orchestration ecosystem, Kubernetes and OpenShift

If you look back at figure 11.1 in the previous chapter, we're now going to continue moving down the branches of the tree and on to tools that take away some of the detail to increase productivity. Most of these are designed with larger deployments across multiple machines in mind, but there's no reason you can't use them on one machine.

As for the last chapter, we recommend trying to come up with a scenario for each tool, to clarify possible use cases in your environment. We'll continue to give examples along the way as starting points.

12.1 *Multi-host Docker*

The best process for moving Docker containers to target machines and starting them up is a matter of much debate in the Docker world. A number of well-known companies have created their own ways of doing things and have released them to the world. You can benefit massively from this, if you can decide what tools to use.

This is a fast moving topic—we've seen the birth and death of multiple orchestration tools for Docker, and we recommend caution when considering whether to move over to a brand-new tool. As a result, we've tried to select tools with significant stability or momentum (or both).

TECHNIQUE 87   **A seamless Docker cluster with swarm mode**

It's great having complete control over your cluster, but sometimes the micromanagement isn't necessary. In fact, if you have a number of applications with no complex requirements, you can take full advantage of the Docker promise of being able to run anywhere—there's no reason you shouldn't be able to throw containers at a cluster and let the cluster decide where to run them.

Swarm mode could be useful for a research lab if the lab were able to split up a computationally intensive problem into bite-size chunks. This would allow them to very easily run their problem on a cluster of machines.

PROBLEM

You have a number of hosts with Docker installed, and you want to be able to start containers without needing to micromanage where they'll run.

SOLUTION

Use swarm mode for Docker, a feature Docker itself has built in to tackle orchestration.

Swarm mode for Docker is the official solution from Docker Inc. to treat a cluster of hosts as a single Docker daemon and deploy services to them. It has a command line quite similar to one you're familiar with from `docker run`. Swarm mode evolved from an official Docker tool that you'd use alongside Docker, and it was integrated into the Docker daemon itself. If you see old references to "Docker Swarm" anywhere, they may be referring to the older tool.

A Docker swarm consists of a number of nodes. Each node may be a manager or a worker, and these roles are flexible and can be changed in the swarm at any time. A manager coordinates the deployment of services to available nodes, whereas workers will only run containers. By default, managers are available to run containers as well, but you'll see how to alter that as well.

When the manager is started, it initializes some state for the swarm and then listens for incoming connections from additional nodes to add to the swarm.

> **NOTE** All versions of Docker used in a swarm must be at least 1.12.0. Ideally you should try to keep all versions exactly the same, or you may encounter issues due to version incompatibilities.

First, let's create a new swarm:

```
h1 $ ip addr show | grep 'inet ' | grep -v 'lo$\|docker0$' # get external IP
    inet 192.168.11.67/23 brd 192.168.11.255 scope global eth0
h1 $ docker swarm init --advertise-addr 192.168.11.67
Swarm initialized: current node (i5vtd3romfl9jg9g4bxtg0kis) is now a
manager.

To add a worker to this swarm, run the following command:

    docker swarm join \
    --token SWMTKN-1-4blo74lo m2bu5p8synq3w4239vxr1pyoa29cgkrjonx0tuid68
➥ -dhl9o1b62vrhhi0m817r6sxp2 \
    192.168.11.67:2377

To add a manager to this swarm, run 'docker swarm join-token manager' and
follow the instructions.
```

This has created a new swarm and set up the Docker daemon of the host h1 to be a manager.

You can now inspect your newly created swarm:

```
h1 $ docker info
[...]
Swarm: active
 NodeID: i5vtd3romfl9jg9g4bxtg0kis
 Is Manager: true
 ClusterID: sg6sfmsa96nir1fbwcf939us1
 Managers: 1
 Nodes: 1
 Orchestration:
  Task History Retention Limit: 5
 Raft:
  Snapshot Interval: 10000
  Number of Old Snapshots to Retain: 0
  Heartbeat Tick: 1
  Election Tick: 3
 Dispatcher:
  Heartbeat Period: 5 seconds
 CA Configuration:
  Expiry Duration: 3 months
 Node Address: 192.168.11.67
 Manager Addresses:
  192.168.11.67:2377
[...]
h1 $ docker node ls
$ docker node ls
ID                             HOSTNAME   STATUS  AVAILABILITY  MANAGER STATUS
i5vtd3romfl9jg9g4bxtg0kis *    h1         Ready   Active        Leader
```

You can now make a Docker daemon on a different host join as a worker by running the command specified after the manager started:

```
h2 $ docker swarm join \
    --token SWMTKN-1-4blo74l0m2bu5p8synq3w4239vxr1pyoa29cgkrjonx0tuid68
➥ -dhl9o1b62vrhhi0m817r6sxp2 \
    192.168.11.67:2377
This node joined a swarm as a worker.
```

h2 has now been added to our cluster as a worker. Running `docker info` on either host will reveal that the `Nodes` count has gone up to 2, and `docker node ls` will list both nodes.

Finally, let's start a container. In swarm mode, this is referred to as deploying a service, because there are additional features that don't make sense with a container. Before deploying the service, we'll mark the manager as having availability `drain`—by default, all managers are available to run containers, but in this technique we want to demonstrate remote machine scheduling capabilities, so we'll constrain things to avoid the manager. Drain will cause any containers already on the node to be redeployed elsewhere, and no new services will be scheduled on the node.

```
h1 $ docker node update --availability drain i5vtd3romfl9jg9g4bxtg0kis
h1 $ docker service create --name server -d -p 8000:8000 ubuntu:14.04 \
        python3 -m http.server 8000
vp0fj8p9khzh72eheoye0y4bn
h1 $ docker service ls
ID              NAME     MODE         REPLICAS  IMAGE         PORTS
vp0fj8p9khzh    server   replicated   1/1       ubuntu:14.04  *:8000->8000/tcp
```

There are a few things to note here. The most important is that the swarm has automatically selected a machine to start the container on—if you had multiple workers, the manager would choose one based on load balancing. You probably also recognize some of the arguments to `docker service create` as familiar from `docker run`—a number of arguments are shared, but it's worth reading the documentation. For example, the `--volume` argument to `docker run` has a different format in the `--mount` argument that you should read the documentation for.

It's now time to check and see if our service is up and running:

```
h1 $ docker service ps server
ID              NAME       IMAGE         NODE  DESIRED STATE  CURRENT STATE
➥      ERROR  PORTS
mixc9w3frple  server.1  ubuntu:14.04  h2    Running        Running 4
minutes ago
h1 $ docker node inspect --pretty h2 | grep Addr
 Address:              192.168.11.50
h1 $ curl -sSL 192.168.11.50:8000 | head -n4
<!DOCTYPE HTML PUBLIC "-//W3C//DTD HTML 4.01//EN"
➥ "http://www.w3.org/TR/html4/strict.dtd">
<html>
<head>
<meta http-equiv="Content-Type" content="text/html; charset=ascii">
```

Swarm mode has a piece of additional functionality it enables by default, called the *routing mesh*. This allows each node in the swarm to appear as if it can serve requests for all services within the swarm that have published ports—any incoming connections are forwarded to an appropriate node.

For example, if you go back on the h1 manager node again (which we know isn't running the service, because it has availability drain), it will still respond on port 8000 to any requests:

```
h1 $ curl -sSL localhost:8000 | head -n4
<!DOCTYPE HTML PUBLIC "-//W3C//DTD HTML 4.01//EN"
➥ "http://www.w3.org/TR/html4/strict.dtd">
<html>
<head>
<meta http-equiv="Content-Type" content="text/html; charset=ascii">
```

This can be particularly useful for a simple kind of service discovery—as long as you know the address of one node, you can access all your services very easily.

Once you're finished with the swarm, you can shut down all services and delete the cluster.

```
$ docker service rm server
server
$ docker swarm leave
Error response from daemon: You are attempting to leave the swarm on a >
node that is participating as a manager. Removing the last manager erases >
all current state of the swarm. Use `--force` to ignore this message.
$ docker swarm leave --force
Node left the swarm.
```

As you can see here, swarm mode will warn you if you're shutting down the last manager in a node, because all information on the swarm will be lost. You can override this warning with --force. You'll need to run docker swarm leave on all worker nodes as well.

DISCUSSION

This has been a brief introduction to swarm mode in Docker, and there's a lot we haven't covered here. For example, you may have noticed that the help text after we initialized the swarm mentioned the ability to connect additional masters to the swarm—this is useful for resilience. Additional subjects of interest are built-in pieces of functionality that store service configuration information (as you did with etcd in technique 74), using constraints to guide placement of containers, and information on how to upgrade containers with rollbacks on failure. We recommend you refer to the official documentation at https://docs.docker.com/engine/swarm/ for more information.

Using a Kubernetes cluster

You've now seen two extremes in approaches to orchestration—the conservative approach of Helios and the much more free-form approach of Docker swarm. But some users and companies will expect a little more sophistication from their tooling.

This need for customizable orchestration can be fulfilled by many options, but there are a few that are used and discussed more than the others. In one case, that's undoubtedly partially due to the company behind it, but one would hope that Google knows how to build orchestration software.

PROBLEM

You want to manage Docker services across hosts.

SOLUTION

Use Kubernetes and its powerful abstractions to manage your fleet of containers.

Kubernetes, a tool created by Google, is for companies that prefer to have clear guidance and best practices on how to arrange applications and state relationships between them. It allows you to use specially designed tools to manage a dynamic infrastructure based on a specified structure.

Before we get going with Kubernetes, let's take a quick look at Kubernetes' high-level architecture in figure 12.1.

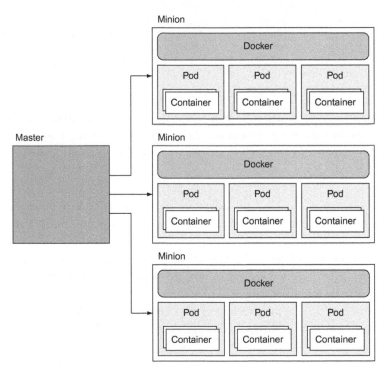

Figure 12.1 Kubernetes high-level view

Kubernetes has a master-minion architecture. Master nodes are responsible for receiving orders about what should be run on the cluster and orchestrating its resources. Each minion has Docker installed on it, along with a *kubelet* service, which manages the pods (sets of containers) running on each node. Information about the cluster is maintained in etcd, a distributed key/value data store (see technique 74), and this is the cluster's source of truth.

> **TIP** We'll go over it again later in this technique, so don't worry about it too much now, but a *pod* is a grouping of related containers. The concept exists to facilitate the management and maintenance of Docker containers.

The end goal of Kubernetes is to make running your containers at scale a simple matter of declaring what you want and letting Kubernetes ensure the cluster meets your needs. In this technique you'll see how to scale a simple service to a given size by running one command.

> **NOTE** Kubernetes was originally developed by Google as a means for managing containers at scale. Google has been running containers for over a decade at scale, and it decided to develop this container orchestration system when Docker became popular. Kubernetes builds on the lessons learned from Google's extensive experience. Kubernetes is also known as "K8s."

A full treatment of Kubernetes' installation, setup, and features is a big and fast-changing topic that's beyond the scope of this book (and no doubt a book in itself, before too long). Here we're going to focus on Kubernetes' core concepts and set up a simple service so you can get a feel for it.

INSTALLING KUBERNETES

You can either install Kubernetes directly on your host via Minikube, which will give you a single-minion cluster, or use Vagrant to install a multi-minion cluster managed with VMs. In this technique we'll focus on the first option—the latter is best achieved with research to identify the correct option for the latest version of Kubernetes.

The recommended approach for getting started locally with Kubernetes is to install a single-minion cluster on your host by following the official documentation for Minikube at https://kubernetes.io/docs/tasks/tools/install-minikube/.

Minikube is a specialized tool from the Kubernetes project created to ease the process of local development, but it's currently a bit limited. If you want to stretch yourself a bit more, we recommend searching for a guide to setting up a multi-node Kubernetes cluster with Vagrant—this process tends to change with the Kubernetes version, so we won't give specific advice here (though, at time of writing, we found https://github.com/Yolean/kubeadm-vagrant to be a reasonable starting point).

Once you have Kubernetes installed, you can follow along from here. The following output will be based on a multi-node cluster. We're going to start by creating a single container and using Kubernetes to scale it up.

SCALING A SINGLE CONTAINER

The command used to manage Kubernetes is `kubectl`. In this case you're going to use the `run` subcommand to run a given image as a container within a pod.

"todo" is the name for the resulting pod, and the image to start is specified with the "--image" flag; here we're using the todo image from chapter I.

The "get pods" subcommand to kubectl lists all pods. We're only interested in the "todo" ones, so we grep for those and the header.

```
$ kubectl run todo --image=dockerinpractice/todo
  $ kubectl get pods | egrep "(POD|todo)"    <─
  POD           IP  CONTAINER(S)  IMAGE(S)  HOST         >
  LABELS          STATUS    CREATED       MESSAGE
  todo-hmj8e                              10.245.1.3/  >   <─
  run=todo  Pending   About a minute
```

"todo-hmj8e" is the pod name.

Labels are name=value pairs associated with the pod, such as the "run" label here. The status of the pod is "Pending", which means Kubernetes is preparing to run it, most likely because it's downloading the image from the Docker Hub.

Kubernetes picks a pod name by taking the name from the `run` command (`todo` in the preceding example), adding a dash and adding a random string. This ensures it doesn't clash with other pod names.

After waiting a few minutes for the todo image to download, you'll eventually see that its status has changed to "Running":

```
$ kubectl get pods | egrep "(POD|todo)"
POD           IP            CONTAINER(S)   IMAGE(S)              >
HOST              LABELS            STATUS    CREATED          MESSAGE
todo-hmj8e  10.246.1.3                                          >
10.245.1.3/10.245.1.3  run=todo  Running   4 minutes
                        todo           dockerinpractice/todo >
                                            Running    About a minute
```

This time the IP, CONTAINER(S), and IMAGE(S) columns are populated. The IP column gives the address of the pod (in this case `10.246.1.3`), and the container column has one row per container in the pod (in this case we have only one, `todo`).

You can test that the container (todo) is indeed up and running and serving requests by hitting the IP address and port directly:

```
$ wget -qO- 10.246.1.3:8000
<html manifest="/todo.appcache">
[...]
```

At this point we haven't seen much difference from running a Docker container directly. To get your first taste of Kubernetes, you can scale up this service by running a `resize` command:

```
$ kubectl resize --replicas=3 replicationController todo
resized
```

This command tells Kubernetes that you want the todo replication controller to ensure that there are three instances of the todo app running across the cluster.

> **TIP** A replication controller is a Kubernetes service that ensures that the right number of pods is running across the cluster.

You can check that the additional instances of the todo app have been started with the kubectl get pods command:

```
$ kubectl get pods | egrep "(POD|todo)"
POD          IP             CONTAINER(S)   IMAGE(S)                  >
HOST                        LABELS             STATUS    CREATED         MESSAGE
todo-2ip3n   10.246.2.2                                             >
10.245.1.4/10.245.1.4    run=todo   Running    10 minutes
                         todo               dockerinpractice/todo  >
                                            Running    8 minutes
todo-4os5b   10.246.1.3                                             >
10.245.1.3/10.245.1.3    run=todo   Running    2 minutes
                         todo               dockerinpractice/todo  >
                                            Running    48 seconds
todo-cuggp   10.246.2.3                                             >
10.245.1.4/10.245.1.4    run=todo   Running    2 minutes
                         todo               dockerinpractice/todo  >
                                            Running    2 minutes
```

Kubernetes has taken the resize instruction and the todo replication controller and ensured that the right number of pods is started up. Notice that it placed two on one host (10.245.1.4) and one on another (10.245.1.3). This is because Kubernetes' default scheduler has an algorithm that spreads pods across nodes by default.

> **TIP** A scheduler is a piece of software that decides where and when items of work should be run. For example, the Linux kernel has a scheduler that decides what task should be run next. Schedulers range from the stupidly simple to the incredibly complex.

You've started to see how Kubernetes can make managing containers easier across multiple hosts. Next we'll dive into the core Kubernetes concept of pods.

USING PODS

A *pod* is a collection of containers that are designed to work together in some way and that share resources.

Each pod gets its own IP address and shares the same volumes and network port range. Because a pod's containers share a localhost, the containers can rely on the different services being available and visible wherever they're deployed.

Figure 12.2 illustrates this with two containers that share a volume. In the figure, container 1 might be a web server that reads data files from the shared volume, which is in turn updated by container 2. Both containers are therefore stateless; state is stored in the shared volume.

Kubernetes pod

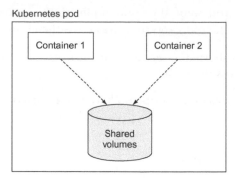

Container 1   Container 2

Shared
volumes

Figure 12.2   A two-container pod

This design of separated responsibilities facilitates a microservices approach by allowing you to manage each part of your service separately. You can upgrade one container within a pod without needing to be concerned with the others.

The following pod specification defines a complex pod with one container that
writes random data (`simplewriter`) to a file every 5 seconds, and another container
that reads from the same file. The file is shared via a volume (`pod-disk`).

Listing 12.1   complexpod.json

```
{
    "id": "complexpod",            Gives the entity a name
    "kind": "Pod",                 Specifies the type of object this is
    "apiVersion": "v1beta1",       Specifies to Kubernetes the version the JSON is targeting
    "desiredState": {
        "manifest": {              The meat of the pod's specification is in the "desiredState" and "manifest" attributes.
            "version": "v1beta1",
            "id": "complexpod",    Gives the entity a name
            "containers": [{       Details of the containers in the pod are stored in this JSON array.
                "name": "simplereader",
                "image": "dockerinpractice/simplereader",     Each container has a name for reference, and the Docker image is specified in the "image" attribute.
                "volumeMounts": [{                              Volume mount points are specified for each container.
                    "mountPath": "/data",                      The mount path is the path to the volume mounted on the filesystem of the container. This could be set to a different location for each container.
                    "name": "pod-disk"                         The volume mount name refers to the name in the pod manifest's "volumes" definition.
                }]
            }, {
                "name": "simplewriter",
                "image": "dockerinpractice/simplewriter",
                "volumeMounts": [{                              Volume mount points are specified for each container.
                    "mountPath": "/data",                      The mount path is the path to the volume mounted on the filesystem of the container. This could be set to a different location for each container.
                    "name": "pod-disk"                         The volume mount name refers to the name in the pod manifest's "volumes" definition.
                }]
            }],
            "volumes": [{                                      The "volumes" attribute defines the volumes created for this pod.
                "name": "pod-disk",                            The name of the volume is referred to in the previous "volumeMounts" entries.
                "emptydir": {}                                 A temporary directory that shares a pod's lifetime
            }]
        }
    }
}
```

To load this pod specification, create a file with the preceding listing and run this command:

```
$ kubectl create -f complexpod.json
pods/complexpod
```

After waiting a minute for the images to download, you'll see the log output of the container by running `kubectl log` and specifying first the pod and then the container you're interested in.

```
$ kubectl log complexpod simplereader
2015-08-04T21:03:36.535014550Z '? U
[2015-08-04T21:03:41.537370907Z] h(^3eSk4y
[2015-08-04T21:03:41.537370907Z] CM(@
[2015-08-04T21:03:46.542871125Z] qm>5
[2015-08-04T21:03:46.542871125Z] {Vv_
[2015-08-04T21:03:51.552111956Z] KH+74      f
[2015-08-04T21:03:56.556372427Z] j?p+!\
```

DISCUSSION

We've only scratched the surface of Kubernetes' capabilities and potential here, but this should give you a sense of what can be done with it and how it can make orchestrating Docker containers simpler.

The next technique looks at directly taking advantage of some more features of Kubernetes. Kubernetes is also used behind the scenes as an orchestration engine by OpenShift in techniques 90 and 99.

TECHNIQUE 89 **Accessing the Kubernetes API from within a pod**

Often it's possible for pods to operate completely independently from each other, not even knowing that they're running as part of a Kubernetes cluster. But Kubernetes does provide a rich API, and giving containers access to this opens the door to introspection and adaptive behavior, as well as the ability for containers to manage the Kubernetes cluster themselves.

PROBLEM

You want to access the Kubernetes API from within a pod.

SOLUTION

Use `curl` to access the Kubernetes API from within a container in a pod, using authorization information made available to the container.

This is one of the shorter techniques in the book, but it contains a lot to unpack. This is one of the reasons it's a useful technique to study. Among other things, we'll cover

- The `kubectl` command
- Starting Kubernetes pods
- Accessing Kubernetes pods
- A Kubernetes anti-pattern

- Bearer tokens
- Kubernetes secrets
- The Kubernetes "downwards API"

NO KUBERNETES CLUSTER?

If you don't have access to a Kubernetes cluster, you have a few options. There are many cloud providers that offer pay-as-you-go Kubernetes clusters. For the fewest dependencies, though, we recommend using Minikube (mentioned in the last technique), which doesn't require a credit card.

For information on how to install Minikube, see the documentation at https://kubernetes.io/docs/tasks/tools/install-minikube/.

CREATING A POD

First you're going to create a container within the fresh `ubuntu` pod using the `kubectl` command, and then you'll access a shell within that container on the command line. (`kubectl run` currently imposes a 1-1 relationship between pods and containers, though pods are more flexible than this in general.)

Listing 12.2   Creating and setting up a container

The kubectl command using the -ti flag, naming the pod "ubuntu", using the by-now familiar ubuntu:16.04 image, and telling Kubernetes not to restart once the pod/container has exited

Kubectl helpfully tells you that your terminal may not show you the prompt unless you press Enter.

```
$ kubectl run -it ubuntu --image=ubuntu:16.04 --restart=Never
  If you don't see a command prompt, try pressing enter.
  root@ubuntu:/# apt-get update -y && apt-get install -y curl
  [...]
  root@ubuntu:/
```

Once the install is complete, the prompt is returned.

This is the prompt from within the container that you'll see if you press Enter, and we're updating the container's package system and installing curl.

You're now in the container created by the `kubectl` command, and you've ensured that curl is installed.

> **WARNING**   Accessing and modifying a pod from a shell is considered a Kubernetes anti-pattern. We use it here to demonstrate what is possible from within a pod, rather than how pods should be used.

Listing 12.3   Access the Kubernetes API from a pod

Uses the curl command to access the Kubernetes API. The -k flag allows curl to work without certificates being deployed on the client, and the HTTP method used to talk to the API is specified as GET by the -X flag.

The -H flag adds an HTTP header to the request. This is an authentication token discussed shortly.

```
root@ubuntu:/# $ curl -k -X GET \
  -H "Authorization: Bearer \
  $(cat /var/run/secrets/kubernetes.io/serviceaccount/token)" <3> \
  https://${KUBERNETES_PORT_443_TCP_ADDR}:${KUBERNETES_SERVICE_PORT_HTTPS}
  {
```

The URL to contact is constructed from environment variables available within the pod.

```
  "paths": [
    "/api",
    "/api/v1",
    "/apis",
    "/apis/apps",
    "/apis/apps/v1beta1",
    "/apis/authentication.k8s.io",
    "/apis/authentication.k8s.io/v1",
    "/apis/authentication.k8s.io/v1beta1",
    "/apis/authorization.k8s.io",
    "/apis/authorization.k8s.io/v1",
    "/apis/authorization.k8s.io/v1beta1",
    "/apis/autoscaling",
    "/apis/autoscaling/v1",
    "/apis/autoscaling/v2alpha1",
    "/apis/batch",
    "/apis/batch/v1",
    "/apis/batch/v2alpha1",
    "/apis/certificates.k8s.io",
    "/apis/certificates.k8s.io/v1beta1",
    "/apis/extensions",
    "/apis/extensions/v1beta1",
    "/apis/policy",
    "/apis/policy/v1beta1",
    "/apis/rbac.authorization.k8s.io",
    "/apis/rbac.authorization.k8s.io/v1alpha1",
    "/apis/rbac.authorization.k8s.io/v1beta1",
    "/apis/settings.k8s.io",
    "/apis/settings.k8s.io/v1alpha1",
    "/apis/storage.k8s.io",
    "/apis/storage.k8s.io/v1",
    "/apis/storage.k8s.io/v1beta1",
    "/healthz",
    "/healthz/ping",
    "/healthz/poststarthook/bootstrap-controller",
    "/healthz/poststarthook/ca-registration",
    "/healthz/poststarthook/extensions/third-party-resources",
    "/logs",
    "/metrics",
    "/swaggerapi/",
    "/ui/",
    "/version"
  ]
}
root@ubuntu:/# curl -k -X GET -H "Authorization: Bearer $(cat
  /var/run/secrets/kubernetes.io/serviceaccount/token)"
  https://${KUBERNETES_PORT_443_TCP_ADDR}:
  ${KUBERNETES_SERVICE_ORT_HTTPS}/version
 {
  "major": "1",
   "minor": "6",
  "gitVersion": "v1.6.4",
  "gitCommit": "d6f433224538d4f9ca2f7ae19b252e6fcb66a3ae",
  "gitTreeState": "dirty",
  "buildDate": "2017-06-22T04:31:09Z",
```

The default response for the API is to list the paths it offers for consumption.

Another request is made, this time to the /version path.

The response to the /version request is to specify the version of Kubernetes that's running.

```
    "goVersion": "go1.7.5",
    "compiler": "gc",
    "platform": "linux/amd64"
}
```

The preceding listing covered a lot of new material, but we hope it gives a flavor of what can be done within Kubernetes pods dynamically, without any setup.

The key point to take from this listing is that information is made available to users within the pod, allowing the pod to make contact with the Kubernetes API. These items of information are collectively called the "downward API." At present, the downward API consists of two classes of data: environment variables, and files exposed to the pod.

A file is used in the preceding example to provide an authentication token to the Kubernetes API. This token is made available in the file /var/run/secrets/kubernetes.io/serviceaccount/token. In listing 12.3, this file is run through cat, and the output of the cat command is supplied as part of the Authorization: HTTP header. This header specifies that the authorization used is of the Bearer type, and the bearer token is the output of cat, so the -H argument to curl is as follows:

```
-H "Authorization: Bearer
⇒ $(cat /var/run/secrets/kubernetes.io/serviceaccount/token)"
```

> **NOTE** *Bearer tokens* are an authentication method that requires only that a specified token is given—no identification is required beyond that (such as username/password). *Bearer shares* operate on a similar principle, where the bearer of the shares is the one who has the right to sell them. Cash money works the same way—indeed on UK cash the notes have the phrase "I promise to pay the bearer on demand the sum of …"

The downward API items exposed are a form of Kubernetes "secret." Any secret can be created using the Kubernetes API and exposed via a file in a pod. This mechanism allows for the separation of secrets from Docker images and Kubernetes pod or deployment configuration, meaning that permissions can be handled separately from those more open items.

DISCUSSION

It's worth paying attention to this technique, as it covers a lot of ground. The key point to grasp is that Kubernetes pods have information made available to them that allows them to interact with the Kubernetes API. This allows applications to run within Kubernetes that monitor and act on activities going on around the cluster. For example, you might have an infrastructure pod that watches the API for newly sprung-up pods, investigates their activities, and records that data somewhere else.

Although role-based access control (RBAC) is outside the scope of this book, it's worth mentioning that this has implications for security, as you don't necessarily want just any user of your cluster to have this level of access. Therefore, parts of the API will require more than just a bearer token to gain access.

These security-related considerations make this technique related half to Kubernetes and half to security. Either way, this is an important technique for anyone looking to use Kubernetes "for real," to help them understand how the API works and how it potentially can be abused.

TECHNIQUE 90 Using OpenShift to run AWS APIs locally

One of the big challenges with local development is testing an application against other services. Docker can help with this if the service can be put in a container, but this leaves the large world of external third-party services unsolved.

A common solution is to have test API instances, but these often provide fake responses—a more complete test of functionality isn't possible if an application is built around a service. For example, imagine you want to use AWS S3 as an upload location for your application, where it then processes the uploads—testing this will cost money.

PROBLEM

You want to have AWS-like APIs available locally to develop against.

SOLUTION

Set up LocalStack and use the available AWS service equivalents.

In this walkthrough you're going to set up an OpenShift system using Minishift, and then run LocalStack in a pod on it. OpenShift is a RedHat-sponsored wrapper around Kubernetes that provides extra functionality more suited to enterprise production deployments of Kubernetes.

In this technique we'll cover

- The creation of routes in OpenShift
- Security context constraints
- Differences between OpenShift and Kubernetes
- Testing AWS services using public Docker images

NOTE To follow this technique you'll need to install Minishift. Minishift is similar to Minikube, which you saw in technique 89. The difference is that it contains an installation of OpenShift (covered comprehensively in technique 99).

LOCALSTACK

LocalStack is a project that aims to give you as complete as possible a set of AWS APIs to develop against without incurring any cost. This is great for testing or trying code out before running it for real against AWS and potentially wasting time and money.

LocalStack spins up the following core Cloud APIs on your local machine:

- API Gateway at http://localhost:4567
- Kinesis at http://localhost:4568
- DynamoDB at http://localhost:4569
- DynamoDB Streams at http://localhost:4570
- Elasticsearch at http://localhost:4571

- S3 at http://localhost:4572
- Firehose at http://localhost:4573
- Lambda at http://localhost:4574
- SNS at http://localhost:4575
- SQS at http://localhost:4576
- Redshift at http://localhost:4577
- ES (Elasticsearch Service) at http://localhost:4578
- SES at http://localhost:4579
- Route53 at http://localhost:4580
- CloudFormation at http://localhost:4581
- CloudWatch at http://localhost:4582

LocalStack supports running in a Docker container, or natively on a machine. It's built on Moto, which is a mocking framework in turn built on Boto, which is a Python AWS SDK.

Running within an OpenShift cluster gives you the capability to run many of these AWS API environments. You can then create distinct endpoints for each set of services, and isolate them from one another. Also, you can worry less about resource usage, as the cluster scheduler will take care of that. But LocalStack doesn't run out of the box, so we'll guide you through what needs to be done to get it to work.

ENSURING MINISHIFT IS SET UP

At this point we assume you have Minishift set up—you should look at the official documentation on getting started at https://docs.openshift.org/latest/minishift/getting-started/index.html.

Listing 12.4   Check Minishift is set up OK

```
$ eval $(minishift oc-env)
$ oc get all
No resources found.
```

CHANGING THE DEFAULT SECURITY CONTEXT CONSTRAINTS

Security context constraints (SCCs) are an OpenShift concept that allows more granular control over Docker containers' powers. They control SELinux contexts (see technique 100), can drop capabilities from running containers (see technique 93), can determine which user the pod can run as, and so on.

To get this running, you're going to change the default `restricted` SCC. You could also create a separate SCC and apply it to a particular project, but you can try that on your own.

To change the 'restricted` SCC, you'll need to become a cluster administrator:

```
$ oc login -u system:admin
```

Then you need to edit the restricted SCC with the following command:

```
$ oc edit scc restricted
```

You'll see the definition of the `restricted` SCC.

At this point you're going to have to do two things:

- Allow containers to run as any user (in this case `root`)
- Prevent the SCC from restricting your capabilities to setuid and setgid

ALLOWING RUNASANY

The LocalStack container runs as root by default, but for security reasons, OpenShift doesn't allow containers to run as root by default. Instead it picks a UID within a very high range, and runs as that UID. Note that UIDs are numbers, as opposed to usernames, which are strings mapped to a UID.

To simplify matters, and to allow the LocalStack container to run as root, change these lines,

```
runAsUser:
 type: MustRunAsRange
```

to read as follows:

```
runAsUser:
 type: RunAsAny
```

This allows containers to run as *any* user, and not within a range of UIDs.

ALLOWING SETUID AND SETGID CAPABILITIES

When LocalStack starts up, it needs to become another user to start ElastiCache. The ElastiCache service doesn't start up as the root user.

To get around this, LocalStack su's the startup command to the LocalStack user in the container. Because the `restricted` SCC explicitly disallows actions that change your user or group ID, you need to remove these restrictions. Do this by deleting these lines:

```
- SETUID
- SETGID
```

SAVING THE FILE

Once you've completed those two steps, save the file.

Make a note of the host. If you run this command,

```
$ minishift console --machine-readable | grep HOST | sed 's/^HOST=\(.*\)/\1/'
```

you'll get the host that the Minishift instance is accessible as from your machine. Note this host, as you'll need to substitute it in later.

DEPLOYING THE POD

Deploying the LocalStack is as easy as running this command:

```
$ oc new-app localstack/localstack --name="localstack"
```

> **NOTE** If you want to take a deeper look at the localstack image, it's available at https://github.com/localstack/localstack.

This takes the localstack/localstack image and creates an OpenShift application around it for you, setting up internal services (based on the exposed ports in the LocalStack Docker image's Dockerfile), running the container in a pod, and performing various other management tasks.

CREATING THE ROUTES

If you want to access the services from outside, you need to create OpenShift routes, which create an external address for accessing services within the OpenShift network. For example, to create a route for the SQS service, create a file like the following, called route.yaml:

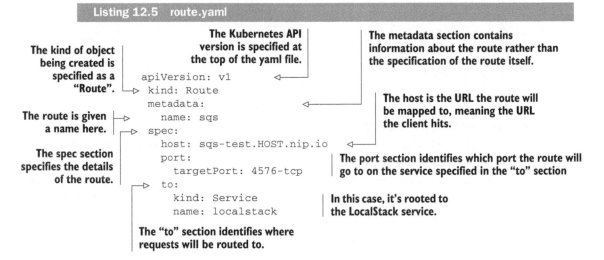

Listing 12.5   route.yaml

The kind of object being created is specified as a "Route".

The Kubernetes API version is specified at the top of the yaml file.

The metadata section contains information about the route rather than the specification of the route itself.

The route is given a name here.

The spec section specifies the details of the route.

The host is the URL the route will be mapped to, meaning the URL the client hits.

The port section identifies which port the route will go to on the service specified in the "to" section

In this case, it's rooted to the LocalStack service.

The "to" section identifies where requests will be routed to.

```
apiVersion: v1
kind: Route
metadata:
  name: sqs
spec:
  host: sqs-test.HOST.nip.io
  port:
    targetPort: 4576-tcp
  to:
    kind: Service
    name: localstack
```

Create the route by running this command,

```
$ oc create -f route.yaml
```

which creates the route from the yaml file you just created. This process is then repeated for each service you want to set up.

Then run `oc get all` to see what you've created within your OpenShift project:

Next, the deployment configs are listed, which specify how a pod should be rolled out to the cluster.

Returns the most significant items in your OpenShift project

First listed are the image streams. These are objects that track the state of local or remote images.

```
$ oc get all
 NAME DOCKER REPO TAGS UPDATED
 is/localstack 172.30.1.1:5000/myproject/localstack latest 15 hours ago
 NAME REVISION DESIRED CURRENT TRIGGERED BY
 dc/localstack 1 1 1 config,image(localstack:latest)
 NAME DESIRED CURRENT READY AGE
 rc/localstack-1 1 1 1 15
 NAME HOST/PORT PATH SERVICES PORT TERMINATION WILDCARD
 routes/sqs sqs-test.192.168.64.2.nip.io localstack 4576-tcp None
 NAME CLUSTER-IP EXTERNAL-IP PORT(S) AGE
 svc/localstack 172.30.187.65  4567/TCP,4568/TCP,4569/TCP,4570/TCP,4571/TCP,
➥ 4572/TCP,4573/TCP,4574/TCP,4575/TCP,4576/TCP,4577/TCP,4578/TCP,
➥ 4579/TCP,4580/TCP,4581/TCP,4582/TCP,8080/TCP 15h
 NAME READY STATUS RESTARTS AGE
 po/localstack-1-hnvpw 1/1 Running 0 15h
```

The third class is the replication configs, which specify the replicated characteristics of the running pods.

The fourth class is the routes set up in your project.

Services are the next class listed. Here you see the ports exposed in the Dockerfile result in exposed ports for the service.

Finally, the pods in the project are listed.

Although technically not *all* the objects available within your project, the oc get all command shows the ones most significant to running applications.

The SQS-like AWS service is now accessible as a URL endpoint to test your code against.

ACCESSING THE SERVICES

You can now hit the services from your host. Here's an example of creating an SQS stream:

The aws client application is used to hit the newly created endpoint, and it asks kinesis to list its streams.

The aws client is called again to create an SQS stream called "teststream" with a shard-count of 2.

```
$ aws --endpoint-url=http://kinesis-test.192.168.64.2.nip.io kinesis
  list-streams
  {
    "StreamNames": []
  }
  $ aws --endpoint-url=http://kinesis-test.192.168.64.2.nip.io kinesis
  create-stream --stream-name teststream --shard-count 2
  $ aws --endpoint-url=http://kinesis-test.192.168.64.2.nip.io kinesis
  list-streams
  {
    "StreamNames": [
    "teststream"
    ]
  }
```

JSON output indicates that no streams exist.

Again, you ask for a list of kinesis streams.

JSON output indicates that a stream exists called "teststream".

NOTE The aws client is an install you'll need to make this work. Alternatively, you can curl the API endpoint directly, but we don't advise this. It's also assumed you have run aws configure and specified your AWS keys and default region. The actual values specified don't matter to LocalStack, as it doesn't do authentication.

Here we've covered only one type of service, but this technique is easily extended to the others listed at the beginning of this technique.

DISCUSSION

This technique has given you a sense of the power of OpenShift (and Kubernetes, on which OpenShift is based). To get a useful application spun up with a usable endpoint and all the internal wiring taken care of is in many ways the realization of the promise of portability that Docker offers, scaled up to the data centre.

 For example, this could be taken further, and multiple instances of LocalStack could be spun up on the same OpenShift cluster. Tests against AWS APIs can be done in parallel without necessarily costing more resources (depending on the size of your OpenShift cluster and the demands of your tests, of course). Because this is all code, continuous integration could be set up to dynamically spin up and spin down LocalStack instances to talk to on each commit of your AWS codebase.

As well as pointing out various aspects of Kubernetes, this particular technique also demonstrates that products such as OpenShift are building on top of Kubernetes to extend its functionality. For example, security context constraints are an OpenShift concept (although security contexts are also in Kubernetes) and "routes" was a concept OpenShift created on top of Kubernetes that was eventually adapted for implementation in Kubernetes directly. Over time, features that have been developed for OpenShift have been upstreamed to Kubernetes and have become part of its offering.

You'll see OpenShift again in technique 99 where we'll look at how it can serve as a platform to securely let users run containers.

TECHNIQUE 91 Building a framework on Mesos

When discussing the multitude of orchestration possibilities, you'll probably find one, in particular, mentioned as an alternative to Kubernetes: Mesos. Typically this is followed by opaque statements like "Mesos is a framework for a framework" and "Kubernetes can be run on top of Mesos."

The most apt analogy we've come across is to think of Mesos as providing the kernel for your data center. You can't do anything useful with it alone—the value comes when you combine it with an init system and applications.

For a low-tech explanation, imagine you have a monkey sitting in front of a panel that controls of all of your machines and has the power to start and stop applications at will. Naturally, you'll need to give the monkey a *very* clear list of instructions about what to do in particular situations, when to start an application up, and so on. You could do it all yourself, but that's time-consuming and monkeys are cheap.

Mesos is the monkey!

Mesos is ideal for a company with a highly dynamic and complex infrastructure, likely with experience at rolling their own production orchestration solutions. If you don't meet these conditions, you may be better served by an off-the-shelf solution rather than spending time tailoring Mesos.

PROBLEM

You have a number of rules for controlling the startup of applications and jobs, and you want to enforce them without manually starting them on remote machines and keeping track of their status.

SOLUTION

Use Mesos, a flexible and powerful tool that provides an abstraction of resource management.

Mesos is a mature piece of software for providing an abstraction of resource management on multiple machines. It's been battle-tested in production by companies you've heard of, and, as a result, it's stable and reliable.

> **NOTE**   You need Docker 1.6.2 or later for Mesos to be able to use the correct Docker API version.

Figure 12.3 shows what a generic production Mesos setup looks like.

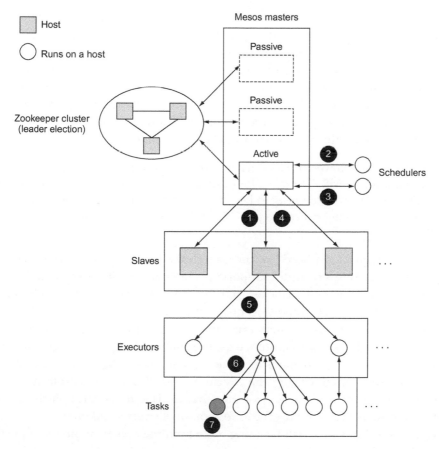

Figure 12.3   A generic production Mesos setup

Referring to this figure, you can see what the basic Mesos lifecycle for starting a task looks like:

1 A slave runs on a node, tracking resource availability and keeping the master informed.

2 The master receives information from one or more slaves about available resources and makes resource offers to schedulers.

3 A scheduler receives resource offers from the master, decides where it wants to run tasks, and communicates this back to the master.

4 The master passes on the task information to the appropriate slaves.

5 Each slave passes the task information to an existing executor on the node or starts a new one.

6 The executor reads the task information and starts the task on the node.

7 The task runs.

The Mesos project provides the master and slave, as well as a built-in shell executor. It's your job to provide a *framework* (or *application*), which consists of a scheduler (the "list of instructions" in our monkey analogy) and optionally a custom executor.

Many third-party projects provide frameworks you can drop into Mesos (and we'll look at one in more detail in the next technique), but to get a better understanding of how you can fully harness the power of Mesos with Docker, we're going to build our own framework consisting only of a scheduler. If you have highly complex logic for starting applications, this may be your final chosen route.

> **NOTE** You don't have to use Docker with Mesos, but since that's what the book is about, we will. There's a lot of detail we won't go into because Mesos is so flexible. We're also going to be running Mesos on a single computer, but we'll try to keep it as realistic as possible and point out what you need to do to go live.

We've not yet explained where Docker fits into the Mesos lifecycle—the final piece to this puzzle is that Mesos provides support for *containerizers*, allowing you to isolate your executors or tasks (or both). Docker isn't the only tool that can be used here, but it's so popular that Mesos has some Docker-specific features to get you started.

Our example will only containerize the tasks we run, because we're using the default executor. If you had a custom executor only running a language environment, where each task involves dynamically loading and executing some code, you might want to consider containerizing the executor instead. As an example use case, you might have a JVM running as an executor that loads and executes pieces of code on the fly, avoiding JVM startup overhead for potentially very small tasks.

Figure 12.4 shows what will be going on behind the scenes in our example when a new dockerized task is created.

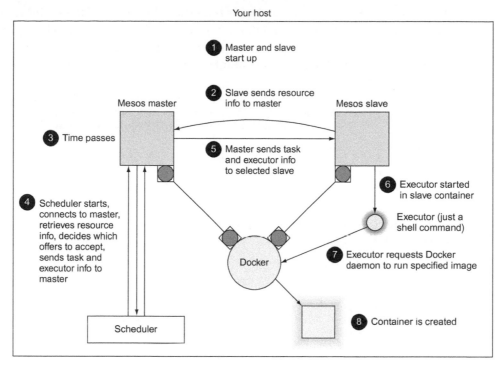

Figure 12.4 A single-host Mesos setup starting a container

Without any further ado, let's get started. First you need to start up a master:

Listing 12.6 Starting a master

```
$ docker run -d --name mesmaster redjack/mesos:0.21.0 mesos-master \
--work_dir=/opt
24e277601260dcc6df35dc20a32a81f0336ae49531c46c2c8db84fe99ac1da35
$ docker inspect -f '{{.NetworkSettings.IPAddress}}' mesmaster
172.17.0.2
$ docker logs -f mesmaster
I0312 01:43:59.182916    1 main.cpp:167] Build: 2014-11-22 05:29:57 by root
I0312 01:43:59.183073    1 main.cpp:169] Version: 0.21.0
I0312 01:43:59.183084    1 main.cpp:172] Git tag: 0.21.0
[...]
```

The master startup is a little verbose, but you should find it stops logging quickly. Keep this terminal open so you can see what happens when you start the other containers.

> **NOTE** Usually a Mesos setup will have multiple Mesos masters (one active and several backups), along with a Zookeeper cluster. Setting this up is documented on the "Mesos High-Availability Mode" page on the Mesos site (http://mesos.apache.org/ documentation/latest/high-availability). You'd also need to expose port 5050 for external communications and use the work_dir folder as a volume to save persistent information.

You also need a slave. Unfortunately this is a little fiddly. One of the defining characteristics of Mesos is the ability to enforce resource limits on tasks, which requires the slave to have the ability to freely inspect and manage processes. As a result, the command to run the slave needs a number of outer system details to be exposed inside the container.

Listing 12.7   Starting a slave

```
$ docker run -d --name messlave --pid=host \
  -v /var/run/docker.sock:/var/run/docker.sock -v /sys:/sys \
  redjack/mesos:0.21.0 mesos-slave \
  --master=172.17.0.2:5050 --executor_registration_timeout=5mins \
  --isolation=cgroups/cpu,cgroups/mem --containerizers=docker,mesos \
  --resources="ports(*):[8000-8100]"
1b88c414527f63e24241691a96e3e3251fbb24996f3bfba3ebba91d7a541a9f5
$ docker inspect -f '{{.NetworkSettings.IPAddress}}' messlave
172.17.0.3
$ docker logs -f messlave
I0312 01:46:43.341621 32398 main.cpp:142] Build: 2014-11-22 05:29:57 by root
I0312 01:46:43.341789 32398 main.cpp:144] Version: 0.21.0
I0312 01:46:43.341795 32398 main.cpp:147] Git tag: 0.21.0
[...]
I0312 01:46:43.554498 32429 slave.cpp:627] No credentials provided. >
Attempting to register without authentication
I0312 01:46:43.554633 32429 slave.cpp:638] Detecting new master
I0312 01:46:44.419646 32424 slave.cpp:756] Registered with master >
master@172.17.0.2:5050; given slave ID 20150312-014359-33558956-5050-1-S0
[...]
```

At this point you should also have seen some activity in the Mesos master terminal, starting with a couple of lines like these:

```
I0312 01:46:44.332494     9 master.cpp:3068] Registering slave at >
slave(1)@172.17.0.3:5051 (8c6c63023050) with id >
20150312-014359-33558956-5050-1-S0
I0312 01:46:44.333772     8 registrar.cpp:445] Applied 1 operations in >
134310ns; attempting to update the 'registry'
```

The output of these two logs shows that your slave has started and is connected to the master. If you don't see these, stop and double-check your master IP address. It can be frustrating later on to try and debug why a framework isn't starting any tasks, when there are no connected slaves to start them on.

Anyway, there's a lot going on in the command in listing 12.7. The arguments after `run` and before `redjack/mesos:0.21.0` are all Docker arguments, and they mainly consist of giving the slave container lots of information about the outside world. The arguments after `mesos-slave` are more interesting. First, `master` tells your slave where to find your master (or your Zookeeper cluster). The next three arguments, `executor _registration_timeout`, `isolation`, and `containerizers`, are all tweaks to Mesos settings that should always be applied when working with Docker. Last, but certainly not least, you need to let the Mesos slave know what ports are acceptable to hand out as resources. By default, Mesos offers 31000–32000, but we want something a bit lower and more memorable.

Now the easy steps are out of the way and we come to the final stage of setting up Mesos—creating a scheduler.

Happily, we have an example framework ready for you to use. Let's try it out, see what it does, and then explore how it works. Keep your two `docker logs -f` commands open on your master and slave containers so you can see the communication as it happens.

The following commands will get the source repository for the example framework from GitHub and start it up.

Listing 12.8   Downloading and starting the example framework

```
$ git clone https://github.com/docker-in-practice/mesos-nc.git
$ docker run -it --rm -v $(pwd)/mesos-nc:/opt redjack/mesos:0.21.0 bash
# apt-get update && apt-get install -y python
# cd /opt
# export PYTHONUSERBASE=/usr/local
# python myframework.py 172.17.0.2:5050
I0312 02:11:07.642227    182 sched.cpp:137] Version: 0.21.0
I0312 02:11:07.645598    176 sched.cpp:234] New master detected at >
master@172.17.0.2:5050
I0312 02:11:07.645800    176 sched.cpp:242] No credentials provided. >
Attempting to register without authentication
I0312 02:11:07.648449    176 sched.cpp:408] Framework registered with >
20150312-014359-33558956-5050-1-0000
Registered with framework ID 20150312-014359-33558956-5050-1-0000
Received offer 20150312-014359-33558956-5050-1-O0. cpus: 4.0, mem: 6686.0, >
ports: 8000-8100
Creating task 0
Task 0 is in state TASK_RUNNING
[...]
Received offer 20150312-014359-33558956-5050-1-O5. cpus: 3.5, mem: 6586.0, >
ports: 8005-8100
Creating task 5
Task 5 is in state TASK_RUNNING
Received offer 20150312-014359-33558956-5050-1-O6. cpus: 3.4, mem: 6566.0, >
ports: 8006-8100
Declining offer
```

You'll note that we've mounted the Git repository inside the Mesos image. This is because it contains all the Mesos libraries we need. Unfortunately, it can be a little painful to install them otherwise.

Our `mesos-nc` framework is designed to run `echo 'hello <task id>' | nc -l <port>` on all available hosts, on all available ports from 8000 to 8005. Because of how netcat works, these "servers" will terminate as soon as you access them, be it by curl, Telnet, nc, or your browser. You can verify this by running `curl localhost:8003` in a new terminal. It will return the expected response, and your Mesos logs will show the spawning of a task to replace the terminated one. You can also keep track of which tasks are running with docker ps.

It's worth pointing out here the evidence of Mesos keeping track of allocated resources and marking them as available when a task terminates. In particular, when you accessed localhost:8003 (feel free to try it again), take a close look at the Received offer line—it shows two port ranges (as they're not connected), including the freshly freed one:

```
Received offer 20150312-014359-33558956-5050-1-O45. cpus: 3.5, mem: 6586.0, >
ports: 8006-8100,8003-8003
```

> **WARNING** The Mesos slave names all the containers it starts with the prefix "mesos-", and it assumes anything like that can be freely managed by the slave. Be careful with your container naming, or you might end up with the Mesos slave killing itself.

The framework code (myframework.py) is well commented, in case you're feeling adventurous. We'll go through some of the high-level design.

```
class TestScheduler
(mesos.interface.Scheduler):
[...]
    def registered(self, driver, frameworkId, masterInfo):
[...]
    def statusUpdate(self, driver, update):
[...]
    def resourceOffers(self, driver, offers):
[...]
```

All Mesos schedulers subclass the base Mesos scheduler class, and they implement a number of methods that Mesos will call at appropriate points to let your framework react to events. Although we've implemented three in the preceding snippet, two of those are optional and have been implemented to add extra logging for demonstration purposes. The only method you *must* implement is resourceOffers—there's not much point in a framework that doesn't know when it can launch tasks. You're free to add any additional methods for your own purposes, such as *init* and _makeTask, as long as they don't conflict with any of the methods Mesos expects to use, so make sure you read the documentation (http://mesos.apache.org/documentation/latest/app-framework-development-guide/).

> **TIP** If you end up writing your own framework, you'll want to look at some documentation of methods and structures. Unfortunately, at time of writing, the only generated documentation is for Java methods. Readers looking for a starting point for digging into the structures may wish to begin with the include/mesos/mesos.proto file in the Mesos source code. Good luck!

Let's look in a bit more detail at the main method of interest: resourceOffers. This is where the decision happens to launch tasks or decline an offer. Figure 12.5 shows the

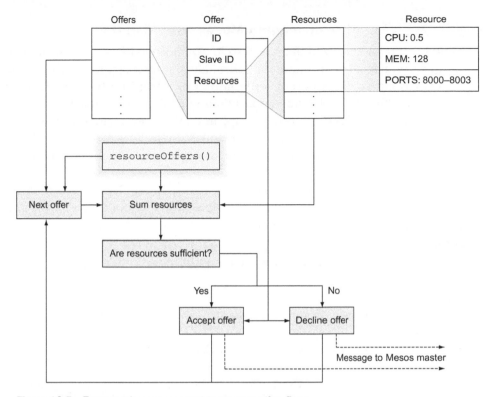

Figure 12.5 Framework `resourceOffers` execution flow

execution flow after `resourceOffers` in our framework is called by Mesos (usually because some resources have become available for use by the framework).

   `resourceOffers` is given a list of offers, where each offer corresponds to a single Mesos slave. The offer contains details about the resources available to a task launched on the slave, and a typical implementation will use this information to identify the most appropriate places to launch the tasks it wants to run. Launching a task sends a message to the Mesos master, which then continues with the lifecycle outlined in figure 12.3.

DISCUSSION

It's important to note the flexibility of `resourceOffers`—your task-launching decisions can depend on any criteria you choose, from health checks of external services to the phase of the moon. This flexibility can be a burden, so premade frameworks exist to take some of this low-level detail away and simplify Mesos usage. One of these frameworks is covered in the next technique.

   You may want to consult Roger Ignazio's *Mesos in Action* (Manning, 2016) for more details on what you can do with Mesos—we've only scratched the surface here, and you've seen how easily Docker slots in.

TECHNIQUE 92   Micromanaging Mesos with Marathon

By now you'll have realized that there's a lot you need to think about with Mesos, even for an extremely simple framework. Being able to rely on applications being deployed correctly is extremely important—the impact of a bug in a framework could range from the inability to deploy new applications to a full service outage.

The stakes get higher as you scale up, and unless your team is used to writing reliable dynamic deployment code, you might want to consider a more battle-tested approach—Mesos itself is very stable, but an in-house bespoke framework may not be as reliable as you'd want.

Marathon is suitable for a company without in-house deployment tooling experience but that needs a well-supported and easy-to-use solution for deploying containers in a somewhat dynamic environment.

PROBLEM

You need a reliable way to harness the power of Mesos without getting bogged down in writing your own framework.

SOLUTION

Use Marathon, a layer on top of Mesos that provides a simpler interface to get you productive faster.

Marathon is an Apache Mesos framework built by Mesosphere for managing long-running applications. The marketing materials describe it as the init or upstart daemon for your datacenter (where Mesos is the kernel). This is not an unreasonable analogy.

Marathon makes it easy to get started by allowing you to start a single container with a Mesos master, Mesos slave, and Marathon itself inside. This is useful for demos, but it isn't suitable for production Marathon deployments. To get a realistic Marathon setup, you'll need a Mesos master and slave (from the previous technique) as well as a Zookeeper instance (from technique 84). Make sure you have all this running, and we'll get started by running the Marathon container.

```
$ docker inspect -f '{{.NetworkSettings.IPAddress}}' mesmaster
172.17.0.2
$ docker inspect -f '{{.NetworkSettings.IPAddress}}' messlave
172.17.0.3
$ docker inspect -f '{{.NetworkSettings.IPAddress}}' zookeeper
172.17.0.4
$ docker pull mesosphere/marathon:v0.8.2
[...]
$ docker run -d -h $(hostname) --name marathon -p 8080:8080 \
mesosphere/marathon:v0.8.2 --master 172.17.0.2:5050 --local_port_min 8000 \
--local_port_max 8100 --zk zk://172.17.0.4:2181/marathon
accd6de46cfab65572539ccffa5c2303009be7ec7dbfb49e3ab8f447453f2b93
$ docker logs -f marathon
MESOS_NATIVE_JAVA_LIBRARY is not set. Searching in /usr/lib /usr/local/lib.
MESOS_NATIVE_LIBRARY, MESOS_NATIVE_JAVA_LIBRARY set to >
'/usr/lib/libmesos.so'
```

```
[2015-06-23 19:42:14,836] INFO Starting Marathon 0.8.2 >
(mesosphere.marathon.Main$:87)
[2015-06-23 19:42:16,270] INFO Connecting to Zookeeper... >
(mesosphere.marathon.Main$:37)
[...]
[2015-06-30 18:20:07,971] INFO started processing 1 offers, >
launching at most 1 tasks per offer and 1000 tasks in total
➥ (mesosphere.marathon.tasks.IterativeOfferMatcher$:124)
[2015-06-30 18:20:07,972] INFO Launched 0 tasks on 0 offers, >
declining 1 (mesosphere.marathon.tasks.IterativeOfferMatcher$:216)
```

Like Mesos itself, Marathon is fairly chatty, but (also like Mesos) it stops fairly quickly. At this point, it will enter the loop you're familiar with from writing your own framework—considering resource offers and deciding what to do with them. Because we haven't launched anything yet, you should see no activity; hence the `declining 1` in the preceding log.

Marathon comes with a nice-looking web interface, which is why we exposed port 8080 on the host—visit http://localhost:8080 in your browser to pull it up.

We're going to dive straight into Marathon, so let's create a new application. To clarify a bit of terminology—an "app" in the Marathon world is a group of one or more tasks with exactly the same definition.

Click the New App button at the top right to bring up a dialog box you can use to define the app you want to start up. We'll continue in the vein of the framework we created ourselves by setting the ID to "marathon-nc", leaving CPU, memory, and disk space at their defaults (to match the resource limits imposed on our mesos-nc framework), and setting the command to `echo "hello $MESOS_TASK_ID" | nc -l $PORT0` (using environment variables available to the task—note, that's the number zero). Set the Ports field to 8000 as an indication of where you want to listen. For now we're going to skip over the other fields. Click Create.

Your newly defined application will now be listed on the web interface. The status will briefly show as "Deploying" before showing as "Running." Your app is now started!

If you click on the "/marathon-nc" entry in the Apps list, you'll see the unique ID of your app. You can get the full configuration from the REST API as shown in the following snippet and also verify that it's running by curling the Mesos slave container on the appropriate port. Make sure you save the full configuration returned by the REST API, as it'll come in handy later—it's been saved to app.json in the following example.

```
$ curl http://localhost:8080/v2/apps/marathon-nc/versions
{"versions":["2015-06-30T19:52:44.649Z"]}
$ curl -s \
http://localhost:8080/v2/apps/marathon-nc/versions/2015-06-30T19:52:44.649Z \
> app.json
$ cat app.json
{"id":"/marathon-nc", >
"cmd":"echo \"hello $MESOS_TASK_ID\" | nc -l $PORT0",[...]
$ curl http://172.17.0.3:8000
hello marathon-nc.f56f140e-19e9-11e5-a44d-0242ac110012
```

Note the text following "hello" in the output from `curl`ing the app—it should match the unique ID in the interface. Be quick with checking, though—running that `curl` command will make the app terminate, Marathon will relaunch it, and the unique ID in the web interface will change. Once you've verified all this, go ahead and click the Destroy App button to remove marathon-nc.

This works OK, but you may have noticed that we've not achieved what we set out to do with Marathon—orchestrate Docker containers. Although our application is within a container, it's been launched in the Mesos slave container rather than in a container of its own. Reading the Marathon documentation reveals that creating tasks inside Docker containers requires a little more configuration (as it did when writing our own framework).

Happily, the Mesos slave we started previously has both the required settings, so we just need to alter some Marathon options—in particular, app options. By taking the Marathon API response from before (saved in app.json), we can focus on adding the Marathon settings that enable Docker usage. To perform the manipulation here, we'll use the handy jq tool, though it's equally easy to do it via a text editor.

```
$ JQ=https://github.com/stedolan/jq/releases/download/jq-1.3/jq-linux-x86_64
$ curl -Os $JQ && mv jq-linux-x86_64 jq && chmod +x jq
$ cat >container.json <<EOF
{
  "container": {
    "type": "DOCKER",
    "docker": {
      "image": "ubuntu:14.04.2",
      "network": "BRIDGE",
      "portMappings": [{"hostPort": 8000, "containerPort": 8000}]
    }
  }
}
$ # merge the app and container details
$ cat app.json container.json | ./jq -s add > newapp.json
```

We can now send the new app definition to the API and see Marathon launch it:

```
$ curl -X POST -H 'Content-Type: application/json; charset=utf-8' \
--data-binary @newapp.json http://localhost:8080/v2/apps
{"id":"/marathon-nc", >
"cmd":"echo \"hello $MESOS_TASK_ID\" | nc -l $PORT0",[...]
$ sleep 10
$ docker ps --since=marathon
CONTAINER ID  IMAGE          COMMAND          CREATED           >
STATUS            PORTS           NAMES
284ced88246c  ubuntu:14.04   "\"/bin/sh -c 'echo  About a minute ago  >
Up About a minute  0.0.0.0:8000->8000/tcp  mesos- >
1da85151-59c0-4469-9c50-2bfc34f1a987
$ curl localhost:8000
hello mesos-nc.675b2dc9-1f88-11e5-bc4d-0242ac11000e
$ docker ps --since=marathon
CONTAINER ID  IMAGE          COMMAND          CREATED           >
```

```
STATUS                         PORTS                    NAMES
851279a9292f  ubuntu:14.04  "\"/bin/sh -c 'echo  44 seconds ago  >
Up 43 seconds                  0.0.0.0:8000->8000/tcp  mesos- >
37d84e5e-3908-405b-aa04-9524b59ba4f6
284ced88246c  ubuntu:14.04  "\"/bin/sh -c 'echo  24 minutes ago  >
Exited (0) 45 seconds ago                           mesos-1da85151-59c0-
➥ 4469-9c50-2bfc34f1a987
```

As with our custom framework in the last technique, Mesos has launched a Docker container for us with the application running. Running `curl` terminates the application and container, and a new one is automatically launched.

DISCUSSION

There are some significant differences between the custom framework from the last technique and Marathon. For example, in the custom framework we had extremely fine-grained control over accepting resource offers, to the point where we could pick and choose individual ports to listen on. In order to do a similar thing in Marathon, you'd need to impose the setting on each individual slave.

By contrast, Marathon comes with a lot of built-in features that would be error-prone to build yourself, including health checking, an event notification system, and a REST API. These aren't trivial things to implement, and using Marathon lets you operate with the assurance that you aren't the first one trying it. If nothing else, it's a lot easier to get support for Marathon than for a bespoke framework, and we've found that the documentation for Marathon is more approachable than that for Mesos.

We've covered the basics of setting up and using Marathon, but there are many more things to see and do. One of the more interesting suggestions we've seen is to use Marathon to start up other Mesos frameworks, potentially including your own bespoke one! We encourage you to explore—Mesos is a high-quality tool for orchestration, and Marathon provides a usable layer on top of it.

Summary

- You can start services on a cluster of machines with Docker swarm mode.
- Writing a custom framework for Mesos can give you fine-grained control over your container scheduling.
- The Marathon framework on top of Mesos provides a simple way to harness some of the power of Mesos.
- Kubernetes is a production-quality orchestration tool and has an API you can leverage.
- OpenShift can be used to set up a local version of some AWS services.

Docker platforms

This chapter covers

- The factors that inform the choice of Docker platform
- The areas of consideration needed when adopting Docker
- The state of the Docker vendor landscape as of 2018

The title of this chapter might seem confusing. Did the previous chapter not cover Docker platforms like Kubernetes and Mesos already?

Well, yes and no. Although Kubernetes and Mesos are arguably platforms on which you can run Docker, in this book we're taking a *platform* to mean a product (or integrated set of technologies) that allows you to run and manage the operation of Docker containers in a structured way. You could think of this chapter as being more infrastructural than purely technical.

As of the time of writing, there are several Docker platforms:

- AWS Fargate
- AWS ECS (Elastic Container Service
- AWS EKS (Elastic Kubernetes Service)
- Azure AKS (Azure Kubernetes Service)
- OpenShift
- Docker Datacenter
- "Native" Kubernetes

NOTE "Native" Kubernetes means running and managing your own cluster on whichever underlying infrastructure you prefer. You might want to run it on dedicated hardware in your own data centre or on VMs on a cloud provider.

The hard part of platform adoption is deciding which platform to choose, and knowing what to consider when looking at Docker adoption across an organization. This chapter will provide a map of the decisions that need to be made in order to make a sensible choice of platform. It'll help you understand why you might choose Open-Shift over Kubernetes, or AWS ECS over Kubernetes, and so on.

This chapter is structured in three parts. The first part discusses the factors that inform decisions about which technologies or solutions are appropriate to an organization looking to adopt Docker. The second part discusses the areas that need to be considered when looking to adopt Docker. The third discusses the state of the vendor landscape as of 2018.

We've deployed Docker in multiple organizations, and we've spoken about the challenges of adoption at numerous conferences as well as within these organizations. What these experiences have taught us is that although the combination of challenges these organizations face are unique, there are patterns of decisions and classes of challenges that need to be understood before you go on the container journey.

13.1 *Organizational choice factors*

This section will outline some of the major factors within your organization that may drive your platform choice for Docker. Figure 13.1 shows some of these factors and their interrelations.

Before discussing these factors in detail, we'll briefly define each and what is meant by it. You may have considered all these factors before and understand what they are, but different terminology within and between organizations can make the terminology unclear, and some terms are more commonly used in some organizations than others.

- *Buy vs. build*—This refers to a difference in approach that organizations have toward new software deployment. Some organizations prefer to buy solutions, and others prefer to build and maintain them themselves. This in turn can influence which platform (or platforms) are chosen.
- *Technical drivers*—Some businesses differentiate themselves on the specific characteristics of their technology, such as high levels of performance or cost efficiency of operation. What underpins these characteristics can be very niche, and specific technical components may not be catered for by commodity services or tooling. This can drive more bespoke solutions that drive a "build" rather than "buy" approach.
- *Monolithic vs. piecemeal*—Again, this is a general cultural approach that organizations can take toward software solutions. Some prefer to centralize solutions in a single monolithic entity (a centralized server or service), and others prefer to tackle problems piece by piece. The latter approach can be seen as more flexible and adaptable, whereas the former can be more efficient at scale.

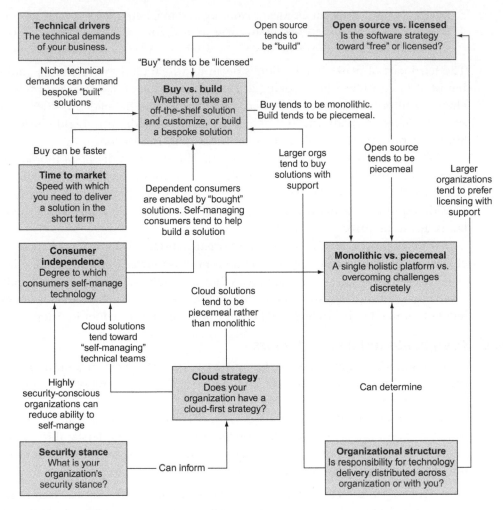

Figure 13.1   Factors driving platform choice

- *Time to market*—Frequently organizations feel a pressure (for commercial or cultural reasons) to deliver a solution to their users quickly. This pressure can favor certain platforms over others at the expense of cost or flexibility in the future.

- *Open source vs. licensed*—Organizations usually have a preference for open source over licensed products these days, but there can still be good reasons to license a product from a vendor. Another related subject that pushes organizations toward open source solutions is fear of lock-in to a particular vendor or platform, leading to increased license costs as dependency on that product persists over time.

- *Consumer independence*—The platform you deploy will have consumers. These could be individuals, teams, or entire business units. Whatever the size of these consumers, they will have a culture and mode of operation. Key questions to ask here are how technically self-managing are they in their operational context, and how bespoke are their development needs? Answers to these questions may determine the character of platform you decide to deploy.

- *Cloud strategy*—Few organizations have no position defined toward cloud computing these days. Whether you're looking to move workloads to the cloud immediately or not, the degree to which a solution is cloud native can be a factor in your decision-making process. Even if you've decided to move to the cloud, you'll still need to consider whether the strategy is limited to one cloud or is designed to be portable across clouds, and even back to the data center.

- *Security stance*—Increasingly, organizations are taking security more seriously as part of their IT strategy. Whether it's state-sponsored actors, amateur (or professional) hackers, industrial espionage, or plain theft, security is something that everyone has a position on. The level of attention devoted to this area can vary, so this can play a part in platform choice.

- *Organizational structure*—Many of the preceding definitions will potentially mean more to you if you work for an enterprise organization than if you work for the opposite kind of organization.

In this book we've defined *enterprise* broadly as an organization in which there's a low degree of independence between the separate functions within it. For example, if you run a centralized IT function, can you deploy solutions without reference to any other part of the business (such as security, development teams, dev tooling teams, finance, operations/DevOps teams) without consequence? If so, we regard that as the opposite of an enterprise organization. Enterprise organizations tend to be larger (so functions are more discrete), and more regulated (internally and externally), which tends to constrain their freedom to enact change with less consequence.

By contrast, a non-enterprise organization (in this book) is one in which functions are free to deploy solutions as they see fit, through a process of self-determination. By this definition, startups are often seen as non-enterprise organizations because they can make decisions quickly and without reference to—or with speedier determination of—others' needs.

Although non-enterprise organizations tend to favor some strategies (such as build over buy), it can still pay to think about the consequences of such decisions for the business over the long term.

Let's look more specifically at how the various factors interact to militate for or against different platforms. Hopefully some of these will resonate with your experience or situation.

After this discussion, we'll go on to look at the specific challenges that running a Docker platform can bring. With these factors as context, you can come to an informed decision about what technology best fits your organization's needs.

13.1.1 *Time to market*

It may be helpful first to consider the simplest of the factors: time to market. Everyone working within an organization feels some pressure to deliver solutions quickly, but the extent to which this is negotiable or desirable can vary.

If a direct competitor has adopted a containerization strategy and is using this successfully to drive down costs, then senior management can get interested in how long your solution is taking to deliver.

Alternatively, if you work for a more conservative organization, a speedily delivered solution might be seen to result in negative effects, such as lock-in to a hastily delivered or flavor-of-the-month platform that can't move with changing needs.

Wiser heads may counsel you to resist the urge to adopt the first credible solution in the face of these dangers.

In general, pressure to deliver quickly drives a move toward "buy" over "build" and "monolithic" over "piecemeal" solutions to complex enterprise challenges. (These choices will be discussed further in the next section.) These challenges can be met by assigning responsibility for solving them to those vendors' solutions. But this isn't always possible, especially if the product isn't mature.

Pressure to deliver can also result in the hasty delivery of bespoke solutions that fulfill the short term needs of the business. This is especially prevalent in organizations with a highly technical focus, and it can be very effective, providing an edge over the competition through control over the core technologies and knowledge of their workings. If technology isn't a critical differentiator for your business, though, this can result in white-elephant technology that becomes difficult to move away from later, should the industry outpace your leading edge.

Similarly, adopting click-and-consume cloud technologies can reduce your time to market significantly. The downside can be a consequent lock-in to that provider's solution, driving up costs as you scale, and the cost of any future move away. It can also reduce flexibility in technical features or solutions, making you dependent on the growth and development of the cloud vendor's product.

13.1.2 *Buy vs. build*

Buying a solution can be an effective strategy in a number of ways. As you've seen, it can result in reducing time to market. If your organization is constrained in terms of development staff, you can also leverage the product's (presumably) expanding feature set to offer more to your customers with relatively little investment.

Buying can also take off the operational cost, if you choose to operate it off-premises, as a service provided by the vendor. The degree to which you're able to take this path may be limited by your security stance: software may be considered safe to run only if it's on hardware owned and operated by the organization using it.

Building a platform yourself, either from scratch or from existing open source software, may appeal to you, since you're reading this book. You would undoubtedly learn a lot from the process, but there are numerous dangers in such an approach from a business point of view.

First, you'll likely need a highly skilled staff to continue to build and maintain this product. It can be much harder than you think (especially if you've been surrounded by computer scientists at work and at university) to source people who can program and operate complex IT systems, especially in recent years when such skills have been in high demand.

Second, as time goes on, the container platform world will mature, with established players offering similar feature sets and commoditized skills around them. Against these offerings, a bespoke solution built for a specific organization's needs some years ago can seem needlessly expensive where once it was a market differentiator.

One strategy that can be adopted is "build, then buy," where an organization builds a platform to meet its immediate needs, but looks to buy when the market has settled on a product that looks to be a standard. Of course, there's a danger that the built platform becomes a "pet" that's difficult to give up. As of the time of writing, Kubernetes appears to have gained almost complete dominance as the basis of most popular Docker platforms. Therefore, you might drop your bespoke solution in favor of a Kubernetes one if you take the view that that's a good bet for the future.

One platform that made two bets early was OpenShift, which embraced Docker soon after it burst onto the tech scene. It rewrote its entire codebase around Docker and Kubernetes. It's currently a very popular option with enterprises as a result. By contrast, Amazon used Mesos as the basis of its ECS solution, which increasingly appeared niche as Kubernetes became more prevalent.

13.1.3 *Monolithic vs. piecemeal*

The question of whether to run a single "monolithic" platform for all your Docker needs or to build functionality up from separate "piecemeal" solutions is closely related to the "buy vs. build" question. When considering buying a monolithic solution from a vendor, time to market can be a compelling reason to throw your lot in with them. Again, there are trade-offs with this approach.

The biggest danger is so-called *lock-in*. Some vendors charge for each machine the solution is deployed on. If your Docker estate grows significantly over time, the licensing costs can become prohibitive, and the platform can become a financial millstone around your neck. Some vendors even refuse to support Docker containers delivered by other vendors, which makes realistic adoption of them almost impossible.

Against this is the piecemeal approach. By piecemeal we mean that you can (for example) have one solution for building containers, another for storing containers (such as a Docker registry), another for scanning containers, and yet another for running containers (perhaps even multiple solutions for this or any of the preceding categories). We'll go into more depth about what "pieces" might need solving for in the next section of this chapter.

Again, if you're a small (and perhaps cash-rich) operation that needs to move quickly, the monolithic approach can deliver for you. The piecemeal approach allows you to adopt different solutions for various pieces as the need arises, giving you more flexibility and focus in your efforts.

13.1.4   *Open source vs. licensed*

Open source has come a long way in the last decade, so that it's now a standard requirement for vendored or supported solutions. This contains within it a danger that's not often obvious. Although many solutions are open source, lock-in isn't necessarily avoided. In theory, the intellectual property of the software is available to use if you fall out with a supporting vendor, but often the skills required to manage and support the codebase are not.

As one conference speaker put it recently, "open source plus vendor support is the new lock-in." One could argue that this is a valid justification for the value the vendor brings to your organization—if it takes a lot of rare skill to manage a required platform, you'll need to pay for it one way or another.

An interesting addition to this mix is cloud computing solutions, which could be regarded as both open sourced and licensed. They're often based on open source software and open standards (such as Amazon's EKS), but they can tie you in to their particular implementation of those standards and technologies, and gain your lock-in that way.

Another interesting mix is seen with platforms like OpenShift from Red Hat. OpenShift is a vendor-supplied platform with licenses required to run it. But its code is available on GitHub, and contributions from the community can be accepted into the main line. What Red Hat supplies as a value-add is support, feature development, and maintenance of the historical codebase. In theory, therefore, you can move off their implementation if you feel you aren't getting value from their offering.

13.1.5   *Security stance*

Security concerns can have a strong influence on platform choice. Enterprise vendors such as Red Hat have a strong history of managing security, and OpenShift adds in SELinux protection for container security on top of protections already supplied by native Kubernetes.

The degree to which security matters to you can vary enormously. We have been involved in companies where developers have full and trusted access to production databases, as well as companies where paranoia about security is at its highest. These different levels of concern drive very different behaviors in development and production, and therefore in platform choices.

To take one simple example: do you trust your data and code to Amazon Web Services' (AWS's) security standards and products? We aren't singling out AWS here—as far as we know and have experienced, their security standards are generally considered second to none in the cloud space. Moreover, do you trust your development teams to manage the responsibilities that necessarily lie with the application teams? There have been enough stories of private data being exposed on AWS S3 buckets for this to be a concern for many companies.

> **NOTE** the responsibility for exposing data on S3 is firmly with the consumer of AWS, and not with AWS itself. AWS gives you comprehensive tools to manage security, but they can't manage your security requirements and operations for you.

13.1.6 Consumer independence

One factor that's not often considered is the degree to which teams wish to self-manage. In smaller organizations this tends to vary less than in larger organizations. In larger organizations you can get development teams ranging from highly skilled ones that demand cutting-edge technological platforms to less skilled ones that simply want a curated way to deploy simple and stable web applications.

These differing demands can lead to different platform choices. For example, we've seen environments where one business unit is happy with a centralized, curated, and monolithic platform, whereas another business unit demands a high degree of control and has specific technical requirements. Such users may push you toward a more bespoke platform than the vendored ones. If those users are willing to help build and maintain the platform, a productive partnership can ensue.

If you're large enough, and your development community is heterogeneous enough, you may even want to consider pursuing multiple options for your Docker platforms.

13.1.7 Cloud strategy

Most companies that deal in IT have some kind of stance toward cloud platforms. Some have embraced it wholeheartedly, and others are still starting their journey toward it, are in the process of moving, or are even moving back to the old fashioned data centre.

Whether your organization adopts a cloud Docker platform can be determined by this stance. Factors to consider center around whether there's a fear of so-called "cloud vendor lock-in," where moving your applications and data from the cloud vendor's data centers becomes too costly to countenance. This can be guarded against by using open standards and products, or even by running existing products atop the generic compute resources supplied by those cloud vendors (rather than using their curated and sometimes cloud vendor–specific products).

13.1.8 Organizational structure

Organizational structure is a fundamental characteristic of any company, and it informs all the other factors here. For example, if development teams are separated from operations teams, this tends to argue for adopting a standardized platform that both teams can manage and work against.

Similarly, if responsibility for different parts of the operation are atomized in different groups, this tends to support a piecemeal approach to platform delivery. One example of this that we've seen is the management of Docker registries in larger organizations. If there's already a centrally managed artifact store, it can make sense to simply upgrade the existing one and use it as a Docker registry (assuming it supports that use case). That way the management and operation of the store is cheaper than building a separate solution for what is essentially the same challenge.

13.1.9 *Multiple platforms?*

One pattern that may be appropriate to mention at this point is that for large organizations with divergent needs, another approach is possible. You may have some consumers that prefer managed platforms they can use, and other consumers in the same organization may demand more bespoke solutions.

In such cases, it can make sense to provide a highly opinionated and easier-to-manage platform for the first set of users, and a more flexible and perhaps more self-managed solution for others. In one case we're aware of, three options are available: a self-managed Nomad cluster, an AWS-managed solution, and an OpenShift option.

The obvious difficulty with this approach is the increased cost of management in running multiple classes of platform and the challenges of communicating these options effectively across the organization.

13.1.10 *Organizational factors conclusion*

Hopefully that discussion resonated with you, and gave some idea of the complexities of choosing an appropriate platform for Docker (or indeed any technology) within organizations with differing needs. Although it may have seemed somewhat abstract, the next section will be much less so, as we look at the specific challenges you may need to consider when choosing solutions for your business. This discussion has given us the appropriate lenses with which to evaluate those problems and their possible solutions.

13.2   *Areas to consider when adopting Docker*

Finally, we get to talking about the specific functional challenges that might need to be addressed when implementing a Docker platform.

It's divided into three sections:

- *Security and control*—Looks at items that will depend on your organization's security and control stance
- *Building and shipping images*—Looks at some of the things you'll need to consider regarding development and delivery of your images and workloads
- *Running containers*—Considers what needs to be thought about as you operate your platform

Along the way we'll consider specific current technologies. Mentioning a product in no way implies our endorsement, nor will the products we mention be exhaustive. Software products can improve and decline, and can be replaced or merged. They're mentioned here only to illustrate the practical consequences of your platform choices.

If many of the items we discuss seem obscure, or irrelevant to your organization, it's likely you don't operate under many constraints and therefore have greater freedom to do as you please. If so, you can consider this chapter as offering insight into some of the challenges seen in large-scale and regulated enterprises.

13.2.1 Security and control

We'll deal with security first, because in many ways your security and control stance will fundamentally affect the way you approach all the other topics. Also, if your organization is less concerned with security than other organizations, you may be less concerned with solving the problems outlined in this section.

> **NOTE** By "control" we mean the systems of governance that are overlaid on the development team's and run team's operations. This includes centrally managed software development life cycles, license management, security audits, general audits, and so on. Some organizations have a very light touch, and others are more heavyweight.

IMAGE SCANNING

Wherever you store your images, you have a golden opportunity at the point of storage to check that these images are as you wish them to be. What you might want to check depends on your use case, but here are some examples of specific questions you might want answered in more or less real time:

- Which images have a shellshock version of bash?
- Is there an out-of-date SSL library on any image?
- Which images are based on a now-suspect base image?
- Which images have nonstandard (or plain wrong) development libraries or tools on them?

> **NOTE** Shellshock was a particularly serious set of security flaws in bash discovered in 2014. Security companies recorded millions of attacks and probes related to the bug in the days following the disclosure of the first of a series of related bugs.

Figure 13.2 shows the basic workflow for an image scan in the software development lifecycle. The image is built and pushed to the registry, and this triggers an image scan. The scanner can either inspect the image in place on the registry or download it and work on it. Depending on the level of paranoia you have about images, you can synchronously check the image and prevent it from being used until it's got the OK, or you can check the image asynchronously and provide a report to the submitting

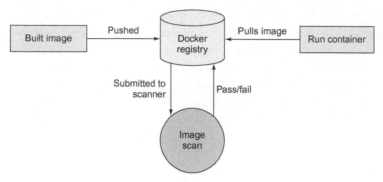

Figure 13.2   Image scanning workflow

user. Usually the paranoid approach is taken for images used in production, and the asynchronous advisory approach is used in development.

In the world of image scanning, there are plenty of options, but they aren't all equal. The most important thing to understand is that scanners roughly divide into two categories: those that focus on packages installed, and those that are primarily designed for deep scanning the software in the image. Examples of the first are Clair and OpenSCAP, and examples of the second are Black Duck Software, Twistlock, Aqua Security, Docker Inc., and many others. There's some overlap between the two categories, but the principal dividing line is cost: it's more expensive to maintain the necessary databases of information to keep up with weaknesses in various types of libraries or binaries, so the deep scanners tend to be far more costly.

This division might be relevant for your decision making. If your images are semi-trusted, you might be able to assume that users aren't being malicious and use a simpler package scanner. This will give you metrics and information about standard packages and their appropriate level of risk without too much cost.

Although scanners can reduce the risk of malicious or unwanted software in your images, they aren't magic bullets. Our experience in evaluating them suggests that even the best ones aren't perfect, and that they tend to be better at identifying issues with some types of binaries or libraries than others. For example, some might more successfully identify npm package issues than (say) ones written in C++, or vice versa. See technique 94 in chapter 14 for an image we've used to exercise and test these scanners.

Another thing to be aware of is that although scanners can work on immutable images and examine the static content of those images, there's still an outstanding risk that containers can build and run malicious software at runtime. Static image analysis can't solve that problem, so you might need to consider runtime control also.

As with all the topics in this section, you must think about what you want to achieve when choosing a scanner. You might want to

- Prevent malicious actors from inserting objects into your builds
- Enforce company-wide standards on software usage
- Quickly patch known and standard CVEs

> **NOTE** A CVE is an identifier for a software vulnerability, to allow for common and unambiguous identification of specific faults.

Finally, you might also want to consider the cost of integrating this tool into your DevOps pipeline. If you find a scanner you're happy with, and it's well-integrated with your platform (or other related DevOps tooling), that might be another factor in its favor.

IMAGE INTEGRITY

Image integrity and image scanning are often confused, but they aren't the same thing. Whereas *image scanning* determines what's *in* an image, *image integrity* ensures that what's *retrieved* from the Docker registry is the same as what was securely placed there. (*Image verification* is another common way to describe this requirement.)

Imagine the following scenario: Alice places an image in a repository (image A), and after it has gone through whatever mandated process exists to check that image, Bob wishes to run that image on a server. Bob requests image A from the server, but unknown to him, an attacker (Carol) has compromised the network, and placed a proxy between Bob and the registry. When Bob downloads the image, he is actually handed a malicious image (image C) that will run code that siphons off confidential data to a third-party IP outside the network. (See figure 13.3.)

The question arises: when a Docker image is downloaded, how can you be sure it's the one you asked for? Being sure of this is what image integrity addresses.

Docker Inc. led the way here with their Content Trust product, also known as Notary. This product signs image manifests with a privately held key that ensures that when the content is decrypted with a public key, the content is the same as what was

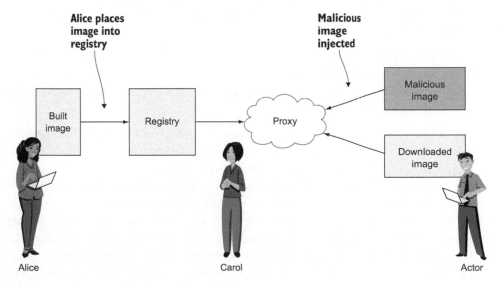

Figure 13.3 Image integrity compromise

uploaded to the registry. Content Trust offers further functionality around delegation of key responsibility that we won't go into here.

Outside of Docker's offering, there's not much to report as of 2018, which is something of a tribute to their engineering lead on this. Leading products like Kubernetes and OpenShift offer very little in this area out of the box, so if you don't buy Docker's products, you may have to integrate these yourself. For many organizations, such an endeavor isn't worth the effort, so they'll rely on existing (likely perimeter) defenses.

If you do manage to implement an image integrity solution, you still must consider how the keys will be managed within your organization. Organizations that care enough to get this far will probably have policies and solutions in place for this.

THIRD-PARTY IMAGES

Keeping on the subject of images, another common challenge when providing a platform is how you're going to approach the subject of external images. Again, the basic difficulty here is one of trust: if you have a vendor that wants to bring a Docker image to your platform, how can you be sure that it's safe to run? This is an especially significant question in a multi-tenant environment, where different teams (who don't necessarily trust each other) must run containers on the same hosts.

One approach is simply to ban all third-party images, and only allow images to be built from known and curated base images using code and artifacts stored within the corporate network. Some vendor images can still be made to work within this regime. If the vendor image is essentially a JAR (Java archive) file running under a standard JVM, the image can be recreated and built within the network from that artifact and run under an approved JVM image.

Inevitably, though, not all images or vendors will be amenable to this approach. If the pressure to allow third-party images is strong enough (and in our experience it is), you have several options:

- Trust your scanner
- Examine the image by eye
- Make the team bringing the image into the organization responsible for its management

It's unlikely you'll entirely trust your scanner to give you sufficient certainty about the safety of a third-party image without the image being fully embedded over time, so responsibility will possibly need to rest somewhere else.

The second option, manually examining images, isn't scalable and is prone to error. The last option is the simplest and easiest to implement.

We've seen environments where all three approaches are taken, with the platform-management team sanity-checking the image, but with final responsibility resting with the application team bringing it. Often there's an existing process for bringing virtual machine images into the organization, so a simple approach is to copy this procedure for Docker images. One key difference worth pointing out here is that although VMs are multi-tenant in that they share a hypervisor with their fellow tenants, Docker images share a fully featured operating system, which gives attacks a much larger surface area (see chapter 14 on security for more about this).

A further option is to sandbox the running of images on their own hardware environment, such as through labeling Kubernetes nodes on a cluster, or using separate instances of cloud products like ECS, or running an entirely separate platform on separate hardware or even networks.

SECRETS

Somehow (and especially when you get to production), privileged information will need to be managed in a secure way. Privileged information includes files or data passed in to builds, such as

- SSL keys
- Username/password combinations
- Customer-identifying data

This passing of secret data into the software lifecycle can be done at several points. One approach is to embed the secrets into your images at build time. This approach is highly frowned upon, as it spreads the privileged data wherever the image goes.

A more approved method is to have the platform place the secrets into your containers at runtime. There are various ways to do this, but several questions that need to be answered:

- Is the secret encrypted when stored?
- Is the secret encrypted in transit?
- Who has access to the secret (in the store or at runtime in the container)?
- How is the secret exposed within the container?
- Can you track or audit who saw or used the secret?

Kubernetes has a so-called "secrets" capability. What surprises many about this is that it's stored in plain text in the persistent store (an etcd database). Technically, it's base64-encoded, but from a security point of view, this is plain text (not encrypted, and easily reversed). If someone were to walk off with a disk containing this information, they could get access to these secrets without difficulty.

As it stands, there are proof-of-concept implementations of applications like HashiCorp's vault to integrate with Kubernetes. Docker Swarm has more secure secrets support out of the box, but Docker Inc. appears to have thrown its lot in with Kubernetes in late 2017.

AUDIT

When running in production (or any other sensitive environment) it can become key to demonstrate that you have control over who ran what command and when. This is something that can be non-obvious to developers, who aren't so concerned with recovering this information.

The reasons for this "root" problem are covered in chapter 14, but they can be briefly covered here by saying that giving users access to the Docker socket effectively gives them root control over the whole host. This is forbidden in many organizations, so access to Docker usually needs to be traceable at the very least.

These are some of the questions you might be required to answer:

- Who (or what) is able to run the docker command?
- What control do you have over who runs it?
- What control do you have over what is run?

Solutions exist for this problem, but they're relatively new and generally part of other larger solutions. OpenShift, for example, has led the way by adding robust RBAC (role-based access control) to Kubernetes. Kubernetes later added this to its core. Cloud providers usually have more cloud-native ways to achieve this kind of control through (in the case of AWS) use of IAM roles or similar features embedded in ECS or EKS.

Container security tools provided by vendors such as Twistlock and Aqua Security offer a means of managing which particular Docker subcommands and flags can be run by whom, usually by adding an intermediary socket or other kind of proxy between you and the Docker socket that can broker access to Docker commands.

In terms of recording who did what, native functionality has been slow in coming in products like OpenShift, but it's there now. If you look at other products, don't assume functionality like this has been fully implemented!

RUNTIME CONTROL

Runtime control can be considered as auditing at a higher level. Regulated enterprises are likely to want to be able to determine what's running across their entire estate and to report on this. The output of such reports can be compared with an existing configuration management database (CMDB) to see whether there are any anomalies or running workloads that can't be accounted for.

At this level, these are the questions you may be asked to answer:

- How can you tell what's running?
- Can you match that content up to your registry/registries and/or your CMDB?
- Have any containers changed critical files since startup?

Again, this comes with some other products that might form part of your Docker strategy, so watch out for them. Or it may be a side-effect of your overall application deployment strategy and network architecture. For example, if you build and run containers with an Amazon VPC, establishing and reporting what's in them is a relatively trivial problem to solve.

Another frequently seen selling point in this space is anomaly detection. Security solutions offer fancy machine-learning solutions that claim to learn what a container is supposed to do, and they alert you if it appears to do something out of the ordinary, like connect to a foreign application port unrelated to the application.

This sounds great, but you need to think about how this will work operationally. You can get a lot of false positives, and these may require a lot of curation—are you resourced to handle that? Generally speaking, the larger and more security-conscious an organization, the more likely they are to be concerned with this.

FORENSICS

Forensics is similar to auditing, but it's much more focused. When a security incident occurs, various parties will want to know what happened. In the old world of physicals and VMs, there were a lot of safeguards in place to assist post-incident investigation. Agents and watcher processes of all descriptions might have been running on the OS, or taps could be placed at a network or even hardware level.

These are some of the questions that a forensic team might want answered following a security incident:

- Can you tell who ran a container?
- Can you tell who built a container?
- Can you determine what a container did once it's gone?
- Can you determine what a container might have done once it's gone?

In this context you might want to mandate the use of specific logging solutions, to ensure that information about system activity persists across container instantiations.

Sysdig and their Falco tool (which is open source) is another interesting and promising product in this area. If you're familiar with tcpdump, this tool looks very similar, allowing you to query syscalls in flight. Here's an example of such a rule:

```
container.id != host and proc.name = bash
```

It matches if a bash shell is run in a container.

Sysdig's commercial offering goes beyond monitoring to allow you to take actions based on the tracked behaviors against your defined rulesets.

13.2.2 *Building and shipping images*

With security covered, we come to building and shipping. This section looks at what you might need to think about when constructing and distributing your images.

BUILDING IMAGES

When it comes to building images, there are a few areas you might want to consider.

First, although Dockerfiles are the standard, other methods of building images exist (see chapter 7), so it might be desirable to mandate a standard if a variety of ways might cause confusion or aren't compatible with each other. You might also have a strategic configuration management tool that you'll want to integrate with your standard OS deployment.

Our real-world experience suggests that the Dockerfile approach is deeply ingrained and popular with developers. The overhead of learning a more sophisticated CM tool to conform to company standards for VMs is often not something developers have time or inclination for. Methods like S2I or Chef/Puppet/Ansible are more generally used for convenience or code reuse. Supporting Dockerfiles will ensure that you'll get fewer questions and pushback from the development community.

Second, in sensitive environments, you may not want the building of images to be open to all users, as images may be trusted by other teams internally or externally.

Building can be limited by appropriate tagging or promotion of images (see below), or through role-based access control.

Third, it's worth thinking about the developer experience. For security reasons, it's not always possible to give users open access to download Docker images from public repositories, nor even the ability to run Docker tools in their local environment (see chapter 14). If this is the case, there are several options you might want to pursue:

- Getting approval for the standard tooling. This can be costly and sometimes too costly to achieve due to the security challenges and demands of the business.
- Creating a throwaway sandbox in which Docker images can be built. If the VM is transient, locked down, and heavily audited, many security concerns are significantly alleviated.
- Offering remote access to the above-mentioned sandbox via any Docker client (but note that this does not necessarily significantly reduce many attack surfaces).

Fourth, it's also worth thinking about the consistency of the developer experience when deploying the application. For example, if developers are using docker-compose on their laptop or test environments, they might balk at switching to Kubernetes deployments in production. (As time goes on, this last point is becoming increasingly moot, as Kubernetes becomes a standard.)

REGISTRY

It should be obvious by now that you'll need a registry. There's an open source example, Docker Distribution, but it is no longer the dominant choice, mainly because a Docker registry is an implementation of a well-known API. There are now numerous offerings out there to choose from if you want to pay for an enterprise registry, or if you want to run an open source one yourself.

Docker Distribution comes as part of Docker's Data Centre product, which has some compelling features (such as Content Trust).

Whichever product you choose, there are some potentially less obvious points to consider:

- Does this registry play nicely with your authentication system?
- Does it have role-based access control (RBAC)?

Authentication and authorization is a big deal for enterprises. A quick and cheap, free-for-all registry solution will do the job in development, but if you have security or RBAC standards to maintain, these requirements will come to the top of your list.

Some tools have less-fine-grained RBAC features, and this can be quite a hole to fill if you suddenly find yourself audited and found wanting.

- *Does it have a means of promoting images?*—All images are not created equal. Some are quick-and-dirty dev experiments where correctness isn't a requirement, whereas others are intended for bulletproof production usage. Your organization's workflows may require that you distinguish between the two, and a registry can help you with this by managing a process via separate instances, or through gates enforced by labels.

- *Does it cohere well with your other artifact stores?*—You likely already have an artifact store for TAR files, internal packages, and the like. In an ideal world, your registry would simply be a feature within that. If that's not an option, integration or management overhead will be a cost you should be aware of.

BASE IMAGES

If you're thinking about standards, the base image (or images) that teams use might need some consideration.

First, what root image do you want to use, and what should go into it? Usually organizations have a standard Linux distribution they prefer to use. If so, that one is likely to be mandated as a base.

Second, how will you build and maintain these images? In the event of a vulnerability being found, who (or what) is responsible for identifying whether you're affected or which images are affected? Who is responsible for patching the affected estate?

Third, what should go into this base image? Is there a common set of tooling that all users will want, or do you want to leave that to individual teams to decide? Do you want to separate these requirements out into separate subimages?

Fourth, how will these images and subimages be rebuilt? Usually some sort of pipeline needs to be created. Typically this will use some kind of CI tool, such as Jenkins, to automatically build the base image (and subsequently from that any subimages) when some trigger is effected.

If you're responsible for a base image, you may be challenged frequently about the size of this image. It's often argued that thin images are better. In some respects (such as security) this might be argued, but this "problem" is more often imagined than real, particularly with respect to performance. The paradoxical nature of this situation is discussed in technique 60.

SOFTWARE DEVELOPMENT LIFECYCLE

A software development lifecycle (SDLC) is the defined process for how software is procured, created, tested, deployed, and retired. In its ideal state, it exists to help reduce inefficiencies by ensuring software is consistently evaluated, bought, and used within a group with a common interest in pooling resources.

If you already have SDLC processes, how does Docker fit in? One can get into philosophical discussions about whether a Docker container is a package (like an rpm) or an entire Linux distribution (because its contents are arguably under the developer's control). Either way, the key point of contention is usually over ownership. Who is responsible for what in the image? This is where Docker's layered filesystem (see chapter 1) comes into its own. Because who created what within the final image is completely auditable (assuming the content is trusted), then tracking back to who is responsible for what part of the software stack is relatively straightforward.

Once responsibility is identified, you can consider how patches will be handled:

- *How do you identify which images need updating?*—A scanner can help here, or any tool that can identify files in artifacts that may be of interest.
- *How do you update them?*—Some platforms allow you to trigger rebuilds and deployments of containers (such as OpenShift, or possibly your hand-rolled pipeline).
- *How do you tell teams to update?*—Is an email sufficient? Or do you need an identifiable person as an owner. Again, your corporate policy will likely be your guide here. Existing policies should exist for more traditional software that's deployed.

The key point in this new world is that the number of teams responsible for containers may be higher than in the past, and the number of containers to assess or update may be significantly higher also. All this can place a high burden on your infrastructure teams if you don't have the processes in place to handle this uptick in software deliveries. If push comes to shove, you may need to force users to update by adding layers to their images if they don't get in line. This is especially important if you run a shared platform. You could even consider using your orchestration tools to put "naughty" containers on specific isolated hosts to reduce risk. Usually these things are considered too late, and an answer must be improvised.

13.2.3 *Running containers*

Now we'll look at the running of containers. In many respects, running containers is little different from running individual processes, but the introduction of Docker can bring its own challenges, and the changes of behavior that Docker enables can also force you to think about other aspects of your infrastructure.

OPERATING SYSTEM

The operating system you run can become significant when running your Docker platform. Enterprise operating systems can lag behind the latest and greatest kernel versions, and as you'll see in chapter 16, the kernel version being run can be very significant for your application.

Historically, Docker has been a very fast-moving codebase, and not all curated OSes have been able to keep up (1.10 was a particularly painful transition for us, with significant changes to the storage format of images). It's worth checking which versions of Docker (and related technologies, such as Kubernetes) are available to you in your package managers before you promise vendors their applications will run on your Kubernetes cluster.

SHARED STORAGE

As soon as your users start deploying applications, one of the first things they'll be concerned about is where their data goes. Docker has in its core the use of volumes (see chapter 5) that are independent of the running containers.

These volumes can be backed by numerous kinds of storage mounted locally or remotely, but the key point is that the storage can be shared by multiple containers, which makes it ideal for running databases that persist across container cycles.

- *Is shared storage easy to provision?*—Shared storage can be expensive to maintain and provision, both in terms of the infrastructure required and the hourly cost. In many organizations, provisioning storage is not simply a matter of calling an API and waiting a few seconds, as it can be with cloud providers like AWS.
- *Is shared storage support ready for increased demand?*—Because it's so easy to deploy Docker containers and fresh environments for development or test, demand on shared storage can increase dramatically. It's worth considering whether you're ready for this.
- *Is shared storage available across deployment locations?*—You might have multiple data centers or cloud providers, or even a mix of the two. Can all these locations talk to each other seamlessly? Is it a requirement that they do? Or is it a requirement that they do not? Regulatory constraints and a desire to enable capabilities to your developers can both create work for you.

NETWORKING

Regarding networking, there are a few things you might need to think about when implementing a Docker platform.

As seen in chapter 10, by default each Docker container has its own IP address allocated from a reserved set of IP addresses. If you're bringing in a product that manages the running of containers on your network, other sets of network addresses may be reserved. For example, Kubernetes' service layer uses a set of network addresses to maintain and route to stable endpoints across its cluster of nodes.

Some organizations reserve IP ranges for their own purposes, so you need to be wary of clashes. If an IP address range is reserved for a particular set of databases, for example, applications that use the IP range within your cluster for their containers or services may take over those IPs and prevent other applications within the cluster from gaining access to that set of databases. Traffic intended for those databases would end up being routed within the cluster to the container or service IPs.

Network performance can also become significant. If you have software-defined networks (SDNs, such as Nuage or Calico) layered on top of your network already, adding more SDNs for Docker platforms (such as OpenVSwitch or even another Calico layer) can noticeably reduce performance.

Containers can also affect networking in ways you might not expect. Many applications have traditionally used a stable source IP address as part of authentication to external services. In the container world, however, the source IP presented from the container may be either the container IP or the IP of the host on which the container runs (which performs network address translation [NAT] back to the container). Furthermore, if it comes from a cluster of hosts, the IP that's presented can't be guaranteed to be stable. There are ways of ensuring the stability of IP presentation, but they usually need some design and implementation effort.

Load balancing is another area that potentially requires a great deal of effort. There's so much to cover on this topic that it might well be the subject for another book, but here's a brief list:

- Which product is preferred/standard (for example, NGinx, F5s, HAProxy, HTTPD)?
- How and where will you handle SSL termination?
- Do you need a mutual authentication TLS solution?
- How will certificates be generated and managed across your platform?
- Does your load balancer affect headers in a way that's consistent with other applications across the business (be prepared to do a lot of debugging here if it doesn't)?

Finally, if you're using a cloud provider in addition to any data centers you already own or use, you may need to consider whether and how users will connect back to on-premises services from the cloud provider.

LOGGING

Pretty much every application will have log files associated with it. Most applications will want to access those logs in a persistent way (especially in production), so some kind of centralized logging service is usually required. Because containers are ephemeral (where VMs and dedicated servers are usually not), such logging data can be lost if the container dies and logs are stored on its filesystem. Moving to the containerized world might bring the logging challenge more to the fore for these reasons.

Because logging is such a core and common piece of application functionality, it often makes sense to centralize and standardize it. Containers can provide an opportunity to do just that.

MONITORING

Most applications will need to be monitored to a greater or lesser extent, and there is a bewildering array of vendors and products related to container monitoring. This is still an emerging area.

One product that has a great deal of traction in the Docker space is Prometheus. Originally developed by SoundCloud, it has grown in popularity over time, particularly since it became part of the Cloud Native Computing Foundation.

Because containers aren't the same as VMs or physical machines, traditional monitoring tools won't necessarily work well inside containers, as sidecars, or on the host if they're not container-aware.

Having said that, if you're running a cluster of hosts and need to maintain them, traditional, established, mature monitoring tools will come in handy. Likely, they'll be relied on heavily as you try to squeeze the maximum performance out of your cluster for the end users. That's assuming the platform is a success. Our experience suggests that demand often far exceeds supply.

13.3　*Vendors, organizations, and products*

There's no shortage of companies and organizations looking to make money from Docker. Here we'll look at the biggest and most significant players as of 2018, and we'll attempt to describe where their efforts are focused and how their products might work for you.

13.3.1　*The Cloud Native Computing Foundation (CNCF)*

The first of these organizations is different in that it's not a company, but it's probably the most influential player in this space. The CNCF was set up in 2015 to promote common standards in container technology. Founding members included

- Google
- Twitter
- Intel
- Cisco
- IBM
- Docker
- VMWare

Its creation coincided with the release of Kubernetes 1.0, which was donated by Google to the CNCF (although it had already been open sourced by Google some time before).

The CNCF's role in the container space is really that of kingmaker. Because the collective might of the various players involved is so great, when the CNCF gets behind a technology, you know two things about it: it's going to have investment and support behind it, and it's unlikely that one vendor will be favored over another. The latter factor is particularly important to the Docker platform consumer, as it means that your technology choice is unlikely to be obsolete in the foreseeable future.

There's a long (and growing) list of technologies that the CNCF has endorsed. We'll look at some of the most significant ones:

- Kubernetes
- CNI
- Containerd
- Envoy
- Notary
- Prometheus

KUBERNETES

Kubernetes was the founding and most significant technology that's part of the CNCF. It was donated by Google to the community, first as open source, and then to the CNCF.

Although it's open source, its donation to the community is part of Google's strategy to commodify cloud technologies and make it easier for consumers to move away from other cloud providers, the most dominant of which is AWS.

Kubernetes is the foundation technology of most Docker platforms, most notably OpenShift, but also Rancher, and even Docker Inc.'s own Docker Datacenter, because they support Kubernetes in addition to Swarm.

CNI

CNI stands for Container Network Interface. This project provides a standard interface for managing network interfaces for containers. As you saw in chapter 10, networking can be a complex area for container management, and this project is an attempt to help simplify its management.

Here's a (very) simple example that defines a loopback interface:

```
{
    "cniVersion": "0.2.0",
    "type": "loopback"
}
```

This file might be placed into /etc/cni/net.d/99-loopback.conf and used to configure the loopback network interface.

More complex examples are available at the Git repository here: https://github.com/containernetworking/cni.

CONTAINERD

Containerd is the community version of the Docker daemon. It manages containers' life cycles. Runc is its sister project, which is the runtime responsible for running the container itself.

ENVOY

Originally built at Lyft to move their architecture away from a monolithic to a microservices architecture, Envoy is a high-performance open source edge and service proxy that makes the network transparent to applications.

It allows straightforward management of key networking and integration challenges such as load balancing, proxying, and distributed tracing.

NOTARY

Notary is the tool originally designed and built by Docker Inc. to sign and verify the integrity of container images. (Please refer to page 317, "Image integrity.")

PROMETHEUS

Prometheus is a monitoring tool that operates nicely with containers. It's gaining currency in the community, with (for example) Red Hat switching from Hawkular to Prometheus in their OpenShift platform.

13.3.2 *Docker, Inc.*

Docker, Inc. is the commercial entity that seeks to profit from the open source Docker project.

> **NOTE** The open source Docker project has been renamed Moby by Docker Inc. in an attempt to reserve the Docker name for profit-making purposes. So far this name hasn't caught on, so you won't see much mention of Moby in this book.

Docker Inc. was an early leader in the Docker product space, as you might expect. They put together several of their products into a monolithic product called Docker Datacenter. This included support, integration, and features for Notary, the registry, Swarm, and several other projects that Docker had open sourced. Latterly, Kubernetes support has been forthcoming.

Because Docker was early to the party and its technical reputation was strong in the early days of Docker, their product was very compelling on the "getting to production quickly" metric. Over time Docker's product has lost ground as others have caught up. Docker's business model has been difficult to sell internally due to its "take it all or leave it" strategy, and to its cost-per server model, which opens up customers to a strong dependency on one vendor that could hold them to ransom for their entire Docker platform.

13.3.3 Google

Kubernetes was created by Google in 2014 after Docker blew up in popularity. It was intended to bring the principles behind Google's internal container platform (Borg) to a wider audience.

At around the same time, the Google Cloud service came into being. The promotion of Kubernetes was part of their cloud strategy. (Please refer to page 327, "Kubernetes.")

Google has a paid service for managing Kubernetes clusters called Google Kubernetes Engine (GKE), similar to AWS's EKS.

Google's cloud offering is a key business priority for them, and Kubernetes support and encouragement is a central part of that strategy.

13.3.4 Microsoft

Microsoft has been involved with Docker on several fronts, all with a view to expanding its Azure cloud offering.

First, Microsoft has implemented the Docker API to containers natively on the Windows platform from Windows 10 onward. This allows Windows containers to be built and run. Kubernetes support for Windows nodes is planned, but at the time of writing it's still in the early stages.

Second, Microsoft has worked on an offering of its .NET platform, called Dotnet Core (or .NET Core if you prefer), that provides support for .NET codebases on Linux. Not all .NET libraries are supported, so moving your Windows application is far from trivial (so far), but many organizations will be interested in the possibility of running their Windows code on a Linux platform, and even in the possibility of building from the ground up to run on either platform.

Third, an Azure offering exists for Kubernetes (AKS), also similar to AWS's EKS and Google Cloud's GKE.

All these efforts can be seen as designed to encourage users to move to the Azure cloud. The ability to run similar workloads on Windows or Linux (or even the same on both) is attractive to many organizations. This is especially true if the data already sits on their data centers. In addition, Microsoft is in a good position to offer attractive license bundles to organizations already heavily invested in Microsoft technologies looking to go to the cloud.

13.3.5 *Amazon*

Amazon now has several container offerings but arguably was somewhat late to the party. Its first offering was the Elastic Container Service (ECS) which used Mesos under the hood to manage the deployment of containers and their hosts.

This had some initial traction but was soon overtaken in the industry by the popularity of Kubernetes. Amazon responded in late 2017 by announcing the Elastic Kubernetes Service (EKS), which (like the GKE and AKS services mentioned previously) is a curated Kubernetes service. ECS is still supported, but it seems only natural to think that EKS will be the more strategic service for them. Also announced in late 2017 was Fargate, a service that runs containers natively without the need to manage any EC2 instances.

All of these services offer tight integration with other AWS services, which is very convenient if you see AWS as a long-term platform for your software. Obviously, AWS's commercial aim is to ensure you want to continue to pay for their services, but their broad support for the Kubernetes API can give consumers some comfort that the ties to the AWS platform can be looser than with other services.

13.3.6 *Red Hat*

Red Hat's commercial strategy is to curate, support, and manage core software for their customers, the so-called "open source sommelier" strategy. Red Hat is different from the other commercial players in that they don't have a generic cloud service to offer consumers (though OpenShift online can be viewed as a cloud offering because it's an externally hosted service).

Red Hat's container focus is in two areas. The first is OpenShift, which is a product wrapping around Kubernetes that can be run and supported in multiple environments, such as on-prem with the cloud providers mentioned here (as well as some others), and as a service with Red Hat's OpenShift Online service.

OpenShift development has introduced various enterprise features (such as RBAC, built-in image storage, and pod deployment triggers), which have found their way into core Kubernetes.

Summary

- Some of the major determining factors that inform your choice of Docker platform might include your "buy" versus "build" stance, your security stance, your cloud strategy, and whether your organization tends to solve technical challenges with "monolithic" or "piecemeal" products.

- These factors can in turn be affected by the technical drivers of your software, time-to-market demands, the level of consumer independence, your open source strategy, and your organizational structure.

- In a larger organization, a multiplatform approach can make sense, but care might need to be taken to ensure consistency of approach across these platforms to reduce later organizational inefficiencies.

- The major functional areas that might be considered when implementing a Docker platform include how images will be built, image scanning and integrity, secrets management, image registries, and the underlying OS.

- The significant players in the Docker platform space include Docker Inc., the three big cloud providers (AWS, Google Cloud Platform, and Microsoft Azure), and the Cloud Native Computing Foundation (CNCF).

- The CNCF is a highly influential organization that incubates and supports the key open source technical components of Docker platforms. Full acceptance by the CNCF is a signal that the technology will be sustainable.

Part 5

Docker in production

At last we're ready to contemplate running Docker in production. In part 5 we'll address the key operational considerations when running Docker on live environments.

Security is the focus of chapter 14. Through practical techniques you'll get a real understanding of the security challenges Docker brings and how you might want to address them.

Backups, logging, and resource management are considered in chapter 15, where we'll show you how these traditional sysadmin tasks can be managed within a Docker context.

Finally, in chapter 16 we'll look at what you can do when things go wrong, covering some common areas where Docker can get into trouble, as well as how you can debug containers in production.

Docker and security

As Docker makes clear in its documentation, access to the Docker API implies access to root privileges, which is why Docker must often be run with sudo, or the user must be added to a user group (which might be called "docker", or "docker-root") that allows access to the Docker API.

In this chapter we're going to look at the issue of security in Docker.

14.1   *Docker access and what it means*

You may be wondering what sort of damage a user can do if they can run Docker. As a simple example, the following command (don't run it!) would delete all the binaries in /sbin on your host machine (if you took out the bogus --donotrunme flag):

```
docker run --donotrunme -v /sbin:/sbin busybox rm -rf /sbin
```

It's worth pointing out that this is true even if you're a non-root user.

The following command will show you the contents of the secure shadow password file from the host system:

```
docker run -v /etc/shadow:/etc/shadow busybox cat /etc/shadow
```

Docker's insecurity is often misunderstood, partly due to a misunderstanding of the benefits of namespaces in the kernel. Linux namespaces provide isolation from other parts of the system, but the level of isolation you have in Docker is at your discretion (as seen in the preceding docker run examples). Furthermore, not all parts of the Linux OS have the ability to be namespaced. Devices and kernel modules are two examples of core Linux features that aren't namespaced.

> **TIP** Linux namespaces were developed to allow processes to have a different view of the system than other processes have. For example, *process namespacing* means that containers can only see processes associated with that container— other processes running on the same host are effectively invisible to them. *Network namespacing* means that containers appear to have their own network stack available to them. Namespaces have been part of the Linux kernel for a number of years.

Also, because you have the ability to interact with the kernel as root from within the container through syscalls, any kernel vulnerability could be exploited by root within the Docker container. Of course, VMs have a similar attack possible through access to the hypervisor, because hypervisors also have security vulnerabilities reported against them.

Another way to understand the risks here is to think of running a Docker container as being no different (from a security perspective) from being able to install any package via a package manager. Your requirement for security when running Docker containers should be the same as for installing packages. If you have Docker, you can install software as root. This is partly why some argue that Docker is best understood as a software packaging system.

> **TIP** Work is underway to remove this risk through user namespacing, which maps root in the container to a non-privileged user on the host.

14.1.1   *Do you care?*

Given that access to the Docker API is equivalent to root access, the next question is "do you care?" Although this might seem an odd line to take, security is all about trust, and if you trust your users to install software in the environment in which they operate, there should be no barrier to them running Docker containers there. Security difficulties primarily arise when considering multi-tenant environments. Because the root user inside your container is in key respects the same as root outside your container, having lots of different users being root on your system is potentially worrying.

> **TIP** A multi-tenant environment is one in which many different users share the same resources. For example, two teams might share the same server with two different VMs. Multi-tenancy offers cost savings through sharing hardware rather than provisioning hardware for specific applications. But it can bring other challenges related to service reliability and security isolation that can offset the cost savings.

Some organizations take the approach of running Docker on a dedicated VM for each user. The VM can be used for security, operational, or resource isolation. Within the VM trust boundary, users run Docker containers for the performance and operational benefits they bring. This is the approach taken by Google Compute Engine, which places a VM between the user's container and the underlying infrastructure for an added level of security and some operational benefits. Google has more than a little compute resources at their disposal, so they don't mind the overhead of doing this.

14.2 Security measures in Docker

Various measures have already been taken by the Docker maintainers to reduce the security risks of running containers. For example,

- Certain core mount points (such as /proc and /sys) are now mounted as read-only.
- Default Linux capabilities have been reduced.
- Support for third-party security systems like SELinux and AppArmor now exists.

In this section, we'll look more deeply at these and at some of the measures you can take to reduce the risks of running containers on your system.

TECHNIQUE 93 Constraining capabilities

As we've already mentioned, the root user on the container is the same user as root on the host. But not all root users are created equal. Linux provides you with the ability to assign more fine-grained privileges to the root user within a process.

These fine-grained privileges are called *capabilities*, and they allow you to limit the damage a user can do, even if they're root. This technique shows you how to manipulate these capabilities when running Docker containers, particularly if you don't fully trust their contents.

PROBLEM

You want to reduce the ability of containers to perform damaging actions on your host machine.

SOLUTION

Drop the capabilities available to the container by using the `--drop-cap` flag.

THE UNIX TRUST MODEL

To understand what "dropping capabilities" means and does, a little bit of background is required. When the Unix system was designed, the trust model wasn't sophisticated. You had admins who were trusted (root users) and users who weren't. Root users could do anything, whereas standard users could only affect their own files. Because the system was typically used in a university lab and was small, this model made sense.

As the Unix model grew and the internet arrived, this model made less and less sense. Programs like web servers needed root permissions to serve content on port 80, but they were also acting effectively as proxies for running commands on the host. Standard patterns were established to handle this, such as binding to port 80 and dropping the effective user ID to a non-root user. Users performing all sorts of roles, from sysadmins to database administrators through to application support engineers and developers, could all potentially need fine-grained access to different resources on a system. Unix groups alleviated this to some degree, but modeling these privilege requirements—as any systems admin will tell you—is a nontrivial problem.

LINUX CAPABILITIES

In an attempt to support a more fine-grained approach to privileged user management, the Linux kernel engineers developed *capabilities*. This was an attempt to break down the monolithic root privilege into slices of functionality that could be granted discretely. You can read about them in more detail by running `man 7 capabilities` (assuming you have the man page installed).

Docker has helpfully switched off certain capabilities by default. This means that even if you have root in the container, there are things you won't be able to do. For example, the `CAP_NET_ADMIN` capability, which allows you to affect the network stack of the host, is disabled by default.

Table 14.1 lists Linux capabilities, gives a brief description of what they allow, and indicates whether they're permitted by default in Docker containers.

Table 14.1   Linux capabilities in Docker containers

Capability	Description	Switched on?
CHOWN	Make ownership changes to any files	Y
DAC_OVERRIDE	Override read, write, and execution checks	Y
FSETID	Don't clear suid and guid bits when modifying files	Y
FOWNER	Override ownership checks when saving files	Y
KILL	Bypass permission checks on signals	Y
MKNOD	Make special files with `mknod`	Y

Table 14.1 Linux capabilities in Docker containers *(continued)*

Capability	Description	Switched on?
NET_RAW	Use raw and packet sockets, and bind to ports for transparent proxying	Y
SETGID	Make changes to group ownership of processes	Y
SETUID	Make changes to user ownership of processes	Y
SETFCAP	Set file capabilities	Y
SETPCAP	If file capabilities aren't supported, apply capability limits to and from other processes	Y
NET_BIND_SERVICE	Bind sockets to ports under 1024	Y
SYS_CHROOT	Use chroot	Y
AUDIT_WRITE	Write to kernel logs	Y
AUDIT_CONTROL	Enable/disable kernel logging	N
BLOCK_SUSPEND	Employ features that block the ability of the system to suspend	N
DAC_READ_SEARCH	Bypass file permission checks on reading files and directories	N
IPC_LOCK	Lock memory	N
IPC_OWNER	Bypass permissions on interprocess communication objects	N
LEASE	Establish leases (watches on attempts to open or truncate) on ordinary files	N
LINUX_IMMUTABLE	Set the FS_APPEND_FL and FS_IMMUTABLE_FL i-node flags	N
MAC_ADMIN	Override mandatory access control (related to the Smack Linux Security Module (SLM))	N
MAC_OVERRIDE	Mandatory access control changes (related to SLM)	N
NET_ADMIN	Various network-related operations, including IP firewall changes and interface configuration	N
NET_BROADCAST	Unused	N
SYS_ADMIN	A range of administrative functions—see man capabilities for more information	N
SYS_BOOT	Rebooting	N
SYS_MODULE	Load/unload kernel modules	N
SYS_NICE	Manipulate nice priority of processes	N
SYS_PACCT	Turn on or off process accounting	N
SYS_PTRACE	Trace processes' system calls and other process manipulation capabilities	N

Table 14.1   Linux capabilities in Docker containers *(continued)*

Capability	Description	Switched on?
SYS_RAWIO	Perform I/O on various core parts of the system, such as memory and SCSI device commands	N
SYS_RESOURCE	Control and override various resource limits	N
SYS_TIME	Set the system clock	N
SYS_TTY_CONFIG	Privileged operations on virtual terminals	N

NOTE If you aren't using Docker's default container engine (libcontainer), these capabilities may be different on your installation. If you have a sysadmin and want to be sure, ask them.

Unfortunately the kernel maintainers only allocated 32 capabilities within the system, so capabilities have grown in scope as more and more fine-grained root privileges have been carved out of the kernel. Most notably, the vaguely named CAP_SYS_ADMIN capability covers actions as varied as changing the host's domain name to exceeding the system-wide limit on the number of open files.

One extreme approach is to remove all the capabilities that are switched on in Docker by default from the container, and see what stops working. Here we start up a bash shell with the capabilities that are enabled by default removed:

```
$ docker run -ti --cap-drop=CHOWN --cap-drop=DAC_OVERRIDE \
--cap-drop=FSETID --cap-drop=FOWNER --cap-drop=KILL --cap-drop=MKNOD \
--cap-drop=NET_RAW --cap-drop=SETGID --cap-drop=SETUID \
--cap-drop=SETFCAP --cap-drop=SETPCAP --cap-drop=NET_BIND_SERVICE \
--cap-drop=SYS_CHROOT --cap-drop=AUDIT_WRITE debian /bin/bash
```

If you run your application from this shell, you can see where it fails to work as desired, and re-add the required capabilities. For example, you may need the capability to change file ownership, so you'll need to lose the dropping of the FOWNER capability in the preceding code to run your application:

```
$ docker run -ti --cap-drop=CHOWN --cap-drop=DAC_OVERRIDE \
--cap-drop=FSETID  --cap-drop=KILL --cap-drop=MKNOD \
--cap-drop=NET_RAW --cap-drop=SETGID --cap-drop=SETUID \
--cap-drop=SETFCAP --cap-drop=SETPCAP --cap-drop=NET_BIND_SERVICE \
--cap-drop=SYS_CHROOT --cap-drop=AUDIT_WRITE debian /bin/bash
```

TIP If you want to enable or disable all capabilities, you can use all instead of a specific capability, such as docker run -ti --cap-drop=all ubuntu bash.

DISCUSSION

If you run a few basic commands in the bash shell with all capabilities disabled, you'll see that it's quite usable. Your mileage may vary when running more complex applications, though.

WARNING It's worth making clear that many of these capabilities relate to the root capabilities to affect *other* users' objects on the system, not root's own objects. A root user could still chown root's files on the host if they were host in the container and had access to the host's files through a volume mount, for example. Therefore, it's still worth ensuring that applications drop to a non-root user as soon as possible to protect the system, even if all these capabilities are switched off.

This ability to fine-tune the capabilities of your container means that using the `--privileged` flag to `docker run` should be unnecessary. Processes that require capabilities will be auditable and under the control of the administrator of the host.

TECHNIQUE 94 **A "bad" Docker image to scan**

One issue quickly recognized in the Docker ecosystem was that of vulnerabilities—if you have an unchanging image, you also won't get any security fixes. This may not be a problem if you're following the Docker best practices of image minimalism, but it can be hard to tell.

Image scanners were created as a solution to this problem—a way to identify issues with an image—but that still leaves open the question of how to evaluate them.

PROBLEM

You want to determine how effective an image scanner is.

SOLUTION

Create a "known-bad" image to test your scanners on.

We were faced with this problem while at work. Plenty of Docker image scanners exist (such as Clair), but commercial offerings claim to go deeper into the image to determine any potential issues lurking within it.

But no image existed that contained known and documented vulnerabilities that we could use to test the efficacy of these scanners. Hardly surprising, as most images don't advertise their own insecurity!

We therefore invented a known bad image. The image is available to download:

```
$ docker pull imiell/bad-dockerfile
```

The principle is simple: create a Dockerfile to build an image riddled with documented vulnerabilities, and point that image at your candidate scanner.

The latest version of the Dockerfile is available at https://github.com/ianmiell/bad-dockerfile. It's still in flux, so it's not printed here. The form of it is, however, quite simple:

Various RUN/COPY/ADD commands install software to the image that are known to be vulnerable.

The reference bad-dockerfile repository uses a centos image, but you might want to replace this with one closer to your base image.

```
FROM <base image>
 RUN <install 'bad' software>
 COPY <copy 'bad' software in>
 [...]
CMD echo 'Vulnerable image' && /bin/false
```

The CMD directive for the image tries its best never to allow itself to be run, for obvious reasons.

The image contains a spectrum of vulnerabilities designed to exercise a scanner to its limits.

At its simplest, the image installs software known to be vulnerable using the package manager. Within each category, the Docker image attempts to contain vulnerabilities of varying degrees of severity.

More sophisticated placement of vulnerabilities is performed by (for example) COPYing vulnerable JavaScript, using language-specific package managers (such as npm for JavaScript, gem for Ruby, and pip for Python) to install vulnerable code, and even compiling a specific version of bash (one with the infamous Shellshock bug) and placing it in an unexpected location to avoid many scanning techniques.

DISCUSSION

You might think that the best scanning solution is one that catches the most CVEs. But this isn't necessarily the case. Obviously, it's good if a scanner can spot that an image has a vulnerability within it. Beyond this, however, scanning for vulnerabilities can become more of an art than a science.

> **TIP** A Common Vulnerability Exposure (CVE) is an identifier for a specific vulnerability discovered in generally available software. An example of a CVE might be CVE-2001-0067, where the first four-digit number is the year of discovery, and the second is the count of the identified vulnerability for that year.

For example, a vulnerability might be very severe (such as gaining root on your host server), but extremely difficult to exploit (such as requiring the resources of a nation-state). You (or the organization you're responsible for) might be less worried about this than about a vulnerability that's less severe, but easy to exploit. If, for example, there's a DoS attack on your system, there's no risk of data leakage or infiltration, but you could be put out of business by it, so you'd be more concerned about patching that than some obscure cipher attack requiring tens of thousands of dollars' worth of computing power.

> **WHAT IS A DOS ATTACK?** DoS stands for "denial of service." This means an attack that results in a reduction in the ability of your system to cope with demand. A denial of service attack could overwhelm your web server to the point where it can't respond to legitimate users.

It's also worth considering whether the vulnerability is actually available on the running container. An old version of the Apache web server may exist on the image, but if it's never actually run by the container, the vulnerability is effectively ignorable. This happens often. Package managers regularly bring in dependencies that aren't really needed just because it makes managing dependencies simpler.

If security is a big concern, this can be another reason to have small images (see chapter 7)—even if a piece of software is unused, it can still show up on a security scan, wasting time as your organization tries to work out whether it needs patching.

This technique hopefully gave you food for thought when considering which scanner is right for you. As always, it's a balance between cost, what you need, and how much you're willing to work to get the right solution.

14.3 Securing access to Docker

The best way to prevent insecure use of a Docker daemon is to prevent any use at all.

You probably first encountered restricted access when you installed Docker and needed to use sudo to run Docker itself. Technique 41 describes how to selectively permit users on the local machine to use Docker without this restriction.

But this doesn't help you if you have users connecting to a Docker daemon from another machine. We'll look at a couple of ways to provide a bit more security in those situations.

TECHNIQUE 95 HTTP auth on your Docker instance

In technique 1 you saw how to open up access to your daemon to the network, and in technique 4 you saw how to snoop the Docker API using socat.

This technique combines those two: you'll be able to access your daemon remotely and view the responses. Access is restricted to those with a username/password combination, so it's slightly safer. As a bonus, you don't have to restart your Docker daemon to achieve it—start up a container daemon.

PROBLEM

You'd like basic authentication with network access available on your Docker daemon.

SOLUTION

Use HTTP authentication to share your Docker daemon with others temporarily.

Figure 14.1 lays out the final architecture of this technique.

> **NOTE** This discussion assumes your Docker daemon is using Docker's default Unix socket method of access in /var/run/docker.sock.

The code in this technique is available at https://github.com/docker-in-practice/docker-authenticate. The following listing shows the contents of the Dockerfile in this repository, used to create the image for this technique.

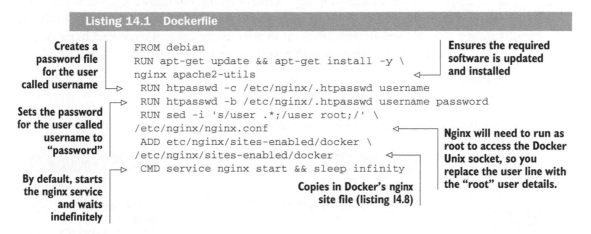

Listing 14.1   Dockerfile

Creates a password file for the user called username

Sets the password for the user called username to "password"

By default, starts the nginx service and waits indefinitely

```
FROM debian
RUN apt-get update && apt-get install -y \
nginx apache2-utils
RUN htpasswd -c /etc/nginx/.htpasswd username
RUN htpasswd -b /etc/nginx/.htpasswd username password
RUN sed -i 's/user .*;/user root;/' \
/etc/nginx/nginx.conf
ADD etc/nginx/sites-enabled/docker \
/etc/nginx/sites-enabled/docker
CMD service nginx start && sleep infinity
```

Ensures the required software is updated and installed

Nginx will need to run as root to access the Docker Unix socket, so you replace the user line with the "root" user details.

Copies in Docker's nginx site file (listing 14.8)

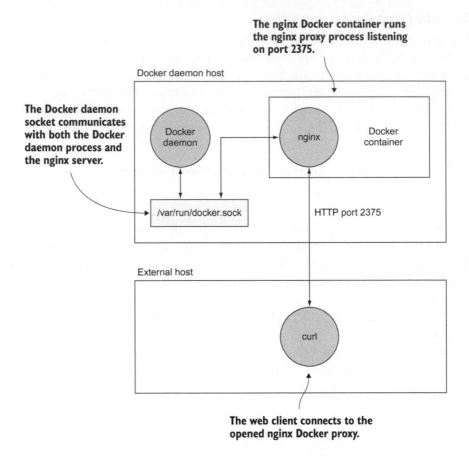

The nginx Docker container runs the nginx proxy process listening on port 2375.

Docker daemon host

The Docker daemon socket communicates with both the Docker daemon process and the nginx server.

Docker daemon

nginx

Docker container

/var/run/docker.sock

HTTP port 2375

External host

curl

The web client connects to the opened nginx Docker proxy.

Figure 14.1   The architecture of a Docker daemon with basic authentication

The .htpasswd file set up with the htpasswd command contains the credentials to be checked before allowing (or rejecting) access to the Docker socket. If you're building this image yourself, you'll probably want to alter username and password in those two steps to customize the credentials with access to the Docker socket.

WARNING   Be careful not to share this image, as it will contain the password you've set!

The nginx site file for Docker is shown in the following listing.

Listing 14.2   /etc/nginx/sites-enabled/docker

```
upstream docker {
  server unix:/var/run/docker.sock;
}

server {
  listen 2375 default_server;
```

Defines the docker location in nginx as pointing to Docker's domain socket

Listens on port 2375 (the standard Docker port)

Proxies these
requests to and
from the
docker location
defined earlier

```
location / {
  proxy_pass http://docker;
    auth_basic_user_file /etc/nginx/.htpasswd;
    auth_basic "Access restricted";
  }
}
```

**Defines the
password file to use**

**Restricts access
by password**

Now run the image as a daemon container, mapping the required resources from the
host machine:

```
$ docker run -d --name docker-authenticate -p 2375:2375 \
  -v /var/run:/var/run dockerinpractice/docker-authenticate
```

This will run the container in the background with the name `docker-authenticate`
so you can refer to it later. Port 2375 of the container is exposed on the host, and the
container is given access to the Docker daemon by mounting the default directory
containing the Docker socket as a volume. If you're using a custom-built image with
your own username and password, you'll need to replace the image name here with
your own.

The web service will now be up and running. If you `curl` the service with the username and password you set, you should see an API response:

**The JSON response from
the Docker daemon**

**Puts the username:
password in the URL to
curl, and the address
after the @ sign. This
request is to the /info
endpoint of the Docker
daemon's API.**

```
$ curl http://username:password@localhost:2375/info
  {"Containers":115,"Debug":0, >
   "DockerRootDir":"/var/lib/docker","Driver":"aufs", >
"DriverStatus":[["Root Dir","/var/lib/docker/aufs"], >
["Backing Filesystem","extfs"],["Dirs","1033"]], >
"ExecutionDriver":"native-0.2", >
"ID":"QSCJ:NLPA:CRS7:WCOI:K23J:6Y2V:G35M:BF55:OA2W:MV3E:RG47:DG23", >
"IPv4Forwarding":1,"Images":792, >
"IndexServerAddress":"https://index.docker.io/v1/", >
"InitPath":"/usr/bin/docker","InitSha1":"", >
"KernelVersion":"3.13.0-45-generic", >
"Labels":null,"MemTotal":5939630080,"MemoryLimit":1, >
"NCPU":4,"NEventsListener":0,"NFd":31,"NGoroutines":30, >
"Name":"rothko","OperatingSystem":"Ubuntu 14.04.2 LTS", >
"RegistryConfig":{"IndexConfigs":{"docker.io": >
{"Mirrors":null,"Name":"docker.io", >
"Official":true,"Secure":true}}, >
"InsecureRegistryCIDRs":["127.0.0.0/8"]},"SwapLimit":0}
```

When you're done, remove the container with this command:

```
$ docker rm -f docker-authenticate
```

Access is now revoked.

USING THE DOCKER COMMAND?

Readers may be wondering whether other users will be able to connect with the docker command—for example, with something like this:

```
docker -H tcp://username:password@localhost:2375 ps
```

At the time of writing, authentication functionality isn't built into Docker itself. But we have created an image that will handle the authentication and allow Docker to connect to a daemon. Simply use the image as follows:

Exposes a port to connect a Docker
daemon to, but only for connections
from the local machine

Runs the client container
in the background and
gives it a name

```
$ docker run -d --name docker-authenticate-client \
    -p 127.0.0.1:12375:12375 \
    dockerinpractice/docker-authenticate-client \
    192.168.1.74:2375 username:password
```

The image we've made to
allow authenticated
connections with Docker

The two arguments to the image: a specification of where the other end of
the authenticated connection should be, and the username and password
(both of these should be replaced as appropriate for your setup)

Note that localhost or 127.0.0.1 won't work for specifying the other end of the authenticated connection—if you want to try it out on one host, you must use ip addr to identify an external IP address for your machine.

You can now use the authenticated connection with the following command:

```
docker -H localhost:12375 ps
```

Be aware that interactive Docker commands (run and exec with the -i argument) won't work over this connection due to some implementation limitations.

DISCUSSION

In this technique we showed you how to set up basic authentication for your Docker server in a trusted network. In the next technique we'll look at encrypting the traffic so snoopers can't take a peek at what you're up to, or even inject evil data or code.

> **WARNING** This technique gives you a basic level of *authentication*, but it doesn't give you a serious level of *security* (in particular, someone able to listen to your network traffic could intercept your username and password). Setting up a server secured with TLS is rather more involved and is covered in the next technique.

TECHNIQUE 96 Securing your Docker API

In this technique we'll show how you can open up your Docker server to others over a TCP port while at the same time ensuring that only trusted clients can connect. This is achieved by creating a secret key that only trusted hosts will be given. As long as that trusted key remains a secret between the server and client machines, the Docker server should remain secure.

PROBLEM

You want your Docker API to be served securely over a port.

SOLUTION

Create a self-signed certificate, and run the Docker daemon with the `--tls-verify` flag.

   This method of security depends on so-called *key files* being created on the server. These files are created using special tools that ensure they're difficult to copy if you don't have the *server key*. Figure 14.2 gives an overview of this how this works.

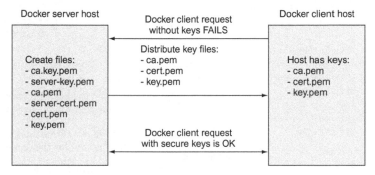

Figure 14.2   Key setup and distribution

TIP   The *server key* is a file that holds a secret number known only to the server, and which is required to read messages encrypted with the secret key files given out by the owner of the server (the so-called *client keys*). Once the keys have been created and distributed, they can be used to make the connection between client and server secure.

SETTING UP THE DOCKER SERVER CERTIFICATE

First you create the certificates and keys.

   Generating keys requires the OpenSSL package, and you can check whether it's installed by running `openssl` in a terminal. If it's not installed, you'll need to install it before generating the certificates and keys with the following code.

Listing 14.3   Creating certificates and keys with OpenSSL

Type in your certificate password and the server name you'll use to connect to the Docker server.

Generate certificate authority (CA) .pem file with 2048-bit security.

```
$ sudo su                ◄─── Ensure you are root.
  $ read -s PASSWORD
  $ read SERVER
  $ mkdir -p /etc/docker        ┐ Create the docker configuration directory
  $ cd /etc/docker              ┘ if it doesn't exist, and move into it.
  $ openssl genrsa -aes256 -passout pass:$PASSWORD \
-out ca-key.pem 2048                                ◄───────┘
  $ openssl req -new -x509 -days 365 -key ca-key.pem -passin pass:$PASSWORD \
-sha256 -out ca.pem -subj "/C=NL/ST=./L=./O=./CN=$SERVER"        ◄───
```

Create the docker configuration directory if it doesn't exist, and move into it.

Sign the CA key with your password and address for a period of one year.

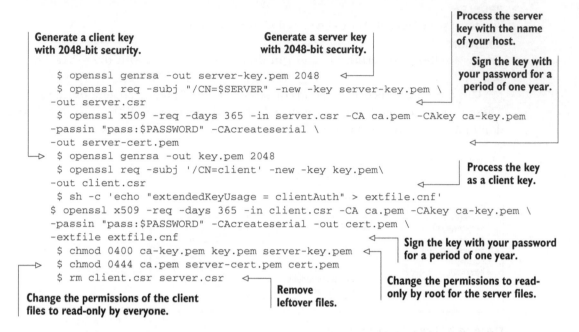

Generate a client key with 2048-bit security.

Generate a server key with 2048-bit security.

Process the server key with the name of your host.

Sign the key with your password for a period of one year.

```
$ openssl genrsa -out server-key.pem 2048
$ openssl req -subj "/CN=$SERVER" -new -key server-key.pem \
-out server.csr
$ openssl x509 -req -days 365 -in server.csr -CA ca.pem -CAkey ca-key.pem
-passin "pass:$PASSWORD" -CAcreateserial \
-out server-cert.pem
$ openssl genrsa -out key.pem 2048
$ openssl req -subj '/CN=client' -new -key key.pem\
-out client.csr
$ sh -c 'echo "extendedKeyUsage = clientAuth" > extfile.cnf'
$ openssl x509 -req -days 365 -in client.csr -CA ca.pem -CAkey ca-key.pem \
-passin "pass:$PASSWORD" -CAcreateserial -out cert.pem \
-extfile extfile.cnf
$ chmod 0400 ca-key.pem key.pem server-key.pem
$ chmod 0444 ca.pem server-cert.pem cert.pem
$ rm client.csr server.csr
```

Process the key as a client key.

Sign the key with your password for a period of one year.

Change the permissions to read-only by root for the server files.

Remove leftover files.

Change the permissions of the client files to read-only by everyone.

> **TIP** A script called CA.pl may be installed on your system that makes this process simpler. Here we've exposed the raw `openssl` commands because they're more instructive.

SETTING UP THE DOCKER SERVER

Next you need to set the Docker opts in your Docker daemon config file to specify which keys are used to encrypt the communications (see appendix B for advice on how to configure and restart your Docker daemon).

Listing 14.4   Docker options for using the new keys and certificates

Specifies the CA file for the Docker server

Tells the Docker daemon that you want to use TLS security to secure connections to it

```
DOCKER_OPTS="$DOCKER_OPTS --tlsverify"
DOCKER_OPTS="$DOCKER_OPTS \
--tlscacert=/etc/docker/ca.pem"
DOCKER_OPTS="$DOCKER_OPTS \
--tlscert=/etc/docker/server-cert.pem"
DOCKER_OPTS="$DOCKER_OPTS \
--tlskey=/etc/docker/server-key.pem"
DOCKER_OPTS="$DOCKER_OPTS -H tcp://0.0.0.0:2376"
DOCKER_OPTS="$DOCKER_OPTS \
-H unix:///var/run/docker.sock"
```

Specifies the certificate for the server

Specifies the private key used by the server

Opens the Docker daemon to external clients over TCP on port 2376

Opens the Docker daemon locally via a Unix socket in the normal way

DISTRIBUTING CLIENT KEYS

Next you need to send the keys to the client host so it can connect to the server and exchange information. You don't want to reveal your secret keys to anyone else, so these need to be passed to the client securely. A relatively safe way to do this is to SCP (secure copy) them direct from the server to the client. The SCP utility uses essentially the same technique to secure the transmission of data that we're demonstrating here, only with different keys that will have already been set up.

On the client host, create the Docker configuration folder in /etc as you did earlier:

```
user@client:~$ sudo su
root@client:~$ mkdir -p /etc/docker
```

Then SCP the files from the server to the client. Make sure you replace "client" in the following commands with the hostname of your client machine. Also make sure that all the files are readable by the user that will run the docker command on the client.

```
user@server:~$ sudo su
root@server:~$ scp /etc/docker/ca.pem client:/etc/docker
root@server:~$ scp /etc/docker/cert.pem client:/etc/docker
root@server:~$ scp /etc/docker/key.pem client:/etc/docker
```

TESTING

To test your setup, first try making a request to the Docker server without any credentials. You should be rejected:

```
root@client~: docker -H myserver.localdomain:2376 info
FATA[0000] Get http://myserver.localdomain:2376/v1.17/info: malformed HTTP >
response "\x15\x03\x01\x00\x02\x02". Are you trying to connect to a >
TLS-enabled daemon without TLS?
```

Then connect with the credentials, which should return useful output:

```
root@client~: docker --tlsverify --tlscacert=/etc/docker/ca.pem \
--tlscert=/etc/docker/cert.pem --tlskey=/etc/docker/key.pem \
-H myserver.localdomain:2376 info
243 info
Containers: 3
Images: 86
Storage Driver: aufs
 Root Dir: /var/lib/docker/aufs
 Backing Filesystem: extfs
 Dirs: 92
Execution Driver: native-0.2
Kernel Version: 3.16.0-34-generic
Operating System: Ubuntu 14.04.2 LTS
CPUs: 4
Total Memory: 11.44 GiB
Name: rothko
ID: 4YQA:KK65:FXON:YVLT:BVVH:Y3KC:UATJ:I4GK:S3E2:UTA6:R43U:DX5T
WARNING: No swap limit support
```

DISCUSSION

This technique gives you the best of both worlds—a Docker daemon open to others to use, and one that's only accessible to trusted users. Make sure you keep those keys safe!

Key management is a critical aspect of most larger organizations' IT management processes. It's definitely a cost, so when it comes to implementing a Docker platform, it can become one that's brought into sharp focus. Deploying keys safely to containers is a challenge that may well need to be considered in most Docker platform designs.

14.4 Security from outside Docker

Security on your host doesn't stop with the `docker` command. In this section you're going to see some other approaches to securing your Docker containers, this time from outside Docker.

We'll start off with a couple of techniques that modify your image to reduce the surface area for external attack once they're up and running. The subsequent two techniques consider how to run containers in a restricted way.

Of these latter two techniques, the first demonstrates the application platform as a service (aPaaS) approach, which ensures Docker runs within a straightjacket set up and controlled by the administrator. As an example, we'll run an OpenShift Origin server (an aPaaS that deploys Docker containers in a managed way) using Docker commands. You'll see that the end user's powers can be limited and managed by the administrator, and access to the Docker runtime can be removed.

The second approach goes beyond this level of security to further limit the freedoms available within running containers using SELinux, a security technology that gives you fine-grained control over who can do what.

> **TIP** SELinux is a tool built and open-sourced by the United States' National Security Agency (NSA) that fulfills their need for strong access control. It has been a security standard for some time now, and it's very powerful. Unfortunately, many people simply switch it off when they encounter problems with it, rather than take the time to understand it. We hope the technique shown here will help make that approach less tempting.

TECHNIQUE 97   **Reducing a container's attack surface with DockerSlim**

In section 7.3 we discussed a few different ways to create a small image in response to reasonable concern about the amount of data being moved around a network. But there's another reason to do this—if your image has less in it, there's less for an attacker to exploit. As one concrete example, there's no way to get a shell in the container if there's no shell installed.

Building up an "expected behavior" profile for your container and then enforcing that at runtime means that unexpected actions have a realistic chance of being detected and prevented.

PROBLEM

You want to reduce an image to the bare essentials to reduce its attack surface.

SOLUTION

Use the DockerSlim tool to analyze your image and modify it for a reduced attack surface.

This tool is intended to take a Docker image and reduce it to its barest essentials. It's available at https://github.com/docker-slim/docker-slim.

DockerSlim reduces your Docker image in at least two distinct ways. First, it reduces your image to only the required files and places these files in a single layer. The end result is an image that's significantly smaller than its original, fat counterpart.

Second, it provides you with a seccomp profile. This is achieved through dynamic analysis of your running image. In lay terms, this means that it runs up your image and tracks which files and system calls are used. While DockerSlim is analyzing your running container, you need to use the app as it would be by all typical users, to ensure that the necessary files and system calls are picked up.

> **WARNING** If you reduce your image using a dynamic analysis tool like this, be absolutely sure you've exercised it enough in the analysis stage. This walk-through uses a trivial image, but you may have a more complex image that's harder to exhaustively profile.

This technique will use a simple web example application to demonstrate the technique. You will

- Set up DockerSlim
- Build an image
- Run the image as a container with the DockerSlim tool
- Hit an endpoint of the application
- Run the slimmed image using the created seccomp profile

> **NOTE** A seccomp profile is essentially a whitelist of which system calls can be made from a container. When running the container, you can specify a seccomp profile with either reduced or raised permissions, depending on what your application needs. The default seccomp profile disables around 45 system calls out of over 300. Most applications need far fewer than this.

SETTING UP DOCKERSLIM

Run these commands to get the docker-slim binary downloaded and set up.

Listing 14.5 Downloading docker-slim and installing it to a directory

Gets the docker-slim zip
file from its release folder

Makes the docker-slim
folder and a bin subfolder

```
$ mkdir -p docker-slim/bin && cd docker-slim/bin
  $ wget https://github.com/docker-slim/docker-slim/releases/download/1.18
/dist_linux.zip
  $ unzip dist_linux.zip          Unzips the retrieved zip file
  $ cd ..
```

Moves to the parent directory, docker-slim

NOTE This technique was tested against the preceding docker-slim version. You may want to visit GitHub at https://github.com/docker-slim/docker-slim/ releases to see whether there have been any updates. This isn't a fast-moving project, so the updates shouldn't be too important.

Now you have the docker-slim binary in a bin subfolder.

BUILDING THE FAT IMAGE

Next you'll build a sample application that uses NodeJS. This is a trivial application that simply serves a string of JSON on port 8000. The following command clones the docker-slim repository, moves to the sample application code, and builds its Dockerfile into an image with the name sample-node-app.

Listing 14.6 Building an example docker-slim application

Checks out a known-working version of the docker-slim repository

Clones the docker-slim repository, which contains the sample application

```
$ git clone https://github.com/docker-slim/docker-slim.git
$ cd docker-slim && git checkout 1.18
$ cd sample/apps/node
$ docker build -t sample-node-app .
$ cd -
```

Moves to the NodeJS sample application folder

Builds the image, giving it the name sample-node-app

Returns to the previous directory, where the docker-slim binary is located

RUNNING THE FAT IMAGE

Now that you've created your fat image, the next step involves running it as a container with the docker-slim wrapper. Once the application has initialized, you then hit the application endpoint to exercise its code. Finally, bring the backgrounded docker-slim application to the foreground and wait for it to terminate.

Runs the docker-slim binary against the sample-node-app image. Backgrounds the process. http-probe will call the application on all exposed ports.

Sleeps for 10 seconds to allow the sample-node-app process to start, and then hits the port the application runs on

```
$ ./docker-slim build --http-probe sample-node-app &
$ sleep 10 && curl localhost:32770
{"status":"success","info":"yes!!!","service":"node"}
$ fg
./docker-slim build --http-probe sample-node-app
INFO[0014] docker-slim: HTTP probe started...
INFO[0014] docker-slim: http probe - GET http://127.0.0.1:32770/ => 200
INFO[0014] docker-slim: HTTP probe done.
INFO[0015] docker-slim: shutting down 'fat' container...
INFO[0015] docker-slim: processing instrumented 'fat' container info...
INFO[0015] docker-slim: generating AppArmor profile...
INFO[0015] docker-slim: building 'slim' image...
```

Sends the application's JSON response to the terminal

Foregrounds the docker-slim process and waits until it completes

The first section of output from docker-slim shows its working logs.

```
Step 1 : FROM scratch                                                Docker-slim
 --->                                                                 builds the
Step 2 : COPY files /                                                   "slim"
 ---> 0953a87c8e4f                                                    container.
Removing intermediate container 51e4e625017e
Step 3 : WORKDIR /opt/my/service
 ---> Running in a2851dce6df7
 ---> 2d82f368c130
Removing intermediate container a2851dce6df7
Step 4 : ENV PATH "/usr/local/sbin:/usr/local/bin:/usr/sbin:/usr/bin:/sbin:
 /bin"
 ---> Running in ae1d211f118e
 ---> 4ef6d57d3230
Removing intermediate container ae1d211f118e
Step 5 : EXPOSE 8000/tcp
 ---> Running in 36e2ced2a1b6
 ---> 2616067ec78d
Removing intermediate container 36e2ced2a1b6
Step 6 : ENTRYPOINT node /opt/my/service/server.js
 ---> Running in 16a35fd2fb1c
 ---> 7451554aa807
Removing intermediate container 16a35fd2fb1c
Successfully built 7451554aa807
INFO[0016] docker-slim: created new image: sample-node-app.slim
$
$                                          When it completes, you may need
                                           to press Return to get a prompt.
```

In this case "exercising the code" just involves hitting one URL and getting a response. More sophisticated apps will need more varied and diverse types of poking and prodding to ensure they've been completely exercised.

Note that according to the documents, we don't need to hit the app on port 32770 ourselves because we've used the http-probe argument. If you enable the HTTP probe, it will default to running an HTTP and HTTPS GET request on the root URL ("/") on every exposed port. We do the curl by hand simply for demonstration purposes.

At this point, you've created the sample-node-app.slim version of your image. If you examine the output of docker images, you can see that its size has been drastically reduced.

                                          The sample-node-app.slim
                                          image is just over 14 MB in size.
```
$ docker images
REPOSITORY            TAG        IMAGE ID        CREATED             SIZE
sample-node-app.slim  latest     7451554aa807    About an hour ago   14.02 MB  <
 sample-node-app      latest     78776db92c2a    About an hour ago   418.5 MB  <
```
                                          The original sample-node-app
                                          image was over 400 MB in size.

If you compare the docker history output of the fat sample app with its slim counterpart, you'll see that they're quite different in structure.

The docker history command is run on the sample-node-app image.

The history of this image shows each command as it was originally created.

```
$ docker history sample-node-app
 IMAGE          CREATED        CREATED BY                                    SIZE
 78776db92c2a   42 hours ago   /bin/sh -c #(nop)    ENTRYPOINT ["node"       0 B
 0f044b6540cd   42 hours ago   /bin/sh -c #(nop)    EXPOSE 8000/tcp          0 B
 555cf79f13e8   42 hours ago   /bin/sh -c npm install                        14.71 MB
 6c62e6b40d47   42 hours ago   /bin/sh -c #(nop)    WORKDIR /opt/my/ser      0 B
 7871fb6df03b   42 hours ago   /bin/sh -c #(nop) COPY dir:298f558c6f2        656 B
 618020744734   42 hours ago   /bin/sh -c apt-get update &&    apt-get       215.8 MB
 dea1945146b9   7 weeks ago    /bin/sh -c #(nop)    CMD ["/bin/bash"]        0 B
 <missing>      7 weeks ago    /bin/sh -c mkdir -p /run/systemd && ec        7 B
 <missing>      7 weeks ago    /bin/sh -c sed -i 's/^#\s*\(deb.*unive        2.753 kB
 <missing>      7 weeks ago    /bin/sh -c rm -rf /var/lib/apt/lists/*        0 B
 <missing>      7 weeks ago    /bin/sh -c set -xe   && echo '#!/bin/s        194.6 kB
 <missing>      7 weeks ago    /bin/sh -c #(nop) ADD file:8f997234193        187.8 MB
$ docker history sample-node-app.slim
 IMAGE          CREATED        CREATED BY                                    SIZE
 7451554aa807   42 hours ago   /bin/sh -c #(nop)    ENTRYPOINT ["node"       0 B
 2616067ec78d   42 hours ago   /bin/sh -c #(nop)    EXPOSE 8000/tcp          0 B
 4ef6d57d3230   42 hours ago   /bin/sh -c #(nop)    ENV PATH=/usr/local      0 B
 2d82f368c130   42 hours ago   /bin/sh -c #(nop)    WORKDIR /opt/my/ser      0 B
 0953a87c8e4f   42 hours ago   /bin/sh -c #(nop) COPY dir:36323da1e97        14.02 MB
```

The docker history command is run on the sample-node-app.slim image.

The history of the slim container consists of fewer commands, including a COPY command not in the original fat image.

The preceding output gives a clue about part of what DockerSlim does. It manages to reduce the image size to (effectively) a single 14 MB layer by taking the final filesystem state, and copying that directory as the final layer of the image.

The other artifact produced by DockerSlim relates to its second purpose as described at the beginning of this technique. A seccomp.json file is produced (in this case, sample-node-app-seccomp.json), which can be used to limit the actions of the running container.

Let's take a look at this file's contents (edited here, as it's rather long).

Listing 14.7   A seccomp profile

Specifies the exit code for the process that tries to call any forbidden syscall

Captures the location of the seccomp file in the variable SECCOMPFILE

```
$ SECCOMPFILE=$(ls $(pwd)/.images/*/artifacts/sample-node-app-seccomp.json)
$ cat ${SECCOMPFILE}
{
"defaultAction": "SCMP_ACT_ERRNO",
  "architectures": [
  "SCMP_ARCH_X86_64"
  ],
  "syscalls": [
    {
      "name": "capset",
```

Cats this file to view it

Specifies the hardware architectures this profile should be applied on

The syscalls controlled are whitelisted here by specifying the SCMP_ACT_ALLOW action against them.

```
      "action": "SCMP_ACT_ALLOW"
   },
   {
     "name": "rt_sigaction",
     "action": "SCMP_ACT_ALLOW"
   },
   {
     "name": "write",
     "action": "SCMP_ACT_ALLOW"
   },
 [...]
   {
     "name": "execve",
     "action": "SCMP_ACT_ALLOW"
   },
   {
     "name": "getcwd",
     "action": "SCMP_ACT_ALLOW"
   }
  ]
}
```

The syscalls controlled are whitelisted here by specifying the SCMP_ACT_ALLOW action against them.

Finally, you're going to run up the slim image again with the seccomp profile and check that it works as expected:

Runs the slim image as a daemon, exposing the same port that DockerSlim exposed in its analysis phase, and applies the seccomp profile to it

Outputs the container ID to the terminal

```
$ docker run -p32770:8000 -d \
--security-opt seccomp=/root/docker-slim-bin/.images/${IMAGEID}/artifacts
/sample-node-app-seccomp.json sample-node-app.slim
4107409b61a03c3422e07973248e564f11c6dc248a6a5753a1db8b4c2902df55
$ sleep 10 && curl localhost:32771
{"status":"success","info":"yes!!!","service":"node"}
```

The output is identical to the fat image you've slimmed.

Reruns the curl command to confirm the application still works as before

DISCUSSION

This simple example has shown how an image can be reduced not just in size, but also in the scope of the actions it can perform. This is achieved by removing inessential files (also discussed in technique 59), and reducing the syscalls available to it to only those that are needed to run the application.

The means of "exercising" the application here was simple (one `curl` request to the default endpoint). For a real application, there are a number of approaches you can take to ensure you've covered all the possibilities. One way is to develop a set of tests against known endpoints, and another is to use a "fuzzer" to throw lots of inputs at the application in an automated way (this is one way to find bugs and security flaws in your software). The simplest way is to leave your application running for a longer period of time in the expectation that all the needed files and system calls will be referenced.

Many enterprise Docker security tools work on this principle, but in a more automated way. Typically they allow an application to run for some time, and track which syscalls are made, which files are accessed, and also (possibly) which operating system capabilities are used. Based on this—and a configurable learning period—they can determine what the expected behavior of an application is, and report any behavior that seems to be out of line. For example, if an attacker gains access to a running container and starts up the bash binary or opens unexpected ports, this might raise an alarm on the system. DockerSlim allows you to take control over this process up-front, reducing what an attacker might be capable of doing even if they got access.

Another way to consider slimming your application's attack surface is to constrain its capabilities. This is covered in technique 93.

TECHNIQUE 98 Removing secrets added during a build

When you're building images in a corporate environment, it's often necessary to use keys and credentials to retrieve data. If you're using a Dockerfile to build an application, these secrets will generally be present in the history, even if you delete it after use.

This can be a security problem: if someone got hold of the image, they might also get hold of the secret in the earlier layers.

PROBLEM

You want to remove a file from an image's history.

SOLUTION

Use `docker-squash` to remove layers from the image.

There are simple ways to solve this problem that work in theory. For example, you might delete the secret while it's being used, as follows.

Listing 14.8 Crude method of not leaving a secret within a layer

```
FROM ubuntu
RUN echo mysecret > secretfile && command_using_secret && rm secretfile
```

This approach suffers from a number of disadvantages. It requires the secret to be put into code in the Dockerfile, so it may be in plain text in your source control.

To avoid this problem, you might add the file to your .gitignore (or similar) file in your source control, and ADD it to the image while it's being built. This adds the file in a separate layer, which can't easily be removed from the resulting image.

Finally, you could use environment variables to store secrets, but this also creates security risks, with these variables being easily set in non-secure persistent stores like Jenkins jobs. In any case, you may be presented with an image by a user and asked to scrub the secret from it. First we're going to demonstrate the problem with a simple example, and then we'll show you a way to remove the secret from the base layer.

AN IMAGE WITH A SECRET

The following Dockerfile will create an image using the file called secret_file as a placeholder for some secret data you've put in your image.

Listing 14.9 Simple Dockerfile with a secret

To save a bit of time, we override the default
command with a file listing command. This will
demonstrate whether the file is in the history.

```
FROM ubuntu
CMD ls /
    ADD /secret_file secret_file
    RUN cat /secret_file
    RUN rm /secret_file
```

Adds the secret file to the image build
(this must exist in your current working
directory along with the Dockerfile)

Uses the secret file as part of the build. In this case, we
use the trivial cat command to output the file, but this
could be a git clone or other more useful command.

Removes the secret file

Now you can build this image, calling the resulting image secret_build.

Listing 14.10 Building the simple Docker image with a secret

```
$ echo mysecret > secret_file
$ docker build -t secret_build .
Sending build context to Docker daemon  5.12 kB
Sending build context to Docker daemon
Step 0 : FROM ubuntu
 ---> 08881219da4a
Step 1 : CMD ls /
 ---> Running in 7864e2311699
 ---> 5b39a3cba0b0
Removing intermediate container 7864e2311699
Step 2 : ADD /secret_file secret_file
 ---> a00886ff1240
Removing intermediate container 4f279a2af398
Step 3 : RUN cat /secret_file
 ---> Running in 601fdf2659dd
My secret
 ---> 2a4238c53408
Removing intermediate container 601fdf2659dd
Step 4 : RUN rm /secret_file
 ---> Running in 240a4e57153b
 ---> b8a62a826ddf
Removing intermediate container 240a4e57153b
Successfully built b8a62a826ddf
```

Once the image is built, you can demonstrate that it has the secret file by using technique 27.

Listing 14.11   Tagging each step and demonstrating the layer with the secret

```
$ x=0; for id in $(docker history -q secret_build:latest);
⮑ do ((x++)); docker tag $id secret_build:step_$x; done       ◁
  $ docker run secret_build:step_3 cat /secret_file'      ◁
mysecret
```

Tags each step of the
build in numerical order

Demonstrates that the
secret file is in this tag
of the image

SQUASHING IMAGES TO REMOVE SECRETS

You've seen that secrets can remain in the history of images even if they're not in the final one. This is where `docker-squash` comes in—it removes the intervening layers but retains the Dockerfile commands (such as `CMD`, `PORT`, `ENV`, and so on) and the original base layer in your history.

The following listing downloads, installs, and uses `docker-squash` to compare the pre- and post-squashed images.

Listing 14.12   Using `docker_squash` to reduce layers of an image

Installs docker-squash. (You may need to refer
to https://github.com/jwilder/docker-squash for
the latest installation instructions.)

Saves the image to a TAR file that docker-squash
operates on, and then loads the resulting image in,
tagging it as "secret_build_squashed"

```
$ wget -qO- https://github.com/jwilder/docker-squash/releases/download
⮑ /v0.2.0/docker-squash-linux-amd64-v0.2.0.tar.gz | \
  tar -zxvf - && mv docker-squash /usr/local/bin
  $ docker save secret_build:latest | \
    docker-squash -t secret_build_squashed | \
    docker load
  $ docker history secret_build_squashed
  IMAGE          CREATED         CREATED BY                          SIZE
  ee41518cca25   2 seconds ago   /bin/sh -c #(nop) CMD ["/bin/sh" "  0 B
  b1c283b3b20a   2 seconds ago   /bin/sh -c #(nop)  CMD ["/bin/bash  0 B
  f443d173e026   2 seconds ago   /bin/sh -c #(squash) from 93c22f56  2.647 kB
  93c22f563196   2 weeks ago     /bin/sh -c #(nop) ADD file:7529d28  128.9 MB
  $ docker history secret_build
  IMAGE          CREATED         CREATED BY                          SIZE
  b8a62a826ddf   3 seconds ago   /bin/sh -c rm /secret_file          0 B
  2a4238c53408   3 seconds ago   /bin/sh -c cat /secret_file         0 B
  a00886ff1240   9 seconds ago   /bin/sh -c #(nop) ADD file:69e77f6  10 B
  5b39a3cba0b0   9 seconds ago   /bin/sh -c #(nop) CMD ["/bin/sh" "  0 B
  08881219da4a   2 weeks ago     /bin/sh -c #(nop)  CMD ["/bin/bash  0 B
  6a4ec4bddc58   2 weeks ago     /bin/sh -c mkdir -p /run/systemd &  7 B
  98697477f76a   2 weeks ago     /bin/sh -c sed -i 's/^#\s*\(deb.*u  1.895 kB
  495ec797e6ba   2 weeks ago     /bin/sh -c rm -rf /var/lib/apt/lis  0 B
  e3aa81f716f6   2 weeks ago     /bin/sh -c set -xe && echo '#!/bin  745 B
  93c22f563196   2 weeks ago     /bin/sh -c #(nop) ADD file:7529d28  128.9 MB
  $ docker run secret_build_squashed ls /secret_file
  ls: cannot access '/secret_file': No such file or directory
  $ docker run f443d173e026 ls /secret_file
  ls: cannot access '/secret_file': No such file or directory
```

The history of the squashed image
has no record of secret_file.

The origin image has the secret_file still in it.

Demonstrates that the secret_file
is not in the squashed image

Demonstrates that the secret_file is not in the
squashed image's "squashed" layer

A NOTE ON "MISSING" IMAGE LAYERS

Docker changed the nature of layering in Docker 1.10. From that point on, images downloaded show up as "<missing>" in the history. This is expected and is because of changes made by Docker to improve the security of images' histories.

You can still get the contents of layers you've downloaded by docker saveing the image and then extracting the TAR files from within that TAR file. Here's an example session that does that for the already-downloaded Ubuntu image.

Listing 14.13 "Missing" layers in downloaded images

Uses the docker save command to output a TAR file of the image layers, which is piped straight to tar and extracted

Uses the docker history command to show the layer history of the Ubuntu image

```
$ docker history ubuntu
IMAGE           CREATED        CREATED BY                            SIZE
104bec311bcd    2 weeks ago    /bin/sh -c #(nop)  CMD ["/bin/bash"]  0 B
<missing>       2 weeks ago    /bin/sh -c mkdir -p /run/systemd && ech  7 B
<missing>       2 weeks ago    /bin/sh -c sed -i 's/^#\s*\(deb.*univer  1.9 kB
<missing>       2 weeks ago    /bin/sh -c rm -rf /var/lib/apt/lists/*   0 B
<missing>       2 weeks ago    /bin/sh -c set -xe   && echo '#!/bin/sh  745 B
<missing>       2 weeks ago    /bin/sh -c #(nop) ADD file:7529d28035b4  129 MB
$ docker save ubuntu | tar -xf -
$ find . | grep tar$
./042e55060780206b2ceabe277a8beb9b10f48262a876fd21b495af318f2f2352/layer.tar
./1037e0a8442d212d5cc63d1bc706e0e82da0eaafd62a2033959cfc629f874b28/layer.tar
./25f649b30070b739bc2aa3dd877986bee4de30e43d6260b8872836cdf549fcfc/layer.tar
./3094e87864d918dfdb2502e3f5dc61ae40974cd957d5759b80f6df37e0e467e4/layer.tar
./41b8111724ab7cb6246c929857b0983a016f11346dcb25a551a778ef0cd8af20/layer.tar
./4c3b7294fe004590676fa2c27a9a952def0b71553cab4305aeed4d06c3b308ea/layer.tar
./5d1be8e6ec27a897e8b732c40911dcc799b6c043a8437149ab021ff713e1044f/layer.tar
./a594214bea5ead6d6774f7a09dbd7410d652f39cc4eba5c8571d5de3bcbe0057/layer.tar
./b18fcc335f7aeefd87c9d43db2888bf6ea0ac12645b7d2c33300744c770bcec7/layer.tar
./d899797a09bfcc6cb8e8a427bb358af546e7c2b18bf8e2f7b743ec36837b42f2/layer.tar
./ubuntu.tar
$ tar -tvf
./4c3b7294fe004590676fa2c27a9a952def0b71553cab4305aeed4d06c3b308ea
/layer.tar
drwxr-xr-x  0 0        0           0 15 Dec 17:45 etc/
drwxr-xr-x  0 0        0           0 15 Dec 17:45 etc/apt/
-rw-r--r--  0 0        0        1895 15 Dec 17:45 etc/apt/sources.list
```

Demonstrates that the TAR files contain only file changes within that layer

---

DISCUSSION

Although somewhat similar in intent to technique 52, the use of a specialized tool has some notable differences in the end result. In the preceding solution, you can see that metadata layers like CMD have been preserved, whereas the previous technique on this subject would discard them entirely, so you'd need to manually recreate those metadata layers through another Dockerfile.

This behavior means the docker-squash utility could be used to automatically clean up images as they arrive in a registry, if you're inclined not to trust your users to use secret data correctly within image builds—they should all work normally.

That said, you should be wary of your users putting secrets in any metadata layers—environment variables in particular are a threat and may well be preserved in the final image.

TECHNIQUE 99   OpenShift: An application platform as a service

OpenShift is a product managed by Red Hat that allows an organization to run an application platform as a service (aPaas). It offers application development teams a platform on which to run code without needing to be concerned about hardware details. Version 3 of the product was a ground-up rewrite in Go, with Docker as the container technology and Kubernetes and etcd for orchestration. On top of this, Red Hat has added enterprise features that enable it to be more easily deployed in a corporate and security-focused environment.

Although OpenShift has many features we could cover, we'll use it here as a means of managing security by taking away the user's ability to run Docker directly, but retaining the benefits of using Docker.

OpenShift is available both as an enterprise-supported product, and as an open source project called Origin, maintained at https://github.com/openshift/origin.

PROBLEM
You want to manage the security risk of untrusted users invoking `docker run`.

SOLUTION
Use an aPaaS tool to manage and mediate the interaction with Docker via a proxying interface.

An aPaaS has many benefits, but the one we'll focus on here is its ability to manage user permissions and run Docker containers on the user's behalf, providing a secure audit point for users running Docker containers.

Why is this important? The users using this aPaaS have no direct access to the `docker` command, so they can't do any damage without subverting the security that OpenShift provides. For example, containers are deployed by non-root users by default, and overcoming this requires permission to be granted by an administrator. If you can't trust your users, using an aPaaS is a effective way of giving them access to Docker.

> **TIP** An aPaaS provides users with the ability to spin up applications on demand for development, testing, or production. Docker is a natural fit for these services, as it provides a reliable and isolated application delivery format, allowing an operations team to take care of the details of deployment.

In short, OpenShift builds on Kubernetes (see technique 88) but adds features to deliver a full-fledged aPaaS. These additional features include

- User management
- Permissioning
- Quotas
- Security contexts
- Routing

INSTALLING OPENSHIFT

A complete overview of OpenShift installation is beyond the scope of this book. If you'd like an automated install, using Vagrant, that we maintain, see https://github.com/docker-in-practice/shutit-openshift-origin. If you need help installing Vagrant, see appendix C.

Other options, such as a Docker-only installation (single-node only), or a full manual build are available and documented on the OpenShift Origin codebase at https://github.com/openshift/origin.git.

> **TIP** OpenShift Origin is the upstream version of OpenShift. *Upstream* means that it's the codebase from which Red Hat takes changes for OpenShift, its supported offering. Origin is open source and can be used and contributed to by anyone, but Red Hat's curated version of it is sold and supported as OpenShift. An upstream version is usually more cutting edge but less stable.

AN OPENSHIFT APPLICATION

In this technique we're going to show a simple example of creating, building, running, and accessing an application using the OpenShift web interface. The application will be a basic NodeJS application that serves a simple web page.

The application will use Docker, Kubernetes, and S2I under the hood. Docker is used to encapsulate the build and deployment environments. The Source to Image (S2I) build method is a technique used by Red Hat in OpenShift to build the Docker container, and Kubernetes is used to run the application on the OpenShift cluster.

LOGGING IN

To get started, run `./run.sh` from the shutit-openshift-origin folder, and then navigate to https://localhost:8443, bypassing all the security warnings. You'll see the login page shown in figure 14.3. Note that if you're using the Vagrant install, you'll need to start up a web browser in your VM. (See appendix C for help on getting a GUI with your VM.)

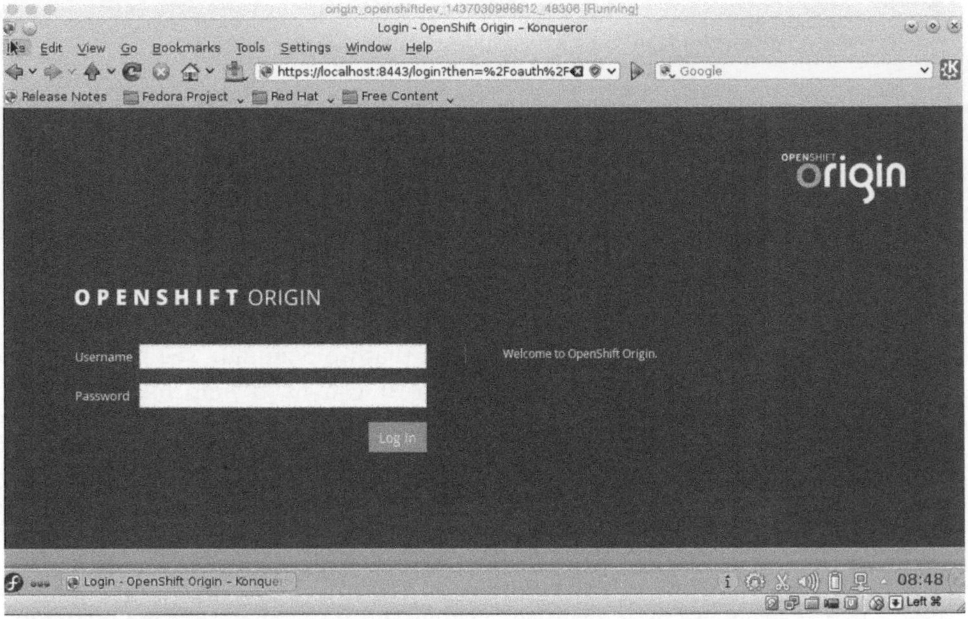

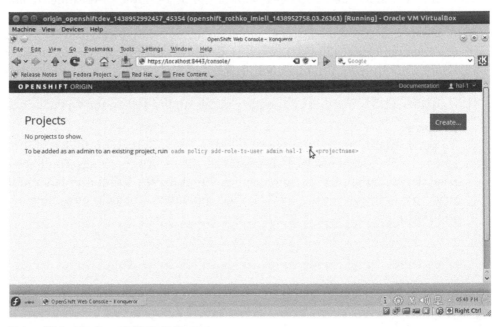

Figure 14.3   The OpenShift login page

Log in as `hal-1` with any password.

BUILDING A NODEJS APP

You're now logged into OpenShift as a developer (see figure 14.4).

Figure 14.4   The OpenShift Projects page

Create a project by clicking Create. Fill out the form, as shown in figure 14.5. Then click Create again.

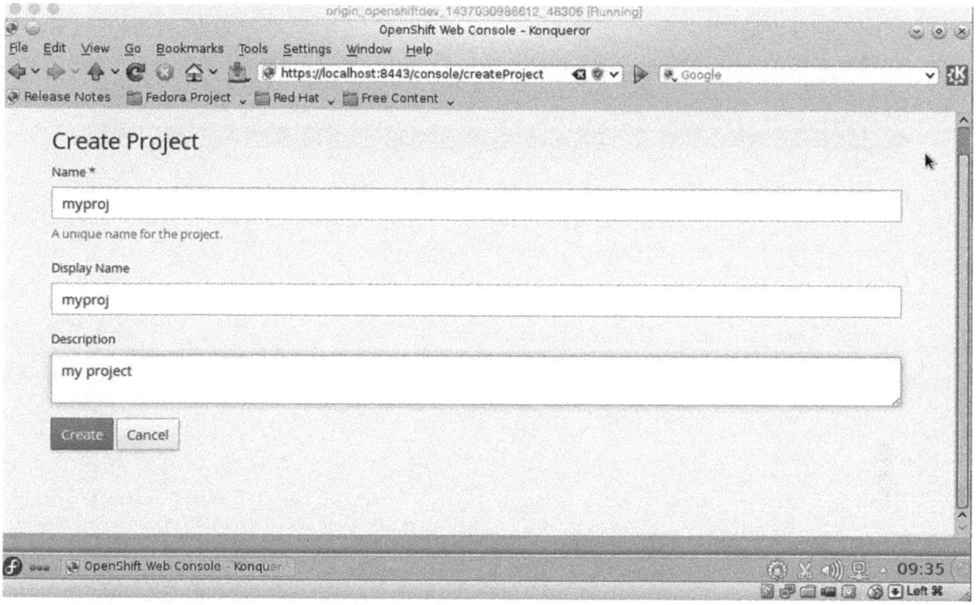

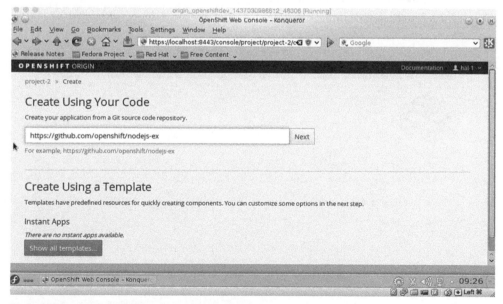

Figure 14.5 The OpenShift project-creation page

Once the project is set up, click Create again and input the suggested GitHub repo (https://github.com/openshift/nodejs-ex), as shown in figure 14.6.

Figure 14.6 The OpenShift project source page

Click Next, and you'll be given a choice of builder images, as shown in figure 14.7. The build image defines the context in which the code will be built. Choose the NodeJS builder image.

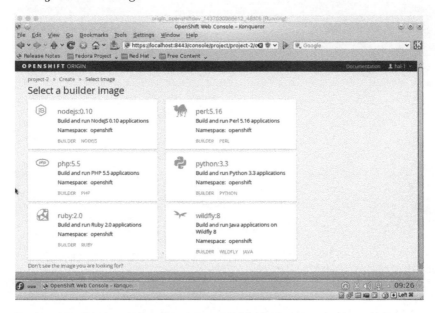

Figure 14.7   The OpenShift builder-image selection page

Now fill out the form, as shown in figure 14.8. Click Create on NodeJS at the bottom of the page as you scroll down the form.

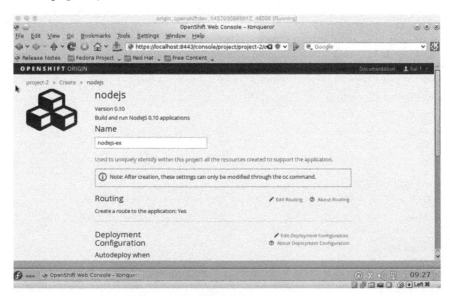

Figure 14.8   The OpenShift NodeJS template form

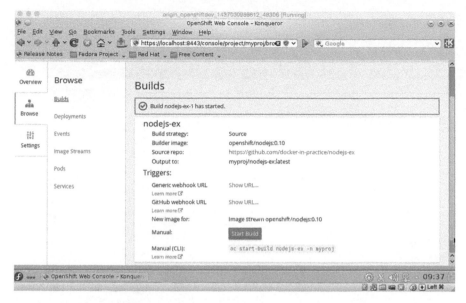

Figure 14.9   The OpenShift build-started page

After a few minutes, you should see a screen like the one in figure 14.9.

In a few moments, if you scroll down, you'll see that the build has started, as shown in figure 14.10.

TIP   In early versions of OpenShift, the build would sometimes not begin automatically. If this is the case, click the Start Build button after a few minutes.

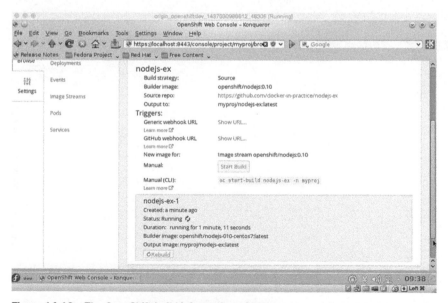

Figure 14.10   The OpenShift build-information window

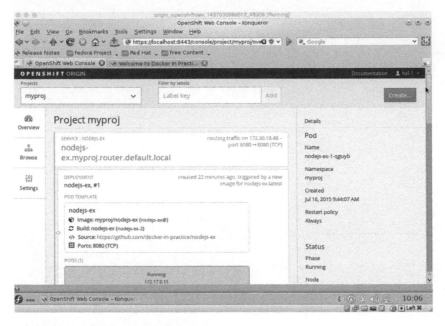

Figure 14.11   Application-running page

After some time you'll see that the app is running, as in figure 14.11.

By clicking Browse and Pods, you can see that the pod has been deployed, as in figure 14.12.

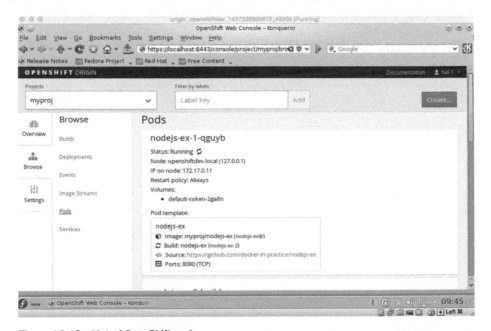

Figure 14.12   List of OpenShift pods

TIP   See technique 88 for an explanation of what a pod is.

How do you access your pod? If you look at the Services tab (see figure 14.13), you'll see an IP address and port number to access.

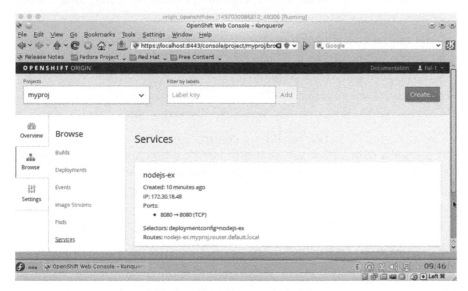

Figure 14.13   The OpenShift NodeJS application service details

Point your browser at that address, and voila, you'll have your NodeJS app, as in figure 14.14.

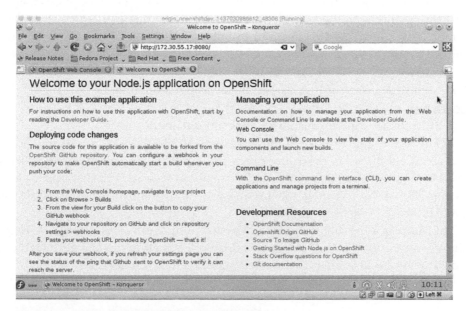

Figure 14.14   The NodeJS application landing page

DISCUSSION

Let's recap what we've achieved here, and why it's important for security.

From the point of view of the user, they logged into a web application and deployed an application using Docker-based technologies without going near a Dockerfile or the `docker run` command.

The administrator of OpenShift can

- Control user access
- Limit resource use by project
- Provision resources centrally
- Ensure code is run with non-privileged status by default

This is far more secure than giving users direct access to `docker run`.

If you want to build on this application and see how an aPaaS facilitates an iterative approach, you can fork the Git repository, change the code in that forked repository, and then create a new application. We've done that here: https://github.com/docker-in-practice/nodejs-ex.

To read more about OpenShift, go to http://www.openshift.org.

TECHNIQUE 100   **Using security options**

You've already seen in previous techniques how, by default, you're given root in the Docker container, and that this user is the same root as the root user on the host. To alleviate this, we've shown you how this user can have its capabilities as root reduced, so that even if it escapes the container, there are still actions the kernel won't allow this user to perform.

But you can go further than this. By using Docker's security-options flag you can protect resources on the host from being affected by actions performed within a container. This constrains the container to only affecting resources it has been given permission to by the host.

PROBLEM

You want to secure your host against the actions of containers.

SOLUTION

Use SELinux to impose constraints on your containers.

Here we're going to use SELinux as our kernel-supported mandatory access control (MAC) tool. SELinux is more or less the industry standard and is most likely to be used by organizations that particularly care about security. It was originally developed by the NSA to protect their systems and was subsequently open-sourced. It's used in Red Hat–based systems as a standard.

SELinux is a big subject, so we can't cover it in depth in this book. We're going to show you how to write and enforce a simple policy so that you can get a feel for how it works. You can take things further and experiment if you need to.

TIP Mandatory access control (MAC) tools in Linux enforce security rules beyond the standard ones you may be used to. Put briefly, they ensure that not only are the *normal* rules of read-write-execute on files and processes enforced, but more fine-grained rules can be applied to processes at the kernel level. For example, a MySQL process may only be allowed to write files under specific directories, such as /var/lib/mysql. The equivalent standard for Debian-based systems is AppArmor.

This technique assumes you have a SELinux-enabled host. This means you must first install SELinux (assuming it's not already installed). If you're running Fedora or some other Red Hat–based system, you likely have it already.

To determine whether you have SELinux enabled, run the command `sestatus`:

```
# sestatus
SELinux status:                 enabled
SELinuxfs mount:                /sys/fs/selinux
SELinux root directory:         /etc/selinux
Loaded policy name:             targeted
Current mode:                   permissive
Mode from config file:          permissive
Policy MLS status:              enabled
Policy deny_unknown status:     allowed
Max kernel policy version:      28
```

The first line of the output will tell you whether SELinux is enabled. If the command isn't available, you don't have SELinux installed on your host.

You'll also need to have the relevant SELinux policy-creation tools available. On a yum-capable machine, for example, you'll need to run `yum -y install selinux-policy -devel`.

SELINUX ON A VAGRANT MACHINE

If you don't have SELinux and want it to be built for you, you can use a ShutIt script to build a VM inside your host machine, with Docker and SELinux preinstalled. What it does is explained at a high level in figure 14.15.

Linux host machine

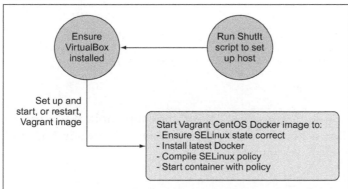

Figure 14.15   Script to provision a SELinux VM

TIP ShutIt is a generic shell automation tool that we created to overcome some limitations of Dockerfiles. If you want to read more about it, see the GitHub page: http://ianmiell.github.io/shutit.

Figure 14.5 identifies the steps required to get a policy set up. The script will do the following:

1 Set up VirtualBox
2 Start an appropriate Vagrant image
3 Log into the VM
4 Ensure the state of SELinux is correct
5 Install the latest version of Docker
6 Install the SELinux policy development tools
7 Give you a shell

Here are the commands to set up and run it (tested on Debian and Red Hat–based distributions):

Listing 14.14   Installing ShutIt

Ensures the required packages are installed on the host

Ensures you are root before starting the run

Clones the SELinux ShutIt script and enters its directory

Installs ShutIt

Configures the script to not compile a SELinux policy, as we'll do this by hand

Runs the ShutIt script. "--delivery bash" means commands are executed in bash rather than via SSH or in a Docker container.

```
sudo su -
 apt-get install -y git python-pip docker.io || \
yum install -y git python-pip docker.io
 pip install shutit
 git clone https://github.com/ianmiell/docker-selinux.git
 cd docker-selinux
 shutit build --delivery bash \
 -s io.dockerinpractice.docker_selinux.docker_selinux \
   compile_policy no
```

After running this script, you should eventually see output like this:

```
Pause point:
Have a shell:
You can now type in commands and alter the state of the target.
Hit return to see the prompt
Hit CTRL and ] at the same time to continue with build

Hit CTRL and u to save the state
```

You now have a shell running inside a VM with SELinux on it. If you type `sestatus`, you'll see that SELinux is enabled in permissive mode (as shown in listing 14.14). To return to your host's shell, press Ctrl-].

COMPILING AN SELINUX POLICY

Whether you used the ShutIt script or not, we assume you now have a host with SELinux enabled. Type `sestatus` to get a status summary.

Listing 14.15   SELinux status once installed and enabled

```
# sestatus
SELinux status:               enabled
SELinuxfs mount:              /sys/fs/selinux
SELinux root directory:       /etc/selinux
Loaded policy name:           targeted
Current mode:                 permissive
Mode from config file:        permissive
Policy MLS status:            enabled
Policy deny_unknown status:   allowed
Max kernel policy version:    28
```

In this case, we're in permissive mode, which means that SELinux is recording violations of security in logs, but isn't enforcing them. This is good for safely testing new policies without rendering your system unusable. To move your SELinux status to permissive, type `setenforce Permissive` as root. If you can't do this on your host for security reasons, don't worry; there's an option to set the policy as permissive outlined in listing 14.15.

> **NOTE** If you're installing SELinux and Docker yourself on a host, ensure that the Docker daemon has `--selinux-enabled` set as a flag. You can check this with `ps -ef | grep 'docker -d.*--selinux-enabled`, which should return a matching process on the output.

Create a folder for your policy and move to it. Then create a policy file with the following content as root, named docker_apache.te. This policy file contains a policy we'll try to apply.

Listing 14.16   Creating a SELinux policy

Creates a folder to store the policy files, and moves into it

Creates the policy file that will be compiled as a "here" document

```
mkdir -p /root/httpd_selinux_policy && >
cd /root/httpd_selinux_policy
cat > docker_apache.te << END
policy_module(docker_apache,1.0)
virt_sandbox_domain_template(docker_apache)
allow docker_apache_t self: capability { chown dac_override kill setgid >
setuid net_bind_service sys_chroot sys_nice >
sys_tty_config } ;
```

Creates the SELinux policy module docker_apache with the policy_module directive

The Apache web server requires these capabilities to run; adds them here with the allow directive.

Uses the provided template to create the docker_apache_t SELinux type, which can be run as a Docker container. This template gives the docker_apache SELinux domain the fewest privileges required to run. We'll add to these privileges to make a useful container environment.

```
 allow docker_apache_t self:tcp_socket >
create_stream_socket_perms;
 allow docker_apache_t self:udp_socket >
create_socket_perms;
 corenet_tcp_bind_all_nodes(docker_apache_t)
 corenet_tcp_bind_http_port(docker_apache_t)
 corenet_udp_bind_all_nodes(docker_apache_t)
 corenet_udp_bind_http_port(docker_apache_t)
 sysnet_dns_name_resolve(docker_apache_t)
 #permissive docker_apache_t
 END
```

These allow and corenet rules give permission for the container to listen to Apache ports on the network.

Allows DNS server resolution with the sysnet directive

Terminates the "here" document, which writes it out to disk

Optionally makes the docker_apache_t type permissive so this policy isn't enforced even if the host is enforcing SELinux. Use this if you can't set the SELinux mode of the host.

TIP For more information about the preceding permissions, and to explore others, you can install the selinux-policy-doc package and use a browser to browse the documentation on file:///usr/share/doc-base/selinux-policy-doc/html/index.html. The docs are also available online at http://oss.tresys.com/docs/refpolicy/api/.

Now you're going to compile this policy and see your application fail to start against this policy in enforcing mode. Then you'll restart it in permissive mode to check the violations and correct it later:

Compiles the docker_apache.te file to a binary SELinux module with a .pp suffix

```
$ make -f /usr/share/selinux/devel/Makefile \
docker_apache.te
 Compiling targeted docker_apache module
/usr/bin/checkmodule:  loading policy configuration from >
tmp/docker_apache.tmp
/usr/bin/checkmodule:  policy configuration loaded
/usr/bin/checkmodule:  writing binary representation (version 17) >
to tmp/docker_apache.mod
Creating targeted docker_apache.pp policy package
rm tmp/docker_apache.mod tmp/docker_apache.mod.fc
$ semodule -i docker_apache.pp
 $ setenforce Enforcing
 $ docker run -ti --name selinuxdock >
--security-opt label:type:docker_apache_t httpd
 Unable to find image 'httpd:latest' locally
latest: Pulling from library/httpd
2a341c7141bd: Pull complete
[...]
Status: Downloaded newer image for httpd:latest
permission denied
Error response from daemon: Cannot start container >
650c446b20da6867e6e13bdd6ab53f3ba3c3c565abb56c4490b487b9e8868985: >
[8] System error: permission denied
$ docker rm -f selinuxdock
 selinuxdock
```

Installs the module

Sets the SELinux mode to "enforcing"

Runs the httpd image as a daemon, applying the security label type of docker_apache_t you defined in the SELinux module. This command should fail because it violates the SELinux security configuration.

Removes the newly created container

```
$ setenforce Permissive
 $ docker run -d --name selinuxdock >
--security-opt label:type:docker_apache_t httpd
```

Sets the SELinux mode to
"permissive" to allow the
application to start up

Runs the httpd image as a daemon, applying the security
label type of docker_apache_t you defined in the SELinux
module. This command should run successfully.

CHECKING FOR VIOLATIONS

Up to this point you've created a SELinux module and applied it to your host.
Because the enforcement mode of SELinux is set to permissive on this host, actions
that would be disallowed in enforcing mode are allowed with a log line in the audit
log. You can check these messages by running the following command:

The type of message in the audit log is always
AVC for SELinux violations, and timestamps are
given as the number of seconds since the epoch
(which is defined as lst Jan 1970).

The type of action denied is
shown in the curly brackets.

The process ID and name of the
command that triggered the violation

The path, device, and
inode of the target file

```
$ grep -w denied /var/log/audit/audit.log
type=AVC msg=audit(1433073250.049:392): avc:  >
 denied { transition } for >
 pid=2379 comm="docker" >
 path="/usr/local/bin/httpd-foreground" dev="dm-1" ino=530204 >
 scontext=system_u:system_r:init_t:s0 >
 tcontext=system_u:system_r:docker_apache_t:s0:c740,c787 >
 tclass=process
  type=AVC msg=audit(1433073250.049:392): avc:  denied { write } for  >
 pid=2379 comm="httpd-foregroun" path="pipe:[19550]" dev="pipefs" >
 ino=19550 scontext=system_u:system_r:docker_apache_t:s0:c740,c787 >
 tcontext=system_u:system_r:init_t:s0 tclass=fifo_file
 type=AVC msg=audit(1433073250.236:394): avc:  denied { append } for  >
 pid=2379 comm="httpd" dev="pipefs" ino=19551 >
 scontext=system_u:system_r:docker_apache_t:s0:c740,c787 >
 tcontext=system_u:system_r:init_t:s0 tclass=fifo_file
 type=AVC msg=audit(1433073250.236:394): avc:  denied { open } for  >
 pid=2379 comm="httpd" path="pipe:[19551]" dev="pipefs" ino=19551 >
 scontext=system_u:system_r:docker_apache_t:s0:c740,c787 >
 tcontext=system_u:system_r:init_t:s0 tclass=fifo_file
 [...]
```

The SELinux context of the target

The class of the target object

Phew! There's a lot of jargon there, and we don't have time to teach you everything you
might need to know about SELinux. If you want to find out more, a good place to start is
with Red Hat's SELinux documentation: https://access.redhat.com/documentation/
en-US/Red_Hat_Enterprise_Linux/5/html/Deployment_Guide/ch-selinux.html.

For now, you need to check that the violations are nothing untoward. What might
look untoward? If an application tries to open a port or a file you didn't expect, you
might think twice about doing what we'll show you next: patch these violations with a
new SELinux module.

In this case, we're happy that the httpd can write pipes. We've worked out that this is what SELinux was preventing because the "denied" actions mentioned are append, write, and open for pipefs files on the VM.

PATCHING SELINUX VIOLATIONS

Once you've decided that the violations you've seen are acceptable, there are tools that can automatically generate the policy file you need to apply, so you don't need to go through the pain and risk of writing one yourself. The following example uses the audit2allow tool to achieve this.

Listing 14.17   Creating a new SELinux policy

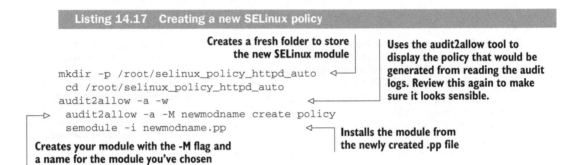

Creates a fresh folder to store the new SELinux module

Uses the audit2allow tool to display the policy that would be generated from reading the audit logs. Review this again to make sure it looks sensible.

```
mkdir -p /root/selinux_policy_httpd_auto
 cd /root/selinux_policy_httpd_auto
audit2allow -a -w
 audit2allow -a -M newmodname create policy
 semodule -i newmodname.pp
```

Creates your module with the -M flag and a name for the module you've chosen

Installs the module from the newly created .pp file

It's important to understand that this new SELinux module we've created "includes" (or "requires") and alters the one we created before by referencing and adding permissions to the docker_apache_t type. You can combine the two into a complete and discrete policy in a single .te file if you choose.

TESTING YOUR NEW MODULE

Now that you have your new module installed, you can try re-enabling SELinux and restarting the container.

> **TIP** If you couldn't set your host to permissive earlier (and you added the hashed-out line to your original docker_apache.te file), then recompile and reinstall the original docker_apache.te file (with the permissive line hashed-out) before continuing.

Listing 14.18   Starting a container with SELinux restrictions

```
docker rm -f selinuxdock
setenforce Enforcing
docker run -d --name selinuxdock \
--security-opt label:type:docker_apache_t httpd
docker logs selinuxdock
grep -w denied /var/log/audit/audit.log
```

There should be no new errors in the audit log. Your application has started within the context of this SELinux regime.

DISCUSSION

SELinux has a reputation for being complex and hard to manage, with the most frequently heard complaint being that it's more often switched off than debugged. That's hardly secure at all. Although the finer points of SELinux do require serious effort to master, we hope this technique has shown you how to create something that a security expert can review—and ideally sign off on—if Docker isn't acceptable out of the box.

Summary

- You can granularly control the power of root within your containers with capabilities.
- You can authenticate people using your Docker API via HTTP.
- Docker has built-in support for API encryption using certificates.
- SELinux is a well-tested way to reduce the danger of containers running as root.
- An application platform as a service (aPaaS) can be used to control access to the Docker runtime.

15

Plain sailing: Running Docker in production

This chapter covers

- Your options for logging container output
- Monitoring your running containers
- Managing your containers' resource usage
- Using Docker's capabilities to help manage traditional sysadmin tasks

In this chapter we're going to cover some of the subjects that come up when running in production. Running Docker in production is a big subject, and production use of Docker is still an evolving area. Many major tools are in the early stages of development and were changing as we wrote this book's first and second editions.

In this chapter we'll focus on showing you some of the key things you should consider when going from volatile environments to stable ones.

15.1   Monitoring

When you run Docker in production, one of the first things you'll want to consider is how to track and measure what your containers are up to. In this section you're going to learn how you can get an operational view of both your live containers' logging activity and their performance.

This is still a developing aspect of the Docker ecosystem, but some tools and techniques are emerging as more mainstream than others. We'll look at redirecting application logs to the host's syslog, at redirecting the output of the `docker logs` command to a single place, and at Google's container-oriented performance monitoring tool, cAdvisor.

TECHNIQUE 101   **Logging your containers to the host's syslog**

Linux distributions typically run a syslog daemon. This daemon is the server part of the system-logging functionality—applications send messages to this daemon, along with metadata like the importance of the message, and the daemon will decide where to save the message (if at all). This functionality is used by a range of applications, from network connection managers to the kernel itself dumping information if it encounters an error.

Because it's so reliable and widely used, it's reasonable for applications you write yourself to log to syslog. Unfortunately, this will stop working once you containerize your application (because there's no syslog daemon in containers, by default). If you do decide to start a syslog daemon in all of your containers, you'll need to go to each individual container to retrieve the logs.

PROBLEM

You want to capture syslogs centrally on your Docker host.

SOLUTION

Run a service container that acts as the syslog daemon for Docker containers.

The basic idea of this technique is to run a service container that runs a syslog daemon, and share the logging touchpoint (/dev/log) via the host's filesystem. The log itself can be retrieved by querying the syslog Docker container, and it's stored in a volume.

Figure 15.1 illustrates how /tmp/syslogdev on the host's filesystem can be used as a touchpoint for all syslogging taking place on containers on the host. The logging containers mount and write their syslog to that location, and the syslogger container collates all those inputs.

> **TIP**   The syslog daemon is a process that runs on a server, collecting and managing messages sent to a central file, which is normally a Unix domain socket. It generally uses /dev/log as a file to receive log messages, and it logs out to /var/log/syslog.

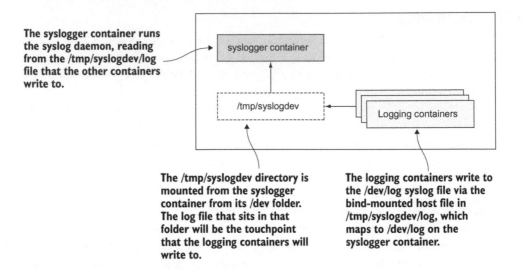

The syslogger container runs the syslog daemon, reading from the /tmp/syslogdev/log file that the other containers write to.

The /tmp/syslogdev directory is mounted from the syslogger container from its /dev folder. The log file that sits in that folder will be the touchpoint that the logging containers will write to.

The logging containers write to the /dev/log syslog file via the bind-mounted host file in /tmp/syslogdev/log, which maps to /dev/log on the syslogger container.

Figure 15.1   Overview of centralized syslogging of Docker containers

The syslogger container can be created with this straightforward Dockerfile.

Listing 15.1   Building a syslogger container

Creates the /dev volume to share with other containers

Installs the rsyslog package, which makes the rsyslogd daemon program available. The "r" stands for "reliable."

```
FROM ubuntu:14.043
RUN apt-get update && apt-get install rsyslog
VOLUME /dev
VOLUME /var/log
CMD rsyslogd -n
```

Creates the /var/log volume to allow the syslog file to persist

Runs the rsyslogd process on startup

Next, you build the container, tagging it with the syslogger tag, and run it:

```
docker build -t syslogger .
docker run --name syslogger -d -v /tmp/syslogdev:/dev syslogger
```

You bind-mounted the container's /dev folder to the host's /tmp/syslogdev folder so you can mount a /dev/log socket into each container as a volume, as you'll see shortly. The container will continue running in the background, reading any messages from the /dev/log file and handling them.

On the host, you'll now see that the /dev folder of the syslog container has been mounted to the host's /tmp/syslogdev folder:

```
$ ls -1 /tmp/syslogdev/
fd
full
fuse
kcore
```

```
log
null
ptmx
random
stderr
stdin
stdout
tty
urandom
zero
```

For this demonstration, we're going to start up 100 daemon containers that log their own starting order from 0 to 100 to the syslog, using the `logger` command. Then you'll be able to see those messages by running a `docker exec` on the host to look at the syslogger container's syslog file.

First, start up the containers.

> **Listing 15.2   Starting up the logger containers**

```
for d in {1..100}
do
    docker run -d -v /tmp/syslogdev/log:/dev/log ubuntu logger hello_$d
done
```

The preceding volume mount links the container's syslog endpoint (/dev/log) to the host's /tmp/syslogdev/log file, which in turn is mapped to the syslogger container's /dev/log file. With this wiring, all syslog outputs are sent to the same file.

When that's complete, you'll see something similar to this (edited) output:

```
$ docker exec -ti syslogger tail -f /var/log/syslog
May 25 11:51:25 f4fb5d829699 logger: hello
May 25 11:55:15 f4fb5d829699 logger: hello_1
May 25 11:55:15 f4fb5d829699 logger: hello_2
May 25 11:55:16 f4fb5d829699 logger: hello_3
[...]
May 25 11:57:38 f4fb5d829699 logger: hello_97
May 25 11:57:38 f4fb5d829699 logger: hello_98
May 25 11:57:39 f4fb5d829699 logger: hello_99
```

You can use a modified exec command to archive these syslogs if you wish. For example, you could run the following command to get all logs for hour 11 on May 25th archived to a compressed file:

```
$ docker exec syslogger bash -c "cat /var/log/syslog | \
grep '^May 25 11'" | xz - > /var/log/archive/May25_11.log.xz
```

> **NOTE**   For the messages to show up in the central syslog container, your programs need to log to syslog. We ensure this here by running the `logger` command, but your applications should do the same for this to work. Most modern logging methods have a means to write to the locally visible syslog.

DISCUSSION

You may be wondering how you can distinguish between different containers' log messages with this technique. Here you have a couple of options. You can change the application's logging to output the hostname of the container, or you can see the next technique to have Docker do this heavy lifting for you.

> **NOTE**   This technique looks similar to the next one, which uses a Docker syslog driver, but it's different. This technique keeps the output of containers' running processes as the output of the `docker logs` command, whereas the next one takes over the `logs` command, rendering this technique redundant.

TECHNIQUE 102   Logging your Docker logs output

As you've seen, Docker offers a basic logging system that captures the output of your container's start command. If you're a system administrator running many services off one host, it can be operationally tiresome to manually track and capture logs using the `docker logs` command on each container in turn.

In this technique, we're going to cover Docker's log driver feature. This lets you use the standard logging systems to track many services on a single host, or even across multiple hosts.

PROBLEM

You want to capture `docker logs` output centrally on your Docker host.

SOLUTION

Use the `--log-driver` flag to redirect logs to the desired location.

By default, Docker logs are captured within the Docker daemon, and you can access these with the `docker logs` command. As you're probably aware, this shows you the output of the container's main process.

At the time of writing, Docker gives you several choices for redirecting this output to multiple *log drivers*, including

- syslog
- journald
- json-file

The default is json-file, but others can be chosen with the `--log-driver` flag. The syslog and journald options send the log output to their respective daemons of the same name. You can find the official documentation on all available log drivers at https://docs.docker.com/engine/reference/logging/.

> **WARNING**   This technique requires Docker version 1.6.1 or higher.

The syslog daemon is a process that runs on a server, collecting and managing messages sent to a central file (normally a Unix domain socket). It generally uses /dev/log as a file to receive log messages on, and logs out to /var/log/syslog.

Journald is a system service that collects and stores logging data. It creates and maintains a structured index of logs received from a variety of sources. The logs can be queried with the `journalctl` command.

LOGGING TO SYSLOG
To direct your output to the syslog, use the `--log-driver` flag:

```
$ docker run --log-driver=syslog ubuntu echo 'outputting to syslog'
outputting to syslog
```

This will record the output in the syslog file. If you have permission to access the file, you can examine the logs using standard Unix tools:

```
$ grep 'outputting to syslog' /var/log/syslog
Jun 23 20:37:50 myhost docker/6239418882b6[2559]: outputting to syslog
```

LOGGING TO JOURNALD
Outputting to a journal daemon looks similar:

```
$ docker run --log-driver=journald ubuntu echo 'outputting to journald'
outputting to journald
$ journalctl | grep 'outputting to journald'
Jun 23 11:49:23 myhost docker[2993]: outputting to journald
```

> **WARNING** Ensure you have a journal daemon running on your host before running the preceding command.

APPLYING ACROSS ALL CONTAINERS
It can be laborious to apply this argument to all containers on your host, so you can change your Docker daemon to log by default to these supported mechanisms.

Change the daemon /etc/default/docker, or /etc/sysconfig/docker, or whichever Docker config file your distribution has set up, such that the `DOCKER_OPTS=""` line is activated and includes the log-driver flag. For example, if the line was

```
DOCKER_OPTS="--dns 8.8.8.8 --dns 8.8.4.4"
```

change it to this:

```
DOCKER_OPTS="--dns 8.8.8.8 --dns 8.8.4.4 --log-driver syslog"
```

> **TIP** See appendix B for details on how to change the Docker daemon's configuration on your host.

If you restart your Docker daemon, containers should then log to the relevant service.

DISCUSSION
Another common choice worth mentioning in this context (but not covered here) is that you can use containers to implement an ELK (Elasticsearch, Logstash, Kibana) logging infrastructure.

> **WARNING** Changing this daemon setting to anything other than `json-file` or `journald` will mean that the standard `docker logs` command will no longer work by default. Users of this Docker daemon may not appreciate this change, especially because the /var/log/syslog file (used by the `syslog` driver) is typically not accessible to non-root users.

TECHNIQUE 103 **Monitoring containers with cAdvisor**

Once you have a serious number of containers running in production, you'll want to monitor their resource usage and performance exactly as you do when you have multiple processes running on a host.

The sphere of monitoring (both generally, and with respect to Docker) is a wide field with many candidates. cAdvisor has been chosen here as it's a popular choice. Open-sourced by Google, it has quickly gained in popularity. If you already use a traditional host-monitoring tool such as Zabbix or Sysdig, then it's worth seeing whether it already offers the functionality you need—many tools are adding container-aware functionality as we write.

PROBLEM

You want to monitor the performance of your containers.

SOLUTION

Use cAdvisor as a monitoring tool.

cAdvisor is a tool developed by Google for monitoring containers. It's open-sourced on GitHub at https://github.com/google/cadvisor.

cAdvisor runs as a daemon that collects performance data on running containers. Among other things, it tracks

- Resource isolation parameters
- Historical resource usage
- Network statistics

cAdvisor can be installed natively on the host or run as a Docker container.

Listing 15.3 Running cAdvisor

Mounts the /var/run folder with read-write access. At most, one instance of cAdvisor is expected to run per host.

Gives cAdvisor read-only access to the root filesystem so it can track information about the host

Gives cAdvisor read-only access to the host's /sys folder, which contains information about the kernel subsystems and devices attached to the host

Gives cAdvisor read-only access to Docker's host directory

```
$ docker run \
--volume /:/rootfs:ro \
--volume /var/run:/var/run:rw \
--volume /sys:/sys:ro \
--volume /var/lib/docker/:/var/lib/docker:ro \
-p 8080:8080 -d --name cadvisor \
--restart on-failure:10 google/cadvisor
```

cAdvisor's web interface is served on port 8080 of the container, so we publish it to the host on the same port. The standard Docker arguments to run the container in the background and give the container a name are also used.

Restarts the container on failure, up to a maximum of 10 times. The image is stored on the Docker Hub within Google's account.

Once you've started the image, you can visit http://localhost:8080 with your browser to start examining the data output. There's information about the host, but by clicking on the Docker Containers link at the top of the homepage, you'll be able to examine graphs of CPU, memory, and other historical data. Just click on the running containers listed under the Subcontainers heading.

The data is collected and retained in memory while the container runs. There is documentation for persisting the data to an InfluxDB instance on the GitHub page. The GitHub repository also has details about the REST API and a sample client written in Go.

> **TIP** InfluxDB is an open source database designed to handle the tracking of time-series data. It's therefore ideal for recording and analyzing monitoring information that's provided in real time.

DISCUSSION

Monitoring is a fast-evolving and splintering space, and cAdvisor is just one component among many now. For example, Prometheus, the fast-emerging standard for Docker, can receive and store data produced by cAdvisor rather than placing it directly in InfluxDB.

Monitoring is also a subject that developers can get very passionate about. It can pay to develop a strategy for monitoring that can be flexible to meet changing fashions.

15.2   *Resource control*

One of the central concerns of running services in production is the fair and functional allocation of resources. Under the hood, Docker uses the core operating system concept of cgroups to manage containers' resource usage. By default, a simple and equal-share algorithm is used when containers contend for resources, but sometimes this isn't enough. You might want to reserve or limit resources for a container, or class of containers, for operational or service reasons.

In this section you'll learn how to tune containers' usage of CPU and memory.

TECHNIQUE 104   **Restricting the cores a container can execute on**

By default, Docker allows containers to execute on any cores on your machine. Containers with a single process and thread will obviously only be able to max out one core, but multithreaded programs in a container (or multiple single-threaded programs) will be able to use all your CPU cores. You might want to change this behavior if you have a container that's more important than others—it's not ideal for customer-facing applications to have to fight for the CPU every time your internal daily reports run. You could also use this technique to prevent runaway containers from locking you out of SSH to a server.

PROBLEM

You want a container to have a minimum CPU allocation, have a hard limit on CPU consumption, or otherwise want to restrict the cores a container can run on.

SOLUTION

Use the --cpuset-cpus option to reserve CPU cores for your container.

To properly explore the --cpuset-cpus option, you'll need to follow this technique on a computer with multiple cores. This may not be the case if you're using a cloud machine.

> **TIP** Older versions of Docker used the flag --cpuset, which is now deprecated. If you can't get --cpuset-cpus to work, try using --cpuset instead.

To look at the effects of the --cpuset-cpus option, we're going to use the htop command, which gives a useful graphical view of the core usage of your computer. Make sure this is installed before continuing—it's typically available as the htop package from your system package manager. Alternatively, you can install it inside an Ubuntu container started with the --pid=host option to expose process information from the host to the container.

If you now run htop, you'll probably see that none of your cores are busy. To simulate some load inside a couple of containers, run the following command in two different terminals:

```
docker run ubuntu:14.04 sh -c 'cat /dev/zero >/dev/null'
```

Looking back at htop, you should see that two of your cores now show 100% use. To restrict this to one core, docker kill the previous containers and then run the following command in two terminals:

```
docker run --cpuset-cpus=0 ubuntu:14.04 sh -c 'cat /dev/zero >/dev/null'
```

Now htop will show that only your first core is being used by these containers.

The --cpuset-cpus option permits multiple core specification as a comma-separated list (0,1,2), a range (0-2), or a combination of the two (0-1,3). Reserving a CPU for the host is therefore a matter of choosing a range for your containers that excludes a core.

DISCUSSION

You can use this functionality in numerous ways. For example, you can reserve specific CPUs for the host processes by consistently allocating the remaining CPUs to running containers. Or you could restrict specific containers to run on their own dedicated CPUs so they don't interfere with the compute used by other containers.

In a multi-tenant environment, this can be a godsend for ensuring that workloads don't interfere with each other.

TECHNIQUE 105 **Giving important containers more CPU**

Containers on a host will normally share CPU usage equally when they compete for it. You've seen how to make absolute guarantees or restrictions, but these can be a little inflexible. If you want a process to be able to use more CPU than others, it's a waste to constantly reserve an entire core for it, and doing so can be limiting if you have a small number of cores.

Docker facilitates multi-tenancy for users who want to bring their applications to a shared server. This can result in the *noisy neighbor* problem well known to those experienced with VMs, where one user eats up resources and affects another user's VM that happens to be running on the same hardware.

As a concrete example, while writing this book we had to use this functionality to reduce the resource use of a particularly hungry Postgres application that ate CPU cycles, robbing a web server on the machine of the ability to serve end users.

PROBLEM

You want to be able to give more important containers a bigger share of CPU or mark some containers as less important.

SOLUTION

Use the `-c/--cpu-shares` argument to the `docker run` command to define the relative share of CPU usage.

When a container is started up, it's given a number (1024 by default) of *CPU shares*. When only one process is running, it will have access to 100% of the CPU if necessary, no matter how many CPU shares it has access to. It's only when competing with other containers for CPU that the number is used.

Imagine we have three containers (A, B, and C) all trying to use all available CPU resources:

- If they've all been given equal CPU shares, they will each be allocated one third of the CPU.
- If A and B are given 512 and C is given 1024, C will get half of the CPU, and A and B will get a quarter each.
- If A is given 10, B is given 100, and C is given 1000, A will get under 1% of the available CPU resources and will only be able to do anything resource-hungry if B and C are idle.

All of this assumes that your containers can use all cores on your machine (or that you only have one core). Docker will spread the load from containers across all cores where possible. If you have two containers running single-threaded applications on a two-core machine, there's obviously no way to apply relative weighting while maximally using the available resources. Each container will be given a core to execute on, regardless of its weight.

If you want to try this out, run the following:

Listing 15.4   Starving a Docker shell of CPU

```
docker run --cpuset-cpus=0 -c 10000 ubuntu:14.04 \
sh -c 'cat /dev/zero > /dev/null' &
docker run --cpuset-cpus=0 -c 1 -it ubuntu:14.04 bash
```

Now see how doing anything in the bash prompt is sluggish. Note that these numbers are relative—you can multiply them all by 10 (for example) and they would mean exactly the same thing. But the default granted is still 1024, so once you start changing these numbers, it's worth considering what will happen to processes that start without a CPU share specified in the command and that run on the same CPU set.

> **TIP**   Finding the right CPU share levels for your use case is something of an art. It's worth looking at the output of programs such as top and vmstat to determine what's using CPU time. When using top, it's particularly useful to hit the "1" key to display what each CPU core is doing separately.

DISCUSSION

Although we haven't seen this technique directly used in the real world very often, and its use is generally seen on the underlying platform, it's good to understand and play with the underlying mechanism to know how it works when tenants are complaining about lack of access (or apparent lack of access) to resources. This happens often in real-world environments, especially if the tenants' workloads are sensitive to fluctuations in infrastructure availability.

TECHNIQUE 106   **Limiting the memory usage of a container**

When you run a container, Docker will allow it to allocate as much memory from the host as possible. Usually this is desirable (and a big advantage over virtual machines, which have an inflexible way of allocating memory). But sometimes applications can go out of control, allocate too much memory, and bring a machine grinding to a halt as it starts swapping. It's annoying, and it's happened to us many times in the past. We want a way of limiting a container's memory consumption to prevent this.

PROBLEM

You want to be able to limit the memory consumption of a container.

SOLUTION

Use the -m/--memory parameter to docker run.

If you're running Ubuntu, chances are that you don't have the memory-limiting capability enabled by default. To check, run docker info. If one of the lines in the output is a warning about No swap limit support, there's unfortunately some setup work you need to do. Be aware that making these changes can have performance implications on your machine for all applications—see the Ubuntu installation documentation for more information (http://docs.docker.com/engine/installation/ubuntulinux/#adjust-memory-and-swap-accounting).

In short, you need to indicate to the kernel at boot that you want these limits to be available. To do this, you'll need to alter /etc/default/grub as follows. If GRUB_CMDLINE _LINUX already has values in it, add the new ones at the end:

```
-GRUB_CMDLINE_LINUX=""
+GRUB_CMDLINE_LINUX="cgroup_enable=memory swapaccount=1"
```

You now need to run sudo update-grub and restart your computer. Running docker info should no longer give you the warning, and you're now ready to proceed with the main attraction.

First, let's crudely demonstrate that the memory limit does work by using a limit of 4 MB, the lowest possible.

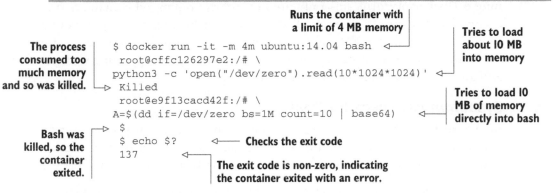

Listing 15.5 Setting the lowest-possible memory limit for a container

```
$ docker run -it -m 4m ubuntu:14.04 bash
  root@cffc126297e2:/# \
python3 -c 'open("/dev/zero").read(10*1024*1024)'
  Killed
  root@e9f13cacd42f:/# \
A=$(dd if=/dev/zero bs=1M count=10 | base64)
$
$ echo $?
137
```

Runs the container with a limit of 4 MB memory

Tries to load about 10 MB into memory

The process consumed too much memory and so was killed.

Tries to load 10 MB of memory directly into bash

Bash was killed, so the container exited.

Checks the exit code

The exit code is non-zero, indicating the container exited with an error.

There's a gotcha with this kind of constraint. To demonstrate this, we'll use the jess/ stress image, which contains stress, a tool designed for testing the limits of a system.

TIP Jess/stress is a helpful image for testing any resource limits you impose on your container. Try out the previous techniques with this image if you want to experiment more.

If you run the following command, you might be surprised to see that it doesn't exit immediately:

```
docker run -m 100m jess/stress --vm 1 --vm-bytes 150M --vm-hang 0
```

You've asked Docker to limit the container to 100 MB, and you've instructed stress to take up 150 MB. You can verify that stress is operating as expected by running this command:

```
docker top <container_id> -eo pid,size,args
```

The size column is in KB and shows that your container is indeed taking about 150 MB of memory, raising the question of why it hasn't been killed. It turns out that Docker double-reserves memory—half for physical memory and half to swap. If you try the following command, the container will terminate immediately:

```
docker run -m 100m jess/stress --vm 1 --vm-bytes 250M --vm-hang 0
```

This double reservation is just a default and can be controlled with the `--memory-swap` argument, which specifies the total virtual memory size (memory + swap). For example, to completely eliminate swap usage, you should set `--memory` and `--memory-swap` to be the same size. You can see more examples in the Docker run reference at https:// docs.docker.com/engine/reference/run/#user-memory-constraints.

DISCUSSION

Memory limits are one of the hottest topics of any operations (or DevOps) team running a Docker platform. Misconfigured or poorly configured containers run out of assigned (or reserved) memory all the time (I'm looking at *you* Java developers!), requiring the writing of FAQs and runbooks to direct users to when they cry foul.

Being aware of what's going on here is a great help to supporting such platforms and giving users the context of what's going on.

15.3   *Sysadmin use cases for Docker*

In this section we're going to take a look at some of the surprising uses to which Docker can be put. Although it may seem strange at first glance, Docker can be used to make your cron job management easier and can be used as a form of backup tool.

> **TIP**   A cron job is a timed, regular command that's run by a daemon included as a service with almost all Linux systems. Each user can specify their own schedule of commands to be run. It's heavily used by sysadmins to run periodic tasks, such as cleaning up log files or running backups.

This is by no means an exhaustive list of potential uses, but it should give you a taste of Docker's flexibility and some insight into how its features can be used in unexpected ways.

TECHNIQUE 107   Using Docker to run cron jobs

If you've ever had to manage cron jobs across multiple hosts, you may have come across the operational headache of having to deploy the same software to multiple places and ensuring the crontab itself has the correct invocation of the program you want to run.

Although there are other solutions to this problem (such as using Chef, Puppet, Ansible, or some other configuration management tool to manage the deployment of software across hosts), one option can be to use a Docker registry to store the correct invocation.

This isn't always the best solution to the problem outlined, but it's a striking illustration of the benefits of having an isolated and portable store of your applications' runtime configurations, and one that comes for free if you already use Docker.

PROBLEM

You want your cron jobs to be centrally managed and auto-updated.

SOLUTION

Pull and run your cron job scripts as Docker containers.

If you have a large estate of machines that need to run jobs regularly, you typically will use crontabs and configure them by hand (yes, that still happens), or you'll use a configuration management tool such as Puppet or Chef. Updating their recipes will ensure that when a machine's config management controller next runs, the changes are applied to the crontab, ready for the run following that.

> **TIP** A *crontab* file is a special file maintained by a user that specifies the times scripts should be run. Typically these will be maintenance tasks, like compressing and archiving log files, but they could be business-critical applications, such as a credit card payment settler.

In this technique, we'll show you how to replace this scheme with Docker images delivered from a registry with 'docker pull'.

In the normal case, shown in figure 15.2, the maintainer updates the configuration management tool, which is then delivered to the servers when the agent is run. Meanwhile, the cron jobs are running with the old and new code while the systems update.

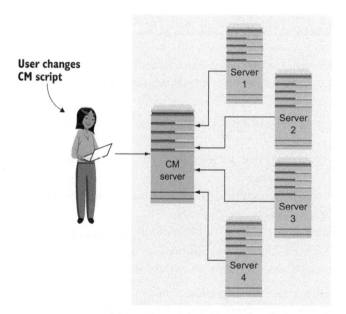

Figure 15.2   Each server updates cron scripts during a CM agent-scheduled run

In the Docker scenario, illustrated in figure 15.3, the servers pull the latest version of the code before the cron jobs run.

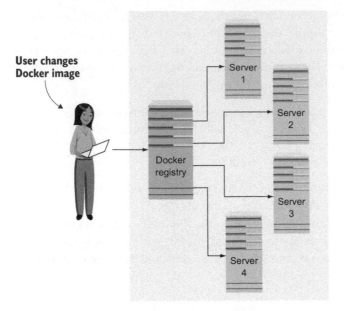

Figure 15.3   Each server pulls the latest image on every cron job run

At this point you may be wondering why it's worth bothering with this, if you already have a solution that works. Here are some advantages of using Docker as the delivery mechanism:

- Whenever a job is run, the job will update itself to the latest version from the central location.
- Your crontab files become much simpler, because the script and the code are encapsulated in a Docker image.
- For larger or more complex changes, only the deltas of the Docker image need be pulled, speeding up delivery and updates.
- You don't have to maintain the code or binaries on the machine itself.
- You can combine Docker with other techniques, such as logging output to the syslog, to simplify and centralize the management of these administration services.

For this example we're going to use the log_cleaner image we created in technique 49. You'll no doubt recall that this image encapsulated a script that cleaned up log files on a server and took a parameter for the number of days of log files to clean up. A crontab that uses Docker as a delivery mechanism would look something like the following listing.

Listing 15.6   Log cleaner crontab entry

Runs the log cleaner over a day's worth of log files →

```
0 0 * * * \                                    ← Runs this at midnight every day
  IMG=dockerinpractice/log_cleaner && \
docker pull $IMG && \                          ←┐ First pulls the latest
  docker run -v /var/log/myapplogs:/log_dir $IMG 1 │ version of the image
```

TIP If you're not familiar with cron, you may want to know that to edit your crontab you can run `crontab -e`. Each line specifies a command to be run at a time specified by the five items at the start of the line. Find out more by looking at the crontab man page.

If there's a failure, the standard cron mechanism of sending an email should kick into effect. If you don't rely on this, add a command with an or operator. In the following example, we assume your bespoke alerting command is `my_alert_command`.

Listing 15.7 Log cleaner crontab entry with alerting on error

```
0 0 * * * \
(IMG=dockerinpractice/log_cleaner && \
docker pull $IMG && \
docker run -v /var/log/myapplogs:/log_dir $IMG 1) \
|| my_alert_command 'log_cleaner failed'
```

TIP An or operator (in this case, the double pipe: `||`) ensures that one of the commands on either side will be run. If the first command fails (in this case, either of the two commands within the parentheses after the cron specification 0 0 * * * joined by the and operator, `&&`), then the second will be run.

The `||` operator ensures that if any part of the log-cleaning job run failed, the alert command gets run.

DISCUSSION

We really like this technique for its simplicity and use of battle-tested technologies to solve a problem in an original way.

Cron has been around for decades (since the late 1970s, according to Wikipedia) and its augmentation by Docker image is a technique we use at home to manage regular jobs in a simple way.

TECHNIQUE 108 **The "save game" approach to backups**

If you've ever run a transactional system, you'll know that when things go wrong, the ability to infer the state of the system at the time of the problem is essential for a root-cause analysis.

Usually this is done through a combination of means:

- Analysis of application logs
- Database forensics (determining the state of data at a given point in time)
- Build history analysis (working out what code and config was running on the service at a given point in time)
- Live system analysis (for example, did anyone log onto the box and change something?)

For such critical systems, it can pay to take the simple but effective approach of backing up the Docker service containers. Although your database is likely to be separate from your Docker infrastructure, the state of config, code, and logs can be stored in a registry with a couple of simple commands.

PROBLEM

You want to keep backups of Docker containers.

SOLUTION

Commit the containers while running, and push the resulting image as a dedicated Docker repository.

Following Docker best practices and taking advantage of some Docker features can help you avoid the need to store container backups. As one example, using a logging driver as described in technique 102 instead of logging to the container filesystem means logs don't need to be retrieved from the container backups.

But sometimes reality dictates that you can't do everything the way you'd like, and you really need to see what a container looked like. The following commands show the entire process of committing and pushing a backup container.

Listing 15.8   Committing and pushing a backup container

Generates a timestamp to the granularity of a second

Generates a tag that points to your registry URL with a tag that includes the hostname and date

```
DATE=$(date +%Y%m%d_%H%M%S)          ◁─┘
 TAG="your_log_registry:5000/live_pmt_svr_backup:$(hostname -s)_${DATE}"   ◁─
 docker commit -m="$DATE" -a="Backup Admin" live_pmt_svr $TAG   ◁─┐
 docker push $TAG
```

Pushes the container to a registry

Commits the container with the date as a message and "Backup Admin" as the author

> **WARNING**   This technique will pause the container while it runs, effectively taking it out of service. Your service should either tolerate outages, or you should have other nodes running at the time that can service requests in a load-balanced fashion.

If this is done in a staggered rotation across all your hosts, you'll have an effective backup system and a means to restore the state for support engineers with as little ambiguity as possible. Figure 15.4 illustrates a simplified view of such a setup.

The backups only push the differences between the base image and the state of the container at the time it's backed up, and the backups are staggered to ensure that the service stays up on at least one host. The registry server only stores one copy of the base image and the diffs at each commit point, saving disk space.

DISCUSSION

You can take this technique one step further by combining this technique with a so-called "Phoenix deployment" model. Phoenix deployment is a model for deployment that emphasizes replacing as much of the system as possible rather than upgrading a deployment in-place. It's a central principle of many Docker tools.

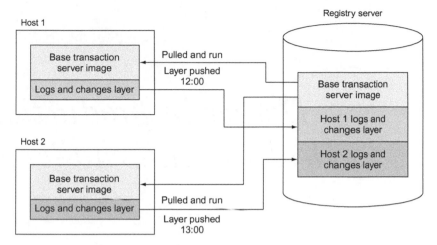

Figure 15.4 Two-host backup of a service

In this case, rather than committing the container and letting it continue on afterward, you can do the following:

1 Pull a fresh copy of the latest image from your registry
2 Stop the running container
3 Start up a new container
4 Commit, tag, and push the old container to the registry

Combining these approaches gives you even more certainty that the live system hasn't drifted from the source image. One of us uses this approach to manage a live system on a home server.

Summary

- You can direct logging from your containers to your host's syslog daemon.
- Docker log output can be captured to a host-level service.
- cAdvisor can be used to monitor the performance of your containers.
- Container usage of CPU, core, and memory can be limited and controlled.
- Docker has some surprising uses, such as being a cron delivery tool and a backup system.

Docker in production: Dealing with challenges

In this chapter we'll discuss what you can do when Docker's abstractions aren't working for you. These topics necessarily involve getting under the hood of Docker to understand why such solutions can be needed, and in the process we aim to provide you with a deeper awareness of what can go wrong when using Docker and how to go about fixing it.

16.1 Performance: You can't ignore the tin

Although Docker seeks to abstract the application from the host it's running on, one can never completely ignore the host. In order to provide its abstractions, Docker must add layers of indirection. These layers can have implications for your running system, and they sometimes need to be understood in order for operational challenges to be fixed or worked around.

In this section we'll look at how you can bypass some of these abstractions, ending up with a Docker container that has little of Docker left in it. We'll also show that although Docker appears to abstract away the details of the storage you use, this can sometimes come back to bite you.

TECHNIQUE 109 Accessing host resources from the container

We covered volumes, the most commonly used Docker abstraction bypass, in technique 34. They're convenient for sharing files from the host and for keeping larger files out of image layers. They can also be significantly faster for filesystem access than the container filesystem, as some storage backends impose significant overheads for certain workloads—this isn't useful for all applications, but it's crucial in some cases.

In addition to the overhead imposed by some storage backends, another performance hit comes about as a result of the network interfaces Docker sets up to give each container its own network. As with filesystem performance, network performance is definitely not a bottleneck for everyone, but it's something you may wish to benchmark for yourself (although the fine details of network tuning are very much outside the scope of this book). Alternatively, you may have other reasons to want to bypass Docker networking entirely—a server that opens random ports to listen on may not be well served by listening on port ranges with Docker, especially because exposing a range of ports will allocate them on the host whether they're in use or not.

Regardless of your reason, sometimes Docker abstractions get in the way, and Docker does offer the ability to opt out if you need to.

PROBLEM

You want to allow access to the host's resources from the container.

SOLUTION

Use the flags Docker offers for docker run to bypass the kernel namespace functionality that Docker uses.

> **TIP** Kernel namespaces are a service the kernel offers to programs, allowing them to get views of global resources in such a way that they appear to have their own separate instances of that resource. For example, a program can request a network namespace that will give you what appears to be a complete network stack. Docker uses and manages these namespaces to create its containers.

Table 16.1 summarizes how Docker uses namespaces, and how you can effectively switch them off.

Table 16.1   Namespaces and Docker

Kernel namespace	Description	Used in Docker?	"Switch off" option
Network	The network subsystem	Yes	`--net=host`
IPC	Inter-process communication: shared memory, semaphores, and so on	Yes	`--ipc=host`
UTS	Hostname and NIS domain	Yes	`--uts=host`
PID	Process IDs	Yes	`--pid=host`
Mount	Mount points	Yes	`--volume, --device`
User	User and group IDs	No	N/A

> **NOTE**   If any of these flags aren't available, it will likely be due to your version of Docker being out of date.

If your application is a heavy user of shared memory, for example, and you want to have your containers share this space with the host, you can use the `--ipc=host` flag to achieve this. This use is relatively advanced, so we'll focus on the other more common ones.

NETWORK AND HOSTNAME

To use the host's network, you run your container with the `--net` flag set to host, like this:

```
user@yourhostname:/$ docker run -ti --net=host ubuntu /bin/bash
root@yourhostname:/#
```

You'll notice that this immediately differs from a network-namespaced container in that the hostname within the container is the same as the host's. On a practical level, this can cause confusion, as it's not obvious that you're in a container.

In a network-isolated container, a quick `netstat` will show that there are no connections on startup:

```
host$ docker run -ti ubuntu
root@b1c4877a00cd:/# netstat
Active Internet connections (w/o servers)
Proto Recv-Q Send-Q Local Address            Foreign Address          State
Active UNIX domain sockets (w/o servers)
Proto RefCnt Flags      Type       State         I-Node    Path
root@b1c4877a00cd:/#
```

A similar run using the host's network shows the usual network-busy host of a similarly busy technical author:

```
$ docker run -ti --net=host ubuntu
root@host:/# netstat -nap | head
Active Internet connections (servers and established)
```

```
Proto Recv-Q Send-Q Local Address     Foreign Address State      PID
⮑ /Program name
tcp        0      0 127.0.0.1:47116 0.0.0.0:*         LISTEN     -
tcp        0      0 127.0.1.1:53    0.0.0.0:*         LISTEN     -
tcp        0      0 127.0.0.1:631   0.0.0.0:*         LISTEN     -
tcp        0      0 0.0.0.0:3000    0.0.0.0:*         LISTEN     -
tcp        0      0 127.0.0.1:54366 0.0.0.0:*         LISTEN     -
tcp        0      0 127.0.0.1:32888 127.0.0.1:47116 ESTABLISHED -
tcp        0      0 127.0.0.1:32889 127.0.0.1:47116 ESTABLISHED -
tcp        0      0 127.0.0.1:47116 127.0.0.1:32888 ESTABLISHED -
root@host:/#
```

NOTE `netstat` is a command that allows you to see information about networking on your local network stack. It's used most commonly to determine the state of network sockets.

The `net=host` flag is the most often used for a couple of reasons. First, it can make connecting containers much easier. But you lose the benefits of port mapping for your containers. If you have two containers that listen on port 80, for example, you can't run them on the same host in this way. The second reason is that network performance is significantly improved over Docker's when using this flag.

Figure 16.1 shows at a high level the layers of overhead a network packet must go through in Docker versus a native network. Whereas the native network need only go through the TCP/IP stack of the host to the network interface card (NIC), Docker has to additionally maintain a virtual Ethernet pair (a "veth pair"—a virtual representation of a physical connection via an Ethernet cable), a network bridge between this veth pair and the host network, and a layer of network address translation (NAT). This overhead can cause the Docker network to be half the speed of a native host network in normal use cases.

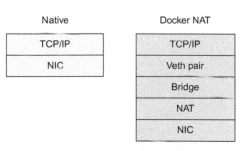

Figure 16.1 Docker networking vs. native networking

PID

The PID namespace flag is similar to the others:

The ps we're running is the only process in this container and is given the PID of I.

Runs the ps command in a containerized environment, showing only the process that has a PID of I

```
imiell@host:/$ docker run ubuntu ps -p 1
    PID TTY          TIME CMD
      1 ?        00:00:00 ps
  imiell@host:/$ docker run --pid=host ubuntu ps -p 1
    PID TTY          TIME CMD
      1 ?        00:00:27 systemd
```

This time the PID of I is the systemd command, which is the startup process of the host's operating system. This may differ for you, depending on your distribution.

Runs the same ps command with the PID namespace removed, giving us a view of the host's processes

The preceding example demonstrates that the systemd process of the host has process ID 1 in the container that has a view of the host PIDs, whereas without that view the only process seen is the ps command itself.

MOUNT

If you want access to the host's devices, use the --device flag to use a specific device, or mount the entire host's filesystem with the --volume flag:

```
docker run -ti --volume /:/host ubuntu /bin/bash
```

The preceding command mounts the host's / directory to the container's /host directory. You may be wondering why you can't mount the host's / directory to the container's / directory. This is explicitly disallowed by the docker command.

You may also be wondering whether you can use these flags to create a container that's virtually indistinguishable from the host. That leads us to the next section…

A HOST-LIKE CONTAINER

You can use the following flags to create a container that has an almost transparent view of the host:

Mounts the root filesystem of the host to a directory /host on the container. Docker disallows the mounting of volumes to the "/" folder, so you must specify the /host subfolder volume.

Runs a container with three host arguments (net, pid, ipc)

```
host:/$ docker run -ti --net=host --pid=host --ipc=host \
  --volume /:/host \
  busybox chroot /host
```

Starts up a BusyBox container. All you need is the chroot command, and this is a small image that contains that. Chroot is executed to make the mounted filesystem appear as the root to you.

It's ironic that Docker has been characterized as "chroot on steroids," and here we're using something characterized as a framework to run chroot in a way that subverts one of the principal purposes of chroot, which is to protect a host filesystem. It's usually at this point that we try not to think about it too hard.

In any case, it's hard to imagine a real-world use of that command (instructive as it is). If you think of one, please drop us a line.

That said, you might want to use it as a basis for more useful commands like this:

```
$ docker run -ti --workdir /host \
   --volume /:/host:ro ubuntu /bin/bash
```

In this example, --workdir /host sets the working directory on container startup to be the root of the host's filesystem, as mounted with the --volume argument. The :ro part of the volume specification means the host filesystem will be mounted as read-only.

With this command, you can give yourself a read-only view of the filesystem while having an environment where you can install tools (with the standard Ubuntu package manager) to inspect it. For example, you could use an image that runs a nifty tool that reports security problems on your host's filesystem, without having to install it on your host.

> **WARNING** As the preceding discussion implies, using these flags opens you up to more security risks. In security terms, using them should be considered equivalent to running with the `--privileged` flag.

DISCUSSION

In this technique you've learned how to bypass Docker's abstractions within the container. Disabling these can give you speedups or other conveniences to make Docker better serve your needs. One variant we've used in the past is to install networking tools (perhaps like tcpflow, mentioned in technique 112) inside a container and expose host network interfaces. This lets you experiment with different tools on a temporary basis without having to install them.

The next technique looks at how you can bypass a restriction of Docker's underlying disk storage.

TECHNIQUE 110 Disabling the OOM killer

The "OOM killer" sounds like a bad horror film or severe disease, but it is in fact a thread within the Linux operating system kernel that decides what to do when the host is running out of memory. After the operating system has run out of hardware memory, used up any available swap space, and removed any cached files out of memory, it invokes the OOM killer to decide which processes should be killed off.

PROBLEM

You want to prevent containers from being killed by the OOM killer.

SOLUTION

Use the `--oom-kill-disable` flag when starting your container.

Solving this challenge is as simple as adding a flag to your Docker container. But as is often the case, the full story isn't that simple.

The following listing shows how you disable the OOM killer for a container:

Listing 16.1 `--oom-kill-disable` shows a warning

```
$ docker run -ti --oom-kill-disable ubuntu sleep 1
 WARNING: Disabling the OOM killer on containers without setting a
'-m/--memory' limit may be dangerous.
```

The `--oom-kill-disable` flag is added to a normal docker run command.

A warning is output regarding another flag that might be set.

The warning you see is important. It tells you that running with this setting is dangerous, but it doesn't tell you why. It's dangerous to set this option because if your host runs out of memory, the operating system will kill all other user processes before yours.

Sometimes that's desirable, such as if you have a critical piece of infrastructure you want to protect from failure—maybe an audit or logging process that runs across (or for) all containers on the host. Even then, you'll want to think twice about how disruptive this will be to your environment. For example, your container might depend on other running infrastructure on the same host. If you're running on a container platform like OpenShift, your container will survive even as key platform processes are killed off. You'd likely want that key infrastructure to stay up before that container.

Listing 16.2 `--oom-kill-disable` without a warning

This time, no warning is seen.

The --memory flag is added to a normal docker run command.

```
$ docker run -ti --oom-kill-disable --memory 4M ubuntu sleep 1
$
```

> **NOTE** The minimum amount of memory you can allocate is 4M, where the "M" stands for megabytes. You can also allocate by "G" for gigabytes.

You may be wondering how to tell whether your container was killed by the OOM killer. This is easily done by using the `docker inspect` command:

Listing 16.3 Determining whether your container was "OOM-killed"

```
$ docker inspect logger | grep OOMKilled
          "OOMKilled": false,
```

This command outputs information about why the container was killed, including whether the OOM killer killed it.

DISCUSSION

The OOM killer doesn't require extended privileges to be set in a container, nor does it require you to be the root user—all you need is access to the `docker` command. This is yet another reason to be wary of giving unprivileged users access to the `docker` command without trusting them with root (see chapter 14 on security).

This is not only a security risk, but a stability risk too. If a user can run `docker`, they could run a process that gradually leaks memory (common in many production environments). If no boundaries are put on that memory, the operating system will step in once its options are exhausted and kill off the user process with the largest memory usage first (this is a simplification of the Linux OOM-killer algorithm, which has been battle-tested and grown over years). If the container has been started with the OOM killer disabled, however, it could trample over all containers on the host, causing far more destruction and instability for its users.

For a more fine-grained approach to memory management, you can adjust the container's "OOM score" with the `--oom-score-adj` flag. Another approach that may suit your purposes is to disable memory overcommit in the kernel. This has the effect of switching off the OOM killer globally, as memory is only granted if it's definitely available. However, this could limit the number of containers that can run on your hosts, which could also be undesirable.

As always, performance management is an art!

16.2 When containers leak—debugging Docker

In this section we'll cover some techniques that will help you understand and fix issues with applications running in Docker containers. We'll cover how to jump into a container's network while using tools from your host to debug issues, and we'll look at an alternative that avoids container manipulation by monitoring network interfaces directly.

Finally, we'll demonstrate how the Docker abstraction can break down, leading to containers working on one host and not another, and how to debug this on live systems.

TECHNIQUE 111 Debugging a container's network with nsenter

In an ideal world, you'd be able to use socat (see technique 4) in an *ambassador container* to diagnose issues with container communication. You'd start the extra container and make sure connections go to this new container, which acts as a proxy. The proxy allows you to diagnose and monitor the connections, and it then forwards them to the right place. Unfortunately it's not always convenient (or possible) to set up a container like this only for debugging purposes.

> **TIP** See technique 74 for a description of the ambassador pattern.

You've already read about docker exec in techniques 15 and 19. This technique discusses *nsenter*, a tool that looks similar but allows you to use tools from your machine inside the container, rather than being limited to what the container has installed.

PROBLEM

You want to debug a network problem in a container, but the tools aren't in the container.

SOLUTION

Use nsenter to jump into the container's network but retain your host's tooling.

If you don't already have nsenter available on your Docker host, you can build it with the following command:

```
$ docker run -v /usr/local/bin:/target jpetazzo/nsenter
```

This will install nsenter in /usr/local/bin, and you'll be able to use it immediately. nsenter might also be available in your distro (in the util-linux package).

You may have noticed by now that the generally useful BusyBox image doesn't come with bash by default. As a demo of nsenter, we're going to show how you can enter a BusyBox container with your host's bash program:

```
$ docker run -ti busybox /bin/bash
FATA[0000] Error response from daemon: Cannot start container >
a81e7e6b2c030c29565ef7adb94de20ad516a6697deeeb617604e652e979fda6: >
```

**Starts up a BusyBox container
and saves the container ID (CID)**

**Inspects the
container,
extracting the
process ID (PID)
(see technique 30)**

```
exec: "/bin/bash": stat /bin/bash: no such file or directory
$ CID=$(docker run -d busybox sleep 9999)
  $ PID=$(docker inspect --format {{.State.Pid}} $CID)
  $ sudo nsenter --target $PID \
  --uts --ipc --net /bin/bash
  root@781c1fed2b18:~#
```

**Runs nsenter, specifying the container
to enter with the --target flag. The
"sudo" may not be required.**

**Specifies the namespaces of the container
to enter with the remaining flags**

See technique 109 for more detail on namespaces that nsenter understands. The critical point in the selection of namespaces is that you don't use the --mount flag, which would use the container's filesystem, because bash wouldn't be available. /bin/bash is specified as the executable to start.

It should be pointed out that you don't get direct access to the container's filesystem, but you do get all the tools your host has.

Something that we've needed before is a way to find out which veth interface device on the host corresponds to which container. For example, sometimes it's desirable to quickly knock a container off the network. An unprivileged container can't bring a network interface down, so you need to do it from the host by finding out the veth interface name.

**We're unable to bring an interface in the container
down. Note that your interface may not be eth0, so
if this doesn't work, you may wish to use ip addr to
find out your principal interface name.**

**Verifies that attempting to ping from
inside a new container succeeds**

```
$ docker run -d --name offlinetest ubuntu:14.04.2 sleep infinity
fad037a77a2fc337b7b12bc484babb2145774fde7718d1b5b53fb7e9dc0ad7b3
$ docker exec offlinetest ping -q -c1 8.8.8.8
 PING 8.8.8.8 (8.8.8.8) 56(84) bytes of data.

--- 8.8.8.8 ping statistics ---
1 packets transmitted, 1 received, 0% packet loss, time 0ms
rtt min/avg/max/mdev = 2.966/2.966/2.966/0.000 ms
$ docker exec offlinetest ifconfig eth0 down
 SIOCSIFFLAGS: Operation not permitted
$ PID=$(docker inspect --format {{.State.Pid}} offlinetest)
$ nsenter --target $PID --net ethtool -S eth0
 NIC statistics:
     peer_ifindex: 53
$ ip addr | grep '^53'
 53: veth2e7d114: <BROADCAST,MULTICAST,UP,LOWER_UP> mtu 1500 qdisc noqueue >
master docker0 state UP
$ sudo ifconfig veth2e7d114 down
 $ docker exec offlinetest ping -q -c1 8.8.8.8
 PING 8.8.8.8 (8.8.8.8) 56(84) bytes of data.

--- 8.8.8.8 ping statistics ---
1 packets transmitted, 0 received, 100% packet loss, time 0ms
```

**Enters into the network
space of the container,
using the ethtool
command from the host to
look up the peer interface
index—the other end of
the virtual interface**

**Looks through the list of interfaces on the host to
find the appropriate veth interface for the container**

Brings down the virtual interface

**Verifies that attempting
to ping from inside the
container fails**

One final example of a program you might want to use from within a container is tcpdump, a tool that records all TCP packets on a network interface. To use it, you need to run nsenter with the --net command, allowing you to "see" the container's network from the host and therefore monitor the packets with tcpdump.

For example, the tcpdump command in the following code records all packets to the /tmp/google.tcpdump file (we assume you're still in the nsenter session you started previously). Some network traffic is then triggered by retrieving a web page:

```
root@781c1fed2b18:/# tcpdump -XXs 0 -w /tmp/google.tcpdump &
root@781c1fed2b18:/# wget google.com
--2015-08-07 15:12:04--  http://google.com/
Resolving google.com (google.com)... 216.58.208.46, 2a00:1450:4009:80d::200e
Connecting to google.com (google.com)|216.58.208.46|:80... connected.
HTTP request sent, awaiting response... 302 Found
Location: http://www.google.co.uk/?gfe_rd=cr&ei=tLzEVcCXN7Lj8wepgarQAQ >
[following]
--2015-08-07 15:12:04--  >
http://www.google.co.uk/?gfe_rd=cr&ei=tLzEVcCXN7Lj8wepgarQAQ
Resolving www.google.co.uk (www.google.co.uk)... 216.58.208.67, >
2a00:1450:4009:80a::2003
Connecting to www.google.co.uk (www.google.co.uk)|216.58.208.67|:80... >
connected.
HTTP request sent, awaiting response... 200 OK
Length: unspecified [text/html]
Saving to: 'index.html'

index.html              [ <=>                ]  18.28K  --.-KB/s    in 0.008s

2015-08-07 15:12:05 (2.18 MB/s) - 'index.html' saved [18720]

root@781c1fed2b18:# 15:12:04.839152 IP 172.17.0.26.52092 > >
google-public-dns-a.google.com.domain: 7950+ A? google.com. (28)
15:12:04.844754 IP 172.17.0.26.52092 > >
google-public-dns-a.google.com.domain: 18121+ AAAA? google.com. (28)
15:12:04.860430 IP google-public-dns-a.google.com.domain > >
172.17.0.26.52092: 7950 1/0/0 A 216.58.208.46 (44)
15:12:04.869571 IP google-public-dns-a.google.com.domain > >
172.17.0.26.52092: 18121 1/0/0 AAAA 2a00:1450:4009:80d::200e (56)
15:12:04.870246 IP 172.17.0.26.47834 > lhr08s07-in-f14.1e100.net.http: >
Flags [S], seq 2242275586, win 29200, options [mss 1460,sackOK,TS val >
49337583 ecr 0,nop,wscale 7], length 0
```

TIP Depending on your network setup, you may need to temporarily change your resolv.conf file to allow the DNS lookup to work. If you get a "Temporary failure in name resolution" error, try adding the line nameserver 8.8.8.8 to the top of your /etc/resolv.conf file. Don't forget to revert it when you're finished.

DISCUSSION

This technique gives you a way to quickly alter the network behavior of containers without having to settle down with any of the tools from chapter 10 (techniques 78 and 79) to simulate network breakage.

You've also seen a compelling use case for Docker—it's much easier to debug network issues in the isolated network environment Docker provides than to do it in an uncontrolled environment. Trying to remember the correct arguments for tcpdump to appropriately filter out irrelevant packets in the middle of the night is an error-prone process. Using nsenter, you can forget about that and capture everything within the container, without tcpdump being installed (or having to install it) on the image.

TECHNIQUE 112   Using tcpflow to debug in flight without reconfiguring

tcpdump is the de facto standard in network investigation, and it's likely the first tool most people reach for if asked to dive into debugging a network issue.

But tcpdump is typically used for displaying packet summaries and examining packet headers and protocol information—it's not quite as full featured for displaying the application-level data flow between two programs. This can be quite important when investigating issues with two applications communicating.

PROBLEM

You need to monitor the communication data of a containerized application.

SOLUTION

Use tcpflow to capture traffic crossing an interface.

tcpflow is similar to tcpdump (accepting the same pattern-matching expressions) but it's designed to give you better insight into application data flows. tcpflow may be available from your system package manager, but, if not, we've prepared a Docker image you can use which should be virtually identical in functionality to an equivalent package manager install:

```
$ IMG=dockerinpractice/tcpflow
$ docker pull $IMG
$ alias tcpflow="docker run --rm --net host $IMG"
```

There are two ways you can use tcpflow with Docker: point it at the docker0 interface and use a packet-filtering expression to retrieve only the packets you want, or use the trick from the previous technique to find the veth interface for the container you're interested in, and capture on that.

> **TIP** You may wish to refer to figure 10.2 in chapter 10 to refresh your memory on how network traffic flows inside Docker and see why capturing on docker0 will capture container traffic.

Expression filtering is a powerful feature of tcpflow to use after attaching to an interface, letting you drill down to the traffic you're interested in. We'll show a simple example to get you started:

```
$ docker run -d --name tcpflowtest alpine:3.2 sleep 30d
fa95f9763ab56e24b3a8f0d9f86204704b770ffb0fd55d4fd37c59dc1601ed11
$ docker inspect -f '{{ .NetworkSettings.IPAddress }}' tcpflowtest
172.17.0.1
$ tcpflow -c -J -i docker0 'host 172.17.0.1 and port 80'
tcpflow: listening on docker0
```

In the preceding example, you ask tcpflow to print a colorized stream of any traffic going to or from your container with a source or destination port of 80 (generally used for HTTP traffic). You can now try this by retrieving a web page in the container in a new terminal:

```
$ docker exec tcpflowtest wget -O /dev/null http://www.example.com/
Connecting to www.example.com (93.184.216.34:80)
null                 100% |*****************************| 1270     0:00:00 ETA
```

You'll see colorized output in the tcpflow terminal. The cumulative output of the command so far will look something like this:

```
$ tcpflow -J -c -i docker0 'host 172.17.0.1 and (src or dst port 80)'
tcpflow: listening on docker0
172.017.000.001.36042-093.184.216.034.00080: >
GET / HTTP/1.1                                     ◁——— Blue coloring starts
 Host: www.example.com
User-Agent: Wget
Connection: close


093.184.216.034.00080-172.017.000.001.36042: >
HTTP/1.0 200 OK                                    ◁——— Red coloring starts
 Accept-Ranges: bytes
Cache-Control: max-age=604800
Content-Type: text/html
Date: Mon, 17 Aug 2015 12:22:21 GMT
[...]

<!doctype html>
<html>
<head>
    <title>Example Domain</title>
[...]
```

DISCUSSION

tcpflow is an excellent addition to your toolbox, given how unobtrusive it is. You can start it against long-running containers to get a bit of insight into what they're transferring right now, or use it alongside tcpdump (the previous technique) to get a more complete picture of the kind of requests your application makes and what information is transferred.

As well as tcpdump, the previous technique also covers using nsenter to monitor traffic on just one container rather than all of them (which is what monitoring docker0 will do).

TECHNIQUE 113 Debugging containers that fail on specific hosts

The previous two techniques have shown how you can start investigating issues caused by the interaction between your containers and other locations (whether those "other locations" are more containers, or third parties on the internet).

If you've isolated a problem to one host, and you're sure that external interaction isn't the cause, the next step should be to try reducing the number of moving parts (removing volumes and ports) and to check the details of the host itself (free disk space, number of open file descriptors, and so on). It's probably also worth checking that each host is on the latest version of Docker.

In some cases, none of the above will help—you've got an image you can run with no arguments (such as `docker run imagename`) which should be perfectly contained, yet it runs differently on different hosts.

PROBLEM

You want to determine why a particular action within a container isn't working on a particular host.

SOLUTION

Strace the process to see what system calls it's making, and compare that to a working system.

Although Docker's stated aim is to allow users to "run any app anywhere," the means by which it tries to achieve this aren't always foolproof.

Docker treats the Linux kernel API as its *host* (the environment in which it can run). When they first learn how Docker works, many people ask how Docker handles changes to the Linux API. As far as we're aware, it doesn't yet. Fortunately, the Linux API is backwards-compatible, but it's not difficult to imagine a scenario in the future where a *new* Linux API call is created and used by a Dockerized application, and for that app to then be deployed to a kernel recent enough to run Docker but old enough to not support that particular API call.

> **NOTE** You may think that the Linux kernel API changing is something of a theoretical problem, but we came across this scenario while writing the first edition of this book. A project we were working on used the `memfd_create` Linux system call, which only exists on kernels versioned 3.17 and above. Because some hosts we were working on had older kernels, our containers failed on some systems and worked on others.

That scenario is not the only way in which the Docker abstraction can fail. Containers can fail on particular kernels because assumptions may be made by the application about files on the host. Although rare, it does happen, and it's important to be alert to that risk.

SELINUX INTERFERENCE WITH CONTAINERS

An example of where the Docker abstraction can break down is with anything that interacts with SELinux. As discussed in chapter 14, SELinux is a layer of security implemented in the kernel that works outside the normal user permissions.

Docker uses this layer to allow container security to be tightened up by managing what actions can be performed from within a container. For example, if you're root within a container, you're the same user as root on the host. Although it's hard to break out of the container so you obtain root on the host, it's not impossible; exploits have been found, and others may exist that the community is unaware of. What SELinux can do is provide another layer of protection so that even if a root user breaks out of the container to the host, there are limits on what actions they can perform on the host.

So far so good, but the problem for Docker is that SELinux is implemented on the host, and not within the container. This means that programs running in containers that query the status of SELinux and find it enabled might make certain assumptions about the environment in which they run, and fail in unexpected ways if these expectations aren't met.

In the following example, we're running a CentOS 7 Vagrant machine with Docker installed, and within that an Ubuntu 12.04 container. If we run a fairly straightforward command to add a user, the exit code is 12, indicating an error, and indeed the user has not been created:

```
[root@centos vagrant]# docker run -ti ubuntu:12.04
Unable to find image 'ubuntu:12.04' locally
Pulling repository ubuntu
78cef618c77e: Download complete
b5da78899d3a: Download complete
87183ecb6716: Download complete
82ed8e312318: Download complete
root@afade8b94d32:/# useradd -m -d /home/dockerinpractice dockerinpractice
root@afade8b94d32:/# echo $?
12
```

The same command run on an ubuntu:14.04 container works just fine. If you want to try to reproduce this result, you'll need a CentOS 7 machine (or similar). But for learning purposes, following the rest of the technique with any command and container will be sufficient.

> **TIP** In bash, $? gives you the exit code of the last-run command. The meaning of the exit code varies from command to command, but typically an exit code of 0 means the call was successful, and a nonzero code indicates an error or exceptional condition of some kind.

DEBUGGING LINUX API CALLS

Because we know that the likely difference between the containers is due to differences between the kernel APIs running on the hosts, strace can help you determine the differences between calls to the kernel API.

strace is a tool that allows you to snoop on the calls made to the Linux API by a process (a.k.a. system calls). It's an extremely useful debugging and educational tool. You can see how it works in figure 16.2.

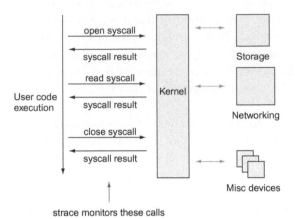

strace monitors these calls   **Figure 16.2   How strace works**

First, you need to install strace on your container using the appropriate package manager, and then run the command that differs, with the strace command prepended. Here's some example output for the failed useradd call:

Runs strace on the command with the -f flag, which ensures that any process spawned by your command and any of its descendants are "followed" by strace

Appends the command you want to debug to the strace invocation

Each line of the strace output starts with the Linux API call. The execve call here executes the command you gave strace. The 0 at the end is the return value from the call (successful).

```
# strace -f \
  useradd -m -d /home/dockerinpractice dockerinpractice
  execve("/usr/sbin/useradd", ["useradd", "-m", "-d", >
  "/home/dockerinpractice", "dockerinpractice"], [/* 9 vars */]) = 0
  [...]
  open("/proc/self/task/39/attr/current", >
  O_RDONLY) = 9
  read(9, "system_u:system_r:svirt_lxc_net_"..., >
  4095) = 46
  close(9)                                     = 0
  [...]
  open("/etc/selinux/config", O_RDONLY)     = >
  -1 ENOENT (No such file or directory)
  open("/etc/selinux/targeted/contexts/files/ >
  file_contexts.subs_dist", O_RDONLY) = -1 ENOENT (No such file or directory)
  open("/etc/selinux/targeted/contexts/files/ >
  file_contexts.subs", O_RDONLY) = -1 ENOENT (No such file or directory)
  open("/etc/selinux/targeted/contexts/files/ >
  file_contexts", O_RDONLY) = -1 ENOENT (No such file or directory)
  [...]
  exit_group(12)
```

The "read" system call works on the previously opened file (with file descriptor 9) and returns the number of bytes read (46).

The "close" system call closes the file referenced with the file descriptor number.

The process exits with the value 12, which for useradd means that the directory couldn't be created.

The "open" system call opens a file for reading. The return value (9) is the file handle number used in subsequent calls to work on the file. In this case, the SELinux information is retrieved from the /proc filesystem, which holds information about running processes.

The program attempts to open the SELinux files it expects to be there, but in each case fails. strace helpfully tells you what the return value means: "No such file or directory."

The preceding output may seem confusing at first, but after a few times it becomes relatively easy to read. Each line represents a call to the Linux kernel to perform some action in what's known as *kernel space* (as opposed to *user space*, where actions are performed by programs without handing over responsibility to the kernel).

> **TIP** If you want to learn more about a specific system call, you can run `man 2 callname`. You may need to install the man pages with `apt-get install manpages-dev` or a similar command for your packaging system. Alternatively, Googling "man 2 callname" will likely get you what you need.

This is an example of where Docker's abstractions break down. In this case, the action fails because the program expects SELinux files to be present, because SELinux appears to be enabled on the container, but the details of enforcement are kept on the host.

> **TIP** It's incredibly useful to read over the `man 2` pages for all the system calls if you're serious about being a developer. At first they might seem full of jargon you don't understand, but as you read around the various subjects, you'll learn a great deal about fundamental Linux concepts. At some point, you'll start to see how most languages derive from this root, and some of their quirks and oddities will make more sense. Be patient, though, as you won't understand it all immediately.

DISCUSSION

Although such situations are rare, the ability to debug and understand how your program is interacting by using strace is an invaluable technique, not only with Docker but for more general development.

If you have very minimal Docker images, perhaps created by leveraging technique 57, and would prefer not to install strace on your container, it's possible to use strace from your host. You'll want to use `docker top <container_id>` to find the PID of the process in the container, and the `-p` argument to strace to attach to a specific running process. Don't forget to use sudo. Attaching to a process potentially allows you to read its secrets, so it requires extra permissions.

TECHNIQUE 114 **Extracting a file from an image**

Copying a file from a container is easily achieved using the `docker cp` command. Not infrequently, you'll want to extract a file from an image, but you don't have a clean container running to copy from. In these cases, you can artificially run a container of the image, run `docker cp`, and then remove the container. This is already three commands, and you may run into trouble if, for example, the image has a default entrypoint that demands a meaningful argument.

This technique gives you a single command alias that you can put into your shell startup scripts to do all this with one command and two arguments.

PROBLEM

You want to copy a file from an image to your host.

SOLUTION

Use an alias to run a container from the image with an entrypoint to cat the file's contents to a file on the host.

First we'll show you how to construct a docker run command to extract a file from an image, and then you'll see how to turn this into an alias for convenience.

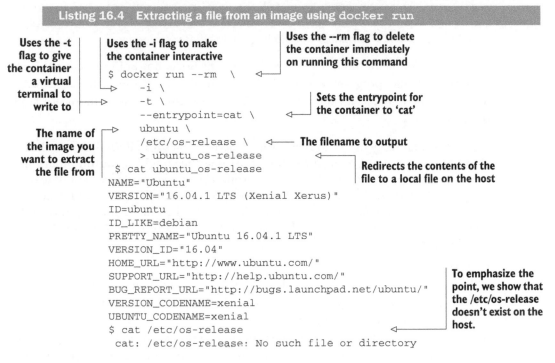

Listing 16.4   Extracting a file from an image using `docker run`

You might be wondering why we use entrypoint here, and don't simply run the cat command to output the file. This is because some images will have set an entrypoint already. When this happens, docker would treat cat as the argument to the entry-point command, resulting in behavior you wouldn't want.

For convenience, you might want to put this command into an alias.

Listing 16.5   Using an alias to extract a file from an image

Aliases the command to the name "imagecat", containing everything in the command from listing 16.4 up to the image and file arguments

```
$ alias imagecat='docker run --rm -i -t --entrypoint=cat'    ◁
 $ imagecat ubuntu /etc/os-release    ◁
 NAME="Ubuntu"                                      Calls "imagecat" with the two
VERSION="16.04.1 LTS (Xenial Xerus)"               arguments (image and filename)
ID=ubuntu
ID_LIKE=debian
PRETTY_NAME="Ubuntu 16.04.1 LTS"
VERSION_ID="16.04"
```

```
HOME_URL="http://www.ubuntu.com/"
SUPPORT_URL="http://help.ubuntu.com/"
BUG_REPORT_URL="http://bugs.launchpad.net/ubuntu/"
VERSION_CODENAME=xenial
UBUNTU_CODENAME=xenial
```

This technique assumes the presence of cat in your containers. If you've been building minimal containers with technique 58, this may not be the case, as only your binary is present in the container—there are no standard Linux tools.

If that's the case, you'll want to consider using docker export from technique 73, but rather than sending them to another machine, you can just extract the file you want from them. Bear in mind that a container doesn't need to successfully start for you to export it—you can attempt to run it with a command that doesn't exist inside the container and then export the stopped container (or just use docker create, which prepares a container for execution without starting it).

Summary

- You can pass arguments to Docker to disable different kinds of isolation, either for greater flexibility of containers or for performance.
- You can disable the Linux OOM killer for individual containers to indicate that Linux should never try to reclaim limited memory by killing this process.
- nsenter can be used to get access to the network context of a container from the host.
- tcpflow allows you to monitor all traffic in and out of your containers without needing to reconfigure or restart anything.
- strace is a vital tool for identifying why a Docker container isn't working on a specific host.

This concludes the book! We hope we've opened your eyes to some of the uses of Docker and given you some ideas for integrating it in your company or personal projects. If you'd like to get in touch with us or give us some feedback, please create a thread in the Manning *Docker in Practice* forum (https://forums.manning.com/forums/docker-in-practice-second-edition) or raise an issue against one of the "docker-in-practice" GitHub repositories.

appendix A
Installing
and using Docker

The techniques in this book sometimes require you to make files and clone repositories from GitHub. To avoid interference, we suggest you create a new empty folder for each technique when you need some working space.

Linux users have it relatively easy when it comes to installing and using Docker, though the fine details can vary significantly between different Linux distributions. Rather than enumerating the different possibilities here, we suggest you check the latest Docker documentation at https://docs.docker.com/installation/. The community edition (CE) of Docker is suitable for use with this book.

Although we assume that you're using a Linux distribution (the containers you'll be looking at are Linux-based, so this keeps things simple), many users interested in Docker work on either Windows- or macOS-based machines. For these users it's worth pointing out that the techniques in this book will still work, as Docker for Linux is officially supported on those platforms. For those who don't want to (or can't) follow the instructions at the preceding link, you can use one of the following approaches to set up the Docker daemon.

> **NOTE** Microsoft is committed to supporting the Docker container paradigm and management interface and has partnered with Docker Inc. to allow the creation of Windows-based containers. Although there are a number of learnings you can take to Windows containers after learning on Linux, there are many things that differ due to the very different ecosystems and underlying layers. We recommend getting started with the free ebook from Microsoft and Docker if you're interested, but be aware that the space is newer and may not be as mature: https://blogs.msdn.microsoft.com/microsoft_press/2017/08/30/free-ebook-introduction-to-windows-containers/.

The virtual machine approach

One approach to using Docker on Windows or macOS is to install a full Linux virtual machine. Once that's achieved, you can use the virtual machine exactly as you would any native Linux machine.

The most common way to achieve this is to install VirtualBox. See http://virtualbox.org for more information and installation guides.

Docker client connected to an external Docker server

If you already have a Docker daemon set up as a server, you can install a client natively on your Windows or macOS machine that talks to it. Be aware that exposed ports will be exposed on the external Docker server, not on your local machine—you may need to alter IP addresses in order to access the exposed services.

See technique 1 for the essentials of this more advanced approach and technique 96 for details on making it secure.

Native Docker client and virtual machine

A common (and officially recommended) approach is to have a minimal virtual machine that runs Linux and Docker, and a Docker client that talks to Docker on that virtual machine.

The currently recommended and supported way of doing this is

- Mac users should install Docker for Mac: https://docs.docker.com/docker-for -mac/
- Windows users should install Docker for Windows: https://docs.docker.com/ docker-for-windows/

Unlike the virtual machine approach described previously, the VM created by the Docker for Mac/Windows tools is very lightweight, as it only runs Docker, but it's worth being aware that you may still need to modify the memory of the VM in the settings if you're running resource-heavy programs.

Docker for Windows shouldn't be confused with Windows Containers (though you can use Windows Containers after installing Docker for Windows). Be aware that Docker for Windows requires Windows 10 (but *not* Windows 10 Home Edition) due to a dependency on recent Hyper-V functionality.

If you're on Windows 10 Home or an older version of Windows, you may also want to try installing the Docker Toolbox, an older take on the same approach. Docker Inc. describes it as legacy, and we strongly recommend pursuing one of the alternative methods of using Docker if possible, as you'll likely stumble across some oddities like these:

- Volumes need a double-slash at the beginning (https://github.com/docker/ docker/issues/12751).
- Because containers are running in a VM that isn't well integrated into the system, if you want to access an exposed port from the host, you'll need to use `docker- machine ip default` in a shell to find the IP of the VM in order to visit it.

- If you want to expose ports to outside of the host, you'll need to use a tool like `socat` to forward the port.

If you've previously been using the Docker Toolbox and are looking to upgrade to the newer tools, you can find migration instructions for both Mac and Windows on the Docker website.

We won't cover the Docker Toolbox beyond noting it as an alternative approach above.

Docker on Windows

Because Windows is a very different operating system from Mac and Linux, we'll go into a bit more detail to highlight some common problems and solutions. You should have installed Docker for Windows from https://docs.docker.com/docker-for -windows/ and made sure *not* to check the Use Windows Containers Instead of Linux Containers box. Starting the newly created Docker for Windows will begin loading Docker, which may take a minute—it will notify you once it's started, and you'll be ready to go!

You can check that it's working by opening PowerShell and running `docker run hello-world`. Docker will automatically pull the `hello-world` image from the Docker Hub and run it. The output of this command gives a brief description of the steps just taken regarding communication between the Docker client and daemon. Don't worry if it doesn't make much sense—there's more detail about what goes on behind the scenes in chapter 2.

Be aware that there will be some unavoidable oddities on Windows because the scripting used throughout this book assumes that you're using `bash` (or a similar shell) and have a number of utilities available, including `git` for downloading code examples throughout the book. We recommend looking into Cygwin and the Windows Subsystem for Linux (WSL) in order to fill this gap—both provide a Linux-like environment with commands like `socat`, `ssh`, and `perl`, though you'll likely find WSL a more complete experience when it comes to very Linux-specific tools like `strace` and `ip` (for `ip addr`).

> **TIP** Cygwin, available at https://www.cygwin.com/, is a collection of tools from Linux made available on Windows. If you want a Linux-like environment to experiment with or want to obtain a Linux tool for use natively on Windows (as a .exe), Cygwin should be top of your list. It comes with a package manager, so you can browse available software. By contrast, WSL (described at https://docs.microsoft.com/en-us/windows/wsl/install-win10) is an attempt from Microsoft to provide a complete emulated Linux environment on Windows, to the extent that you can copy executables from actual Linux machines and run them in WSL. It's not perfect yet (you can't run the Docker daemon, for example), but you can effectively treat it as a Linux machine for most purposes. A complete treatment of each of these is beyond the scope of this appendix.

A couple of Windows replacements for some commands and components is listed below, but it's worth bearing in mind that some of these will be noticeably imperfect replacements—this book focuses on using Docker to run Linux containers, and it makes sense that a "full" Linux installation (be it a fat VM, a box in the cloud, or an installation on your local machine) will be more capable at teasing out the full potential of Docker.

- `ip addr`—This command is typically used in this book to find the IP address of your machine on the local network. The Windows equivalent is `ipconfig`.
- `strace`—This is used in the book to attach to a process running in a container. Take a look at the "A host-like container" section in technique 109 for details on how to bypass Docker containerization and get host-like access inside the virtual machine running Docker—you'll want to start a shell rather than run `chroot` and also use a Linux distribution with a package manager, like Ubuntu, rather than BusyBox. From there you can install and run commands as if you're running on the host. This tip applies to many commands, and it almost lets you treat your Docker VM as a fat VM.

Exposing ports externally on Windows

Ports forwarding is handled automatically when using Docker for Windows, so you should be able to use `localhost` to access exposed ports as you'd expect. The Windows firewall may get in the way if you're attempting to connect from external machines.

If you're on a trusted and firewalled network, you can work around this problem by temporarily disabling the Windows firewall, but remember to re-enable it again afterwards! One of us found that on a particular network this didn't help, eventually determining that the network was set up in Windows as a "Domain" network, requiring a trip into the Windows Firewall advanced settings to perform the temporary disabling.

Graphical applications on Windows

Running Linux graphical applications on Windows can be challenging—not only do you have to make all the code work on Windows, you also need to decide how to display it. The windowing system used on Linux (known as the *X Window System* or *X11*) isn't built into Windows. Fortunately, X allows you to display an application window over a network, so you can use an implementation of X on Windows to display applications running in a Docker container.

There are a few different implementations of X on Windows, so we're just going to cover the installation you can obtain with Cygwin. The official documentation is at http://x.cygwin.com/docs/ug/setup.html#setup-cygwin-x-installing, which you should follow. When selecting packages to install, you must ensure `xorg-server`, `xinit`, and `xhost` are selected.

Once the installation has completed, open a Cygwin terminal and run `XWin :0 -listen tcp -multiwindow`. This will start an X server on your Windows machine with the ability to listen to connections from the network (`-listen tcp`) and display each application in its own window (`-multiwindow`) rather than a single window acting as a virtual screen to display applications on. Once it's started, you should see an "X" icon in your system tray area.

> **NOTE** Although this X server can listen to the network, it currently only trusts the local machine. In all cases we've seen, this allows access from your Docker VM, but if you see issues with authorization you may want to try running the insecure xhost + command to permit access from all machines. If you do this, be sure your firewall is configured to reject any connection attempts from the network—under no circumstances run it with the Windows firewall disabled! If you do run this command, remember to run xhost- later to resecure it.

It's time to try out your X server. Find out the IP address of your local machine with ipconfig. We generally have success when using the IP address on the external facing adapter, be it a wireless or wired connection, as this seems to be where connections from your containers look like they're coming from. If you have multiple adapters like this, you may need to try the IP address for each in turn.

Starting your first graphical application should be as simple as running docker run -e DISPLAY=$MY_IP:0 --rm fr3nd/xeyes in PowerShell, where $MY_IP is the IP address you've found.

If you're not connected to a network, you can simplify matters by using the insecure xhost + command to allow you to use the DockerNAT interface. As before, remember to run xhost + when you're done.

Getting help

If you run a non-Linux operating system and want to get further help or advice, the Docker documentation (https://docs.dockcr.com/install/) has the latest officially recommended advice for Windows and macOS users.

appendix B
Docker configuration

At various points in this book you're advised to change your Docker configuration to make changes permanent on starting up your Docker host machines. Appendix B will advise you on the best practices to achieve this. The operating system distribution you use will be significant in this context.

Configuring Docker

The location of the config files for most mainstream distributions is listed in table B.1.

Table B.1   Docker configuration file locations

Distribution	Configuration
Ubuntu, Debian, Gentoo	/etc/default/docker
OpenSuse, CentOS, Red Hat	/etc/sysconfg/docker

Note that some distributions keep the configuration to a single file, whereas others use a directory and multiple files. For example, on Red Hat Enterprise License, there's a file called /etc/sysconfig/docker/docker-storage, which by convention contains configuration relating to storage options for the Docker daemon.

If your distribution doesn't have any files that match the names in table B.1, it's worth checking for an /etc/docker folder, as there may be relevant files in there.

Within these files, arguments to the Docker daemon's startup command are managed. For example, when edited, a line such as the following allows you to set the starting arguments for the Docker daemon on your host.

```
DOCKER_OPTS=""
```

For example, if you want to change the location of Docker's root directory from the default (which is /var/lib/docker), you might change the preceding line as follows:

```
DOCKER_OPTS="-g /mnt/bigdisk/docker"
```

If your distribution uses systemd config files (as opposed to /etc), you can also search for the `ExecStart` line in the docker file under the systemd folder, and change that if you want. This file might be located at /usr/lib/systemd/system/service/docker or /lib/systemd/system/docker.service, for example. Here's an example file:

```
[Unit]
Description=Docker Application Container Engine
Documentation=http://docs.docker.io
After=network.target

[Service]
Type=notify
EnvironmentFile=-/etc/sysconfig/docker
ExecStart=/usr/bin/docker -d --selinux-enabled
Restart=on-failure
LimitNOFILE=1048576
LimitNPROC=1048576

[Install]
WantedBy=multi-user.target
```

The `EnvironmentFile` line refers the startup script to the file with the `DOCKER_OPTS` entry we discussed earlier. If you change the systemctl file directly, you'll need to run `systemctl daemon-reload` to ensure that the change is picked up by the systemd daemon.

Restarting Docker

Altering the configuration for the Docker daemon isn't sufficient—in order to apply the changes, the daemon must be restarted. Be aware that this will stop any running containers and cancel any in-progress image downloads.

Restarting with systemctl

Most modern Linux distributions use systemd to manage the startup of services on the machine. If you run `systemctl` on the command line and get pages of output, then your host is running systemd. If you get a "command not found" message, go to the next section.

If you want to make changes to your configuration, you can stop and start Docker as follows:

```
$ systemctl stop docker
$ systemctl start docker
```

Or you can just restart:

```
$ systemctl restart docker
```

Check the progress by running these commands:

```
$ journalctl -u docker
$ journalctl -u docker -f
```

The first line here outputs available logs for the docker daemon process. The second follows the logs for any new entries.

Restarting with service

If your system is running a System V-based set of init scripts, try running `service --status-all`. If that returns a list of services, you can use `service` to restart Docker with your new configuration.

```
$ service docker stop
$ service docker start
```

appendix C
Vagrant

At various points in this book we use virtual machines to demonstrate a technique for Docker that requires a full machine representation, or even multiple virtual-machine orchestration. Vagrant offers a simple way to start, provision, and manage virtual machines from the command line, and it's available on several platforms.

Setting up

Go to https://www.vagrantup.com and follow the instructions from there to get set up.

GUIs

When running `vagrant up` to start up a virtual machine, Vagrant reads the local file called Vagrantfile to determine the settings.

A useful setting that you can create or change within the section for your provider is the `gui` one:

```
v.gui = true
```

For example, if your provider is VirtualBox, a typical config section might look like this:

```
Vagrant.configure(2) do |config|
  config.vm.box = "hashicorp/precise64"

  config.vm.provider "virtualbox" do |v|
    v.memory = 1024
    v.cpus = 2
    v.gui = false
  end
end
```

You could change the `v.gui` line's `false` setting to `true` (or add it if it isn't already there) before running `vagrant up` to get a GUI for the running VM.

> **TIP**   A *provider* within Vagrant is the name of the program that provides the VM environment. For most users, this will be `virtualbox`, but it might also be `libvirt`, `openstack`, or `vmware_fusion` (among others).

Memory

Vagrant uses VMs to create its environments, and these can be very memory-hungry. If you're running a three-node cluster with each VM taking up 2 GB of memory, your machine will require 6 GB of available memory. If your machine is struggling to run, this lack of memory is most likely why—the only solution is to stop any non-essential VMs or buy more memory. Being able to avoid this is one of the reasons Docker is more powerful than a VM—you don't need to preallocate resources to containers—they'll just consume what they need.

index